Human Communication Theory

Applications and Case Studies

James W. Neuliep
St. Norbert College

Allyn and Bacon
Boston • London • Toronto • Sydney • Tokyo • Singapore

Vice President, Humanities: Joseph Opiela
Series Editor: Carla F. Daves
Editorial Assistant: Mary Visco
Marketing Manager: Karon Bowers
Production Administrator: Susan McIntyre
Editorial-Production Service: Ruttle, Shaw & Wetherill, Inc.
Cover Administrator: Suzanne Harbison
Composition Buyer: Linda Cox
Manufacturing Buyer: Megan Cochran

Library of Congress Cataloging-in-Publication Data

Neuliep, James William, [date]
    Human communication theory : applications and case studies / James W. Neuliep.
        p.   cm.
    Includes bibliographical references (p.   ) and index.
    ISBN 0-13-142226-X
    1. Communication–Philosophy–Case studies.   I. Title.
P90.N47   1996
302.2'01–dc20
                            95-12860
                            CIP

Printed in the United States of America
10 9 8 7 6 5 4 3 2 1   00 99 98 97 96 95

Good Night Roxanne, Good Morning Josephine

Contents

Preface

As the field of communication evolves, so do the theoretical perspectives that guide it. This book attempts to describe those perspectives as they exist at this particular point in the field's evolution. Readers will find an approach to human communication that focuses on the application of theory, especially in our personal and professional lives. This book provides numerous examples and case studies of communication theory in application, demonstrates how students can use communication theory in the construction of their personal and professional realities. In this sense, the book presents human communication theory as user friendly.

The book contains eighteen case studies with at least one in each chapter, except Chapter 3. Some focus on actual communication events that are politically, socially, or culturally significant, such as *Roe v. Wade,* President Bush's Operation Desert Storm speech, and the Los Angeles riots. Others emphasize naturally occurring verbal and nonverbal conversation in dyadic, small group, and organizational contexts. Although they may not follow the traditional format, these case studies propose a way of applying theory to our everyday lives.

Chapter 1 offers an introduction to the study of human communication and traces the historical roots of the discipline. The chapter presents the similarities and differences between the two major approaches—scientific and humanistic—and argues that they should not be viewed in polar opposition to one another but as degrees on a theoretical continuum. Some approaches are more scientific while others are more humanistic, but neither approach operates in complete isolation. The chapter closes with a case study about how a communication scholar from a scientific perspective and another with a humanistic/critical perspective might approach an advertising campaign.

Chapter 2 introduces theory as a cyclic process of deduction and induction. The central thesis of the chapter is that human communication theories can be used to explain, predict, and control human interaction. Two oft-forgotten dimensions of theory—replication and ethics—are presented as critical elements in theory use and application. The case study in this chapter focuses on how theories can be used unethically.

Chapter 3 may be the most controversial chapter in the book. Over seventy theories are annotated within an overarching organizational scheme. The point is not to have students memorize each individual theory, but to demonstrate the immense diversity within the discipline and to offer one way of organizing it. The chapter, which presents a kind of "book within a book," should serve as a valuable reference for students beginning and developing their study of human communication.

Chapters 4 and 5 are devoted to the humanistic/critical theories of human communication. In Chapter 4 the roots of classical rhetorical theory are examined beginning with ancient Greek society and the Sophists, and moving on to Plato and Aristotle. This chapter also includes a discussion of Roman rhetoric and closes with a brief introduction to neoclassical rhetoric. Mario Cuomo's noteworthy speech to the 1984 Democratic National Convention serves as the vehicle for a case study. Chapter 5 outlines a variety of perspectives labeled contemporary rhetorical theory. Included here are the traditional contemporary theories of Burke, Richards, and Toulmin. Also included are detailed accounts of Marxist/critical theory and feminist approaches to human communication. George Bush's Operation Desert Storm speech and the Supreme Court's *Roe v. Wade* serve as case studies.

Chapters 6 and 7 profile causal process theories. Chapter 6 traces the concept of causality and the structure of causal process theories. Many of the dominant research programs operating in our discipline assume, either implicitly or explicitly, a causal process approach. The chapter finishes with a description of the laws approach as one example of a causal process theory. Chapter 7 focuses on several of the principal causal process theories in the field, including uncertainty reduction theory, nonverbal expectancy violation theory, and trait approaches. Both chapters offer case studies.

Chapters 8 and 9 emphasize the human action orientation of human communication theory. Chapter 8 outlines the fundamental assumptions of the perspective and provides a detailed account of the notion of rule-governed communicative behavior. Chapter 9 presents a variety of human action centered theories of human communication, including the coordinated management of meaning, contingency rules theory, and conversation analysis. Several case studies, one from an intercultural communication context, appear in these chapters.

Chapters 10 and 11 focus on a systems-interactional approach. Chapter 10 traces the roots of general systems theory and von Bertalanffy. Chapter 11 explains human communication as a social system. The chapter presents the systems approach in three communication contexts, including interpersonal, small group, and organizational. The Los Angeles riots serve as a case study.

Throughout the past three years, several publishers, editors, developmental editors, reviewers, colleagues, and friends told me that communication theory was the most difficult book in the curricula to write. I believe them. There are some extremely strong and differing opinions about the topic of communication theory. I have tried to accurately represent the field as I see it. To be sure, some will agree, others will not. Let's keep the dialogue open.

Though my name appears alone on the cover this book, many people were instrumental in helping me complete it. My friends and colleagues at St. Norbert College have been very supportive of my efforts. Thanks to the Faculty Development Committee of St. Norbert College for the summer grant that motivated the earlier stages of the book. Thanks to the past and present communication majors of St. Norbert College who offered their opinions. This book is really for you. Thank you B.D. Thanks also to the many theorists mentioned in this book. Without their work, no book would be written. Several times throughout the past few years I impulsively picked up the phone and called them to ask about their particular approach or view. Almost without exception they would stop whatever they were doing to talk to me at length. They were incredibly helpful. Thanks to Charles R. Berger, Judee Burgoon, James C. McCroskey, John Searle, Don Stacks, and William Wilmot.

This book has been reviewed by over twenty anonymous reviewers throughout the various stages of development. I don't know who you are but thank you very much. Thanks to Stephen Dalphin, executive editor of Prentice-Hall, who originally signed the project. Thanks to Carla Daves, editor at Allyn and Bacon, who picked up the project after it was transferred from Prentice-Hall. Special thanks to Ruttle, Shaw, & Wetherill, Inc. who were extremely helpful and cordial throughout the editorial production of the book. Special thanks also to Ferald Bryan of Northern Illinois University, Alan Cirlin of St. Mary's University, Kenneth Frandsen of the University of New Mexico, Gordon Nakagawa of California State University-Northridge, and Thomas Socha of Old Dominion University whose reviews were extremely helpful.

Those people who deserve the most thanks are the ones who sat with me day after day during the whole process. This book could not have been completed without their tolerance, endurance, and sustenance. Thank you. To Rick Crandall for the many hours of expertise, advice, perspective, and balance. You've opened some important doors for me. To Kevin "Ginger" Hutchinson, my colleague, counsel, and friend. You have been the voice of rationality. I have depended on you for so much and you gave so willingly. Your insight, analysis, and interpretation have guided me throughout the entire process. To Jan, my lover, my best friend, and my partner in life. No one is more important than you. Thank you for the strength. Thank you for holding me up. This book is dedicated to you.

J. W. N.
DePere, Wisconsin

Chapter 1

The Study of Human Communication

> *Communication is essentially a social affair.*[1]
> ——COLIN CHERRY

Communication is everywhere. Even when they are alone, people are bombarded with different types of communication. One advertising magazine estimates that the average American is exposed to over 5,000 persuasive messages every day![2] To imagine our lives without the ability to communicate is difficult, perhaps even impossible. In fact, human communication—that is, the ability to symbolize and use language—separates us from animals. Communicating messages with language is the essence of what it means to be human.

Communication, a major topic of study in the contemporary world, has a profound effect on humans. Through it people conduct their lives—they initiate, maintain, and terminate relationships; they influence and persuade others; and they manage and resolve local, regional, national, and international conflicts. However, communication can be the source of many problems. Marriage counselors indicate that a breakdown in communication is the most frequently cited reason for divorce in the United States.[3] A specific form of communication—making speeches in public—is one of the most frequently cited fears, sometimes feared more than death.

This book is about theories of human communication. Such theories are extremely important because they help us to understand how and why communication operates; they identify and examine the numerous dimensions that embody the communication process; and they help people predict their communication with others in an effort to develop appropriate interactive strategies and messages. For example, theories of persuasive communication help people to understand and construct messages designed to influence others (e.g., political campaigns, advertisements). Interpersonal communication theories help people understand and manage their relationships with family members, friends, and spouses. Theories of organizational communication enable managers and workers to effectively interact with each other and with consumers and producers. There are myriad theories about communication. This book focuses specifically on theories of "human" communication. Theories of how animals and/or machines communicate are not included, nor are theories of mass communication.

This first chapter introduces the contemporary study of human communication, and is divided into four sections. Section one outlines some definitional boundaries of communication and describes nine "dimensions" of communication. Section two introduces two different, but equally valid, ways of approaching the study and theory of human communication—the scientific and humanistic approaches. Section three presents a detailed analysis of the scientific study of communication and section four discusses the humanistic study of communication.

Dimensions of Communication

Because of its ubiquitous nature communication is difficult to define. About twenty-five years ago, Frank Dance who, at the time, was teaching communication at the University of Wisconsin-Milwaukee, compiled a list of ninety-eight different definitions of communication.[4] A few years later he and Carl Larson presented a listing of over 125 such definitions.[5] The late B. Aubrey Fisher, who was a leading communication scholar/theorist, wrote that if a person were to randomly select any ten communication scholars from around the country and ask them for their definition of communication, the chances are excellent that each scholar would provide a different one.[6] But such differences are important because they indicate how each person thinks and theorizes about communication.

Although no universally agreed-upon definition exists, there are certain dimensions of communication that most communication scholars agree describe its nature. The following list presents nine of these dimensions along with their definitions, which come from various scholars with diverse backgrounds in the communication field.

Nine Dimensions and Definitions of Communication

1. Process. "Communication theory reflects a process point of view...you cannot talk about the beginning or the end of communication..." (Berlo).[7]

2. Dynamic. "Communication is a transaction among symbol users in which meanings are dynamic, changing as a function of earlier usages and of changes in perceptions and metaperceptions. Common to both meanings is the notion that communication is time-bound and irreversible" (Bowers & Bradac).[8]

3. Interactive. "Communication occurs when two or more people interact through the exchange of messages" (Goss).[9]

4. Transactional. "Communication is a personal transactional process" (Wenburg & Wilmot).[10]

5. Symbolic. "All the symbols of the mind, together with the means of conveying them through space and preserving them in time" (Cooley).[11]

6. Intentional. "Communication has as its central interest those behavioral situations in which source transmits a message to a receiver(s) with conscious intent to affect the latter's behavior" (Miller).[12]

7. Contextual. "Communication always and inevitably occurs within some context" (Fisher).[13]

8. Ubiquitous. "Communication is the discriminatory response of an organism to a stimulus" (Stevens).[14]

9. Cultural. "Culture is communication . . . communication is culture" (Hall).[15]

Process

Perhaps the most widely held truism about the nature of communication is that it is a process. David Berlo's treatment of communication as a process was one of the first to appear and it made a significant contribution to the field.[16] At the time of his writing, Berlo was the head of the Department of Communication Arts at Michigan State University and he later became the president of Illinois State University. According to Berlo, a process is anything that is ongoing, ever-changing, and continuous. Processes do not have a fixed sequence of events. A process cannot be said to have "a" beginning or "an" ending point. A process is not static or at rest, it is always moving. Certainly individual verbal messages have definite beginning and ending points, but the process of communication does not.

For example, Jim and Jan meet in the hallway and greet each other. Jim says, "Hello, Jan" and Jan says, "Oh, hi Jim." Both Jim's and Jan's verbal messages have exact beginning and ending points. But it is virtually impossible to point out exactly when and where the communication of either Jim or Jan begins and stops because they continue to communicate, nonverbally at least. They may not be communicating with each other, but they are still communicating. Even if they walk away from each other they are communicating that they are no longer talking with each other. Keep in mind that a process is something that is timebound and irreversible. Jim and Jan's greeting interaction is transient, meaning that it exists at the here-and-now moment but is irretrievable the very next moment. Also remember that because communication is irreversible, it affects future communication. How Jim and Jan interact with each other today is very much influenced by how they interacted yesterday, last week, or even years ago. Think about your own relationships with others and how what you have said in the past influences what you say today. Imagine the last time you had an argument with your boyfriend or girlfriend, for example. You may have said some things you now regret, which influences how you interact today. The idea of process was perhaps best said many centuries ago when Heraclitus stated that "a man can never step in the same river twice; the man is different and so is the river."

Dynamic

Inextricably bound to the notion of communication as a process is the argument that communication is dynamic. By definition, something that is dynamic is considered active and/ or forceful. Unfortunately, communication is typically talked about it as if it were some physical entity or "thing" that could be held in the palm of one's hand. Because communication is a dynamic process, it is impossible to capture its true essence in a sentence or a model. This problem is not unlike that faced by a photographer who tries to capture the essence of a running horse with a photograph. Certainly the photograph can be very informative about the horse, but the camera cannot make a complete reproduction of the object photographed. The relationship between the forward and hind legs, the beautiful "dynamic" muscular motions, cannot be truly represented in a photograph. Hence, any discussion of communication as a dynamic process is subject to the same kind of limitations as the photographer.[17] We can certainly discuss the source, receiver, message, and channel, but to fully appreciate the process one must be a part of it or witness it in motion. As a dynamic process communication is flexible, adaptive, and fluid. Communication is a psychological dynamic process and hence is impossible to identically replicate in a picture, drawing, or model, although certain communication elements can be graphically represented (see Chapter 2).

Interactive

That communication is interactive means that it occurs between people. While some might argue that people can communicate with themselves (i.e., intrapersonal communication), most scholars accept the notion of interaction—the active participation of both sender and receiver—as a fundamental dimension of communication. As Michael Motley, a professor of communication at the University of California–Davis, argues, a minimum requirement for active participation by a communicator is "other-directedness," or the conscious directing of one's attention to the other person.[18] Communication is a two-way process—it is interactive. For example, if Jim interprets Jan's behavior in the absence of Jan's motive to have that behavior interpreted, then Jim is engaged in a one-way process that is not truly interactive and Jan is not other-directed.

Inherent in the notion that communication is interactive is the encoding of messages. Encoding, which refers to a person's ability to speak and write, is putting one's thoughts and ideas into some symbol system (i.e., verbal and/or nonverbal language). Once a thought or an idea is encoded, it is a message.[19] Interaction, then, is the process of sending and receiving messages between people.

Transactional

The above discussion of communication as interactive implies that communication occurs when Person A encodes a message and sends it to Person B, who decodes it and sends a message back to Person A. This represents a rather static (i.e., not dynamic) view of the communication process. Although communication is certainly interactive, it is also transactional. This simply means that while Person A is encoding a message for Person B, Person A is simultaneously decoding messages from Person B. Each person in an interactional setting simultaneously sends (encodes) and receives (decodes) messages. For example, as you listen to your professor lecture, it is obvious that the professor is encoding messages and sending them to the class. At the same time, however, the professor is decoding the messages from individual students. For example, if the student behind you yawns out loud, you can be sure the professor will notice it. As the professor sends messages (e.g., lectures) he or she is also receiving messages (e.g., yawns) from the class. Most professors are well aware of how their lecture is progressing, because they can simultaneously send and receive messages.

Symbolic

That communication is symbolic is another fundamental assumption guiding most communication scholars. Gary Chronkhite argues that symbolic behavior is the common thread attaching communication researchers.[20] A symbol is an arbitrarily selected and learned stimulus that represents something else. Symbols are the vehicle by which the thoughts and ideas of one person can be communicated to another person. Symbols are not the same as signs and the two should not be confused. Unlike signs, which are naturally connected to their referents, symbols have no natural relationship with what they represent (they are arbitrarily selected and learned). For example, the symbols "b o o k" have no natural connection with what you are currently reading. The symbols "b o o k" have no meaning in Russia, for example. They are only meaningful to you because you have learned to associate them with the object in front of you. The letters "b o o k" are arbitrarily selected and learned stimuli representing something else. You allow the symbols to represent something else. If you really wanted to, you could allow just about any symbols you want to represent your book. For example, you and your friends probably communicate with each other using private symbols that no one else understands. You have phrases and names for other people, things, and activities that only you know and use. This allows you to communicate with each other almost with your own private "foreign" language. Drug dealers and users, for example, have an elaborate and highly rule governed language that allows them to communicate about their illegal activities. In drug language, the phrase "blow a splif" means to "smoke a marijuana cigarette."

Signs, on the other hand, are naturally connected to their referents; they are a part of their referent. Thunder, for example, is a sign of a storm; sweating is a sign of being hot; shivering is a sign of being cold. Each sign is intrinsically and naturally a part of the referent. Hence, a stop sign is really a "stop symbol" telling you to stop before you cross the road.

Intentional

Perhaps one of the most hotly debated issues regarding the communication process centers around intentionality. On one side of the debate are those who argue that for communication to exist there must be intention by one person to send a message to another. On the other side are those who insist that communication can occur unintentionally. Frank Dance, for example, argues that communication is defined as the eliciting of a response.[21] Intentional communication exists whenever two or more people engage in interaction consciously and with some purpose. For example, if Jim says to Jan, "Hey, do you want to go out to eat tonight?" and Jan responds by saying, "Yeah, that sounds like a good idea!" intentional communication has taken place. Unintentional communication exists when someone may think that another is consciously sending them a message when, in reality, the sender is not consciously intending to send any specific message. For example, at a party, Jan thinks that Jim is intentionally trying to ignore her because he interacts with several other people. Jan senses that Jim is sending her a message when, in fact, Jim's intention is simply to talk with new friends. Jim is not sending Jan an intentional message although she thinks that he is (i.e., a nonverbal message). Since a response has been elicited in Jan, communication has occurred. Some scholars argue that only the first example of Jim and Jan constitutes communication while others argue that any time a message is perceived, communication has occurred.

Much of this debate began many years ago with an article published by the late Gerald R. Miller, a professor of communication at Michigan State University and one of the most prominent and published scholars in the communication field. In his article, Miller argued that "in the main, communication has as its central interest those behavioral situations in which a source transmits a message to a receiver(s) with conscious intent to affect the latter's behaviors."[22] To Miller (and many others) intentionality is a central dimension of the communication process. Others, such as Paul Watzlawick, Janet Beavin, and Don Jackson, contend that all behavior, intentional or not, is informative and meaningful, and thus is communicative.[23] Indeed, S. S. Stevens argues that communication is "the discriminatory response of an organism to a stimulus."[24] Thus, whenever a person (e.g., Jan in the above example) responds to some stimulus (e.g., Jim talking with other people) communication has occurred. Most communication scholars agree that when messages are intentionally sent by one person and received by another, communication has taken place. The debate lies in whether unintentional messages perceived by someone constitute communication. When thinking about this dilemma, keep in mind that if you accept the notion that communication is (a) interactive, (b) transactional, and (c) symbolic then you should also recognize that each of these activities requires a certain degree of intention.

Contextual

The process of communication is dependent on the context. The effects and outcomes, styles and fashions, and the resulting meaning are all dependent on the context in which the communication occurs. B. A. Fisher argues that the context in which communication occurs serves to "constrain" the people interacting.[25] In other words, the context limits the number of potential interpretations that one might perceive from a message. For example, the context of the classroom defines the kind of communication that will occur. Most students sit quietly while the professor psychologically stimulates them with a brilliant lecture.

Essentially three different kinds of context influence the process of communication, including (a) the physiological environment, (b) sociological roles, and (c) psychological dispositions. The physiological context is the actual geographical space or territory in which the communication takes place. For example, communication between Jim and Jan will be different if they are interacting on a busy street in a big city or if they are in front of a fireplace in the privacy of their own home. The sociological context refers to the group membership of the interactants (e.g., demographics). That Jim is male and Jan is female places them in different sociological groups and hence affects their communication with each other. Religious affiliation, education level, economic status, and one's level in the hierarchy of employment all affect how one communicates and represents the sociological context.

Finally, the psychological context includes all of the motivations, intentions, and personality traits a person brings to the communication event. Thus, if Jim is considered arrogant and has hidden agendas regarding Jan, this would certainly affect his communication with her and contribute to the psychological context.

Ubiquitous

That communication is ubiquitous simply means that communication is everywhere, done by everyone, all of the time. Though it is theoretically possible not to communicate, it is practically impossible. Humans are constantly bombarded with and bombard others with messages of some kind, both verbal and nonverbal. This implies that wherever one goes some communication is happening. For at least three decades communication scholars have debated whether it is possible to *not* communicate. The debate began when Paul Watzlawick, Janet Beavin, and Don Jackson, published what is now a seminal book in the field titled *Pragmatics of Human Communication: A Study of Interactional Patterns, Pathologies, and Paradoxes*. One of the key points made in their book was that one cannot not communicate. Their argument was that: (a) behavior had no opposite—one cannot not behave; (b) in an interactional setting, all behavior has informational value and/or message value—it is informative; (c) since behavior is informative, it is communicative; and (d) if behavior is communicative, and one cannot not behave, then one cannot not communicate.[26] Scholars are divided on this issue. At the core of the disagreement is the notion of intentionality as discussed earlier in this chapter. If one cannot not communicate, then people are always communicating whether they intend to or not. Recently, the debate has heated up again and a scholarly forum involving three communication scholars was published. In that forum, Janet Beavin-Bavelas, one of the three original authors of the book, argued that all behavior is not communicative but that one probably cannot avoid communicating in social settings. Beavin-Bavelas now argues that the mere presence of others may require an individual to communicate about his or her relationship with them, even if that relationship is going to be one of not communicating, as in the case of strangers. Beavin-Bavelas points out that this does not mean that all of the individual's behaviors are communicative, just that some must be; hence one cannot not communicate. Beavin-Bavelas contends that the statement "All behavior in an interactional setting is communication" is a universal statement ascribing communicative properties to all behavior occurring in such situations where people interact. The statement "One cannot not communicate," on the other hand, means that in the presence of others (not necessarily interacting), some behavior is communicative. Thus, Beavin-Bavelas appears to be saying that at certain times, people can choose not to communicate.[27]

In that same forum, Motley argues that the phrase "in an interactional setting" has important implications because not all behavior is communication, only interactive behavior; hence in noninteractive contexts, one might not communicate. Also, as shown earlier, Motley argues that if people accept the notion that communication is (a) interactive, (b) symbolic, and (c) involves encoding, all of which require intention, then certainly people can choose not to communicate.[28]

Cultural

Culture shapes communication and communication is culture bound. The verbal and nonverbal symbols we use to communicate with our friends and families are strongly influenced by our culture. Perhaps the most obvious verbal communication difference between two cultures is language. Even cultures speaking the same language have different meanings for different symbols, however. For example, although English is the dominant language spoken in the United States and in England, many words and phrases have different meanings in these two cultures. In England, to "bomb" an examination is to have performed very well. To receive an "overdraft" from the bank is good because it means one has good enough credit to have obtained a loan. When in London, do not bother to ask for directions to the nearest bathroom or restroom. In England it is called the "water closet" or the "WC."

Culture also has a dramatic effect on nonverbal communication. Nonverbal symbols, gestures, and perceptions of personal space and time vary significantly from culture to culture. In the United States, for example, people generally stand about two and a half feet, or an arm's length, away from others when communicating. In many Middle Eastern cultures people stand very close to one another, especially men, in order to smell each other's breath. In Saudi Arabia, two men walking together are likely to be holding hands as a sign of trust.

The words and gestures you have learned since childhood are representative of your unique cultural upbringing. Remember when you travel to other cultures that your communication is different because it is culture bound. Your way of communicating is not the only way.

Hopefully at this point you have some notion of what the term communication means. Perhaps more important than devising a single definition is an understanding of the dimensions of the process. The following section includes a discussion of the various approaches to the study of communication. In other words, given its dynamic properties, how do scholars go about studying this ubiquitous process?

The Study of Communication: An Eclectic Discipline

Because of its processual, dynamic, and ubiquitous nature, the study of communication can be approached from a variety of perspectives. Even outside the academic world, the word "communication" has become very popular. For example, problems between labor unions and management are described as "communication" problems. A recent survey indicates that the number one skill managers desire of their employees is the ability to "communicate." As mentioned earlier in this chapter, marriage counselors identify breakdowns in "communication" as the number one reason why couples divorce.[29] Bruskin Associates reveals that the most frequently cited fear people have is speaking before a group.[30] The technological revolution is frequently discussed as the "communications" explosion. Anyone involved in radio or television is in the "communications" field. As Berlo noted over thirty years ago, "communication" concerns are broad in scope and permeate much of contemporary society.[31]

The academic study of communication is composed of elements drawn from many sources and academic disciplines. Some of the earliest known studies of communication, for example, date back to the fifth century B.C. during what is called the classical period of communication study. Such well-known scholars as Plato and Aristotle studied rhetoric—the study and delivery of public speeches—and/or public oratory during this period. Aristotle and his contemporaries were interested in the role of public oratory as it functioned in the government of newly formed democracies. This emphasis on oratory dominated the study of communication for centuries.

A second line of research and theory began in earnest during the beginning of the twentieth century with the formation of the National Association of Academic Teachers of Public Speaking in 1914. Speech teachers, whose roots were frequently in rhetoric, concerned themselves with the study of the elements of discourse and public address. These scholars focused on the source of ideas, the place of logic and reason in speeches, elocution, the structure of ideas, and the relation of speaker to the audience. During this time communication was not an academic discipline in its own right. Rhetoricians and speech teachers were generally housed in English departments. Eventually they began to break away to form their own departments. Both rhetoricians and speech teachers practiced a humanistic brand of scholarship; that is, the study of the achievements of creative people, art, and literature.[32]

A third tradition has its roots in scientific disciplines. Many of the leading social scientists between the 1930s and the 1950s who were interested in communication came from a diverse group of scientific disciplines such as anthropology, economics, psychology, political science, and sociology. Even scientists in the natural sciences had an interest in the study of communication. Thirty years ago, Wilbur Schramm, who was responsible for the foundation of the very first institutes of communication at the University of Illinois in 1947 and at Stanford University in 1955, wrote that communication was "an academic crossroad where many have passed, but few have tarried."[33]

At the time scientists were becoming interested in communication, no "Departments of Communication" existed nor could one receive a college degree in that discipline. Many scientists studied communication from their own academic perspective and then returned to their respective fields of study. For example, Carl Hovland, whose doctorate was in psychology, studied communication by examining how people used messages to produce changes in the attitudes of others (e.g., fear appeals, persuasibility). Harold Lasswell, whose doctorate was in political science, studied the communication effects of propaganda. Paul Lazarsfeld, whose doctorate was in mathematics, focused his study on mass communication with an emphasis not on how many people were listening but rather on who was listening and why.[34] Such people introduced scientific methods to the study of communication. Eventually doctorates in the scientific study of communication were offered (e.g., at the Universities of Illinois, Minnesota, and Wisconsin and at Stanford University) and finally, during the 1960s and 1970s, departments of communication began emerging throughout the country.[35] Since that time, as Charles Berger and Steven Chaffee note, "so many have tarried at the crossroad that a relatively large urban center has developed."[36]

The formation of departments of communication typically was accomplished by combining rhetoricians and speech teachers with communication scientists, or by combining schools of journalism with communication scientists. In some cases, such as Marquette University in Milwaukee, Wisconsin, students can enroll in the College of Communication, Journalism, and the Performing Arts. A few colleges and universities have departments of speech (e.g., Central Oregon Community College, Saddleback College). Many colleges and universities have departments of speech communication (e.g., California State University, Iowa State University, Indiana University) or departments of communication (Indiana State University, University of Nebraska, University of Oklahoma). Some schools have departments of communication studies (New Mexico State University, San Jose State University).

TABLE 1.1   Theoretical Continuum of Scientific and Humanistic Approaches to Communication

Scientific ◄──────────────────────────────────► Humanistic	
Objective knowledge is sought	Some knowledge is subjective
Search for regularity in communication behavior and quantification of concepts	Focus on individuals and how they create meaning
Systematic observation of communication behaviors that can be measured and quantified	Nonstandardized methods
Knowledge of communication through empirical means	Knowledge gained via introspection and interpretation
Goal of generalization	Goal of creative individuality

The diverse historical nature of the field and the various perspectives represented therein have led to the development of a whole host of communication theories. The theories generally adopted by rhetoricians and speech teachers are rooted in the humanities. The theories advanced by communication scientists come from a social scientific perspective. Chances are very good that in your own communication department, you have professors adopting one of these perspectives. Please note that neither perspective is necessarily "better" than the other—each approach is just as scholarly. In fact, as Fisher points out, there are very few purely scientific or purely humanistic approaches to the study of human communication.[37] Neither approach can proceed to the absolute exclusion of the other and very similar research questions can be formulated from each perspective. Perhaps the perspectives are best viewed as degrees on a theoretical continuum. On the left side of the continuum are those theoretical ideals representing the scientific perspective and on the right side are those assumptions guiding the humanistic perspective. Theories falling toward the left side are more scientifically based and those toward the right are humanistically based. Because the ideals are represented on a continuum, no theory is purely scientific or humanistic. In fact, many theories adopt certain ideals from both perspectives and they would fall in the middle of the continuum. Table 1.1 outlines some of the theoretical ideals associated with the scientific and humanistic approaches to theories of human communication.

As you will see throughout the remaining chapters, some theories emphasize scientific ideals, others focus on humanistic ideals, and still others integrate ideas from both approaches.

The Scientific Study of Communication

The word science conjures up images of such subject matters as physics, zoology, or chemistry. A practicing scientist can be involved in much more than the study of physical properties, animal kingdoms, or chemical analysis. In fact, many academic departments at your college or university are, in their own way, scientific and legitimate members in the class of disciplines comprising the field of science.

Most people have some notion of the meaning of the word science. Unfortunately, because of its complex multidisciplinary nature, science is very difficult to define in only a few sentences. Science is abstract and means different things to different people, especially scientists. Aristotle argued that "science starts with a certain department of the real, and investigates within that department the necessary interconnexions of subjects and attributes (substances, or things), and properties."[38] Aristotle believed that the object of science is to see the truth. To Aristotle, the scientist is entirely concerned with knowing and/or understanding.

Science and Objectivity

One of the foremost, yet probably unattainable, goals of science is to obtain objective knowledge. René Descartes, often regarded as the father of modern philosophy, argued that science should lead to absolute certainty. He once wrote, "All science is certain, evident knowledge. We reject all knowledge which is merely probable and judge that only those things should be believed which are perfectly known and about which there can be no doubts."[39] According to Descartes, all phenomena can be reduced to mathematical and/or mechanical principles. The body of an animal, the properties of wood, and the characteristics of the sky are viewed as machinelike qualities that can be measured and studied according to the laws of mathematics. The concept that nature works according to mechanical laws has since become known as the mechanistic view of science. This perspective on science reduces the quality of phenomena into quantitative dimensions that can be studied objectively. Nature is viewed in much the same way as math where the adding of two numbers results in one, and only one, sum. For example, the human body, though inhabited by a rational soul, is viewed as similar to a machine. Descartes explained the functions and motions of the body in mathematical terms just as he would those of a machine. In his time, clockmaking had become an important development and he often compared the workings of the human body to those of a clock. Thus, human hands work in much the same way as the hands of the clock and the mathematical principles used in making clocks were applied to the motions and workings of the human body. In fact, Descartes once wrote that "I consider the human body as a machine.... My thought... compares a sick man and an ill made clock with my idea of a healthy man and a well made clock."[40] Because of the precision of mathematical principles, there is no room for human error or subjectivity in Cartesian (i.e., Descartes's) philosophy. Descartes's mechanistic view of nature, the view of nature as a perfect machine governed by exact mathematical laws, dominated science for centuries.[41]

Science as Subjective

In opposition to the view that science is absolutely objective is the perspective stressing that science should be as objective as possible, but that its objectivity cannot be absolute since science is the result of human reasoning and human creativity. As Max Weber has written: "There is no absolutely 'objective' scientific analysis of culture—or put perhaps more narrowly but certainly not essentially different for our purposes—of 'social phe-nomena.'"[42] Perhaps this viewpoint was expressed best by David Hume, who argued that all sciences, including mathematics, are dependent upon the reasoning skills of humans, thus are inherently subjective. Hume stressed that scientists should be as objective as pos-sible but cannot be totally objective.[43]

Similar to Hume's notion of the nature of science is that of Jacob Bronowski, a noted poet, mathematician, physicist, playwright and philosopher, who argues that science is es-sentially a creative process and that scientists are more than collectors of objective facts. They are personally a part of their science and impose order on that which appears to be disordered. The great scientists see order where others do not. Thus, when engaged in sci-ence a scientist is creative.[44]

Like Bronowski, Michael Polanyi, an eminent physical chemist and philosopher, con-tends that the scientist's personal participation in science is a valuable part of the scientific process. Polanyi states that "complete objectivity as usually attributed to the exact sciences is a delusion and is in fact a false ideal."[45] Scientists are guided by their personal commit-ment and their passion for increased understanding of reality. Thus, science, either in the natural or social realm, is not objective.

Communication scientists understand that they are not absolutely objective in their ap-proach toward human communication. They try, however, to be as objective as they can through the use of standardized methodology.

Science as the Search for Order and Regularity

A fundamental assumption guiding scientists is that events do not happen accidentally or randomly but rather that there is some degree of regularity and orderliness in all of nature and that natural and social phenomena recur over time.[46] For example, the revolution of the earth around the sun is not haphazard, but consistent and predictable. There are definite and clear weather patterns such that every year, with a certain degree of regularity, it snows in certain parts of the United States. Communication scientists believe that there is a certain degree of order in the way people communicate as well. Many of our daily conversations sound remarkably similar to ones we have had before and we repeat many of our nonverbal behaviors. Note, for example, how most of your classmates sit in the same seat day after day. You may have observed students becoming angry when someone sits in their seats. The goal of the scientist is to seek out and uncover such order and regularity whether the subject is physics, mathematics, or human communication. Hence, the communication scientist's goal is to discover order and regularity in the ways that humans communicate with each other. Discovering regularity allows scientists to explain events and to predict them with some degree of precision just as you can predict where your classmates will sit in tomor-row's class.

Science and Observation

Most scientists engage in their search for regularity by means of systematic observation. Generally, the principle of observation is the foundation upon which most of modern science is based. As Brodbeck states: "All scientific concepts, whether they concern things, persons, or groups of persons, must ultimately be defined in terms of observable characters."[47] The belief that scientific evidence must be based on careful observation is known as empiricism. Empiricists (scientists practicing empiricism) believe that all knowledge originates from experience and that it is only through sensation (seeing, hearing, touching, tasting, smelling) that one experiences the natural or social world and can thus make an observation. You observed (via sight) your classmates sitting in the same seats day after day. Bronowski argues that of the five human senses two dominate the scientist's search for order: seeing and hearing. The sense of sight, according to Bronowski, dominates our view of the outside world whereas the sense of hearing is used by humans to make contact with other humans. Specifically, the world of science, as stated by Bronowski, is "wholly dominated by the sense of sight."[48]

Perhaps Aristotle was the first to argue that any knowable reality lies within the sensible world. That is to say that any knowable reality lies within that which can be sensed (i.e., seen, heard, smelled, felt, or tasted), and thus, is observable. Other noteworthy empiricists include Sir Isaac Newton and David Hume. To an empiricist, intuitions, superstitions, and extrasensory perceptions (ESP) are not empirical and are not considered scientific.

Depending on their method of study, scientists can directly and/or indirectly observe phenomena. Sometimes scientists directly observe their subject as in the case of a biologist observing the mating rituals of a particular animal. Archaeologists would also be considered empiricists since they directly observe ancient dwellings or human bones either through actually digging or via photographs taken by other archaeologists. The communication scientist can directly observe humans interacting with each other via one-way mirrors or hidden cameras. When you noticed the seating patterns of your classmates, you made a direct observation. Other times scientists rely on indirect observations. For example, many political scientists rely on the reported experiences of others on surveys and questionnaires for their source of observation. Many communication scientists also employ questionnaires in their research. For example, to determine seating patterns in classrooms, you might simply ask students, by means of a questionnaire or survey, where they sit when they attend particular classes. In this case you would have indirectly observed their preference for the same seat day after day. In other cases, scientists (e.g., sociologists) might use census reports for their studies. In either case, direct or indirect, the scientists utilize the principles of observation in their search for regularity.

Closely linked with the idea of systematic observation is quantification. Once a behavior has been observed, scientists believe its characteristics and properties can be precisely measured and quantified. To quantify a behavior is to assign a numerical value to its size, amount, degree, strength, duration, or magnitude. Once a number has been assigned to a behavior or concept, it has been operationalized. For example, a student's behavior in the classroom (e.g., participation, performance on examinations and quizzes, presentations) is assigned a numerical value. One's level of intelligence can be operationalized via an IQ (e.g., intelligence quotient), which is expressed in numerical values. In communication, one's degree of speech anxiety might be operationalized by the number of times the speaker gestures. You could count the number of times a student sits in the same seat in your classroom.

Science and Methodology

The scientific search for regularity should not be confused with everyday commonsense observations of order and/or patterns. That you may have noticed your classmates sit in the same seat day after day in your communication class would not be considered a truly scientific discovery. What separates the commonsense observation of order and a scientific discovery is something called methodology, which refers to the procedures, rules, guidelines, methods, and standards scientists employ in their search for order. Methodology allows scientists to search for order in a systematic methodical fashion. Kuhn refers to such methods as paradigms, like road maps that instruct the scientist how to uncover regularity and order.[49]

The discoveries scientists make are highly dependent on the type of methods they follow. Ideally we would expect two scientists observing the same phenomenon to reach the same conclusions regarding the nature of the phenomenon, its characteristics or its effects on other phenomena, etc. If the two scientists employ different observation methods, however, their results may be quite different. For example, say Communication Scientist A was interested in how people communicate when they first meet each other. In his or her study he or she uses a hidden camera to film people during their very first communication encounter and then transcribes the audio portion of film. Communication Scientist B is interested in the very same subject but instead of filming people, decides to have people fill out surveys about their communication during initial communication encounters. It is quite possible, perhaps even likely, that the results of these two studies will be different. People filling out surveys may not accurately remember what they say during initial encounters, for example.

Scientists within the same academic disciplines do not necessarily follow the same methods in discovering regularity and making predictions. In many communication departments, for example, different professors use different methods for discovering order about the way humans communicate with each other. In some academic fields (e.g., communication) there is considerable debate regarding which methodology is the best. Some communication scientists might prefer the direct observation method employed by Communication Scientist A whereas others might prefer the methods used by Communication Scientist B.

Science as Criticism

Karl Popper, a well-known philosopher and professor at the London School of Economics, argues that science is essentially a critical process of discovering order. What Popper means is that whenever scientists become engaged in their search for regularity they must, from time to time, step back and evaluate their work critically. To be critical is to exercise careful judgment about the truth and value of a set of results. In fact, scientists should never accept their findings as absolute. Doing so, according to Popper, stagnates scientific advancement. Popper warns that scientists can become so dependent on their methodologies that it is the method, rather than their own drive and motivation, that leads them toward scientific discovery. For science to progress, according to Popper, scientists must adopt a critical approach to theory building. That is to say that they should develop competing theories and not regard any one theory as absolute or certain. The aim of the scientist is to find theories, in light of critical discussion, that get nearer to the truth. Scientists, then, are obliged to evaluate (i.e., critique) their own and others' theories so that they do not become entrenched in only one view of the truth.[50]

Popper believes that it is the striving for knowledge and the critical search for truth that are the strongest motives for scientific discovery. Indeed, he contends that once put forward, our discoveries should not be dogmatically (narrow-mindedly) upheld but that as scientists we should try to overthrow them and try to prove them false—in order to advance new and unjustified ideas, thoughts, and discoveries. Scientists should constantly be critical (evaluative) of their own and others' findings because it is through this critical evaluative process that science advances and new knowledge is gained. This process, according to Popper, is the essence of science.

The Role of the Communication Scientist

Like scientists in other academic disciplines, communication scientists strive toward objectivity in their search for order and regularity via the use of standardized methods. Given these criteria, from a scientific perspective communication scholars conduct systematic observations of human communication as objectively as possible with the goal of discovering some sort of regularity. As Peter Andersen points out, communication scientists observe how humans think, feel, plan, create, act, and react in the communication process in a variety of contexts,[51] which might involve humans engaged in interpersonal, small group, organizational, or mediated communication environments. Some communication scientists may only observe certain types of communication such as persuasive, nonverbal, or intercultural. The point is that there are many different kinds of communication the scientist can observe. Typically, communication scientists focus their observations in one or two areas. Very few scientists in the field study all kinds of communication phenomena.

Another important characteristic of communication scientists is that they spend a great deal of their time making controlled observations of communication, which is where the scientist tries to isolate and minimize as much error and subjectivity as possible while measuring communication behavior. This usually occurs in some sort of laboratory setting whereby the scientist can "control" for external variables that may interfere with or contaminate the observation (e.g., other people getting in the way, external noise, weather). In this way, the observations are very systematic.

Another dimension of communication science is the notion of generalization. Obviously, communication scientists cannot observe every human engaged in communication, thus a subset, or a sample, of people is selected. After observing the sample, scientists assume that its communication activities are generalizable to other large groups of people (e.g., populations). Thus, it is critical that scientists observe a sample representative of the larger group of people to whom they want to generalize.

For example, Communication Scientist A is interested in how stage fright affects students' nonverbal communication while delivering a speech. So she devises an experiment whereby she will observe twenty-five student speakers with stage fright and twenty-five student speakers without stage fright delivering speeches. At this point keep in mind that the only larger group to which Communication Scientist A can generalize is students. It would not be fair (or scientific) to generalize to any other group since students are the only people she is observing. Note also that she is not going to observe all students, only a subset of them. During her careful observation of the speeches she decides to count the number of times (quantify) a speaker looks at the audience and how many times the speaker uses hand gestures. During her observation she notices that, on average, the speakers with stage fright give much less eye contact and gesture less than the speakers without stage fright. After careful analysis of her results, she concludes that, in general, students with stage fright give less eye contact and gesture less than students without stage fright. Communication Scientist A's ability to generalize, based on methodical systematic observation, is at the crux of science. As Berger and Chaffee argue, "Science seeks to explain by developing general principles that can be used to account for specific events or classes of events."[52] Keep in mind that these generalizations are based on the systematic observation of regularity. Communication Scientist A, in the above example, observed that with a certain degree of regularity, speakers with stage fright gave less eye contact and gestured less than the speakers without stage fright. A part of what allows her to make such generalizations is the careful method by which the observations were made. The experiment should be conducted so carefully that if Communication Scientist B were to come along and perform the same experiment he would find the same results. Hence three key characteristics of the study of communication as a science include (1) the systematic search for order by (2) making observations that (3) allow for generalization.

The Humanistic Study of Communication

Unlike the scientific study of communication, which is relatively young, the roots of the humanistic study of communication (i.e., rhetoric) date back as far as 500 B.C.[53] Communication scholars who study the rhetoric of ancient times are usually called classical rhetorical theorists. At the beginning of this century a "new" rhetoric emerged that moved beyond classical rhetoric and scholars studying this are usually called contemporary rhetorical theorists. Recently, however, the term interpretive-critical theorist has been used to describe contemporary rhetorical theorists. Dilip Parameshwar Gaonkar argues:

> *Contemporary rhetoric differs from its classical counterpart in two important ways. First, we have extended the range of rhetoric to include discourse types such as scientific texts that the ancients would have regarded as falling outside its purview. . . . This brings me to the second key difference between contemporary and classical views of rhetoric. We have reversed the priority the ancients accorded to rhetoric as a practical/productive activity over rhetoric as a critical/interpretive activity. As academics, we are more interested in rhetoric as interpretive theory than as a cultural practice.[54]*

Humanists, who emphasize individual differences in communication behavior, do not necessarily rely on standardized observation methods with objectivity as a goal. They do, however, rely on observations and therefore on empirical data. Humanists are interested in interpreting communication events. As mentioned earlier, most if not all, scientific research is grounded on the tenet of empiricism; that is, information is gained via the senses. Humanistic scholars contend that when concepts such as communication are reduced to an empirical or quantifiable base, important nonempirical aspects are eliminated. Humanists contend that internal psychological meanings drive behavior. Thomas Farrell maintains that communication is a process and a practice that is done consciously and unconsciously. The unconscious component is very difficult, if not impossible, to verify or falsify empirically. In addition, Farrell argues that the process of communication may be larger than the quantity of its individual parts (i.e., sender, receiver, message, etc.), rendering it not subject to empirical validation or quantification. Hence, Farrell asserts that communication science always leaves something out. The task of the humanistic scholar in communication, then, is to articulate these nonempirical aspects of communication.[55]

Generalization is not a necessary goal of humanistic scholarship. The true nature of what it means to be human is gained via introspection and is reflected in criticism, poetry, speeches, playwriting, and rhetoric. Humanists make aesthetic, historical, and philosophical inquiries into communication and how people construct meaning.

There are at least three humanistic approaches to the study of communication, including (a) philosophical, (b) aesthetic-allegorical, and (c) interpretive-critical.[56] Philosophical approaches focus on some important aspect of communication via an identifiable school of philosophy. Recently, for example, existentialism, the branch of philosophy that holds that humans are totally free and responsible for their own acts, was employed to examine contemporary journalistic practices.[57] Aesthetic-allegorical approaches examine how the process of communication actually works aesthetically and are guided by traditions of taste and judgment. Using an aesthetic-allegorical approach, some communication scholars have analyzed the communicative performances of evangelical television ministers and compared them to performances on soap operas. Interpretive-critical approaches examine actual forms of communication (e.g., speeches or texts) and interpret or criticize them according to some nonstandardized and/or individualized set of criteria. A fairly large group of communication scholars interpret and criticize communication events or happenings using the writings and teachings of Karl Marx as standards by which to criticize and interpret communication events, and their results are called Marxist critiques. Many of these scholars prefer the title critical theorists rather than rhetorical. Whatever their title, they have offered much to the basic understanding of human communication.

Other examples of interpretive-critical research in communication include those scholars engaged in criticizing the media, researchers who make ethical or moral judgments about the communicative output of politicians or political institutions, or scholars who seek to explain individual communication events using their own, nonstandard means of observation.[58] For example, a rhetorician might be interested in analyzing the political speeches of the president of the United States. Recently, two scholars, Steven Goldzwig and George Dionisopoulos, published an article titled "John F. Kennedy's Civil Rights Discourse: The Evolution from 'Principled Bystander' to Public Advocate." In this article, Goldzwig and Dionisopoulos highlight two of Kennedy's speeches as evidence of an evolutionary change in his position on civil rights. Their work offers an insight into the communication behavior of an important American historical figure.[59]

Another key element to humanistic scholarship is that while the scientist seeks to discover knowledge, humanists, especially contemporary rhetorical theorists, venture to produce knowledge. In this sense, the humanist goes beyond science by not only uncovering knowledge but by offering some sort of interpretation or critique of what has been found. Critical theorists, for example, articulate the present state of society (i.e., discover knowledge) then proceed to point out the problems with it and how it should be changed (production of knowledge via critique). Obviously, the production of knowledge relies heavily on subjective insight, something the scientist tends to avoid.

CASE STUDY 1   Scientific and Humanistic Approaches in Advertising

One of the most pervasive forms of communication in modern American culture is print and electronic advertising. Charles Larson indicates that the average American is exposed to over 1,700 advertising messages per day and that the average expenditure on advertising in the United States exceeds $400 per person per year.[a] Advertisers have much to gain by understanding communication theories, especially persuasive communication theories.

This first case study focuses on an advertising agency, which has just hired two consultants to assist them in producing advertisements for a client who sells a brand of running shoes. The two consultants are both experts in communication. Consultant A has a background in scientific communication theory while Consultant B's background is in the humanities. Both have very valuable, yet quite different, advice for the ad company.

Consultant A's Advice

Consultant A advises the ad company to conduct a marketing survey. One type of marketing survey includes a number of surveys to assess a product's consumer demographics, psychographics, and sociographics.[b] Demographics are used in the study of groups of consumers on the basis of some quantifiable variable or variables, including such things as income, political preference, age group, or gender. Based on these statistics, the ad company can design an ad that features the certain characteristics found in the survey. For example, are certain kinds of people more interested in running shoes than others? Psychographics concerns the consumers' life-styles and provides quantitative data as to how consumers spend their time and in what kinds of activities. A psychographic survey is conducted by having large groups of people respond to questionnaires about their activities, interests, and opinions. In this case, how many people actually spend time running? Is running something people do as a daily, weekly, or monthly activity? Sociographics is the study of how, why, and where people gather together and form groups. Research in sociographics might sample persons in the same ZIP code. The ad company can then analyze the data and look for patterns. Is there a particular region where there are more runners than in another?

Once the demographic, psychographic, and sociographic surveys are completed, Consultant A advises the ad company to conduct a number of tests on the shoe and to communicate the results of the tests in the ad. For example, test the shoe for its level of comfort, durability, stability, and attractiveness. If the results are favorable, communicate them in the ad perhaps even comparing the results against a competitor's shoe.

Finally, Consultant A advises the ad company to provide in the ad a detailed description of the shoe, perhaps via a diagram or drawing that outlines its dimensions, and to name the material from which the shoe is made.

Consultant B's Advice

Consultant B, who was excited about the opportunity to offer advice, suggested the agency create an advertisement that would establish a mood and atmosphere that captures the essence of running. He argued that to focus on the context of running, rather than the individual shoe, would trigger the affective component of running and would emphasize that running is a very physical, emotional, and personal activity. Each runner has a unique attitude and feeling about the sport. He argued that even though there might be some demographic similarities with runners, most probably train by themselves and run for different reasons. Consultant B reminded the ad company of the drama contained in the pictures and videos of Olympic athletes as they finish a race or marathon and suggested that the ad depict the silhouettes of two runners, a male and a female, running together against the backdrop of a beautiful mountain scene. He argued that most runners, professional or amateur, could imagine themselves, or would like to imagine themselves, in the same circumstances. Underneath the image of the runners the name of the shoe and the company that produces it should be shown, perhaps accompanied with the phrase, "Our shoes will take you wherever you want to be." The focus then allows individual runners to see themselves in their own ideal environment.

Consultants A and B have offered the ad company some useful advice. Based on what you have read in the chapter and in the case study, consider the following questions:

1. How is the advice of Consultant A representative of a scientific perspective?
2. How is the advice of Consultant B representative of a humanistic perspective?
3. What are the advantages and disadvantages of the scientific perspective?
4. What are the advantages and disadvantages of the humanistic perspective?
5. Which perspective do you prefer? Why?

a. Larson, C. U. (1995). *Persuasion: Reception and Responsibility,* (7th Ed.), Belmont, CA: Wadsworth.
b. Ibid.

State of the Field: Science or Art?

Both the scientific and humanistic approaches offer much to the understanding of communication. One approach is not necessarily "better" than the other and there is certainly no one dominant theory. In fact, because there are many kinds—both humanistic and scientific—communication theory is seen as eclectic (i.e., selecting from what appears to be the best in various doctrines, methods, or styles). Scholars adopting this position believe that theoretical diversity is desirable. John Bowers and James Bradac, for example, argue that scientific maturity cannot be forced and that conflict among the various schools should not be suppressed.[60] Karl Rosengren believes that open dialogues between scientists working within different quasi paradigms is advantageous.[61] Brenda Dervin, Larry Grossberg, Bar-

bara O'Keefe, and Ellen Wartella note that one advantage of theoretical diversity is that it fosters an appreciation for multidisciplinary efforts and intellectual mobility.[62] One of the negative consequences of such theoretical pluralism is fragmentation. Typically, different theories have different vocabularies, different criteria for evaluating research, and are unable to integrate other kinds of research and scholarship. The effects of such diversity are unknown and whether theoretical pluralism advances or hinders progress remains to be seen.[63]

Summary

The purpose of this chapter was to introduce you to some of the fundamental aspects of studying human communication. While a specific definition of communication was not offered, several dimensions of communication that capture its essence were presented and discussed. Communication is a dynamic, interactive, transactional, symbolic, mostly intentional, contextually driven, ubiquitous culture bound process. The academic discipline of communication is a diverse combination of many schools of thought, each offering a unique perspective. In this way, the study of communication is eclectic. Communication theories, then, are vital in order to function in the contemporary world. Chapter 2 discusses the nature of theory and demonstrates how theories function to help us understand, predict, and control our world.

Glossary

Classical Rhetorical Theorist: A person who approaches communication from a humanistic point of view and who studies rhetoric from approximately 500 B.C. to the beginning of this century.

Communication Science: The systematic search for order in the ways humans interact with each other.

Contemporary Rhetorical Theorist: A person who approaches communication from a humanistic point of view and who studies rhetoric from the beginning of this century to the present, including such areas as critical theory, interpretive approaches, and deconstruction. Many of these persons refer to themselves as critical theorists.

Context: The physiological, sociological, and psychological environment in which communication occurs.

Controlled Observation: To directly or indirectly observe something (e.g., people in communication) while eliminating extraneous variables that may affect how the people communicate. To study something without the influence of its natural environment.

Critical Process: To exercise careful judgment. To evaluate judiciously. To express reasoned opinion on any matter regarding its value or truth.

Dynamic: Something described as dynamic is forceful and active, generally not static but taking on new dimensions. Communication is considered dynamic because it constantly changes.

Empiricism: The branch of philosophy and science that adheres to the notion that all knowable reality is gained via observation. All knowable reality is sensible and gained via experience.

Generalization: To make inferences about large groups of things, objects, or people based on a sampling of only a few. Communication scientists generalize to populations of people by studying a small subset of the population—that is, a sample.

Interactive: That which occurs between at least two objects or people. Communication occurs between people which renders it interactive.

Marxist Critique: To analyze and critique something using the ideas of Karl Marx. Contemporary rhetorical theorists apply Marxist ideology to judge/critique communication events.

Methodology: The procedures, rules, guidelines, and standards that scientists employ in their search for order.

Observation: The act of recognizing or noting phenomena via the senses of sight, smell, sound, taste, and touch. The natural and social sciences are dominated by sight and sound.

Order/Regularity: A fundamental assumption among most scientists is that events in nature and human nature are not random but are marked by regularity, order, and patterns. Nature and human nature have a degree of symmetry and uniformity such that relationships can be observed.

Paradigm: Generally accepted examples of scientific practice. A model for normal science.

Process: Something that is continuously developing, ongoing, and dynamic.

Quantification: To assign a numerical value to a behavior or concept.

Rhetoric: In communication, the study of rhetoric is the study of persuasive oratory from classical and contemporary times.

Symbol: An arbitrarily selected and learned stimulus representing something else. Communication is inherently symbolic. The symbols we use represent our thoughts and ideas.

Transactional: In communication, transactional refers to the *simultaneous* encoding and decoding of messages by a communicator interacting with someone else, who also sends and receives simultaneously.

Ubiquitous: Something that is everywhere, universal, and pervasive.

References

1. Cherry, C. (1966). *On Human Communication,* (2nd Ed.), Cambridge, MA: MIT Press, (p. 3).

2. Larson, C. U. (1995). *Persuasion: Reception and Responsibility,* (7th Ed.), Belmont, CA: Wadsworth, (p. 5).

3. Safran, C. (1979). "Troubles That Pull Couples Apart: A Redbook Report," *Redbook, 83,* 138–141.

4. Dance, F. E. X. (1970). "The 'Concept' of Communication," *Journal of Communication, 20,* 201–210.

5. Dance, F. E. X., & Larson, C. E. (1976). *The Function of Human Communication: A Theoretical Approach,* New York: Holt, Rinehart and Winston.

6. Fisher, B. A. (1978). *Perspectives on Human Communication,* New York: Macmillan.

7. Berlo, D. K. (1960). *The Process of Communication,* New York: Holt, Rinehart & Winston, (p. 24).

8. Bowers, J. W., & Bradac, J. J. (1982). "Issues in Communication Theory: A Metatheoretical Analysis," in M. Burgoon, (Ed.), *Communication Yearbook 5,* (p. 3), New Brunswick: Transaction Books.

9. Goss, B. (1983). *Communication in Everyday Life,* Belmont, CA: Wadsworth, (p. 6).

10. Wenburg, J. R., & Wilmot, W. W. (1973). *The Personal Communication Process,* New York: Wiley, (p. 7).

11. Cooley, C. (1909). *Social Organization,* New York: Scribner, (p. 61).

12. Miller, G. R. (1966). "On Defining Communication: Another Stab," *Journal of Communication, 16,* 88–99, (p. 92).

13. Fisher, B. A. (1987). *Interpersonal Communication: Pragmatics of Human Relationships,* New York: Random House, (p. 22).

14. Stevens, S. S. (1950). "Introduction: A Definition of Communication," *The Journal of the Acoustical Society of America, 22,* (p. 689).

15. Hall, E. T. (1959). *The Silent Language,* New York: Doubleday, (p. 93).

16. Berlo, *The Process of Communication,* (p. 24).

17. Ibid.

18. Motley, M. T. (1990). "On Whether One Can(not) Not Communicate: An Examination Via Traditional Communication Postulates," *Western Journal of Speech Communication, 54,* 1–20.

19. Goss, *Communication in Everyday Life.*

20. Cronkhite, G. (1986). "On the Focus, Scope, and Coherence of the Study of Human Symbolic Activity," *Quarterly Journal of Speech, 72,* 231–246.

21. Dance, F. E. X. (1967). "Toward a Theory of Human Communication," in F. E. X. Dance, (Ed.), *Human Communication Theory: Original Essays,* (pp. 288–309), New York: Holt, Rinehart & Winston.

22. Miller, "On Defining Communication," (pp. 88–99, 92).

23. Watzlawick, P., Beavin, J., & Jackson, D. (1967). *Pragmatics of Human Communication: A Study of Interactional Patterns, Pathologies, and Paradoxes,* New York: Norton.

24. Stevens, "A Definition of Communication," (p. 689).

25. Fisher, *Interpersonal Communication.*

26. Watzlawick, Beavin, & Jackson, *Pragmatics of Human Communication. A Study of Interactional Patterns, Pathologies, and Paradoxes.*

27. Beavin-Bavelas, J. (1990). "Behaving and Communicating: A Reply to Motley," *Western Journal of Speech Communication,* 54, 593–602.

28. Motley, "On Whether One Can(not) Not Communicate," 1–20.

29. Safran, "Troubles That Pull Couples Apart," 138–141.

30. R. H. Bruskin Associates (1973). "Fears," *Spectra, 9,* 4.

31. Berlo, *The Process of Communication,* (p. 24).

32. Frey, L. R., Botan, C. H., Friedman, P. G., & Kreps, G. L. (1991). *Investigating Communication: An Introduction to Research Methods.* Englewood Cliffs, NJ: Prentice-Hall.

33. Schramm, W. (1963). *The Science of Human Communication,* New York: Basic Books, (p. 2).

34. Schramm, W. (1980). "The Beginnings of Communication Study in the United States," in D. Nimmo, (Ed.), *Communication Yearbook 4,* (pp. 73–82), New Brunswick: Transaction Books.

35. Reardon, K. K. (1987). *Interpersonal Communication: Where Minds Meet,* Belmont, CA: Wadsworth.

36. Berger, C. R., & Chaffee, S. H. (1987). "The Study of Communication as a Science," in C. R. Berger & S. H. Chaffee, (Eds.), *Handbook of Communication Science,* (pp. 15–19), Newbury Park, CA: Sage.

37. Fisher, *Interpersonal Communication.*

38. Joachim, H. H. (1966). *Aristotle: The Nicomachean Ethics,* Oxford: Clarendon Press, (p. 5).

39. Capra, F. (1988). *The Turning Point: Science, Society, and the Rising Culture,* Toronto: Bantam.

40. Capra, F., *The Turning Point: Science, Society, and the Rising Culture,* (p. 62).

41. Ibid.

42. Weber, M. (1968). "'Objectivity' in Social Science," in M. Brodbeck, (Ed.), *Readings in the Philosophy of the Social Sciences,* (pp. 85–97), New York: Macmillan.

43. Hume, D. (1896). *A Treatise of Human Nature,* (2nd Ed.), Oxford: Clarendon.

44. Bronowski, J. (1956). *Science and Human Values,* New York: Harper.

45. Polyani, M. (1962). *Personal Knowledge: Towards a Post-Critical Philosophy,* Chicago: The University of Chicago Press.

46. Andersen, P. (1989). "Philosophy of Science," in P. Emmert & L. Barker, (Eds.), *Measurement of Communication Behavior,* (pp. 3–17), White Plains, NY: Longman.

47. Brodbeck, M. (1968). "General Introduction," in May Brodbeck (Ed.), *Readings in the Philosophy of the Social Sciences,* (pp. 1–12), New York: Macmillan, (p. 6).

48. Bronowski, J. (1977). *A Sense of the Future: Essays in Natural Philosophy,* Cambridge: MIT Press, (p. 11).

49. Kuhn, T. (1962). *The Structure of Scientific Revolutions,* Chicago: The University of Chicago Press.

50. Popper, K. (1959). *The Logic of Scientific Discovery,* New York: Harper.

51. Andersen, "Philosophy of Science," (pp. 3–17).

52. Berger & Chaffee, "The Study of Communication," (p. 18).

53. Reardon, *Interpersonal Communication.*

54. D. P. Gaonkar, (1993). "The Idea of Rhetoric in the Rhetoric of Science," *The Southern Communication Journal, 58,* 258–295, (pp. 258–259).

55. Farrell, T. B. (1987). "Beyond Science: Humanities Contributions to Communication Theory," in Berger & Chaffee, *Handbook of Communication Science,* (pp. 123–142).

56. Ibid.

57. Dalamia, S. (1991). *Existentialism in New Journalism.* Paper presented at the Annual Convention of the International Communication Association, Chicago.

58. Berger, & Chaffee, "The Study of Communication," (pp. 15–19).

59. Goldzwig, S. R., & Dionisopoulos, G. N. (1989). "John F. Kennedy's Civil Rights Discourse: The Evolution from 'Principled Bystander' to Public Advocate," *Communication Monographs, 56,* 179–198.

60. Bowers & Bradac, "Issues in Communication Theory," (p. 3).

61. Rosengren, K. E. (1989). "Paradigms Lost and Regained," in Dervin, B., Grossberg, L., O'Keefe, B., & Wartella, E. (Eds.), Rethinking Communication (Vol. 1), (pp. 21–39), Newbury Park, CA: Sage.

62. Dervin, B., Grossberg, L., O'Keefe, B., & Wartella, E. (1989). "Introduction," in Dervin et al., *Rethinking Communication,* (Vol. 1), (pp. 13–17).

63. Ibid.

Chapter **2**

The Nature of Theory

All knowledge is theory-impregnated, including our observations.[1]—SIR KARL R. POPPER

In the year 1543 an event took place that would forever change how human beings viewed themselves and their world. For at least 1,000 years, the Eastern peoples, whose culture was at the base of Greek intellectual development, viewed the earth as at the center of God's creation, the universe. They conceived the earth as a motionless spherical platform around which all other bodies in the universe revolved.[2] In 1543 Nicolas Copernicus, an astronomer, mathematician, linguist, amateur artist, and now considered the father of the scientific revolution, published a series of six books called *De revolutionibus* that refuted geocentric dogma and argued that the earth was not at the center of the universe but was only one of several other planets circling a minor star (i.e., the sun) at the edge of the galaxy. Copernicus, fully aware that his position would greatly upset the religious conservatism of the time, dedicated his writings to the Pope. Indeed, so conscious was Copernicus of offending the church he delayed the publication of *De revolutionibus* until 1543, the year that he died, and even then he outlined his view merely as a theory, without any empirical support. Thus, because of a mere theory, what is now known as the scientific revolution began and to this day remains a cardinal concept of classical astronomy.[3]

The above illustration demonstrates the potential influence of a "mere" theory. The goal of this chapter is to profile the importance of theories and how they are developed. In doing so, this chapter will present a model of the process of theory construction and development as well as some definitions of theory. Finally, this chapter will outline and discuss three fundamental functions of theory, including explanation, prediction, and control.

Defining and Developing Theory

Though a theory is defined in many ways, one simple definition is any serious attempt to explain something. Fred Kerlinger defines a theory as:

23

a set of interrelated constructs (concepts), definitions, and propositions that present a systematic view of phenomena by specifying relations among variables, with the purpose of explaining and predicting the phenomena.[4]

All of us at some time in our lives have formulated our own personal theories of why things happen and why people act as they do. We rely heavily on our theories in making decisions that greatly affect our lives. As a high school student you may have had a theory about which parent, mom or dad, was the most likely to comply with your request to borrow the car. Your decision to attend college may have been guided by the theory that a college education would increase your chances for gainful employment. Some of our theories develop out of common sense, others by experience, and others by sheer intuition. Theories are an active component in most aspects of our lives. The kinds of theories developed through common sense and those constructed by trained scholars within some academic setting are paradoxically quite different and similar. Like the average person using naive theories to help make everyday decisions, theorists use theories to guide much of their scholarly decision making. Unlike a layperson, whose theories are sometimes mere hunches, a scholar's theories are based on careful, systematic, logically consistent sets of propositions subject to tests of verification and falsification. Figure 2.1 presents a model of how theorists construct theories.

As indicated in Figure 2.1, many variables play a role in the construction and development of theory. At the early stages of theory building, theorists are guided by their life experiences and intuition. Albert Einstein, for example, the creator of the theory of relativity, said that theories "can only be reached by intuition, based upon something like an intellectual love of the objects of experience."[5] The starting point for most theories lies in the theorist's past experiences and creative intuition. Indeed, Karl Popper maintains that of 1,000

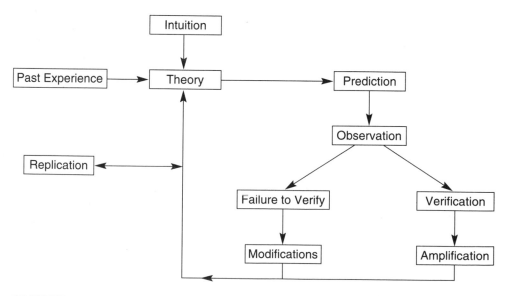

FIGURE 2.1   A Model of Theory Construction and Development

units of knowledge a person possesses, 999 of them are inherited or inborn. Popper alleges that all acquired knowledge consists of the modification of some form of knowledge that was there previously.[6]

Using their past experience and intuition as their initial guide, theorists then state their theory, which represents their explanation of the topic. Based on this explanation, the theorist should be able to make predictions. As the model in Figure 2.1 outlines, the theorist then makes observations to see if the predictions are correct. If the observations confirm the prediction, then the theory is supported. If they do not, then the theory is not supported and the theorist has to decide whether the theory needs refinement or whether additional observations are needed.

An important part of the theory-building process is replication. Additional observations should always be made regardless of whether a theorist's predictions are confirmed. The rest of this chapter will discuss the nature of theory, especially the concepts of explanation, prediction, and control.

What Do Theories Look Like?

Humanistic and scientific theories are constructed by humans, and thus, are limited and restricted views of reality. The only vehicle by which theorists can communicate their theories is language. Some theorists may use very sophisticated and technical language while others may be rather casual in their presentation. Rom Harré asserts that descriptive sentences are an important ingredient of any theory. Descriptive sentences are those that: (a) identify something to be the subject of the theory including the use of a referring expression, such as a name, which is conventionally correlated with it, and (b) the recognition of the thing selected as belonging to a certain class of objects or possessing a certain property.[7] Once contained in a descriptive sentence, the described object is typically referred to as a theoretical "concept," which represents the foundation of any theory. Some examples of descriptive statements and their corresponding theoretical concepts appear in Table 2.1 on page 26.

In addition to descriptive statements, most theories will contain a set of sentences called propositions, postulates, or axioms. Though different in name, these statements, which are typically based on theorists' past experiences or intuition, all outline the general assumptions guiding theorists and describe the nature of things as they see them. Einstein's relativity theory, for example, was guided by his general belief of nature's inherent harmony. Isaac Newton was led by some of his beliefs in the occult and esoteric knowledge. A central tenet of feminist theory is that society is androcentric (i.e., male-oriented). In developing his theory of universal pragmatics, Jürgen Habermas asserts that "I start from the assumption that other forms of social action—for example, conflict, competition, strategic action in general—are derivative of action oriented to reach understanding."[8] These types of general assumptions, held to be true by one or more theorists, serve as the starting point for theory.

To some, theories are of little use. Many people think that theories only deal in the abstract and are only of use to scholars. In today's society, many people, especially students, would rather learn how to apply some skill than study the theory behind the application. Simply mention to your friends that you are currently enrolled in a communication theory

TABLE 2.1   Descriptive Theoretical Statements

Theory	Concept	Description
Newtonian Mechanics	Gravity	Gravity is a force that tends to draw all objects in earth's sphere toward the center of the earth.
Behaviorism	Operant Conditioning	Operant conditioning is a learning process whereby a stimulus is presented to some organism and when the desired response is made by the organism, some reinforcement or reward is given in order to either fix or strengthen the response.
Coordinated Management of Meaning	Speech Acts	Speech acts are the things that people do to each other with word gestures.
General Systems	System	A system is a set of objects or entities that interrelate with one another to form a whole.
Marxism	Materialism	A conception of history and the way a society organizes itself. Everything is shaped by the economic system of a society which subtly affects the ideas people have.

class and they may react with a long, stifling yawn. But without theories to guide scientists, there would be no application. As Kurt Lewin noted many years ago, there is nothing so practical as a good theory. The applicability of any theory is dependent on two fundamental functions, including (a) its explanation of some phenomena, and (b) its ability to predict. In addition, some theorists argue that theories should perform a third function of control.

The First Fundamental Function: Explanation

Perhaps the foremost objective of scholarly inquiry is to go beyond answering the question *what* to answering the question *why*. Answering *why* requires theorists to construct explanations and thus to endeavor to go beyond the simple description of subject matter. Instead, theorists seek to understand the unknown. While few would dispute that the major aim of theory is explanation, there is considerable debate surrounding the logic of explanation and what type of explanation is best. How does one go about explaining phenomena? Is there any logic associated with explaining something? What should an explanation look like? These questions, and others like them, constitute the battleground for debate among philosophers and theorists alike.

Generally, a theory begins by describing and defining its topic. For example, a theory of nonverbal communication would begin by offering a detailed account of what it means to communicate without words. In this example, nonverbal communication is the central concept. Rom Harré argues that the theory should identify regularities about the concept and its association with other concepts. Recall from Chapter 1 that one of the assumptions guiding theorists is that there is a certain degree of order and regularity in the world. For example, assume that we have noticed consistently that when people give public speeches they tend to engage in certain nonverbal behaviors such as fidgeting, hand tremors, and so on. We have seen this type of behavior so often that we conclude there is a consistent and regular relationship between nonverbal behavior and public speeches. Identifying this regularity involves mere description. The descriptive component of an explanation does two jobs—it isolates and refers to a certain subject, and it ascribes to this subject a certain property. To identify regularity is simply to answer the "what" of phenomena.[9]

The next step in formulating an explanation is to articulate the reasons why the observed regularity occurs. We ask ourselves, "Why do people fidget when they give speeches?" This is sometimes called designating the force that makes the regularity necessary.[10] If fidgeting is observed with some degree of regularity, then there must be some reason for it; that is, a force. Communication theorists generally recognize three types of necessity in communication theories, including causal, practical, and logical. Each type of necessity has a different type of force.[11]

Causal Necessity

In the natural sciences it is assumed that the force which makes certain regularities necessary is causal. In our nonverbal communication example, we might conclude that public speeches cause people to be nervous which causes them to fidget. In many cases, the concept of causality is defined in terms of predictability according to a scientific law.[12] Laws are statements that express regularities. A law describes a universal invariant by expressing that one instance of a concept is always connected with an instance of another (i.e., cause-effect).[13] In the physical sciences, laws are usually stated in universal conditional form—that is, the if-then statement—which is capable of being confirmed or disconfirmed through empirical testing. For example, the statement, "If water is heated to the temperature of 212 degrees Fahrenheit, then it will boil," would be considered a law. The main function of laws in the natural sciences is to provide an explanation of why some event occurred. The high temperature caused the water to boil (i.e., the effect).

Laws are established through the observation of and the articulation of those conditions that are present before the regularity is observed and absent after it occurs. When natural scientists are asked to account for or give reasons for some regularity, they observe the events or conditions that lead up to the regularity. These are sometimes called the antecedent conditions, which, if they meet certain criteria, are then assumed to be the cause of the regularity. Each of the conditions, to be considered a cause of the regularity, must be both necessary and sufficient. A necessary condition is one that must be present when regularity occurs; that is, without its presence, the regularity could not occur. If a scientist heats water to only 150 degrees Fahrenheit, the water will not boil. Without reaching 212 degrees Fahrenheit water cannot boil; it is a natural law. Hence, water temperature of 212 degrees Fahrenheit is a necessary condition for boiling. A sufficient condition, on the other hand, is one that may be adequate to produce the regularity but is not absolutely necessary for the regularity to occur. For example, throwing a rock toward a window with great force is a sufficient condition to break the window. The same act is not a necessary condition, however, since there are any number of ways to break a window.[14] The law governing the breaking of a window is that when a certain amount of pressure is applied to glass, the glass will shatter or fracture. Thus, this law explains why the window broke, but note that this law does not specify the particular cause of the breakage. In this case the cause is a rock being thrown with a certain degree of force.

Not all theories based on causal necessity include laws. There are no recognized laws in communication theories, for example. But, as we shall see in subsequent chapters, many theories of communication rely on causal necessity as a part of their explanation of communication.

Practical Necessity

Many communication theorists eschew theoretical explanations based on laws and/or causal necessity, because they argue that social phenomena cannot meet the criteria of causal necessity. When asked, for example, "Why do people fidget during public speeches?" we can state any number of sufficient causes (e.g., nervous disorders, habits, anxiety, etc.), none of which are absolutely necessary. Instead, many communication theorists believe that people are teleological and that our theories should include teleological explanations. Questions about teleology—the doctrine or study of ends or purposes[15]—have to do with whether a thing, object, or person has a goal or is acting to accomplish some goal, and, if so, the identification of the goal. If social phenomena are goal directed, then social processes, especially behavior, must serve some function in the attainment of that goal.[16] Theories including teleological explanations rely on practical necessity.

Practical necessity refers to the amount of normative force people feel to act or behave in some way in order to achieve their goal.[17] For example, there is a certain degree of pressure for you to get good grades in college that comes from society, your parents, peers, and your own personal goals. You could achieve your goal of getting good grades by taking easy classes, by cheating, or by studying very hard. Any of these three options are sufficient but none, individually, are absolutely necessary for you to get good grades. In most cases, goals can be achieved in a number of ways or by performing a number of different kinds of behaviors, all of which might be sufficient in achieving a goal, but which are not necessary to obtain the goal. In this way, the force that makes the regularity is sufficient but not necessary.

Since we can meet the sufficiency criteria, our explanations are said to be based on practical necessity and are the result of some rule. A rule, unlike a law, is a followable prescription that indicates what is preferred, obligated, or prohibited.[18] People follow rules to attain goals. One rule is that if you want to get good grades, then you should study hard. Rules prescribe appropriate behaviors to achieve goals. That rules are followable implies that they can be broken. You could break the rule regarding studying hard and follow a different rule that says that cheating can get you good grades. Laws, however, cannot be broken. Water cannot choose whether to boil once it reaches 212 degrees Fahrenheit. The temperature causes water to boil.

In some ways causal and practical necessity are conceptually related. For example, let's assume that you have an examination in your communication theory class tomorrow. Since there is a test tomorrow, you decide to study tonight. One could argue that your scheduled test tomorrow represents a sufficient antecedent condition "causing" you to study tonight. In this way, social scientific explanation, based on practical necessity, implies causal relationships.[19] One of the major differences between causation as expressed in natural laws and the implied causation in social rules is the temporal placement of the cause. For a natural law to apply, certain conditions must be met prior to the observed regularity; the cause must occur before the effect. Water must be heated to 212 degrees Fahrenheit before it will boil. This temporal dimension is reversed in practical necessity, however. In some ways, the cause of social phenomena actually occurs in the future. You are studying tonight because your test is tomorrow. In essence, the effect occurs before the cause. In viewing your exam tomorrow as the cause of your studying tonight, the idea of a necessary condition is discarded. You could prepare for your exam in a number of ways, studying being only one of them. As Fisher points out, "The necessity criterion is often ignored in social scientific explanations."[20]

In any event, as Richard Rudner argues, causation is not necessary for explanation, regularity is. The more frequent the regularity, the stronger the explanation, with or without causation. As Rudner contends, "Laws of atemporal correlation are just as much laws of nature or just as much scientific laws as are laws of succession."[21] Thus, if 85 percent of the time you study the night before an examination, there is sufficient justification to warrant the statement, "If you have an exam tomorrow, you will probably study tonight." The explanatory force, then, rests with the stability and consistency of the observed regularity.

Logical Necessity

A third type of necessity employed by communication theorists, and often used in humanist accounts, is called logical, conceptual, and/or isological necessity.[22] Here the force lies not with any law or rule but with the conceptual power of a set of internally consistent definitions furnished by the theorist. Mathematicians rely heavily on logical necessity to prove their theories. For example, the statement, "This is a triangle because it is a three-sided closed figure," is representative of logical necessity.[23] If we observe two people and conclude that Person A is taller than Person B, then we must logically conclude that Person B is the shorter of the two since, by definition, if someone is "taller" then someone must be "shorter." The power of logical necessity is contingent on the theorist's commitment to sustain the logic of the definitions. For example, Karl Marx argued that materialism, the mode of production, and economic relationships define the social, political, and spiritual character of people. Marx continued to offer a detailed analysis of how such factors define the structure of society. His theory is not based on any kind of causal or practical necessity but rather on the consistency in which he defines his concepts and describes their relationship with other concepts.

Theories and Model Building

One important tool used by theorists to represent their theories and explanations is modeling. A model is a graphic representation of an object or process. Models are not theories or explanations, but they can be extremely useful to theorists in representing their theories. In many cases models are not identical replicas of what they depict but can be thought of as well-developed analogies of some object or process. Objects are analogous to each other to the extent that the physical or logical structure of one is similar to the physical or logical structure of the other.[24] Theorists use models because they can describe and simulate physical, logical, or conceptual processes that may not otherwise be observable or presentable. For example, several communication scholars have developed theories of listening. Because listening is a psychological phenomena that is impossible to touch or hold, models can provide a critical method of indirect observation. Models enable theorists to illustrate, delineate, and depict the structural (i.e., what the object or process looks like) and functional (i.e., what the object or process actually does) features, properties, or characteristics of their theories (e.g., descriptive statements, general assumptions, and explanations) in various degrees of abstractness and detail. Some models may be very detailed and literal and others rather general and abstract.

Some models, usually called scale models, involve no substantive change in medium and are virtually able to identically replicate some physical object due to their detailed and literal representations. Models of cars or airplanes, for instance, are scale models and differ only in size from the original. You may recall a scale model of the human body or skeleton used by your biology or anatomy teacher in high school. Models of this type, while accurate in depiction, offer little more than simple description.[25]

Conceptual models, on the other hand, involve a change in medium and are sometimes quite abstract. Physical, psychological, and logical processes can be represented conceptually in models and because communication is a psychological process, communication models are conceptual models.[26]

Linear Models of Communication

One model that dominated the communication field for some time is called the Aristotelian or linear model of communication. As its name implies, the model is based on the writings of Aristotle, one of the very first and most influential theorists in communication. To the best of our knowledge Aristotle did not present a graphic depiction of his idea of communication, but we can extrapolate from his writings how he conceived of the communication process.

$$\text{Speaker} \longrightarrow \text{Message} \longrightarrow \text{Audience}$$

From this model, we can see that communication occurs when a speaker sends a message to an audience within some setting. The model depicts communication as a one-way process, that is, linear. We know that Aristotle was concerned primarily with rhetoric (i.e., persuasion) and focused almost exclusively on public oratory. The above model, while informative to a point, leaves out many important aspects of communication, especially the concept of feedback.

Information Theory Model

Another model of communication that dominated the field for some time was developed by Claude Shannon and Warren Weaver and was based on their "Mathematical Theory of Communication."[27] Their goal in developing the model was to show what happens to information from the time it is transmitted until it is received (see Figure 2.2).

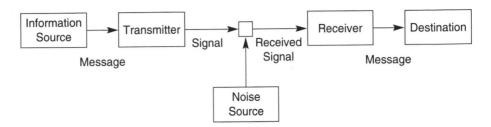

FIGURE 2.2   Mathematical Model of Communication

Shannon and Weaver's Model of Communication from *Mathematical Model of Communication,* by Claude Shannon and Warren Weaver. Copyright © 1949 by the Board of Trustees, University of Illinois Press. Reprinted with permission of the University of Illinois Press.

An important feature of this model is the concept of noise. Noise, of course, is anything that interferes with the transmission of the message. Like Aristotle's model, Shanon and Weaver's information model excludes feedback.

Goss Model of Communication

Blaine Goss has developed a model of communication that takes into account social and psychological concepts of communication.[28]

The Goss model emphasizes that communication involves at least two people who simultaneously encode and decode messages. The communication process is depicted as circular. Note in Figure 2.3 that the top level of the communicator on the left begins with encoding while the communicator on the right is decoding. Both communicators then interpret the message. The three lines represent the levels of which messages can be encoded and decoded, including a verbal, vocal, and nonverbal level. "Relationship" in the middle denotes that the communicators have a social relationship with each other. The large box

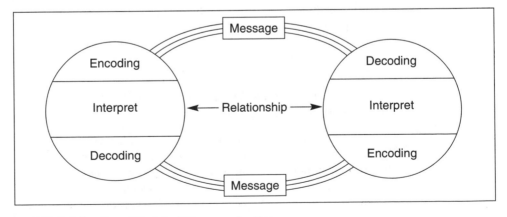

FIGURE 2.3   Goss Model of Communication

Goss Model of Communication, from *Communication in Everyday Life,* by Blaine Goss. Copyright © 1983 by Wadsworth Publishing. Reprinted by permission from Wadsworth Publishing.

Source		Message		Channel		Receiver
Source ⟶		**Message** ⟶		**Channel** ⟶		**Receiver**
Communication Skills		Elements		Seeing		Communication Skills
Attitudes		Contents		Hearing		Attitudes
Knowledge		Treatment		Touching		Knowledge
Social System		Structure		Smelling		Social System
Culture		Code		Tasting		Culture

FIGURE 2.4   Berlo's Model of Communication

A model of the ingredients of communication, from *The Process of Communication,* by David K. Berlo. Copyright © 1960 by Holt, Rinehart and Winston. Reprinted by permission from Holt, Rinehart and Winston.

around the two denotes that communication occurs within a context. As one communicator encodes, the other decodes, and interprets the message while simultaneously encoding a different message. They both encode and decode simultaneously. The model depicts an ongoing cyclical process of encoding, decoding, and interpreting.

Berlo's SMCR Model

One model of communication that influenced the communication field for decades is David Berlo's model of communication (see Figure 2.4).[29]

Berlo's model is rather static and abstract but can offer much to our understanding of the communication process. A particular advantage of this model is that it outlines many of the factors that affect how we communicate with others. For example, the model indicates that as a source or receiver of communication, our communication skills, attitudes, knowledge, social system, and culture will influence our interaction with others. The model also demonstrates that our messages contain a certain content, can be sent in a particular code, have structure, and may be treated differently by others. Finally, the model shows that our messages can be sent through a number of different channels. The model does not favor one type of communication over another. Messages sent through the mail, in person, over television, radio, telephone, or computer, will be affected by the very same source, message, channel, and receiver variables.

Habermas's Model of the Distinction between Observation and Communicative Experience

In Figure 2.5, Habermas distinguishes between sensory experience (seeing, hearing, touching, smelling, tasting) and communicative experience or understanding.[30] Observation is directed to perceptible things and objects whereas understanding is directed to meanings. Level 1 depicts the relationship between the actual object of observation and the observer. The act of understanding relates to the symbols used to express the event. Level 2 depicts the relationship between the symbolic expression of the object or event and the meaning of the observation sentence. The interpretation represents the meaning as the observation sen-

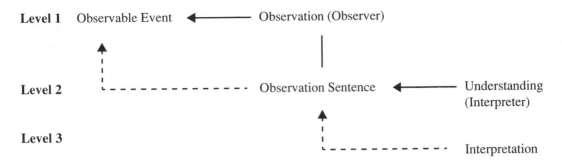

**FIGURE 2.5   Habermas's Model of the Distinction between Observation
and Communicative Experience**

From *Communication and the Evolution of Society* by Jürgen Habermas. Copyright © 1979 by Beacon Press. Reprinted by permission of Beacon Press.

tence in turn represents the object or event. Level 3 demonstrates that the understanding (of the observation sentence) is expressed in the content of the interpretation, as the observation is expressed in the content of the observation sentence.

While models serve the theorist well by illustrating difficult descriptions and explanations, we should exercise caution in our interpretation of them. Again, models are not theories or explanations; they are only representations of theories. Both theorists and students must avoid confusing the model with the actual object or theory. Models, by definition, are limited and restricted but can be of immense help to theorists in describing, explicating, and simulating their theories.

The Second Fundamental Function: Prediction

Second only to explanation, prediction is another primary function of theory. As indicated in Figure 2.1, the theory leads the scientist to make predictions. In many ways explanations and predictions are intrinsically linked because if you are able to explain a phenomenon, then you should be able to predict it. May Brodbeck, a leading social science philosopher, argues that if anything can be explained deductively by a set of premises after it has occurred, it could, in principle, be predicted from the same premises before it occurred.[31] For example, if the theorist knows that water boils at 212 degrees Fahrenheit, he or she can go to the stove, set a pot of water on the heating element, and predict that when the temperature of the water reaches 212 degrees, the water will boil. Indeed, the natural scientist can make such a prediction with a high degree of confidence, perhaps with 100 percent accuracy. If the social scientist explains that your studying is correlated with scheduled exams, then he or she can predict that if you have an exam scheduled for tomorrow, you will study tonight. The social scientist's prediction, however, cannot be stated with the same degree of certainty as in the case of the natural scientist; the former is based on causal necessity while the latter is based on practical necessity.

Most theorists use the term hypothesis instead of prediction. A hypothesis is a statement proposing a relationship between two or more different concepts.[32] A hypothesis should be general enough to apply to more than one event but it is not usually universal (i.e., applying to all events). One way theorists derive their hypotheses is by using a system of deductive logic to proceed from general statements of accepted fact to less general or more specific judgments that, in relation to the general statements, must necessarily be true. Aristotle defined the syllogism as a formal presentation of deductive reasoning. A standard example of a syllogism is:

All men are mortal.
Socrates is a man.
Therefore, Socrates is mortal.

For example, assume we have a theory that tells us that, in most cases, students gesture during public speeches. In syllogistic terms, this assumption is called the major premise. In order for the syllogism to work, the major premise must be valid. Assume also that we know Jan is a student and that she has a speech in her communication class tomorrow. This assumption, in syllogistic terms, is called the minor premise. Given these two statements, assumed to be true, we can deduce that Jan will gesture during her speech. The syllogism would look something like this:

Major Premise: Students gesture during public speeches.
Minor Premise: Jan is a student who will deliver a speech tomorrow.
Conclusion: Jan will gesture in her speech.

Observation

As indicated in Figure 2.1, once the theorist formulates a hypothesis, the next step is to make observations in order to test the accuracy of the prediction. How communication theorists test their hypotheses is a source of much debate in communication. Peter Andersen argues that all scientific research is grounded in the principles of observation.[33] Remember from Chapter 1 that the belief that scientific evidence must be based on observation is known as empiricism and that empiricists believe all knowledge originates from experience. Social scientists adhere to strict rules of methodology when making their observations and they typically engage in measurement and the use of statistics to test their hypotheses. Humanists, too, make observations but do so without the use of standardized methods and statistics, relying more heavily on personal experience, case study examples, or historical accounts to assist them in rendering judgments about their predictions. The basic purpose of making observations is to either confirm or deny one's predictions.

Verification and Falsification

The ability to make accurate predictions rests with the soundness of one's theory and explanation. The structure of one's theory, ironically, is ultimately dependent on the ability to confirm predictions. Theoretical predictions can be tested to confirm or refute the theory on which they are based. Thus, as Figure 2.1 demonstrates, theoretic verification, adaptation, or rejection is contingent on the ability to predict.[34] For example, if we predict that if Jan has a speech tomorrow she will gesture during it, the next step would be to test the prediction. As mentioned above, hypothesis testing relies on observation, so we would establish a set of conditions whereby we could observe Jan's behavior during her speech. If we observed Jan gesturing during the speech, our hypothesis is supported. The more times we support or confirm our hypothesis, the more faith we have in our theory. Cases such as these lead to greater confidence in our theory and our ability to predict. In Figure 2.1, this is called amplification. If, however, Jan did not gesture during her speech, our prediction has been falsified. In the case of hypotheses falsification, we would have to either modify or abandon our theory about the gesturing habits of students. In either case, the nature of the theory has changed.

When theorists use the verification or falsification of their predictions to modify or amplify their theories, they are using a form of induction, or the process of proceeding from specific statements, such as accounts from the results of observations, to general statements, such as hypotheses or theories.[35] An inductive argument might look like this:

Observation 1: Student A gestured during his speech.
Observation 2: Student B gestured during her speech.
Observation 3: Student C gestured during her speech.

.

.

.

N No student is known to not gesture during his or her speech.

Conclusion: Students gesture during speeches.

When theorists use their past experience and observations in constructing theories, as indicated in Figure 2.1, much of this is based on induction. Probably most of our commonsense theories are inductively based. If you decide to ask your dad instead of your mom for the keys to the car, it is probably because he has said yes in the past. Your theory about who to ask is based on past experience, induction. To be sure, much of scientific theory building progresses in the same way. In this case, however, the induction is based on careful observation. The model followed by most theorists in modifying theory is induction.

The use of inductive reasoning poses some knotty problems for philosophers who contend that there is no justification for expecting and believing that instances of which they have had no experience will conform to those of which they have had experience. In addressing the problem of induction John Maynard Keynes contends that an inductive argument affirms, not with absolute certainty, that a certain event will recur, but that relative to certain evidence there is a probability in its favor. The validity of the induction is not eliminated if the prediction is not confirmed, however. In fact, the failure to confirm may supply the theorist with added information by which to amend and sharpen the theory.[36] If Jan is observed numerous times gesturing during her speeches, you can predict that she will probably gesture in her next speech because she has done so in the past. The inductive inference is based on repeated observations and our faith in regularity is justified by those repeated observations. When the prediction is confirmed, the theory, or induction, is said to have been verified.

In sharp contrast, Karl Popper asserts that there can be no such thing as verification via induction. Popper contends that we are never justified in inferring universal statements from singular ones because any conclusion drawn from singular statements, no matter how numerous, may at any time turn out to be false. For example, no matter how many students we observe reading the night before an examination we cannot justify the conclusion that all students, or even one student, will read the night before examinations. To Popper, theories can never be verified. Instead, Popper contends that observations are able to inform the scientist whether some explanatory theory is true or "false." Particularly in the face of competing theories, observations may be informative to the extent that they reveal the falsity of some theoretical statements. Since theorists are looking for the true theory, they will naturally prefer those whose falsity has not been established empirically. For example, the theorist that predicts "all flowers are yellow" and subsequently observes several yellow flowers has not verified the prediction. In theory, the theorist would have to observe every flower on earth to verify that prediction, a practical impossibility. The observation of only one green flower, on the other hand, falsifies the prediction and informs the scientist that this particular theory is false and to look to alternative theories. This position is typically called "falsificationist" advocacy. According to such advocacy, theories can never be verified by observation but they can, in fact, be falsified. Theorists are attracted to those theories whose falsification has yet to be determined.[37]

Replication

Scientific or humanistic theories cannot be verified or falsified based on only one observation. A critical process in the development of theory is replication, an attempt to identically, partially, or conceptually repeat the procedures of prediction and observation made earlier.[38] The Federal Drug Administration, for example, requires drug companies to repeatedly demonstrate the efficacy of newly developed drugs before allowing them to be marketed. Whether a prediction is confirmed or denied, it must be replicated before we can have much faith in it. How often an experiment is replicated, and by whom, is a topic of debate among theorists. Robert Rosenthal argues, for example, that the first replication doubles our information about that particular topic, the fifth replication adds 20 percent to our information level, and the fiftieth replication adds only 2 percent. Rosenthal also argues that someone other than the original investigator should perform replications to ensure as much objectivity as possible.[39]

The Third Fundamental Function: Control

The third and perhaps most controversial function of theory is control. If a theory adequately explains and predicts phenomena, then the theorist or whomever knows of the theory can use it to control events or happenings—to direct, regulate, and manage the explained phenomena. For example, if my theory tells me that water boils at 212 degrees Fahrenheit, and I do not want the water to boil, then I will try to control the temperature. This does not seem too controversial, but what about other types of theories? When people eventually accepted the theory of the universe posited by Copernicus they gained control over solar eclipses of the sun. They no longer had to succumb to witch doctors and religious fanatics that demanded agricultural or human sacrifices simply to make the gods happy once again. Indeed, the theory of atomic energy, if used peacefully, can be beneficial in many ways, but when used to create nuclear weapons, such as the bomb dropped on Hiroshima, its usefulness seems questionable. Some of the scientists involved in the construction of the atomic bomb have since publicly announced their disapproval of its use.

Theories of persuasion explain and predict how people will react to advertising messages. Armed with this type of theory, people can control and manipulate the types of messages sent to be more persuasive. Many theories of communication, for instance, explain how to structure messages in such a way as to make them most effective. In the hands of propaganda ministers, brainwashers, and false advertisers, this may be a negative consequence of the theory. In the hands of free speech advocates, therapeutic counselors, and political negotiators, this may produce positive outcomes.[40] Once theories are developed, the theorists, scientists, and laypersons who ultimately apply the theories are responsible for the outcomes. Control is not inherently good or bad. The ethical issues arise over how the control is exercised.

Because communication theories explain the process of communication, users of communication theories have a special responsibility regarding the ethics of control. Ethical issues are inherent in almost any communicative exchange between humans, whether it's in interpersonal or group settings, public speeches, communications from government to citizens, or advertising or political campaigns. As Richard Johannesen argues:

> *Whether a communicator seeks to present information, increase someone's level of understanding, facilitate independent decision in another person, persuade about important values, demonstrate the existence and relevance of a societal problem, advocate a solution or program of action, or stimulate conflict—potential ethical issues inhere in the communicator's symbolic efforts.*[41]

Issues of control arise when someone decides to use/apply a communication theory. In communication it could be as simple as using a particular persuasive appeal known to gain compliance or as complex as an entire government misleading its citizenry about its misuse of nuclear weapons tests. Whether or not the application of a theory is ethical depends on one's perception of what is good or bad, right or wrong, moral or immoral. Richard Johannesen, a professor of communication at Northern Illinois University, has written extensively about the ethical standards communicators should use in judging choices of communicative techniques, contents, and purposes. Johannesen outlines seven perspectives for the ethical assessment of human communication, including political, human nature, dialogical, situational, religious, utilitarian, and legal perspectives. As categories, these perspectives are not necessarily mutually exclusive.[42]

Most political systems or governments adhere to an ideology that posits explicit or implicit sets of values and/or procedures accepted as essential to the functioning of the particular political government. In the United States, for example, democracy is valued where freedom of choice, freedom of press, freedom of religion, access to information, and tolerance of diversity is professed. Criteria such as this can be used to judge the ethicality of communication—that which suppresses such freedoms would be seen as unethical.

Human nature perspectives emphasize the essence of what it means to be human. The unique qualities of human nature—such as the capacity to reason, the capacity to create and use symbols, and the capacity to make value judgments—become the standard by which communication is evaluated. Messages that undermine such human characteristics are deemed unethical.

The dialogical perspective focuses on the attitudes interactants hold toward each other as the basis of ethical communication. Such attitudes as honesty, concern for the welfare of others, trust, open-mindedness, equality, directness, lack of pretense, and sincerity represent communication as dialogue. Communication as monologue, by contrast, is seen as one-way, unidirectional. Characteristics of such communication might include deception, exploitation, concern for self, and even coercion. Communication as monologue is seen as unethical.

The situational perspective uses the elements of the specific situation at hand as its base for making ethical decisions. Such situational dimensions are the role of or function of the communicator and the audience, audience expectations regarding the speaker's reasonableness, degree of awareness by the audience of the speaker's techniques, audience goals and values, and audience standards for ethical communication.

Religious perspectives are based on the teachings, rules, and moral codes found in the sacred literature of a particular religion. Many Christian ethics, for example, are based on the Ten Commandments found in the Bible. The moral codes of Islam are found in the Koran which spells out the rules of behavior and conduct for Muslims.

Utilitarian perspectives focus on whatever promotes usefulness, pleasure, and happiness for the greatest number of people as ethical. Ethical communications would be those that promote the greatest good for the greatest number. What constitutes "good" and the "greatest" number of people is certainly open to speculation. Such answers may be found in other ethical perspectives. A social utilitarian perspective sees as ethical that which promotes the good of the group, rather than the individual.

Legal perspectives operate under the premise that whatever is permitted within the legal code of a particular society is ethical; that which is illegal is unethical. Legal codes often conflict with other ethical perspectives. In the United States, for example, abortion is legal, but considered unethical by many religious perspectives. False advertising is also illegal and thus would be considered unethical.

Summary

Many of the communication theories presented in this book will explain how communication works. Equipped with this knowledge, you will have to make decisions on how to apply such theories. When you do apply them, you have made an ethical decision. Which ethical perspective will guide your decision?

CASE STUDY 2   Explanation, Prediction, and Control

Colon cancer is the second leading cause of cancer deaths—fifty-five thousand people die of it every year in the United States alone. Physicians have long observed that some kinds of cancer, including colon cancer, tend to run in families, which suggests that susceptibility to such cancers may be inherited genetically. Over the past few years, the genes that might cause those cancers have been the focus of much research. Recently, an international team of scientists believes they have discovered the underlying genetic basis for a common type of colon cancer. They narrowed their search to a precise stretch of DNA on chromosome 2 where they found consistent irregularities (mutancies) with colon cancer patients. The co-discoverers of the susceptibility gene, Albert de la Chapelle of the University of Helsinki, Finland, and Bert Vogelstein of Johns Hopkins University of Medicine, estimate that as many as one in every 200 people carry the gene.[a] Such a frequency is ten times greater than those genes causing more conventional genetic diseases. Scientists hope that the newly discovered gene will serve as a tool for identifying high-risk individuals before they get colon cancer. Knowing that the gene predisposes persons to the disease, scientists can predict who is susceptible to it. Scientists are hopeful that a blood test will be developed that can identify those people with the susceptibility gene and that early detection might eventually help reduce the death toll.

The discovery of the colon cancer susceptibility gene is a major medical breakthrough, one that can save thousands of lives each year. By explaining how the susceptibility gene works, scientists can predict who is likely to get colon cancer. By explaining and predicting, scientists can control the spread of the disease. By understanding how the gene works, and by being able to predict that those with the gene will develop colon cancer, the medical profession is faced with some very serious ethical issues. Most treatments for cancer are very costly and many of those costs are covered by an individual's health insurance. If it is possible to identify those people who are likely to develop colon cancer (estimates are that 160,000 people develop a type of colon cancer annually in the United States), insurance companies might use such information to deny coverage to those people carrying the gene they will simply apply the theory. Insurance companies, which routinely require that applicants complete a physical examination prior to coverage, could require all applicants to undergo a screening for the susceptibility gene. In essence, insurance companies could use the theory to control who they will and will not cover.

1. If you were an executive for an insurance company, would you require persons to submit to the blood test that locates the potential gene for colon cancer?
2. Should insurance companies have the right to force potential clients to submit to the blood test?
3. What kinds of theories do you use on a daily basis?
4. How do you use the theories to control aspects of your life?

a. Marx, J. (1993). "New Colon Cancer Gene Discovered," Science, 260, 751–753.

Glossary

Causal Necessity: A force that is the origin of some unavoidable outcome or regularity. A cause is the antecedent condition producing some effect.

Control: To guide or manage the actions or behaviors of animate or inanimate phenomenon.

Deductive Logic: The deriving of a conclusion based on logical inference. Proceeding from general statements (i.e., major premise) and inferring specific conclusions.

Explanation: A set of theoretical statements describing a phenomenon, identifying regularity about the phenomenon, and the force which makes the regularity necessary.

Inductive Logic: The act of reasoning from particulars to a whole or from specific instances to general conclusions.

Logical Necessity: A force of conceptually consistent facts leading to some inevitable or predictable conclusion or outcome.

Model: A graphic representation of an object or process.

Practical Necessity: The amount of normative force that motivates a person to act or behave in order to achieve some goal or end state.

Prediction: To forecast the future based on available information, observations, or scientific reason.

Regularity: Recurring, patterned, nonrandom, and consistent behavior or action.

Replication: The attempt to identically, partially, or conceptually repeat or duplicate the procedures of some earlier conducted test or observation.

Syllogism: A formal scheme or presentation of deductive logic consisting of a major and minor premise and a conclusion.

Theory: A serious and systematic attempt to explain something. A theory presents a systematic view of some phenomenon (i.e., concept).

References

1. Popper, K. R. (1972). *Objective Knowledge: An Evolutionary Approach,* Oxford: Clarendon.

2. Armitage, A. (1962). *Copernicus: The Founder of Modern Astronomy,* New York: A. S. Barnes and Company, Inc.

3. Capra, F. (1988). *The Turning Point: Science, Society, and the Rising Culture,* Toronto: Bantam.

4. Kerlinger, F. N. (1973). *Research Methods in the Behavioral Sciences,* (2nd ed.), New York: Holt, Rinehart and Winston, (p. 9).

5. Einstein, A. (1953). *Ideas and Opinions,* New York: Bonanza, (p. 226).

6. Popper, *Objective Knowledge.*

7. Harré, R. (1967). *An Introduction to the Logic of the Sciences,* New York: St. Martin's Press, (p. 8).

8. Habermas, J. (1979). *Communication and the Evolution of Society,* Boston: Beacon Press.

9. Harré, *The Logic of the Sciences.*

10. Cushman, D. P., & Pearce, W. B. (1977). "Generality and Necessity in Three Types of Theory about Human Communication, with Special Attention to Rules Theory," *Human Communication Research, 3,* 344–353.

11. Ibid.

12. Feigl, E. (1953). "Notes of Causality," in H. Feigl & M. Brodbeck, (Eds.), *Readings in the Philosophy of Science,* (pp. 408–418), New York: Appleton, Century, Crofts, Inc.

13. Brodbeck, M. (1968). "General Introduction," in M. Brodbeck, (Ed.), *Readings in the Philosophy of the Social Sciences,* (p. 7), New York: Macmillan.

14. Fisher, B. A. (1978). *Perspectives on Human Communication,* New York: Macmillan.

15. Woodfield, A. (1976). *Teleology,* Cambridge: Cambridge University Press.

16. Nagel, E. (1953). "Teleological Explanation and Teleological Systems," in Feigl & Brodbeck, *Readings in the Philosophy of Science,* (pp. 537–558).

17. Cushman & Pearce, "Generality and Necessity," 344–353.

18. Shimanoff, S. B. (1980). *Communication Rules: Theory and Research,* Beverly Hills: Sage.

19. Fisher, *Perspectives on Human Communication.*

20. Ibid.

21. Rudner, R. S. (1966). *Philosophy of Social Science,* Englewood Cliffs, NJ: Prentice-Hall, (pp. 64–65).

22. Ducasse, C. J. (1969). *Causation and the Types of Necessity,* New York: Dover.

23. Ibid.

24. Hawes, L. C. (1975). *Pragmatics of Analoguing: Theory and Model Construction in Communication.* Reading, MA: Addison-Wesley.

25. Ibid.

26. Ibid.

27. Shannon, C. E., & Weaver, W. (1949). *The Mathematical Theory of Communication,* Urbana, IL: University of Illinois Press.

28. Goss, B. (1983). *Communication in Everyday Life,* Belmont, CA: Wadsworth.

29. Berlo, D. K. (1960). *The Process of Communication,* New York: Holt, Rinehart and Winston.

30. Habermas, J. (1979). *Communication and the Evolution of Society,* Boston: Beacon Press.

31. Brodbeck, M., (1968). "Explanation, Prediction, and 'Imperfect' Knowledge," in Brodbeck, *Readings in the Philosophy of the Social Sciences,* (pp. 363–397).

32. Hawes, *Pragmatics of Analoguing,* (p. 35).

33. Andersen, P. A. (1989). "Philosophy of Science," in P. Emmert & L. L. Barker, (Eds.), *Measurement of Communication Behavior,* (pp. 3–17), New York: Longman.

34. Ibid.

35. Popper, K. R. (1959). *The Logic of Scientific Discovery,* New York: Harper and Row.

36. Keynes, J. M. (1957). *A Treatise on Probability,* London: Macmillan.

37. Popper, *The Logic of Scientific Discovery.*

38. Hendrick, C. (1991). "Replications, Strict Replications, and Conceptual Replications: Are They Important?" in J. W. Neuliep, (Ed.), *Replication Research in the Social Sciences,* (pp. 41–50), Newbury Park, CA: Sage.

39. Rosenthal, R. (1991). "Replication in Behavioral Research," in Neuliep, *Replication Research in the Social Sciences,* (pp. 1–30).

40. Andersen, "Philosophy of Science," (pp. 3–17).

41. Johannesen, R. L. (1990). *Ethics in Human Communication,* Prospect Heights, IL: Waveland Press, (p. 2).

42. Johannesen, R. L. (1990) *Ethics in Human Communication,* Prospect Heights, IL: Waveland Press.

$Chapter$ 3

Building Communication Theory

Perhaps the most striking feature which all the social sciences
share is their internal diversity.[1]—W. BARNETT PEARCE

This chapter will profile the current state of communication theory. The study of human communication theory is the study of a very diverse group of theories. Many communication scholars view such theoretical diversity as a strength, while others view it as a sign of weakness and incoherence. Whether seen as a positive or negative aspect of the field, few would disagree that diversity of theory abounds in communication.

Many communication theories have their roots in other academic disciplines such as psychology and sociology. Because of such variance, no single textbook can adequately cover all of them. This chapter will, however, provide a broad overview of these theories and will outline criteria for evaluating them.

Classifying Communication Theories

In order to manage the vast number of communication theories, scholars have created classification schemes, although many theorists dislike having their theory categorized at all. B. Aubrey Fisher, Leonard Hawes, and Stephen Littlejohn, all respected communication scholars, have devised methods of classification that can serve as examples. Fisher classifies communication theories into four general categories, including (a) mechanistic, (b) psychological, (c) interactional, and (d) pragmatic.[2] Hawes also categorizes theories into four basic groups, including (a) literary, (b) academic, (c) eristic, and (d) symbolic.[3] Littlejohn classifies communication theories into at least nine different categories, including theories of (a) signs and language, (b) discourse, (c) message production, (d) message reception and processing, (e) symbolic interaction, dramatism, and narrative, (f) social and cultural reality, (g) experience and interpretation, (h) critical theories, and (i) four kinds contextual theories.[4] In this book, communication theories are classified into the following four categories.

1. General/Metatheory: Theories that describe the basic underlying structure of communication and/or other social or natural phenomena, that present a grand scheme of the nature of things, and that differ in terms of necessity (e.g., causal, practical, and logical). Although there are only a few of these types of theories, they provide the blueprint for most others. Examples include causal process, systems, and social-action theories.

2. Topical: These theories describe topical forms of communication found in most communication settings and explain the underlying structure of different types of communication (e.g., verbal, nonverbal, persuasive).

3. Contextual: These theories describe communication that occurs in particular settings/contexts. A context is defined by its physical, social, and psychological environment. Communication contexts also can be defined by the number of people in the setting (e.g., dyadic, small group, organizational) and the type of feedback (immediate, delayed).

4. Humanistic: Humanistic theories are rhetorical, aesthetic, critical, historical, interpretative, and philosophical theories of communication that generally do not rely on scientific standardized empirical confirmation and/or falsification. Some of these theories may assume a sociopolitical reference for explaining communication.

General/Metatheories

This first category is important because it outlines the basic assumptions about the underlying structure of communication, regardless of context. These theories, which serve as the foundation for other communication theories, are sometimes called "metatheories" because, in a sense, they are theories about how to theorize. Most topical and contextual theories are dependent on the general metatheoretical approach adopted by the theorist. Three traditional metatheoretical approaches include causal process, systems, and social-action theories. An important difference between these theories is the principle of necessity upon which their method of explanation is based—causal process theories rely on the principle of causal necessity, the social-action (rules) approach emphasizes practical necessity, and the systems approach favors logical necessity.

A critical point to make here is that most theories do not rely exclusively on either causal, practical, or logical necessity but tend to favor one approach over another. Several theories actually use a combination of causal and practical necessity to explain communication. Causal process theories generally apply classical scientific assumptions and contend there are causal processes that can explain communicative behavior. Advocates of the social-action (rules) perspective contend that communication phenomena are governed by societal and contextual norms and prescriptions of which they call "rules." These researchers, who see human communicative behavior as goal driven and rules as internally generated decisions about how to accomplish goals, focus their theoretical work around identifying those rules. Systems thinkers treat the process of communication as a social system; that is, in terms of relationships and integration. Like natural, biological, sociological, and psychological systems, communication is seen as open living system and is an integrated whole whose properties cannot be reduced into smaller units.

A new and emerging metatheoretical perspective in communication is called the "biosocial" approach. These theorists contend that some behavior is caused by biological factors and some is the result of free choice and the drive to achieve goals. Hence, these theories employ a combination of causal and practical necessity in their explanations of human communication. Because these general metatheories direct and influence the communication theorist and researcher they are a critical ingredient to the development of topical and contextual theories.

Topical Theories

Topical theories, which are greater in number and more specific than metatheories, focus on general themes or topics of communication that are present in most, but not necessarily all, communication settings.[5] For example, since just about any communication setting involves the use of language, theories of language and nonverbal and persuasive communication are examples of topical theories.

Theories of Language and Verbal Communication

Many topical theories of language have their roots outside the field of communication, in areas such as linguistics, psycholinguistics, and sociolinguistics. Because language is a central component of communication these theories are important to understand. The following list presents some of the dominant theories of language.

   1. Conversation Analysis: Conversation analysis theories focus on the relationship between conversation and language. Many theorists see conversation as a form of game playing that involves moves, turns, goals, and strategy. Many of these theorists maintain that conversation, like language, is a highly rule-governed form of communicative behavior. Conversation analysts try to discover the rules of conversation and guide people in their conversations with others. Communication scholars engaged in conversation analysis include Robert T. Craig, Margaret McLaughlin, Robert Nofsinger, Sandra Ragan, and Karen Tracy.[6]

   2. Ethnography of Communication: Developed initially by Dell Hymes, this perspective assumes that the nature of communication, especially speech, is systematically patterned and needs to be studied on its own and for its own sake. The nature of communication is culture specific and cross-culturally diverse. Ethnographers typically examine ways of speaking within a particular culture or community and through the use of case studies and fieldwork, search for specific patterns of communication that are distinctive to a particular culture and for general principles of communication that are cross-culturally valid. Ethnographers generally do not rely on scientific method in their scholarship. Donal Carbaugh, Gerry Philipsen, Steven Pratt, and Lawrence Weider are representative scholars in this tradition.[7]

3. Face Work /Model of Politeness: Developed by sociologist Irving Goffman, "Face-Work" is based on the idea that social interaction revolves around maintaining one's face, or a socially approved identity. People claim face by taking a "line" during interaction. A "line" is a verbal or nonverbal act which expresses people's definition of the situation and themselves. Penelope Brown and Stephen Levinson extended the notion of face to include positive and negative face. Positive face is the want to be thought of as desirable. Negative face is the want not to be imposed on by others. Communication, especially speech acts, are expected to attend to both positive and negative face.[8]

4. General Semantics/Functional Theories: These theories focus on how language takes on meaning. The guiding principle here is that symbols are arbitrarily learned stimuli representing something else and that there is no natural connection between a symbol and that which it represents. Meanings are culturally learned. Theories in this group include Ogden and Richard's theory of meaning; Sapir and Whorf's cultural theory of language; Morris's theory of signs, language and behavior; Langer's theory of symbols; and Korzybski's theory of general semantics.[9]

5. Generative Grammar: A type of language acquisition theory, Noam Chomsky's theory argues that language has a deep structure grammar innate in all humans and that it consists of subject-predicate relations, verb-object relations, and modifications. Chomsky suggested that there is a universal grammar to which any human language conforms. Such grammar corresponds with the nature and scope of the human cognitive organization. All humans, regardless of culture, are born with a mental representation of the universal grammar. Chomsky also distinguished between language performance and language competence; performance being the behavioral output and competence the inherent knowledge of language. Chomsky defined language as all of the possible sentences generated by syntax.[10]

6. Semiology: This is a theory of signs and how they are used to represent meanings. A sign is a socially agreed upon convention that represents something else. The process of representing things by signs is called signification or semiosis.[11]

7. Speech Act Theory: Speech act theorists maintain that in order to understand language, one must understand a speaker's intentions. Any statement uttered is called a speech act. Five types of speech acts include commissives, directives, assertives, expressives, and declarations. Speech acts are governed by constitutive and regulative rules. Constitutive rules prescribe the meaning of an act whereas regulative rules guide the sequence of acts. The theory was developed by John Searle.[12]

8. Speech Accommodation Theory: According to this theory, during interaction, people try to adapt or adjust their style of speech to others in order to increase efficiency, gain approval, and maintain positive social identity. Major theorists here include Howard Giles, Anthony Mulac, James Bradac, and Richard L. Street.[13]

9. Structural Theories/Classical Linguistics: These theories outline the hierarchical framework of verbal language. Structural linguistics, for example, divide a sentence into four component parts including sounds, words, phrases, and clauses. Phrase structure grammar breaks down a sentence into noun and verb phrases. Finite state theory contends that sentences are produced from left to right, one word at a time. Ferdinand Saussure's analysis of signs was a major contribution to structural linguistics.[14]

10. Symbolic Interactionism: Developed mainly from the works of George Herbert Mead, this theory's central premise is that human behavior and interaction are carried on through the medium of symbols and their meanings. Individuals become human through interaction with others. Core concepts in the theory include society, self, and mind which evolve from the social act of communicating. Mead argued that the self is created by an individual's acting toward it as though it is a social object. The self is designated symbolically and thus gains meaning. The meanings of objects or people are created when people treat them similarly through their symbols. Other theorists in this tradition include Herbert Blumer, Manford Kuhn, Jerome Manis, and Bernard Meltzer.[15]

Conversation analysts, who study the ways in which people use rules to guide their conversation with others, might focus on turn taking, action sequences, and speech acts. Other areas of study deal with conversational alignment—the strategies people use to correct mistakes made during conversation—and conversational competence and the ways people become efficient in conversation. Many theorists spend much of their time articulating the different rules of conversation.[16]

Ethnography of communication is as much a method of conducting research as it is a theory of language. Individual ethnographers might actually live within a particular speech community and study their unique styles and patterns of verbal communication. Gerry Philipsen, for example, spent considerable time in a Chicago community of labor workers and discovered a unique set of rules for how the men communicate among themselves, with their spouses and children, and with outsiders. Lawrence Weider and Steven Pratt studied the rules for language use among a Native American Osage tribe.[17]

Functional theories, also called general semantics, focus on how language takes on meaning; that is, how symbols can and do derive their meaning. Count Alfred Korzybski, regarded as the father of general semantics, argued that words are only maps of reality, not the actual territory; that is, they only depict part of the territory while simultaneously condensing it.[18]

Noam Chomsky, a linguist, mathematician, and philosopher, developed one of the most influential theories of language in the area of generative grammar. He believes that humans are born with an innate biologically determined capacity to acquire language. In addition, humans learn language, not by memorizing all of the possible sentences, but through the unconscious acquisition of a deep structure grammar that allows them to generate an infinite number of sentences.[19]

Speech accommodation theory focuses on how people try to adapt their conversation to whomever they are speaking. Generally people will try to converge (i.e., adjust toward the other person's style) or diverge (i.e., adjust away from the other's style) with their conversational partners depending on the situation.[20]

Structural theories of language, sometimes called descriptive linguistics, focus on how language is structured and how it is used. The standard structural model of linguistics breaks down a sentence into parts, including phonemes (sounds), morphemes (words), and syntax (the rules for combining morphemes).[21]

Symbolic interactionism, which contends that society is a cluster of cooperative behaviors by a group of societal members, grew out the work of George Herbert Mead and his followers. The core concepts here include society, self, and mind. Humans are active in shaping their own behavior but the self becomes humanized through interaction with others. Symbolic interactionists believe that human behavior and interaction are carried out through the medium of symbols and meaning. Methodologically, symbolic interactionsists believe that an understanding of human behavior requires the study of covert behavior.[22]

Nonverbal Communication Theories

Topical theories of nonverbal communication focus on the type of communication that occurs without the use of spoken or written words, including kinesics (i.e., body movement), occulesics (i.e., eye behavior), paralinguistics (i.e., use of the voice), proxemics (i.e., use of space), and chronemics (i.e., use of time). The following list presents some such theories.

1. Action Theory: Developed by D. Morris, this theory categorizes kinesic behaviors as inborn, discovered, absorbed, trained, and mixed actions. Inborn behaviors are instinctive, discovered behaviors are essentially unconscious, absorbed behaviors are those actions we imitate, trained behaviors are learned, and mixed actions are acquired by combining the other four.[23]

2. Adaption Theory: People use nonverbal communication to adapt to various situations and to maintain the self.[24]

3. Arousal Labeling Theory: Proposed by M. L. Patterson, this theory argues that nonverbal intimacy behaviors arouse others who interpret them as positive or negative. The other's interpretation of the behaviors determines their subsequent behavior (i.e., either reciprocation or avoidance).[25]

4. Ethological Approaches: Ethology is the comparative study of animal behavior. This approach to nonverbal communication began with Charles Darwin in the late 1800s. One assumption guiding this approach is that human beings represent a level of biological evolution in the animal kingdom and that certain nonverbal behaviors are innate response patterns. The origin of these behaviors predates verbal communication.[26]

5. Equilibrium Theory (Affiliative Conflict Theory): Proposed by Argyle and Dean, this theory maintains that interaction is tied to a conflict between approach and avoidance forces. Interactants try to establish and maintain a comfortable equilibrium point during interaction. Equilibrium is reached by compromising approach and avoidance behaviors, which are communicated nonverbally through distance, eye contact, touch, and gestures.[27]

6. Expectancy Violation Theory: This is one of the more dominant nonverbal communication theories developed by Judee Burgoon, who argues that people have well-established expectations about the interaction distances others will adopt. These expectations are generally learned culturally and are occasionally violated by others which causes arousal in the recipient. There are circumstances under which violations of social norms may be perceived positively particularly if enacted by a person of higher status.[28]

7. Functional Theories: These theories focus on how nonverbal communication actually communicates. Knapp contends that nonverbal communication functions to accent, complement, contradict, regulate, and repeat verbal messages. Patterson's functional approach suggests that nonverbal communication functions to provide information, express intimacy, regulate interaction, express social control, and facilitate service or task goals. Mehrabian's metaphorical functional approach divides nonverbal behaviors into three functional groups, including dominance-submissiveness, pleasure-displeasure, and arousal-nonarousal. These functions vary according to one's power, status, liking, and responsiveness.[29]

8. Structural Theories: These theories outline the basic organizational composition of nonverbal communication and are mostly descriptive rather than explanatory. Structural theories include Birdwhistell's theory of kinesics which contends that the structure of nonverbal language is analogous to the structure of verbal language. Also in this group of theories is Hall's theory of proxemics and Ekman and Friesen's theory of nonverbal signs.[30]

Some of the earliest treatment of nonverbal communication dates back as far as Aristotle and Cicero, with his work on "pronunciatio," or delivery, that focused on how the voice and body are used in public address. Many of the early approaches to nonverbal communication emphasized delivery's importance to the public speaker. Gilbert Austin, for example, developed a complete taxonomy of the appropriate gestures and body movements that should accompany certain types of speech events. This type of study is typically referred to as the study of elocution and is not the focus of modern scientific approaches to nonverbal communication.[31]

Contemporary approaches to nonverbal behavior began in earnest with Darwin's publication of *The Expression of Emotion in Man and Animals* in 1872. Darwin was convinced that nonverbal expressions of emotion are instinctive and innate. He was also well aware of the communicative function of nonverbal behaviors, particularly the movements of the face and body. To Darwin, nonverbal behaviors are not learned and are not culturally bound.[32] Another influential theory of nonverbal behavior came from Ray Birdwhistell, an anthropologist who argued that nonverbal behaviors are learned and differ from cultural to culture; that is, there are no universal meanings behind any nonverbal behaviors, including the smile. Birdwhistell also argued for what is called the linguistic-kinesic analogy. The argument holds that verbal and nonverbal language are structurally analogous.[33] Contemporary scientific theories of nonverbal communication began in the late 1960s and early 1970s. Here, several different approaches have been offered, including the equilibrium theory, the expectancy violation theory, and some aspects of functional theories. These approaches tend to focus on the communicative function of nonverbal actions and how nonverbal behaviors serve as indicators of attitudes and affect. These theories also look at how nonverbal behaviors are decoded and the impact they have on receivers in terms of perceptions of competency, intimacy, and persuasiveness.

Persuasive Communication Theories

The following is a list and brief description of topical theories of persuasion:

1. Attribution Theory: According to attribution theory, when people observe the actions of others they make attributions about why people behaved in such a way. People attribute the behavior of others to personal or situational factors. We are more likely to send persuasive messages to those whose action we attribute to personal factors than situational factors. In addition, how we respond to a persuasive message depends on our attribution of the speaker's motivation for sending the message. Attribution theorists include Fritz Heider, Edward Jones, Harold H. Kelley, Robert E. Nisbett, and Alan Sillars.[34]

2. Classical Learning Theories: Based on Skinner's classical and operant conditioning models, these theories focus on the relationship between the responses people make to specific persuasive stimuli and positive and negative reinforcement their responses foster. Persuasive messages serve as stimuli whereas attitudinal, affective, or behavioral change serves as the response.[35]

3. Cognitive Consistency Theories: People desire consistency and when their thoughts, behaviors, or feelings are inconsistent they will strive to resolve it, usually by changing their attitudes, beliefs, or behaviors. Hence, inconsistent states are susceptible to persuasion. There are several variations of the consistency premise, including balance theory, congruency theory, and cognitive dissonance theory. Noteworthy theorists here include Fritz Heider and Leon Festinger.[36]

4. Counterattitudinal Advocacy: Gerald Miller and Michael Burgoon posit that persuasion can occur when people advocate that which is counter to what they do not really believe. If you can get people to espouse an idea or act in a way counter to their beliefs, they may actually begin to believe in what they have said or done. This is actually a form of consistency theory.[37]

5. Elaboration Likelihood Model: According to Richard E. Petty and John T. Cacioppo, the model's originators, people process persuasion messages via one of two routes, either centrally or peripherally. Centrally processed messages involve the active assessment of the persuasive message, its content, logic, and rationale. Peripherally processed messages involve focusing on external variables such as source attractiveness, delivery, and style.[38]

6. Information-Integration Theory: Attitude formation, reinforcement, or change is a function of how an individual combines, or integrates, all the available information relevant to an attitudinal object. People assign parameters to each item of information they process—that is, weight and valence. Weight is the person's subjective belief in the truth of the information and valence is the person's positive or negative evaluation of the information.[39]

7. Social Learning Theory: Albert Bandura argued that people learn new behaviors and attitudes by perceiving the way people around them respond to their own behavior. If people are socially rewarded for their behaviors and attitudes, they will continue to hold them. If people are socially punished for their behaviors and attitudes, they will discontinue them.[40]

8. Social Judgment Theory: This theory, first articulated by Carolyn and Muzafer Sherif and Robert Nebergall, deals specifically with ego-involvement. People are persuaded by messages depending on their level of ego-involvement with the issue. The more ego involved the less amount of change. Ego-involvement serves as a reference point by which persuasive messages are judged.[41]

9. Yale Theories of Attitude Change: Named after the university where Carl Hovland, Irving Janis, and Harold Kelley advanced the research, these theories focus on the adoption of new attitudes as a consequence of learning new information. Persuasion is the result of who says what to whom with what effect. These theories focus on source, message, channel, and receiver variables that enhance the adoption of new attitudes.[42]

Though defined in many ways, persuasion is generally known as the communicative process by which people try to influence others with messages. Persuasive communication theories are those that either describe or explain how people send messages that influence others to act, think, or feel a certain way. The study of persuasion, the oldest subdiscipline in communication, began as far back as 500 B.C.,[43] when it was actually called rhetoric, which Aristotle defined as "the available means of persuasion." Contemporary scientific study of persuasion began in earnest during the 1930s with its focus on the effects of propaganda during World War I. Research blossomed during the 1950s at Yale University when Carl Hovland and his associates in the psychology department studied attitude change and argued that attitudes are learned predispositions of behavior. Their research focused on a chain of learning responses consisting of the source (who says it), the message (what is said), the receiver (who listens), and with what effect (behavioral, attitudinal, or emotional shaping, reinforcement, or change). In the 1960s more cognitively based theories and the notion of consistency came to the fore. This group of theories assumes that people mentally organize their attitudes in consistent patterns and when incoming persuasive messages are inconsistent with their frame of reference, they must either change their attitudes or ignore the persuasive stimuli. The guiding notion here is that inconsistent states are susceptible to persuasion. In the 1980s and still today, much attention is paid to individual persuasive message strategies, known as compliance-gaining strategies, which focus on how personality, culture, and situational dimensions affect the sending and receiving of individual persuasive messages. Because this approach is relatively new, few theories have been formulated. Note that many of the persuasive communication theories were begun outside the field of communication by psychologists.

Contextual Theories

A fundamental dimension of communication is its contextual nature, because all communication occurs within and is affected by a context. Remember from Chapter 1 that a context is the physical, social, and psychological aspects of a communication situation. Of the four basic categories of communication theories, perhaps most can be classified as contextual. These theories attempt to explain communication that occurs in particular settings or situations. Most communication theorists agree on four basic contexts of communication, including dyadic/interpersonal, group, organizational, and mediated/mass, which are typically defined according to the number of people communicating and the type of feedback communicated. For example, dyadic/interpersonal communication contexts are usually those consisting of two people interacting with direct and immediate feedback. Group communication contexts consist of anywhere from three to ten people communicating with relatively less direct and immediate feedback. Mass or mediated communication contexts are characterized by over twenty people with delayed and indirect feedback as in the case of a public speech or television program. Organizational contexts fall in between group and mediated contexts. These contexts form a hierarchy whereby each of the higher contexts include aspects of the lower levels but also adds something individual of its own.[44] For example, there is certainly dyadic/interpersonal communication within group or organizational communication contexts.

Dyadic/Interpersonal Theories

Following is an annotated list of several dyadic/interpersonal communication theories. Please note that the annotations are not comprehensive and are designed to provide only a brief introduction to the theory.

1. Attribution Theory: Developed by psychologists Fritz Heider, Harold Kelley, and Edward Jones, this theory accounts for the way people explain their own and others' behavior by making attributions. Behavior is attributed to either the personal dispositions of the actor or to uncontrollable situational constraints. Personal disposition attributions are more meaningful and informative about the other person than are situational attributions.[45]

2. Constructivism: Formulated by Jesse Delia and his associates, this theory, which is based in impression formation and personal construct theory, says that all social processes occur through a cognitive system of constructs (i.e., pattern or templates that facilitate the interpretation of reality). Constructs used to perceive others are called interpersonal constructs and construct systems vary from simple to complex. Individuals with complex cognitive systems are more positively disposed to communication than cognitively simple persons.[46]

3. Fundamental Interpersonal Relations Orientation Theory (FIRO): Originated by psychologist William Schutz, this theory holds that people are attracted to and interact with people in order to fulfill three basic needs, including (a) inclusion, the need to belong; (b) control, the need to be in charge and have power; and (c) affection, the need to be loved. This theory also applies to group communication contexts.[47]

4. Impression Formation Theory: Actually a group of theories could be called impression formation theory (e.g., constructivism, uncertainty reduction). Impression formation theory describes how individuals use perception and information to form impressions of others and what we do with that information in making decisions about others, especially the decision to interact with them.[48]

5. Interpersonal Attraction Theory (Reinforcement Theory): Articulated by psychologist Donn Byrne, this theory outlines the forces that attract and/or repel us from others. One hypothesis is that we are attracted to people who reward us (positive reinforcement) and are repelled from those who punish us (negative reinforcement).[49]

6. Objective Self-Awareness Theory (Interpersonal Knowledge Theory): Developed by Charles Berger and his colleagues, this theory contends that individuals are aware of themselves in two ways—objectively and subjectively. Objective self-awareness occurs when one's self is the focus of attention. Subjective self-awareness is when one is more aware of his or her surroundings than him- or herself. The degree of self-awareness is important regarding interpersonal communication.[50]

7. Relational Development Theory: Relational development theory has been advanced by many communication scholars including Mark Knapp, William Wilmot, Gerald Phillips, and Steve Duck. These theorists contend that relationships develop in a gradual stage-by-stage process. Each stage of the relationship is characterized by the interaction between the relational partners. Many of these theorists have created their own models of relational stages.[51]

8. Rhetorical Sensitivity Theory: Developed by Roderick Hart, this theory states interpersonal relationships are more satisfying and healthy if the interactants are rhetorically sensitive; that is, if they are concerned about themselves and others and can adapt to situational needs. The theory also outlines two other types of people called Noble Selves and Rhetorical Reflectors. Noble Selves typically do not adapt well to others whereas Rhetorical Reflectors conform at will to the desires of others.[52]

9. Social Exchange Theory: Developed by psychologists Thibaut and Kelley, this is a theory of how people maintain their interpersonal relationships. According to the theory, relationships are said to revolve around the exchange of resources (e.g., money, time, sex, communication, self-disclosure). To give up a resource is a cost, to receive a resource is a reward. As long as relational partners perceive there to be a balanced exchange of resources, the relationship remains stable. When one member perceives there to be an imbalance of exchange, relational dissatisfaction may occur.[53]

10. Social Penetration Theory: Originally conceived by psychologists Altman and Taylor and further developed by communication scholars Miller and Steinberg, this is a theory very much akin to relational development theory but with a twist. According to this theory, as relationships develop, they grow closer in intimacy and Miller and Steinberg contend that the closer two people become depends in large part on the type of information they communicate to each other. Noninterpersonal relationships are characterized by communication that is either culturally (e.g., race, language) or sociologically (group membership) based. Interpersonal relationships are characterized by the exchange of psychological information (e.g., attitudes, motivations, beliefs, values, etc.).[54]

11. Self-Perception Theory: Proposed by psychologist Daryl Bem, this theory advances the notion that individuals come to know themselves and their attitudes and emotions by making observations of their own behavior. According to Bem, our inner thoughts do not provide an accurate picture of ourselves so we must observe our own actions. This is considered an interpersonal theory because how we view ourselves determines in large part the other people with whom we choose to develop interpersonal relationships.[55]

12. Social Comparison Theory: Originally proposed by Leon Festinger, this theory argues that people have a need to evaluate themselves and their attitudes, emotions, and behaviors and one way to do this is by comparing them with others' attitudes, behaviors and emotions. In a sense, we use the thoughts, actions, and emotions of others as a reference or a barometer for our own. Typically we compare ourselves to others who are similar to us.[56]

13. Theory of Relational Control: Actually a part of a larger systems theory of interpersonal communication, the theory of relational control was developed by Frank Millar, Edna Rogers and their associates. These theorists assert that relational partners maintain their relationships by negotiating metaphorical distance between each other. The vertical distance between partners is relational control. The control distance is exercised when a partner tries to direct, delimit, and define the actions of the relationship.[57]

14. Uncertainty Reduction Theory: This theory, formulated by Charles Berger and Richard Calabrese, is a perspective that deals with initial entry stages of relational development. Central to the theory is the fundamental assumption that when people meet for the first time, their primary concern is the reduction of uncertainty or the increase of predictability about the behavior of both themselves and the others in the interaction. A basic axiom of the theory is that as interaction increases, uncertainty decreases.[58]

Theories of interpersonal communication center on communication between two people and many focus on relationships. Many theorists in this area contend that a major function of communication is to initiate, maintain, and terminate relationships. Other theorists argue that the only way one can define a relationship is via communication. Note that several of these have their roots in psychology including attribution, fundamental interpersonal relations orientation, impression formation, interpersonal attraction, self-perception, social comparison, and social exchange theory. Though based in psychology, these theories have been applied to communication.

Theories of Group Communication

Following is an annotated listing of the group communication theories, designed to be only a brief introduction and not an exhaustive treatment. Group theories are generally concerned with those settings in which three to ten people are interacting and one of the major foci of these theories is on group decision making. Many scholars contend that a major function of groups is to make decisions. Groupthink, structuration theory, task contingency theory, and social decisions schemes theory are decision-making based theories. Interestingly, one theory, proposed by communication scholar Dean Hewes, argues that group decisions are not a function of communication but result from what is called socioegocentric interaction. Other group theories, such as field theory, FIRO, and group syntality theory, focus on the physical and psychological characteristics of groups.

    1. Exchange Theory: See "Social Exchange Theory" on page 53. The same assumptions apply but in relation to group settings.

    2. Field Theory: This theory was developed by Kurt Lewin who maintains that group behavior is the result of a field of positive and negative interdependent forces inside and outside of the group. Each force affects the individual and the total group. Central to field theory is the notion of lifespace; that is, the physical space in which the group activity takes place. Individual lifespaces are subjective to the extent that they represent the perceptions group members have about the other group members and the group's activities. Lifespace is shared by group members.[59]

    3. Fundamental Interpersonal Relations Orientation Theory (FIRO): See "FIRO" in the previous list. The same assumptions apply but in relation to group settings.

    4. Groupthink: This classic theory was developed by psychologist Irving Janis who defined groupthink as "a mode of thinking that people engage in when they are deeply involved in a cohesive in-group, when members' striving for unanimity override their motivation to realistically appraise alternative courses of action." Janis asserts that overly cohesive groups are prone to this phenomena and outlines eight symptoms of groupthink, including the illusion of invulnerability, a belief in the inherent morality of the group, collective rationalization, the creation of out-group stereotypes, members' self-censorship, the illusion of unanimity, the application of pressure on group members who dissent from the group, and self-appointed mindguards.[60]

    5. Group Syntality Theory: Created by psychologist Raymond Cattell, this theory is related to field theory in that it stresses the interrelationships within a group. Syntality theory also specifies that groups have three interdependent characteristics that distinguish them from other groups, including (a) population traits; that is, the group's demographic makeup; (b) internal structure; group size, membership roles, the physical setting of group meetings; and (c) syntality; the group's personality. Cattell argued that group syntality is a function of the population traits and internal structure.[61]

6. Socioegocentric Theory: This theory questions the relationship between communication and group decision making and offers an alternative explanation of how groups make decisions. The basic assumption is that group communication is epiphenomenal. In other words, decision making occurs with and seems to result from communication but actually does not; decision making stems from noninteractive factors called socioegocentric speech. Advanced by Dean Hewes, this theory contends that decisions are made through purely structural, content-free resources such as turn taking and nonsubstantive connecting devices that allow group members to interact with each other and make decisions though their individual contributions are essentially unrelated.[62]

7. Symbolic Convergence Theory: Developed by Ernest Bormann and his associates, this theory centers around fantasy themes. Bormann alleges that groups create their own miniculture through the sharing of stories, anecdotes, jokes, and reminiscences. These narratives are called fantasy themes and help the group build its own consciousness. Typically, fantasy themes are stories about the group or the organization in which the group functions and through the sharing of them, group members jointly experience emotions and learn to become a part of the group.[63]

8. Structuration Theory: This theory offers a framework for the study of group decision making. Based on the writings of Giddens, Marshall Scott Poole and his associates state that the basic unit of analysis in this theory is the social practices of the group. These practices include group decision making, courtship, conversation, or religious and civil ceremonies. Such practices result in structures; that is, the unobservable rules and resources used to generate observable patterns of behavior. Structures are both the medium of action and an outcome of action. The structures of any particular group stem from the social institution in which the group exists.[64]

9. Task Contingency Theory: This theory was developed by Randy Hirokawa who argues that the relationships between communication and group performance is a function of three variables, including task difficulty, cooperation between members, and the number of potential solutions that the group might choose. Group communication will vary as the three variables do. For example, in a situation where there is high task difficulty, high cooperation, but low a number of potential solutions, the group should try to centralize important information and develop a decision-making strategy.[65]

10. Theory of Social Decisions Schemes: Developed by psychologist James H. Davis, this theory is aimed at accounting for the distribution of group decisions while focusing on individual-group differences. A central theme is that groups provide a mechanism for recognizing diverse personal opinion and preferences in the decision-making process. When an individual group member contributes an idea that opinion, though not technically a vote, is much like a vote. As more and more members contribute their individual ideas, the distribution of opinion is revealed and the group reaches a decision without actually voting. However any particular group achieves this is called its social decision scheme. There can be any number of different types of social decision schemes depending on the group. An advantage of these schemes is that no formal vote has to be taken.[66]

Organizational Communication Theories

The following list outlines the major theories of organizations, and although many of these are not communication theories per se, they are important for the organizational communication scholar to know and understand because of the organization's inherent relationship with communication. The classical school, for example, is not a theory of communication but rather a theory of organizational structure. On the other hand, a scientific management approach sees communication as relatively unimportant. Again, please note that the annotations accompanying these theories are brief introductions and are not intended as exhaustive treatises on any one particular theory.

1. Classical Theory: The classical theory of organizations, frequently called the classical school, is not a communication theory per se but is recognized as the first standardized attempt to analyze organizational activities. Classical theory focuses almost entirely on the structure of the formal organizations and is based on three distinct but related theories, including Max Weber's bureaucracy theory, Henri Fayol's administrative theory, and Frederick Taylor's scientific management theory.[67]

2. Bureaucracy Theory: Developed by sociologist Max Weber, bureaucracy theory provides a descriptive account of the nature of effective hierarchical organizations with strong emphasis on authority and power. Weber outlines three types of authority, including traditional, bureaucratic, and charismatic. In addition, Weber outlines eight, now considered classic, structural characteristics of bureaucracies.[68]

3. Administrative Theory: Henri Fayol, another classical theorist, developed what is sometimes called administrative theory. Fayol's central thesis is that management is common to all human undertakings, including business, government, and social systems such as the family. Fayol categorized organizations into six activities, including (a) technical, (b) commercial, (c) financial, (d) security, (e) accounting, and (f) managerial. Fayol is very well known for his fourteen principles of management.[69]

1. Division of Work
2. Authority & Responsibility
3. Discipline
4. Unity of Command
5. Unity of Direction
6. Subordination of Individuals
7. Remuneration
8. Centralization
9. Scalar Chain
10. Order
11. Equity
12. Stability of Tenure
13. Exercise of Initiative
14. Esprit de Corps

4. Scientific Management Theory: This theory was developed by Frederick Taylor, whose book, *Principles of Scientific Management,* proposes four principles of management, including (a) rule-of-thumb methods of management should be replaced with scientific knowledge about the work world, (b) the scientific selection of "first-class" workers who are trained for their task, (c) a hearty cooperation between management and workers, and (d) equally distributed work between managers and workers.[70]

5. Functional Theory: The functional theory of organizational communication focuses on what communication actually does and how it contributes to the overall operation of the organization. Functional theorists suggest that communication (a) transmits information throughout the organization, (b) defines relationships between organizational members, and (c) facilitates change. Functional theory also focuses on networks; that is, the formal and informal patterns of communication that bind organizational members.[71]

6. Human Relations Theory: Sometimes called the human relations school or movement, this theory challenged the idea that productivity is the function of organizational structure. Theorists of the human relations school assert that more emphasis should be placed on the social dimensions of the workplace. This includes worker morale, worker attitudes, and the work environment. This movement started with the famous Hawthorne studies which found that productivity actually increased with reduced lighting.[72]

7. Independent Mindedness Theory: This theory, as applied to organizational communication, stresses that Americans tend to have their own thoughts and opinions (i.e., have independent minds) and are not likely to passively accept the opinions and orders of others (e.g., managers). Thus, workers will be more productive and satisfied and will also perceive their supervisors as more effective when they are allowed their independent mindedness in making decisions and carrying out tasks.[73]

8. Organizational Culture Theory: Based on the work of anthropologist Clifford Geertz, this theory looks at an organization as a culture all its own; that is, it is a way of life for its members with its own set of shared meanings. The underlying premise is that communication defines a culture by means of communication performances such as industry vocabulary usages, storytelling, and organizational rites and rituals. The basic goal of communication theorists here is to understand how organizational life is accomplished through communication.[74]

9. Organizational Information Theory: Based on the writing of Karl Weick, this theory emphasizes organizing over organization. Weick equates organizing with information processing and views organizing as a process of reducing uncertainty. Weick contends that much of the information received by an organization is equivocal and creates uncertainty. To reduce the uncertainty, members must progress through a communication-behavior cycle. This cycle has three stages, including (a) the enactment—reception of equivocal information, (b) selection—making decisions about the information, and (c) retention—making copies of the information for storage.[75]

Critical/Humanistic Theories

Humanistic theories of communication are different from the other three types because they are not scientifically based. Some are perhaps among the oldest communication theories and are no less scholarly than scientific ones. Whereas scientific theories emphasize the identification of regularity, standardized methods of observation, quantification of concepts, and generalization, humanistic theories stress individualism, interpretation, and nonstandardized methods. Some of these theories are called interpretive while others are called critical and they try to explain and interpret the meaning of communicative behavior. Sometimes interpretive theorists will focus their attention on a single speech or book and try to explain (i.e., interpret) what it means. But since a given book or speech may mean any number of things, interpretive scholars often disagree with one another. Critical theories typically establish a set of criteria, often with specific political orientations, by which a communication event can be judged or "critiqued." For example, many critical theorists, employing a Marxist perspective, critique communication events using the ideas and standards set forth in the writings of Karl Marx. The following list presents several of the critical/humanistic theories of communication along with a brief description of them.

1. Classical Rhetorical Theory: Classical rhetorical theory is a historical look at how people communicate through oratory. The primary focus is on persuasive oratory. Rhetorical theorists focus their attention on the work of Socrates, Plato, Aristotle, Cicero, Quintilian, and others as they pertain to public discourse, with particular attention to persuasion. Ancient rhetoricians sought to understand what makes a speaker persuasive. Much of the field of communication, as we know it today, is based on this line of research.[76]

2. Contemporary Rhetorical Theory: These theories, which focus on how people and institutions communicate and influence other people, investigate and study how mass media, newspapers, books, magazines, radio, and television affect their audience. Contemporary rhetorical scholars have moved away from classical rhetorical theory and its emphasis on public speaking by recognizing that communication is not one-way (e.g., speaker to audience) but is transactional. Contemporary theorists understand the importance of audience and of the interplay between communicants.[77]

3. Deconstruction: Unlike phenomenology or hermeneutics, wherein language is thought to refer to some actual object or thing, deconstruction denies meaning altogether. According to this perspective, all language refers to nothing but itself. Thus, language is totally relativistic. A body of literature is viewed as a system of relationships between texts instead of a picture of the real world. These theorists aim to deconstruct any absolute meaning of a literary text. This is not a communication theory per se, but, with its emphasis on the nature of language, has important implications for the interpretive and critical theorist. Well-known deconstruction theorists include Jacque Derrida, Jacques Lacan, and Michel Foucault.[78]

4. Feminist Theory: A type of critical theory, feminist theory centers around the role of the sexes and gender. These theorists study how gender affects physical, social, and political reality with particular emphasis on the androcentric society that dominates life and the oppression of women. As a communication perspective, feminist theorists examine male bias in language and the differences between male and female communication patterns. An emerging theorist in this line of theory is Starhawk.[79]

5. Hermeneutics: An interpretive approach to the study of understanding action and text, hermeneutics is considered a part of communication theory because interpretation is regarded as a linguistic activity. Hermeneutic scholars contend that language forms the reality of the interpreter. The five basic categories of hermeneutics include (a) exegesis—the interpretation of the Bible, (b) philology—the interpretation of ancient books, (c) technical—

the interpretation through the use of linguistic rules, (d) social—the interpretation of social action, and (e) philosophical—the process of understanding itself.[80]

6. Marxist Social Theory: Referred to as "critical theory," this approach has as its basis the fundamental assumptions of Karl Marx. Critical theorists focus on who controls communication, why people want control over communication, and who benefits from such control. Early critical theorists questioned capitalistic society and the role of mass communication within that society. A central focus of critical theorists is the sociopolitical-economic context of communication as described in the writings and teachings of Karl Marx.[81]

7. Phenomenology: Like hermeneutics, this is an interpretive method of understanding how objects acquire meaning. Phenomenology began as a branch of philosophy that classifies and describes objects without the benefit of theoretical orientations. Contemporary phenomenologists believe that no conceptual or theoretical premises can adequately explain experience. An individual's consciousness is what eventually leads one to the discovery of truth.[82]

Evaluating Communication Theory

Believe it or not, the over seventy theories discussed in this chapter do not include all of the research that is being done in communication study. In fact, the professor teaching your class may lament that his or her favorite approach was not included. However, not everyone studying or doing research in communication is developing or using a theory; some are pursuing "lines of research" instead. These lines of research may be atheoretical (without a theory). Indeed, many scholars have developed "models" of communication processes that, although important to the field, are not really theories. Essentially, the difference between a theory and a line of research depends on how well one or the other explains and predicts communicative phenomena. Recall from Chapter 2 that two of the fundamental functions of a theory are to explain and to predict. The body of work that accomplishes these functions is regarded as a theory and the following list names criteria one can use to assess how well our theories explain and predict. These criteria apply to both scientific and humanistic theories, though in different ways.

Criteria for Evaluating a Theory

Criteria Related to Explanation

1. Organization of Concepts
2. Scope of Concepts
3. Summary of Concepts
4. Focus of Concepts
5. Clarification of Concepts
6. Parsimony of Explanation[83]

Criteria Related to Prediction

1. Heuristic
2. Testable
3. Anticipatory
4. Observable[84]

Criteria Related to Explanation

Recall that the primary purpose of an explanation is to identify regularity and the force which makes the regularity necessary and that explanations are composed of descriptive statements that identify something to be the object of an explanation (i.e., a concept). The first criteria by which one can judge the value of an explanation is the organization of concepts. While identifying the concepts, the explanation should also present them in a well-organized manner, which means in a logically consistent pattern or structure that facilitates comprehension. Theorists frequently rely on models, for example, to organize their concepts. In this sense, models are graphic representations or organizational schemes symbolic of the concepts and their relationship to other concepts.[85]

The second standard by which to evaluate an explanation is the scope of concepts. Scope refers to the range of concepts encompassed by the explanation. Most explanations, for example, should attempt to explain more than a single concept. As Littlejohn asserts, scientists frequently provide explanations for individual events but the explanations are not considered theoretical because they only explain one event. The scope criteria may be the criteria that most frequently distinguishes between a line of research and a theory.[86]

The third criteria is the summarization of concepts. The explanation should offer a complete account of its concepts, including their definition and any past related research. Scientists or theorists should not have to turn to other sources for information.[87]

The fourth yardstick of an explanation is its focus on concepts. The theory should point out the more relevant and significant concepts that deserve special attention.[88] Any particular theory may have several concepts, not equally relevant or consequential. The explanation should concentrate on those concepts most significant in understanding the concepts.

The fifth criteria is the clarification of concepts. The utility of any theory is determined by the ability of others to interpret the concepts and use them in the real world. An important job of the theorist is to spell out how the concept can be applied in the everyday lives of its users.[89]

The final criteria related to the evaluation of explanation is parsimony. By definition, to exercise parsimony is to be stingy or overcareful in spending. Although it may sound a little awkward, the theorist, too, should be stingy. The explanation should include only that to which it applies, nothing more or less. In essence, the explanation should be simple.[90]

Criteria Related to Prediction

Once theorists judge whether their explanations are useful, they can them move on to the second primary function of a theory—that is, prediction. Predictions can be evaluated along four criteria, including their heuristic value, their testability, their anticipatory nature, and their observability. Heuristic prediction generates research and gives other theorists new insights into the topic area. They specify what concepts are to be investigated and which should be ignored. Any single prediction should assist the scientist in formulating new and related predictions.[91]

Theoretical predictions should be testable; that is, subject to verifiability and falsifiability. For example, the prediction "All people will communicate at some time in their lives" is impossible to verify since you would have to observe "all" people. The same prediction, however, is falsifiable with the observation of only one person who does not communicate. The prediction "People will communicate" is verified by the observation of one person communicating but is impossible to falsify since you would have to observe all people; something practically impossible. However, the prediction "Ten percent of the people in your class will raise their hand during today's class" is testable, since it is verifiable and falsifiable. By simply counting the number of people who raise their hand during class, you will either verify or falsify your prediction.

Strange as it sounds, valid theoretical predictions should not surprise theorists, because if they believe in the substance of their theories then they should be able to anticipate or expect certain outcomes. Theoretical predictions should explicitly state what is to be expected given a certain set of theoretical statements. This criteria is especially important for laypersons who might attempt to apply the theory.

The observable criteria, which is closely related to the testable criteria, simply means that whatever is predicted can be observed in some way; that is, in the same way by a number of different people. Ideally, any two theorists using the same method of observation should be able to make observations and reach the same conclusion. This criteria is at the essence of theoretic activity. The methods used to make observations and the object of observation are what separates scientific theories from humanistic ones.

Application of Criteria

To evaluate a particular theory is to apply the above-mentioned criteria to its explanation and prediction. Not all theories will meet each of the criteria specified. Some theories, for example, will not be very parsimonious whereas others will be too simple. Some theories, especially contextual ones, will have very limited scope and application. Indeed, many theories, perhaps all of the nonscientific theories, are not scientifically testable. There is one group of theories that seems to meet most the aforementioned criteria, however—the general/metatheories. Because of this, they are the major focus of this text.

Summary

As undergraduate students in communication, a complete comprehension of the seventy plus theories is less important than the understanding of the general theories, because they are the ones that have led to the development of the thematic and contextual theories. This chapter provided a kind of book within a book of communication theory and demonstrated the great diversity of theories in our field. Remember that there are many different ways to theorize about communication. Given this introduction to the nature of theory, and communication theory, it is now time to look a some of the actual general theories operating in communication. We begin by looking at humanistic theories with classical rhetorical theory, since it really is at the very core of the field. Then, we will look at contemporary rhetorical theory and from there we take up the scientific theories, including causal process, social-action, and systems based theories.

Glossary

Contextual Theories: These are theories based on the particular physical, social, and psychological setting in which communication occurs, including dyadic, group, and organizational contexts.

Dyadic/Interpersonal Theories: Theories of how two people communicate. Many of these theories focus on communication as relationships begin, develop, and end. Such theories include uncertainty reduction theory, social penetration theory, social exchange theory, and others.

Group Communication Theories: These theories explain how groups of people communicate, including decision making, conflict, and agenda setting. Such theories include field theory, task contingency theory, and syntality theory.

Humanistic Theories: These are rhetorical, critical, historical, or philosophical theories that generally do not rely on standardized empirical methods of observation.

Language Theories: Theories that focus on the topic of verbal language, including conversational analysis, general semantics, generative grammar, speech act, and speech accommodation theories.

Metatheory: A metatheory is a theory about how to theorize. In communication, metatheories describe the general structure of communication processes.

Nonverbal Communication Theories: Theories that focus on the use of communication without words, including kinesics and proxemics, among others. Representative theories here include expectancy violation theory and arousal labeling theory.

Organizational Communication Theories: Theories that describe internal and external communication processes with organizations. Such theories include scientific management, human relations, and organizational culture.

Persuasive Communication Theories: Theories that describe the ways messages influence the ways humans act, feel, or think. Sometimes these theories are called attitude change theories. Such theories include attribution theory, consistency theory, and cognitive dissonance theory, among others.

Topical Theories: Topical theories describe the structure of particular types of communication found in most contexts, such as nonverbal or persuasive communication.

References

1. Pearce, W. B. (1977). "Metatheoretical Concerns in Communication," *Communication Quarterly, 25,* 3–18.

2. Fisher, B. A. (1978). *Perspectives on Human Communication,* New York: Macmillan.

3. Hawes, L. (1975). *Pragmatics of Analoguing: Theory and Model Construction in Communication,* Reading, MA: Addison-Wesley.

4. Littlejohn, S. W. (1992). *Theories of Human Communication,* (4th Ed.), Belmont, CA: Wadsworth.

5. Ibid.

6. Nofsinger, R. E. (1991). *Everyday Conversation,* Newbury Park, CA: Sage.

7. Carbaugh, D. (Ed.) (1990). *Cultural Communication and Intercultural Contact,* Hillsdale, NJ: Erlbaum.

8. Goffman, I. (1955). "On Face-Work: An Analysis of Ritual Elements in Social interaction," *Psychiatry, 18,* 213–231; Goffman, I. (1959). *The Presentation of Self in Everyday Life,* Garden City, NY: Doubleday; Brown, P., & Levinson, S. (1978). "Universals in Language Usage: Politeness Phenomena," in E. Goody, (Ed.), *Questions and Politeness: Strategies in Social Interaction,* (pp. 56–289), Cambridge: Cambridge University Press; Craig, R. T., Tracy, K., & Spisak, F. (1986). "The Discourse of Requests: Assessment of a Politeness Approach," *Human Communication Research, 12,* 437–468.

9. Stacks, D., Hickson, M., III, & Hill, S. R., Jr. (1991). *An Introduction to Communication Theory,* New York: Holt, Rinehart and Winston.

10. Lyons, J. (1970). *Noam Chomsky,* New York: Viking Press.

11. Silverman, K. (1983). *The Subject of Semiotics,* New York: Oxford University Press.

12. Searle, J. (1969). *Speech Acts: An Essay in the Philosophy of Language,* Cambridge: Cambridge University Press.

13. Giles, H., Mulac, A., Bradac, J. J., & Johnson, P. (1987). *Speech Accommodation Theory: The First*

Decade and Beyond, in M. McLaughlin, (Ed.), *Communication Yearbook 10,* (pp. 13–48), Newbury Park, CA: Sage.

14. Littlejohn, *Theories of Human Communication.*
15. Manis, J. G., & Meltzer, B. N. (Eds.) (1978). *Symbolic Interaction,* Boston: Allyn & Bacon.
16. Nofsinger, *Everyday Conversation.*
17. Philipsen, G. (1975). "Speaking 'Like a Man' in Teamsterville: Culture Patterns of Role Enactment in an Urban Neighborhood," *Quarterly Journal of Speech, 61,* 13–22; Wieder, D. L., & Pratt, S. (1990). "On Being a Recognizable Indian among Indians," in D. Carbaugh, (Ed.), *Cultural Communication and Intercultural Contact,* (pp. 45–64), Hillsdale, NJ: Erlbaum.
18. Korzbski, A. (1958). *Science and Sanity: An Introduction to Non-Aristotelian Systems and General Semantics,* Lakeville, CT: The Institute of General Semantics.
19. Lyons, *Noam Chomsky.*
20. Giles et al., *Speech Accommodation Theory,* (pp. 13–48).
21. Harris, Z. (1951). *Structural Linguistics,* Chicago: University of Chicago Press.
22. Manis, & Meltzer, *Symbolic Interaction.*
23. Morris, D. (1971). *Manwatching: A Field Guide to Human Behavior,* New York: Abrams.
24. Stacks, Hickson, & Hill, (1991). *An Introduction to Communication Theory.*
25. Patterson, M. L. (1976). "An Arousal Model of Interpersonal Intimacy," *Psychological Review, 83,* 235–245.
26. Burgoon, J. K., & Saine, T. (1978). *The Unspoken Dialogue: An Introduction to Nonverbal Communication,* Boston, MA: Houghton Mifflin Company.
27. Argyle, M., & Dean, J. (1965). "Eye Contact, Distance, and Affiliation." *Sociometry, 28,* 289–304.
28. Burgoon, J. K. (1978). "A Communication Model of Personal Space Violations: Explication and an Initial Test," *Human Communication Research, 4,* 129–142; Burgoon, J. K., & Jones, S. (1976). "Toward a Theory of Personal Space Expectations and Their Violations," *Human Communication Research, 2,* 131–146.
29. Knapp, M. L. (1978). *Nonverbal Communication in Human Interaction,* (2nd Ed.), New York: Holt, Rinehart and Winston; Stacks, Hickson, & Hill, *An Introduction to Communication Theory.*
30. Birdwhistell, R. L. (1970). *Kinesics and Context: Essays on Body Motion and Communication,* New York: Ballatine; Hall, E. (1959). *Silent Language,*

Greenwich: Fawcett; Ekman, P., & Friesen, W. (1969). "The Repertoire of Nonverbal Behavior: Categories, Origins, Usage, and Coding," *Semiotica, 1,* 49–98.
31. Stacks, Hickson, & Hill, *An Introduction to Communication Theory.*
32. Darwin, C. (1872). *Expression of the Emotions in Man and Animals,* London: Murray.
33. Birdwhistell, *Kinesics and Context.*
34. Eagly, A. H., Chaiken, S., & Wood, W. (1981). "An Attribution Analysis in Persuasion," in J. H. Harvey, W. J. Ickes, & R. F. Kidd, (Eds.), *New Directions in Attribution Research* (Vol. 3), (pp. 37–62), Hillsdale, NJ: Erlbaum.
35. Lulofs, R. S. (1991). *Persuasion: Contexts, People, and Messages,* Scottsdale, AZ: Gorsuch Scarisbrick.
36. Bettinghaus, E. P., & Cody, M. J. (1994). *Persuasive Communication,* (5th Ed.), Fort Worth: Harcourt Brace.
37. Miller, G. R. (1973). "Counterattitudinal Advocacy: A Current Appraisal," in D. Mortenson & K. Sereno, (Eds.), *Advances in Communication Research,* (pp. 105–151), New York: Harper & Row.
38. Petty, R. E., & Cacioppo, J. T. (1986). "The Elaboration Likelihood Model of Persuasion," in L. Berkowitz, (Ed.), *Advances in Experimental Social Psychology* (Vol. 19), (pp. 124–205), Orlando: Academic Press.
39. Smith, M. J. (1982). *Persuasion and Human Action: A Review and Critique of Social Influence Theories,* Belmont, CA: Wadsworth.
40. Bandura, A. (1977). *Social Learning Theory,* Englewood Cliffs, NJ: Prentice-Hall.
41. Sherif, C., Sherif, M., & Nebergall, R. (1965). *Attitudes and Attitude Change: The Social Judgement-Involvement Approach,* Philadelphia: Saunders.
42. Hovland, C., Janis, I., & Kelley, H. (1953). *Communication and Persuasion,* New Haven: Yale University Press.
43. Reardon, K. K. (1987). *Interpersonal Communication: Where Minds Meet,* Belmont, CA: Wadsworth.
44. Lulofs, *Persuasion: Contexts, People, and Messages.*
45. Eagly, Chaiken, & Wood, "An Attribution Analysis in Persuasion," (pp. 37–62).
46. Neuliep, J. W., & Hazleton, V. Jr. (1986). "Enhanced Conversational Recall and Reduced Conversational Interference as a Function of Cognitive *Complexity,*" *Human Communication Research, 13,* 211–224.

47. Schutz, W. C. (1966). *The Interpersonal Underworld,* (2nd Ed.), Palo Alto, CA: Science and Behavior Books.

48. Trenholm, S. (1986). *Human Communication Theory,* (2nd Ed.), Englewood Cliffs, NJ: Prentice-Hall.

49. Byrne, D., & Nelson, D. (1965). "Attraction as a Linear Function of Proportion of Positive Reinforcements," *Journal of Personality and Social Psychology, 1,* 659–663.

50. Berger, C. R., & Douglas, W. (1982). "Thought and Talk: 'Excuse Me, But Have I Been Talking to Myself?'" in F. E. X. Dance, (Ed.), *Human Communication Theory: Comparative Essays,* (pp. 42–60), New York: Harper & Row.

51. Knapp, M. L., & Vangelisti, A. L. (1992). *Interpersonal Communication and Human Relationships,* (2nd Ed.), Boston: Allyn & Bacon; Phillips, G., & Wood, J. T. (1983). *Communication and Human Relationships,* New York: Macmillan; Wilmot, W. W. (1987). *Dyadic Communication,* (3rd Ed.), New York: Random House.

52. Hart, R., & Burks, D. (1972). "Rhetorical Sensitivity and Social Interaction," *Speech Monographs, 39,* 75–91.

53. Thibaut, J. W., & Kelley, H. H. (1959). *The Social Psychology of Groups,* New York: Wiley.

54. Miller, G. R., & Steinberg, M. (1975). *Between People: A New Analysis of Interpersonal Communication,* Chicago: Science Research Associates.

55. Bem, D. (1972). "Self-Perception Theory," in L. Berkowitz, (Ed.), *Advances in Experimental Social Psychology,* (Vol. 6), (pp. 2–17), New York: Academic Press.

56. Festinger, L. (1954). "A Theory of Social Comparison Processes," *Human Relations, 7,* 117–140.

57. Millar, F. E., & Rogers, E. L. (1987). "Relational Dimensions in Interpersonal Dynamics," in M. E. Roloff & G. R. Miller, (Eds.), *Interpersonal Processes: New Directions in Communication Research,* (pp. 117–139), Newbury Park, CA: Sage.

58. Berger, C. R., & Calabrese, R. J. (1975). "Some Explorations in Initial Interaction and Beyond: Toward a Developmental Theory of Interpersonal Communication," *Human Communication Research, 1,* 99–112.

59. Lewin, K. (1951). *Field Theory in Social Science,* New York: Harper and Row.

60. Janis, I. (1967). *Victims of Groupthink: A Psychological Study of Foreign Decisions and Fiascoes,* Boston: Houghton Mifflin.

61. Cattell, R. (1948). "Concepts and Methods in the Measurement of Group Syntality," *Psychological Review, 55,* 48–63.

62. Hewes, D. E. (1986). "A Socio-Egocentric Model of Group Decision-Making," in R. Y. Hirokawa and M. S. Poole, (Eds.), *Communication and Group Decision-Making,* (pp. 265–292), Beverly Hills, CA: Sage.

63. Bormann, E. (1983). "Symbolic Convergence: Organizational Communication and Culture," in L. Putnam & M. Pacanowsky, (Eds.), *Communication and Organizations: An Interpretive Approach,* (pp. 99–122), Beverly Hills: Sage.

64. Poole, M. S., Seibold, D. S., & McPhee, R. D. (1986). "A Structurational Approach to Theory-Building in Group Decision-Making Research," in Hirokawa and Poole, *Communication and Group Decision-Making,* (pp. 237–264).

65. Beebe, S. A., & Masterson, J. T. (1994). *Communicating in Small Groups: Principles and Practices,* (4th Ed.), New York: HarperCollins.

66. Davis, J. H. (1973). "Group Decision and Social Interaction: A Theory of Social Decision Schemes," *Psychological Review, 80,* 97–109.

67. Cortez, C. A. (1990). Unpublished manuscript, De Pere, WI: St. Norbert College); Goldhaber, G. M. (1993). *Organizational Communication,* (6th Ed.), Madison, WI: Brown & Benchmark.

68. Cortez, Unpublished manuscript.

69. Tompkins, P. K. (1984). "The Function of Human Communication in Organization," in C. C. Arnold & J. W. Bowers, (Eds.), *Handbook of Rhetorical and Communication Theory,* (pp. 659–719), Boston: Allyn & Bacon.

70. Ibid.

71. Shockley-Zalabek, P. (1991). *Fundamentals of Organizational Communication: Knowledge, Sensitivity, Skills, Values,* (2nd Ed.), New York: Longman.

72. Tompkins, "The Function of Human Communication in Organization," (pp. 659–719); Goldhaber, G. M. (1993). *Organizational Communication,* (6th Ed.), Madison, WI: Brown & Benchmark.

73. Infante, D. A., Rancer, A. S., & Womack, D. F. (1993). *Building Communication Theory,* (2nd Ed.), Prospect Heights, IL: Waveland Press.

74. Geertz, C. (1973). *The Interpretation of Cultures,* New York: Basic Books.

75. Weick, K. (1979). *The Social Psychology of Organizing,* Reading, MA: Addison-Wesley.

76. Kennedy, G. (1980). *Classical Rhetoric and Its Christian and Secular Tradition from Ancient to Modern Times,* Chapel Hill, NC: University of North Carolina.

77. Foss, S. K., Foss, K. A., & Trapp, R. (1991). *Contemporary Perspectives on Rhetoric,* (2nd Ed.), Prospect Heights, IL: Waveland.

78. Neary, J. (1988). "A Primer on Deconstructionism," Unpublished manuscript, DePere, WI: St. Norbert College.

79. Foss, S. K., & Griffin, C. L. (1992). "A Feminist Perspective on Rhetorical Theory: Toward a Classification of Boundaries," *Western Journal of Communication, 56,* 330–349.

80. Littlejohn, *Theories of Human Communication.*

81. Rogers, E. M. (1982). "The Empirical and the Critical Schools of Communicative Research," in M. Burgoon, (Ed.), *Communication Yearbook 5,* (pp. 125–144), New Brunswick, NJ: Transaction Books.

82. Husserl, E. (1964). *The Idea of Phenomenology,* The Hague, Netherlands: Martinus Hijhoff.

83. Littlejohn, *Theories of Human Communication;* Shaw, M. E., & Costanzo, P. R. (1970). *Theories of Social Psychology,* New York: McGraw-Hill.

84. Infante, Rancer, & Womack, *Building Communication Theory;* Miller, G. R., (1981). "Models and Speech Communication," in J. M. Civikly, (Ed.), *Contexts of Communication,* (pp. 4–13), New York: Holt, Rinehart and Winston.

85. Hawes, L. (1975). *The Pragmatics of Analoguing: Theory and Model Construction in Communication,* Reading, MA: Addison-Wesley.

86. Shaw, & Costanzo, *Theories of Social Psychology.*

87. Littlejohn, *Theories of Human Communication.*

88. Ibid.

89. Ibid.

90. Infante, Rancer, & Womack, *Building Communication Theory.*

91. Miller, "Models and Speech Communication," (pp. 4–13).

Chapter 4

Classical Rhetorical Theory

Rhetoric has occupied the attention of man ever since he has been able to communicate with his fellows by language.[1]
—*LIONELL CROCKER & PAUL A. CARMACK*

At the heart of the communication discipline is the study of classical rhetoric and at the heart of that study is public speaking. Books of epic proportions have been written about rhetoric. This chapter will introduce the undergraduate student in communication, who probably knows little about classical rhetoric, to a historical perspective of this very important topic. The study of classical rhetorical theory covers almost twenty-five hundred years, beginning some five hundred years before the birth of Christ and ending at the close of the nineteenth century. The emphasis of this chapter is on the major events and persons in the study of classical rhetorical theory.

The first part of the chapter offers some definitions of rhetoric and offers several reasons why students should be studying it in their communication theory class. Part two traces the beginnings of the study of rhetoric. Next, a group of teachers, called Sophists, are discussed followed by a discussion of Socrates, Plato, and Aristotle. In the next sections the rhetoric of Cicero and Quintilian are outlined. Finally, moving beyond the rhetoric of Greece and Rome, the study of rhetoric in the Middle Ages, the Renaissance, and into the seventeenth and eighteenth centuries is briefly covered. In this chapter much emphasis is placed on the beginnings of rhetoric, especially Plato and Aristotle, and less on the later stages, because their work served as the foundation for the study of rhetoric.

Definitions of Rhetoric

What does it mean to study "rhetoric?" What is a "rhetorical" theory? The term *rhetoric* refers to one of the most fascinating and important areas of study in human communication, but unfortunately, it is one of those words that sometimes invokes negative connotations. For example, in our attempts to discredit distrustful politicians we may accuse them of employing "empty rhetoric" or "mere rhetoric." Many dictionaries define rhetoric as that which is devoid of content or a type of speech that emphasizes style at the expense of thought.[2]

As a communication student, rhetoric is a key part of your academic discipline—it is at the very heart and soul of the field. Unfortunately, many communication students have very limited and/or distorted views of rhetoric because they have only studied communication from the social scientific perspective that emerged in the 1940s and 1950s. The formal study of communication, then called rhetoric, began some twenty-five hundred years ago, however. Students must have at least an introduction to their field's historical roots in order to have a complete understanding, and for this field that is the study of rhetoric.

The etymology (i.e., the origin and/or derivation) of the word *rhetoric* comes from the Greek notion of "words" or "speech." Obviously, "words" and "speech" are core concepts in the study of communication. In Greek, the word *rhema* means "a word" where *rhetor* refers to "a teacher of oratory." Both *rhema* and *rhetor* stem from the Greek verb *eiro* which means "I say." Specifically, the English noun "rhetoric" has its origin in the Greek feminine adjective *rhetorike,* translated as "the art of the rhetor or oratory." Technically, English got the term "rhetoric" from the French word *rhetorique.*[3]

In its original sense, the term *rhetoric* refers to aspects of public speaking and/or oratory. Over the centuries, however, principles of rhetoric have been applied to composition (i.e., written communication) as well. Today, rhetoric is associated primarily with persuasive speaking. As Corbett notes: "From its beginnings and throughout its history, classical rhetoric was thought of as the art of persuasive speech. Its end was to convince or persuade an audience to think in a certain way or to act in a certain way."[4]

Perhaps the most famous definition of rhetoric comes from Aristotle. Aristotle, who was born in 384 B.C., defined rhetoric not as the art of persuasion but "to discover the available means of persuasion in a given case."[5] To Aristotle the pure rhetorician is not a practitioner of persuasion but a strategist. Like the army general who creates the battle plan but leaves the fighting to soldiers, the pure rhetorician determines the available means of persuasion, the rationale, the arguments and appeals, but leaves it to others to apply such information. To Aristotle, rhetoric is the pure science whereas speaking and writing are the applied science or the art of rhetoric. Although Aristotle distinguishes between art and science, many others do not. To most scholars, both past and present, the rhetorician and practitioner are one and the same; that is, they see rhetoric as the whole art of persuasion.[6]

If rhetoric is defined as persuasion, then why do we have some courses in rhetoric and other courses in persuasion? Is there are difference between the two? Perhaps the simplest answer to this question is that, to some, there is no difference between rhetoric and persuasion or even between rhetoric and communication. Some scholars argue, for example, that the terms *communication* and *rhetoric* are essentially synonymous. Indeed, Foss, Foss, and Trapp define rhetoric as the "uniquely human ability to use symbols to communicate with one another."[7] For those who distinguish between rhetoric and persuasion, the difference probably lies in method. By some, the study of rhetoric, unlike the study of persuasion, is not regarded as scientific. When we speak of courses in persuasion we are typically referring to those courses whose content is based on discoveries made since the social scientific method was introduced to communication some fifty years ago. Such a distinction is unfortunate since contemporary approaches to persuasion (i.e., based on social scientific method) owe their origins to ancient times and the study of rhetoric.

Historically, however, there is a difference in the focus of what is taught in a course on rhetoric and one on persuasion. Classical rhetorical theory, for example, focuses almost exclusively on persuasion as it relates to the public speaker. On the other hand, a course in persuasion will focus on the process of persuasion not only as it relates to the public speech but in many other contexts as well; that is, interpersonal, small group, organizational, and perhaps even intercultural settings.

The Beginnings of Rhetoric: Corax and Tisias

Although some rhetorical theorists disagree, many concur that the study of rhetoric began in about 465 B.C. with a person by the name of Corax and his student Tisias. Although there are conflicting accounts of the relationship between the two men, several sources indicate that both lived in Syracuse, a Greek colony on the island of Sicily.[8] During this time Europe was breaking its ties with Asia and democracies were being established on the European continent. Prior to the establishment of democracies on Sicily, however, tyrants, such as Thrasydaeus, Hiero, Phalaris, and Thrasybulus, ruled the island. Many of these rulers were particularly brutal. Thrasybulus, for example, customarily boasted about arresting citizens, seizing their property, falsely accusing them of crimes, and then executing them. Eventually the people successfully rebelled against such rulers, banished them, and established democracies.[9]

In their infancy, the democracies, like any new government, went through growing pains. One of biggest problems faced by the young democracies was the ownership of land. Many citizens claimed their right to the land, including descendants of the original owners, the people to whom the tyrants had given such land, and the peasants who, under the rule of tyrants, worked the land themselves. In order to handle such disputes, legal courts were established where citizens could plead their cases. Those citizens who won their cases possessed something that the others did not—that is, the effective and persuasive use of words. Corax made that discovery and decided to observe the citizens while pleading their cases and record their actions. His recorded observations became the first known book on the art of persuasive speaking and began what we now know as the study of rhetoric. Actually Corax and his student Tisias are both credited with the first book on rhetoric wherein they defined rhetoric as "the art of persuasion."[10]

Corax and Tisias are also credited with two other monumental achievements that would forever shape the study of rhetoric by influencing such rhetorical giants as Plato and Aristotle: naming the parts of discourse (i.e., *dispositio*) and outlining, for the first time, the principle of probability.

After listening to hundreds, perhaps thousands, of speeches in the courts, Corax perceived that the majority of the speeches had five parts, or divisions. These include (a) an introduction, (b) a narration, (c) the presentation of an argument or proof, (d) subsidiary remarks, and (e) a conclusion. Sometimes these five parts, taken together, are called a quintuplex.[11]

The second crowning achievement by Corax, and probably his most important contribution, is the introduction of the principle of probability. Corax understood that in many cases absolute truth could not be known but that the probabilities of something being true could be established and argued in court. To Corax, probability simply referred to the likelihood that something is true. In other words, some things are more likely to be true than are others. He understood that the likelihood of something being true must be established in order to be persuasive. He asserted that probability could be established via the invention of argument or proofs. Probability may be based on one's own observation and experience or on the testimony others who profess from their observations and experience. Corax claimed that any argument has two sides, each with its own probabilities. The most gifted speakers could compose the most compelling arguments establishing probabilities and thus persuading juries to vote in their favor.

The Rise of the Sophists

Although we can never be absolutely certain, it is widely believed that Tisias introduced his (and Corax's) books on rhetoric to Greek society.[12] Some scholars contend that the Sophist Gorgias, not Corax and Tisias, first introduced rhetoric in ancient Athens. During this time in Greece democracies were being established and there was a great cultural interchange between Sicily and Athens. As the young democracies flourished, particularly in Athens, the need for instruction in oratory grew as a result of the application of democratic principles in the newly founded courts of law. Even before the democracies were established, oratory had been one of the oldest and most widely practiced activities in Greek culture. Poetry, for example, was learned orally and reading was considered secondary to speech and memory. Even when reading to oneself, one was to read out loud.[13] Hence, when the books of rhetoric were introduced by Tisias, they were in great demand. Also in demand were people who could teach what these new books prescribed. Hence, the rise of a group of teachers, called Sophists, began.[14]

The Greek words *sophos* and *sophia,* meaning "wise" and "wisdom," were commonly used in Greece for many years. Initially they stood for an intellectual and/or spiritual quality among men. Eventually, however, they connoted primarily skill in a particular craft. For example, a sculptor was *sophos* with his chisel, a musician *sophos* with his lyre (a stringed instrument of the harp class used by ancient Greeks). As many words do, *sophos* and *sophia* continued to acquire new meanings and eventually they meant "to be clever" or "to trick and deceive."[15] From *sophos* and *sophia* derived the noun *sophistes* meaning "Sophist." A Sophist was a teacher; specifically, a poet. In Greece, poets instructed and provided moral advice to the citizens.

Some time during the fifth century B.C. the word was used to refer to professional educators who instructed the young men for the exchange of fees.[16] Instruction was accomplished in a variety of ways, including large lectures where the Sophist would engage in eloquent oratory, small groups or seminars with students discussing some issue under the direction of the Sophist, short lectures on particular topics, and finally, a sort of argument in question and answer form where the goal was to win, not necessarily to find the truth.[17]

The Sophists often competed with one another for students but shared a similar philosophy about human nature. They believed that certain, absolute knowledge could not exist. They believed that what is known is subject to the limitations of the human senses. Although each of the Sophists had his own specialty, one subject they each practiced and taught was the art of rhetoric. To be successful in Greece meant to be skilled in politics and in the art of persuasion, sometimes called "forensics." As Guthrie notes:

> [O]ne might assign to rhetoric the place now occupied by advertising. Certainly the art of persuasion, often by dubious means, was no less powerful then, and, as we have our business schools and schools of advertising, so the Greeks had their teachers of politics and rhetoric: the Sophists. Peitho, Persuasion, was for them a powerful Goddess; 'the charmer to whom nothing is denied.'[18]

In their teachings, the Sophists trained their students to argue both sides of an issue. In many cases, pupils were taught to strongly support the weaker of the two sides so that it appeared stronger. To the Sophists, truth was relative and no one knew anything for certain except that of which they could be persuaded. The Sophists believed that "there can be belief, but never knowledge."[19]

Like the word rhetoric, the label "Sophist" developed negative connotations. Many Greeks felt that what the Sophists taught should be known as a kind of second nature or instinct that one passes on to their sons, not through formal education. Sophists were also criticized for fee taking. Socrates, for example, called them prostitutes, arguing that selling one's mind is no different than selling one's body.[20] Sophists were also strangers to the Greeks; because they were not from Athens, many were distrusted.[21] Finally, Sophists were criticized for teaching practice without theory and even committing deception. Thus, sophistry began to take on its negative connotation. Many dictionaries define sophism as an argument meant to deceive, and a Sophist as one who engages in fallacious reasoning.[22]

The Sophists: The Men

Although it is not always possible to attribute a particular philosophy or perspective to one individual with certainty, there are several Sophists about whom we know a great deal. Much of what we know about these men comes not from their own writings but from the writings of others, especially Plato. Five of the most prominent Sophists include Protagoras, Isocrates, Gorgias, Prodicus, and Thrasymachus. A brief biography and summary of their contributions appears in Box 4.1 on pages 72–73. Many other important Sophists could be introduced here, but these particular men were chosen for their unique and important contributions to rhetoric.

Socrates, the Sophists, and Philosophical Rhetoric

As the success of the Sophists grew, so did a dissatisfaction with their method of instruction and rhetoric in general. Some people began to distrust the Sophists because of their style and their relativistic perspective. As Kennedy notes:

(text continues on page 73)

BOX 4.1   Five Great Sophists

Protagoras

Protagoras was born in approximately 485 B.C. in Abdera, in northeast Greece, and is widely considered the most famous and perhaps first professional Sophist. Protagoras believed and professed that absolute truth was unknowable. He is best known for his assertion that "man is the measure and measurer of all things." This statement serves as the basis for philosophical relativism which sees truth as subjective in each individual. To Protagoras, there are no universal principles. He believed that rhetoric played a key role in determining the closest approximation to truth, and like Corax before him, that any case had two sides of which both could be argued persuasively. The most persuasively argued side was to be accepted as the most truthful. Though highly regarded by his contemporaries, including Plato, Protagoras is thought to have drowned in a shipwreck after being tried and banished from Athens for his agnostic beliefs.[a]

Gorgias

Born in approximately 490 B.C., Gorgias, who lived to be over one hundred years old, is another first-generation Sophist and contemporary with Protagoras. Like Protagoras, Gorgias believed in a relativistic philosophy. His primary interest was in persuasive speech and his secondary interest was in medicine. His brother, a doctor, is said to have brought his patients to Gorgias to have him persuade them to take their medicine. Gorgias, who is considered the father of impromptu speaking, would elicit questions from the audience during his public exhibitions and provide impromptu replies. Gorgias's first concern, however, was to train his pupils to become masters of persuasion. He was the first to write about how speakers must adapt their words to the audience and the occasion. To him, persuasion was the queen of all science and the source of all power. Gorgias is said to have asked: "Of what use is the surgeon's skill if the patient will not submit to the knife?" To Gorgias, persuasion may have been an art of deceit, but deceit can be employed in a good cause. For him the means justified the ends. The truth is whatever we can be persuaded to believe.[b]

Isocrates

Born in Athens in 436 B.C., Isocrates was the most famous student of Gorgias and a friend of Socrates. Before becoming a Sophist, Isocrates was a logographer (speech writer). In about 392 B.C. he opened his own school of rhetoric and wrote an essay entitled "Against the Sophists" in which he criticized his contemporaries for practicing deceit and fee taking. Isocrates considered rhetoric to be the science of persuasion, meaning that it can alter our perceptions of things, allow us to dispute with others, and seek knowledge for ourselves. Persuasion was also that which separated man from beasts. He wrote that "none of the things which are done with intelligence take place without the help of speech, but that in all our actions as well as in all our thoughts speech is our guide, and most employed by those who have the most wisdom."[c]

Prodicus

Prodicus was born between 470 and 460 B.C. and was a contemporary with Gorgias. Socrates and Aristotle are thought to have studied under him. Prodicus is known mostly for his treatment of semantics, especially for making fine distinctions between words commonly used as synonyms. To Prodicus correct language was a prerequisite for correct living and productive government. Prodicus's main contribution was to dialectic and he is attributed with the paradoxical view of the impossibility of contradiction. When two people contradict only one is speaking the truth, hence the other is not saying anything, hence there is no contradiction.[d]

Thrasymachus

Though the exact date is not known, Thrasymachus is thought to have been born sometime between 440 and 420 B.C. Thought to be a harsh and an unlikable personality, some believe he committed suicide. Primarily a teacher of prose and rhetorical style, he is known as the first to pay attention to varied rhythmic patterns in his writings and oratory. He is credited as the first to have used rhythm as an emotional appeal. Thrasymachus was known for his ability to bring his audience to tears with emotional descriptions in his oratory. His book *Eleoi* is thought to be the first on dramatic delivery techniques for orators.[e]

a. Kennedy, G. A. (1963). *The Art of Persuasion in Greece,* Princeton, NJ: Princeton University Press; Guthrie, W. K. C. (1971). *The Sophists,* Cambridge: Cambridge University Press; Stacks, D., Hickson, M., III, & Hill, S. R., Jr. (1991). *Introduction to Communication Theory,* Fort Worth, TX: Holt, Rinehart, and Winston.
b. Guthrie, *The Sophists*; Foss, S. K., Foss, K. A., & Trapp, R. (1991). *Contemporary Perspectives on Rhetoric,* (2nd Ed.), Prospect Heights, IL: Waveland.
c. Benoit, W. L. (1984). "Isocrates on Rhetorical Education," *Communication Education,* 33, (pp. 109–120).
d. Rankin, H. D. (1983). *Sophists, Socratics, and Cynics,* Totowa, NJ: Barnes & Noble; Guthrie, *The Sophists.*
e. Rankin, *Sophists, Socratics, and Cynics*; Guthrie, *The Sophists*; Kennedy, *The Art of Persuasion in Greece.*

Bold claims about the role of the orator and the power of speech replaced tacit assumptions about aristocratic leaders, and rhetoric could now be learned by anyone interested.... Not only did it easily seem vulgar or tasteless, it could seem to treat the truth with indifference and to make the worse seem the better case.[23]

Such a reaction produced a new kind of rhetoric, called philosophical rhetoric. This new school of thought was first introduced by Socrates and then by his most famous student, Plato. Although none of his writings exist, we know that Socrates lived from 469–399 B.C. He was similar to the Sophists in that he taught orally and was interested in many of the same subjects. He was also quite different from them in that he did not accept fees and he promoted a method of teaching called *dialectic,* whereby instruction was accomplished via a dialogue of questions and answers. Today, this is called the Socratic method of teaching. Perhaps most importantly, Socrates rejected the relativistic position of the Sophists and doubted that much good had come from the rhetoric used in the courts. In 399 B.C. Socrates was charged with atheism when he refused to acknowledge the gods recognized by the government. He was also charged with corrupting the youth. He was found guilty of both and executed.[24]

Plato

Plato is regarded as the most important and influential student of Socrates. According to Kennedy: "Plato is the greatest Greek prose writer, a master of structure, characterization, and style, as well as one of the greatest thinkers of all time."[25] Plato was born to an upper-class family in Athens in 427 B.C. and is thought to have lived to the age of eighty. As a youth, Plato's life was filled with tragedy. He witnessed the violent years of the Peloponnesian War and the decline and fall of the Athenian empire.[26] In addition, as mentioned above, Plato's teacher, Socrates, was put to death. Because of these events, Plato was quite hostile to the democracy of Athens, especially its legal system and the orators with all their rhetoric.[27]

Like his teacher, Socrates, Plato started his own school, called the Academy, where he instructed the likes of Aristotle. Unlike the Sophists, however, he did not charge for his instruction. Plato taught and wrote about many subjects, especially mathematics and philosophy, and is regarded as one of the most influential contributors to Western thought. In addition, he held very strong views about rhetoric.

Controversy surrounds the interpretation of Plato's works, particularly those expressing his views of rhetoric. As Hare notes, "It is safe to say that no single statement can be made in interpretation of Plato which some scholars will not dispute."[28] Even his writing style receives contradictory reviews. Hare notes, for example, that "Plato is a very clear writer; and he certainly writes in a delightfully readable style."[29] Conversely, Edwin Black, an expert of Platonic writings says, "Of course, Plato is difficult to understand. He is complicated, variegated, audacious, and sometimes paradoxical."[30]

One reason for the difficulty in interpreting Plato may be that his writings are in the form of dialogues (i.e., a written composition in which two or more characters are represented as conversing), thus it is unclear whether the views expressed by the characters in the dialogues are those of Plato. Most, if not all, of Plato's dialogues address rhetoric. Those focusing particularly on rhetoric are presented through the character of Socrates. Though historians disagree about how to interpret Plato, his views on rhetoric are well known. As Black states, "Indeed, the only uniformity which crystallizes from this diversity of interpretation is the judgment that Plato disapproved of rhetoric, and was, in fact, rhetoric's most effective historical opponent."[31] Plato was a harsh critic of the Sophists and felt that there was no place for rhetoric in political debate or in the courts. Three of his dialogues, *The Apology, Gorgias,* and *The Phaedrus,* outline his views on rhetoric.[32]

The Apology

The Apology is Plato's portrayal of the events that took place at Socrates' trial. In 399 B.C. Socrates was charged with atheism and corrupting youth. During that time in Athens, charges against citizens could be brought up by any person or group of persons. There were no public prosecutors or judges in the American sense and juries typically consisted of five hundred or so citizens selected by lottery. Trials proceeded in two stages. The first began with the accusers presenting their case. Following this, the defendant was allowed a rebuttal. A rebuttal or defense speech is called *apologia* in Greek. After the apologia the first stage ended with the jury voting. The second stage begins after the vote. In the case of a guilty verdict, a determination of penalty is made by the jury, usually by vote also since there were no predetermined penalties in those times. In Socrates' case, he was found guilty by a vote of 280 to 221 and sentenced to death. Plato's *Apology,* sometimes called the *Apology of Socrates,* is not an exact transcript of the trial but rather Plato's dramatization of what occurred.[33] In several places, Socrates criticizes rhetoric and particularly the role of the orator who practices it. *The Apology* begins with Socrates addressing the jury in his own defense: "How you, men of Athens, have been affected by my accusers, I do not know. For my part, I nearly forget myself because of them, so persuasively did they speak. And yet they have said, so to speak, nothing true."[34]

The accusers have warned the jury they should beware of Socrates and his clever style of speech. To this Socrates responds: "I was most amazed by one of the many falsehoods they told, when they said that you should beware that you are not deceived by me, since I am a clever speaker."[35]

Socrates then distinguishes between a clever speaker; that is, a Sophist employing rhetoric, and a truthful speaker: "[T]his seemed to me the most shameless of them, unless perhaps they call a clever speaker the one who speaks the truth. If this is what they are saying, then I too would agree that I am an orator—but not of their sort."[36]

Now Socrates contrasts truthful speech from rhetoric. "[F]rom me you will hear the whole truth—not beautifully spoken speeches like theirs, ordered and adorned with phrases and words; rather what you will hear will be spoken at random in the words that I happen upon—for I trust that the things I say are just."[37]

In addition to attacking the Sophists' rhetorical style, these passages are said to reflect the basic philosophy of Socrates, now shared by Plato, that absolute truth can be known and should be sought. Remember that the philosophy of the Sophists was relativistic; that is, whatever one can be persuaded as true determines what is, in fact, true. Socrates and Plato profoundly disagreed with such a perspective.

After Socrates is found guilty and sentenced to death he addresses the jury and again attacks orators who use rhetoric and says he would rather die than to live their lives. He says:

> *Perhaps you suppose, you men of Athens, that I have been convicted because I was at a loss for the sort of speeches that would have persuaded you, if I had supposed that I should do and say anything at all to escape the penalty. Far from it. But I have been convicted because I was at a loss, not however for speeches, but for daring and shamelessness and for not being willing to say the sorts of things to you that you would have been pleased to hear.*[38]

In Plato's mind, Socrates would rather die than act as the Sophists did.

Gorgias

Plato's *Gorgias* is a dialogue in three sections. In each section Socrates is conversing with a proponent of rhetoric, including (a) the famous Sophist Gorgias, (b) a young and relatively inexperienced Sophist named Polus, and (c) an advocate of political power achieved through rhetoric, Callides. In each case, Socrates makes each man appear foolish.

An important part of the *Gorgias* is Plato's use of his favored method of teaching called dialectic. Unlike the Sophists' method of long, drawn-out rhetorical discourse, dialectic proceeds by having the leader ask questions of the student eventually leading to a conclusion. In the first part of *Gorgias,* Socrates is asking Gorgias for a definition of rhetoric and in so doing, distinguishes rhetoric from art. Following is a portion of this dialogue.

Socrates: With what is rhetoric concerned?

Gorgias: With discourse.

Socrates: What sort of discourse, Gorgias?—such as discourse as would teach the sick under what treatment they might get well?

Gorgias: No.

Socrates: The rhetoric does not treat all kinds of discourse?

Gorgias: Certainly not.

Socrates: And yet rhetoric makes men able to speak?

Gorgias: Yes.

Socrates: And to understand about which they speak?

Gorgias: Of course.

Socrates: But does not the art of medicine, which we were just now mentioning, also make men able to understand and speak about the sick?

Gorgias: Certainly.

Socrates: The medicine also treats of discourse?

Gorgias: Yes.

Socrates: Of discourse concerning disease?

Gorgias: Just so.

Socrates: And does not the gymnastic also treat of discourse concerning the good or evil condition of the body?

Gorgias: Very true.

Socrates: And the same, Gorgias, is true of the other arts:—all of them treat of discourse concerning the subjects with which they severally have to do.

Gorgias: Clearly.

Socrates: Then why, if you call rhetoric the art which treats discourse, and all the other arts treat of discourse, do you not call them arts of rhetoric?[39]

Eventually Socrates demonstrates to Gorgias, who is portrayed as a naive, that rhetoric is not art but is simply the artificer (i.e., one that makes or contrives) of persuasion. Following the dialectic, Socrates now demonstrates that rhetoric is essentially devoid of content. This portion of the dialogue follows.

Socrates: Now I want to know about rhetoric in the same way; is rhetoric the only art which brings persuasion, or do other arts have the same effect? I mean to say—Does he who teaches anything persuade men of that which he teaches or not?

Gorgias: He persuades Socrates, there can be no mistake about that.

Socrates: Again, if we take the arts of which we were just now speaking: do not arithmetic and the arithmeticians teach us the properties of number?

Gorgias: Certainly.

Socrates: And therefore persuade us of them?

Gorgias: Yes.

Socrates: Then arithmetic as well as rhetoric is an artificer of persuasion?

Gorgias: Clearly.

Socrates: And if any one asks us what sort of persuasion, and about what, we shall answer, persuasion which teaches the quantity of odd and even; and we shall be able to show that all of the other arts of which we were just now speaking are artificers of persuasion, and what of what sort, and what about.

Gorgias: Very true.

Socrates: Then rhetoric is not the only artificer of persuasion.

Gorgias: True.

Socrates: Seeing, then, that not only rhetoric works by persuasion, but that other arts do the same, as in the case of a painter, a question has arisen which is a very fair one: Of what persuasion is rhetoric the artificer, and about what?—is not that a fair way of putting the question?

Gorgias: I think so.

Socrates: Then, if you approve of the question, Gorgias, what is the answer?

Gorgias: I answer, Socrates, that rhetoric is the art of persuasion in courts of law and other assemblies, as I was just now saying, and about the just and the unjust.[40]

At this point Socrates points out that there is a difference between "having learned" something and "having believed" something. Socrates gets Gorgias to admit that rhetoric cannot persuade others of knowledge in something but can only produce beliefs in something. When Gorgias agrees, Socrates says: "Then rhetoric, as would appear, is the artificer of persuasion which creates belief about the just and unjust, but gives no instruction about them?"[41] Finally, Socrates leads Gorgias to the conclusion that because the rhetorician gives no instruction about that which he persuades, the rhetorician cannot discuss matters of the just and unjust.

Socrates: Then, when the rhetorician is more persuasive than the physician, the ignorant is more persuasive with the ignorant than he who has knowledge?—is that not the inference?

Gorgias: In the case supposed: Yes.

Socrates: And the same holds of the relation of rhetoric to all the other arts: the rhetorician need not know the truth about things: he has only to discover some way of persuading the ignorant that he has more knowledge than those who know.[42]

Clearly Socrates has succeeded pointing out the faults of rhetoric. But many literary scholars agree that what Socrates was really doing was not criticizing rhetoric in its pure sense, but only Gorgias's definition of rhetoric. In *The Phaedrus,* Plato spells out the criteria for true rhetoric.

The Phaedrus

There is considerable disagreement over the interpretation of *The Phaedrus.* Most scholars agree, however, that this piece was the catalyst for Aristotle's later work called *Rhetoric.* Actually, *The Phaedrus* deals with two subjects, including rhetoric and love. The dialogue is between Socrates and Phaedrus and is divided into two parts. The first part is in three speeches. In the first speech Socrates continues his attack on rhetoric. Socrates begins by stating that writing speeches, in itself, is not disgraceful. He argues: "But the disgrace, I fancy, consists in speaking or writing not well, but disgracefully and badly."[43] Good rhetoric, according to Socrates, is having knowledge of the truth:

Socrates: If a speech is to be good, must not the mind of the speaker know the truth about the matters of which he is to speak?

Phaedrus: On that point, Socrates, I have heard that one who is to be an orator does not need to know what is really just, but what would seem just to the multitude who are to pass judgement, and not what is really good or noble, but what will seem to be so; for they say that persuasion comes from what seems to be true, not from the truth.[44]

At this point Socrates argues that bad rhetoric, as is used in the Athenian courts, is: "[N]ot an art but a craft devoid of art. The real art of speaking, says the Laconian, which does not seize hold of truth, does not exist and never will."[45] As the dialogue continues, Socrates begins to articulate the true nature of rhetoric. He says: "Is not rhetoric in its entire nature an art which leads the soul by means of words, not only in law courts and the various public assemblages, but in private companies as well?"[46] The good orator, when using true rhetoric, will be able to define his topic and present it in an organized fashion. Regarding definition he states:

> That of perceiving and bringing together one idea the scattered particulars, that one may make clear by definition the particular thing he wishes to explain; just as now, in speaking of Love, we said what he is and defined it, whether well or ill. Certainly by this means the discourse acquired clearness and consistency.[47]

Regarding organization Socrates says:

> Then he who is to develop an art of rhetoric must first make a methodical division and acquire a clear impression of each class, that in which people must be in doubt and that in which they are not.[48]

[E]very discourse must be organised, like a living being, with a body of its own, as it were, so as not to be headless or footless, but to have a middle and members, composed in fitting relation to each other and the whole.[49]

[T]here must be an introduction first, at the beginning of the discourse.[50]

And the narrative must come second with the testimony after it, and third the proofs, and fourth the probabilities; and confirmation and further confirmation are mentioned.[51]

Socrates summarizes:

A man must know the truth about all the particular things of which he speaks or writes, and must be able to define everything separately; then when he has defined them, he must know how to divide them by classes until further division is impossible; and in the same way he must understand the nature of the soul, must find out the class of speech adapted to each nature, and must arrange and adorn his discourse accordingly, offering to the complex soul elaborate and harmonious discourses, and simple talks to the simple soul. Until he has attained to all this, he will not be able to speak by the method of art, so far as speech can be controlled by method, either for purposes of instruction or of persuasion. This has been taught by our whole preceding discussion.[52]

In his summary, Socrates emphasizes the importance of the orator's knowledge of the topic, its definition, and its organization. Another key element of the summary includes Socrates' mention of the importance of audience analysis (e.g., simple versus complex audiences).

To contemporary students of communication, especially those who have never read Plato, the above discussion may seem trivial—everyone knows that speeches must be organized. But in Plato's dialogues we find the very first articulation of these principles. Plato distinguishes between true rhetoric and the kind of "crafty" rhetoric practiced by the Sophists. Moreover, Plato's work would lead his most famous student, Aristotle, to pen what is considered the most important treatise on speech making and one that serves as the very basis of the field of communication.

Aristotle's Rhetoric

The work of Aristotle is the very foundation of the discipline of speech communication.[53] Lane Cooper, a noted Aristotelian scholar, writes that "Aristotle's treatise on Rhetoric is one of the world's best and wisest books."[54] Of Aristotle, Voltaire writes, "I do not believe there is a single refinement of the art that escapes him." [55] Dante asserted that Aristotle is the "master of those who know."[56] Put simply, any student of communication must have some knowledge of the work of Aristotle.

Born in 384 B.C. in Stagira, a Greek colony, Aristotle was the son of a physician. Although very little is known about his childhood, we do know that at the age of seventeen he went to Athens and entered Plato's school called The Academy. By most accounts, he was Plato's most famous student. He stayed there for twenty years until Plato's death in 367 B.C. It is said that both Athens and Plato were his teachers and that Aristotle accepted and rejected much from each.[57]

To be sure, rhetoric was not the only subject about which Aristotle wrote. In fact, as Kennedy notes, "Rhetoric was hardly a major interest with Aristotle. He seems to have taught it as a kind of extracurricular subject. . . ."[58] The complete works of Aristotle include topics that address nearly every area of human inquiry, such as logic, philosophy of science, biology, meteorology, memory, sleep, dreams, sensation, metaphysics, politics, economics, ethics, poetry, and, of course, rhetoric.[59]

Aristotle's initial work on rhetoric was called *Gryllus.* Unfortunately, very little is known about this work since it has never been found. Apparently, *Gryllus* presents a case against viewing rhetoric as an art.[60] The surviving writings about rhetoric come in the form of three books called the *Rhetoric,* which serve as a kind of guide for speakers. As Cooper notes:

> *The Rhetoric of Aristotle is a practical psychology, and the most helpful book extant for writers of prose and for speakers of every sort. Everyone whose business it is to persuade others—lawyers, legislators, statesmen, clergymen, editors, teachers—will find the book useful when it is read with attention.[61]*

Aristotle's *Rhetoric* is the very first systematic treatment regarding how to construct a speech.

Book I

Book I of the *Rhetoric* consists of fifteen chapters. Chapter 1 begins by stating that rhetoric is the counterpart of dialectic (i.e., Plato's method of finding truth). Aristotle contends that rhetoric (i.e., the art of public speaking) and dialectic (i.e., the art of logical discussion) are coordinated but contrasted activities. To Aristotle, engaging in dialectic is to search for the truth. Engaging in rhetoric, on the other hand, is to persuade someone (i.e., an audience) of the truth. He argues that everybody makes use of both.

In Book I, Aristotle attacks the Sophists' style of rhetoric by asserting that the essence of rhetoric lies in arguments or proofs, not solely in arousing the emotions. Discarding the rhetoric of the Sophists, Aristotle argues that when used properly, rhetoric is valuable because: (a) it prevents the triumph of fraud and injustice by advancing truth, (b) it offers a means of instruction by method of logic, (c) it can argue either side of a case not to advance injustice but to refute it, and (d) it offers a means by which men can defend themselves.[62] In Chapter 2 of Book I, Aristotle defines rhetoric "as the faculty of discovering in the particular case what are the available means of persuasion. This is the function of no other art."[63] Persuasion is accomplished by means of proofs, of which there are two kinds—artistic (scientific) and nonartistic (unscientific). Nonartistic proofs are outside the realm of the rhetorician and include such things as witnesses, admissions under torture, etc. Nonartistic proofs are used by the speaker, whereas artistic proofs are created by the speaker.

Artistic proofs of persuasion, according to Aristotle, are of three kinds, including the character of the speaker (ethos), the right attitude in the hearer (pathos), and the proper argument (logos). Of ethos, Aristotle writes:

> *The character of the speaker is a cause of persuasion when the speech is so uttered as to make him worthy of belief; for as a rule we trust men of probity more, and more quickly, about things in general, while on points outside the realm of exact knowledge, where opinion is divided, we trust them absolutely. This trust, however, should be created by the speech itself, and not left to depend upon the antecedent impression that the speaker is this or that kind of man.*[64]

In contemporary social scientific communication studies, ethos is called "credibility." A great deal of contemporary communication research has focused on credibility, especially in studies in persuasion. Later, in Book II of the *Rhetoric,* Aristotle prescribes that a person possessing ethos is a person of intelligence, virtue, and good will. Regarding the second artistic proof, pathos, Aristotle writes: "Secondly, persuasion is effected through the audience, when they are brought by the speech into a state of emotion; for we give very different decisions under the sway of pain or joy, and liking and hatred."[65] Pathos, of course, refers to emotional appeals. Again, much contemporary research has investigated the effects of emotional appeals, such as humor, warmth, and fear appeal research. Much of Book II of the *Rhetoric* is devoted to emotions. Concerning the use of rational appeals and evidence, called logos, Aristotle writes: "Thirdly, persuasion is effected by the arguments, when we demonstrate the truth, real or apparent, by such means as inhere in particular cases."[66]

Logos, or logical appeals, refers to the type of rational argument the speaker presents the audience. Aristotle identified two types: argument by example and by enthymeme. To make one's case by example is to argue inductively. Recall from Chapter 2 that an inductive argument derives a general law or statement from a number of specific instances; to move from specific to general. To argue by enthymeme is to argue deductively; to move from general principles regarded as true and apply them to specific cases. To Aristotle, the enthymeme took on the form of a syllogism. Aristotle felt that while arguments by example were no less persuasive than arguments by enthymeme, arguments by enthymeme were the preferred method of persuasion.

In Chapter 3 of Book I, Aristotle distinguishes between three kinds of rhetoric corresponding to the three types of audiences to which speeches are addressed, including (a) deliberative, (b) forensic, and (c) epideictic. Deliberative rhetoric refers to political speeches addressed to a legislative body or some political ruler. The purpose of deliberative rhetoric is to recommend a certain course of action or to dissuade from some action or plan. Forensic rhetoric includes judicial speeches used in prosecution and defense cases where a jury is the audience. The third type of rhetoric, called epideictic, refers to ceremonial speeches, sometimes called declamation, in which the speaker praises or blames someone else for the benefit of the audience. Lincoln's Gettysburg Address is a form of epideictic rhetoric.

The rest of Book I, including Chapters 4 through 15, elaborate on much of what is presented in Chapters 1, 2, and 3 regarding the types of argument and the forms of rhetoric. Particular attention is paid to constructing arguments by enthymeme.

Book II

Book II of the *Rhetoric* is, by the admission of several Aristotelian scholars, awkwardly organized. It is composed of twenty-six chapters, of which most deal with ethos and pathos. Chapter 1 begins with:

> *Now Rhetoric finds its end in judgment—for the audience judges the counsels that are given, and the decision is a judgment; and hence the speaker must not only see to it that his speech shall be convincing and persuasive, but he must give the right impression of himself, and get his judge into the right state of mind.*[67]

In Chapters 2 through 11, audience emotions are defined in regard to the circumstances under which they are felt, the persons toward whom they are felt, and the things that arouse them. In many cases Aristotle prescribes how to arouse such emotions. Specifically anger, mildness, love, fear, confidence, shame and shamelessness, benevolence and the lack of it, pity, indignation, envy, and emulation and contempt are discussed.[68]

Chapters 12 through 17 focus specifically on ethos. Here, Aristotle ponders how such aspects as age, wealth, and power (and their opposites) contribute to one's credibility (though he never used that word). For example, concerning age, Aristotle writes that the physical body is at its best from thirty to thirty-five years and that the mind is at its best at the age of forty-nine. The final chapters of Book II revert back to the study of enthymemes. Much of Chapter 18, for example, is a summary of Book I.

Book III

The final part of the *Rhetoric,* Book III, is made up of nineteen chapters dealing specifically with style and delivery. In Chapter 1, Aristotle says, "it is not enough to know what to say—one must also know how to say it."[69] The art of delivery, according to Aristotle, has to do with the voice; specifically, volume, modulation of pitch, and rhythm. In Chapter 2, Aristotle argues that one's style should be clear and appropriate; that one should use the current idiom of the day, avoid unusual and coined words, and use metaphors. In Chapter 3 Aristotle warns that a speaker should avoid the misuse of words, specifically the use of unusual words and ridiculous metaphors. In Chapter 4 the relation of simile to metaphor is discussed. Good similes are proportional. In Chapter 5, it is argued that stylistic purity is gained through the correct use of words, the avoidance of vague and/or ambiguous words, attention to gender, and attention to the singular and plural. In Chapter 6, Aristotle recommends that speakers should describe their object rather than simply naming it. Speakers should use metaphors, substitute plural for singular, and use negatives; that is, say what a thing is not and what it does not do. Chapters 7 through 12 deal with the use of language, including the use of prose, and two chapters on lively sayings; that is, dramatic presentation.

The final part of Book III, including Chapters 13 through 19, deal specifically with the order of the parts of speech. In Chapter 13 Aristotle initially writes that a speech has only two parts, including a statement and an argument. Speakers must state their case and then prove it. Later, however, he concedes that, at most, a speech has four parts, including a proem (Introduction), statement (of the case), argument (support for the case), and epilogue (conclusion).

In Chapter 14 the nature of the proem, or introduction, is discussed. Aristotle maintains that the function of the introduction is to make clear the purpose of the speech and to arouse the audience in favor of the speaker. In case the audience is prejudiced against the speaker, Aristotle, in Chapter 15, spells out nine possible solutions. In Chapter 16, Aristotle heeds advice for advancing one's ethos. Chapters 17 and 18 deal with how to present one's argument, including refutation of the opposition. Finally, Chapter 19 outlines the epilogue as having four parts, including making the audience well-disposed to the speaker, pointing out the strengths of the speaker's arguments and the weaknesses of the opposition, putting the audience in the right frame of mind, and refreshing the audience's memories.

Aristotle is credited with the first systematic articulation of what are called the major canons of rhetoric, including invention (the discovery of ideas), organization (the arrangement of ideas), elocution (style), and delivery (how the speech is presented). As Griffin notes: "For many teachers of public speaking, criticizing Aristotle's *Rhetoric* is like doubting Einstein's theory of relativity or belittling Shakespeare's "King Lear."[70] The *Rhetoric* was the first systematic treatment of the art of public speaking. The work has remained a dominant influence in our field for over twenty-five hundred years. To be sure, much of what undergraduate students read in their public speaking and persuasion textbooks is based on the work of Aristotle. Without this important book, our field would not exist as it does.

CASE STUDY 3   A Neo-Aristotelian Application to Modern Political Oratory

Key Terms

Artistic Proofs (Ethos, Pathos, & Logos)

Deliberative Speaking

Proem, Statement, Argument, & Epilogue

Although Aristotle's work is some 2,500 years old, it can easily be applied to contemporary public speaking, especially modern political debate and discourse. The case study is labeled "neo-Aristotelian" because the application is derived from the ancient works of Aristotle's *Rhetoric*. This type of application is called traditional rhetorical criticism.

The ideal neo-Aristotelian criticism focuses on several dimensions of oratory, including the speaker's personality, the speaker's public perception, the speaker's motivation, a transcript of the actual speech, the audience, the speaker's mode of arrangement and expression, the speaker's delivery, and finally, the speaker's effect on the audience.[a]

Continued

CASE STUDY 3   *Continued*

This case study focuses on a speech delivered by Mario M. Cuomo, governor of New York state. The speech was delivered to the 1984 Democratic National Convention (DNC) in San Francisco, California. Prior to the speech, Cuomo was relatively unknown as a national politician. At the time of the speech, in July 1984, Cuomo had been the governor of New York for only two years and was just beginning his rise to national recognition. His keynote speech at the convention made him an instant political celebrity. About his speech, one source wrote that "Mario Cuomo emerged after this speech as a political star and potential standard bearer of his party."[b] Some observers rank the speech with the likes of John F. Kennedy's inaugural address.[c]

In the months prior to presidential elections, the dominant political parties convene formally to nominate their candidate. At the 1984 DNC, the Democrats nominated former Vice President Walter Mondale. The Democrats were keenly aware that theirs was an uphill battle if they were to win the White House in 1984. At the time, President Ronald Reagan, who was very popular, was completing his first term in office and was the sure nominee for the Republicans. In fact, only 35 percent of the delegates at the DNC believed that their candidate, Walter Mondale, could win in their own home states.[d] Cuomo's task, as the keynote speaker, was to unite the party.

Historically Democrats have been perceived as a disorganized party of special interests. For example, they left their 1980 convention as divided as ever with special interest factions fighting for their own individual agendas. In 1984 the Democratic leadership desperately wanted to unify the party, knowing that unification was key if there was any hope of winning the November election.

On June 14, 1984, only a few weeks away from the convention, Mondale phoned Cuomo to ask him to deliver the keynote speech. At the time many insiders felt, including Cuomo himself, that Senator Ted Kennedy should give the speech. At the time, Kennedy had not endorsed Mondale and many felt that they could get Kennedy's endorsement in exchange for the speech. Nevertheless, Mondale was convinced that it should be Cuomo. After discussing the issue with Kennedy, Cuomo agreed to give the speech although he told Mondale that he still thought it was a mistake.[e]

In the days and weeks prior to the convention Cuomo worked hard on the speech, writing much of it himself. In fact, he spent so much time on it that he thought it was too predictable and dull. He was convinced that he would not be able to reach the high expectations that were created about his speech.[f]

On the night of the speech former President Jimmy Carter delivered a brief address to the delegates. Following that, a film tribute about Harry Truman was shown. Instead of having someone introduce Cuomo personally, a six-minute movie about Cuomo and his upbringing in New York and his subsequent accomplishments was shown. At the movie's end, the houselights were dimmed and a spotlight focused on Cuomo as he approached the speaker's podium.[g] The audience consisted of over 3,900 DNC delegates. A transcript of Cuomo's speech appears below. Each paragraph is numbered to facilitate reference.

On behalf of the Empire State and the family of New York, I thank you for the great privilege of being allowed to address this convention. Please allow me to skip the stories and the poetry and the temptation to deal in nice but vague rhetoric. Let me instead use this valuable opportunity to deal with the questions that should determine this election and that are vital to the American people.

Ten days ago, President Reagan admitted that although some people in this country seemed to be doing well nowadays, others were unhappy, and even worried, about themselves, their families and their futures. The President said he didn't understand that fear. He said, "Why, this country is a shining city on a hill." The President is right. In many ways we are "a shining city on a hill." But the hard truth is that not everyone is sharing in this city's splendor and glory.

A shining city is perhaps all the President sees from the portico of the White House and the veranda of his ranch, where everyone seems to be doing well. But there's another part of the city, the part where some people can't pay their mortgages and most young people can't afford one, where students can't afford the education they need and middle-class parents watch dreams they hold for their children evaporate.

In this part of the city there are more poor than ever, more families in trouble. More and more people who need help but can't find it. Even worse: there are elderly people who tremble in the basements of the houses there. There are people who sleep in the city's streets, in the gutter, where the glitter doesn't show. There are ghettos where thousands of young people, without an education or a job, give their lives away to drug dealers every day. There is despair, Mr. President, in faces you never see, in places you never visit in your shining city.

In fact, Mr. President, this nation is more a "Tale of Two Cities" than it is a "Shining City on a Hill." Maybe if you visited more places, Mr. President, you'd understand.

Maybe if you went to Appalachia where some people still live in sheds and to Lackawanna where thousands of unemployed steel workers wonder why we subsidized foreign steel while we surrender their dignity to unemployment and to welfare checks; maybe if you stepped into a shelter in Chicago and talked with some of the homeless there.

Maybe, Mr. President, if you asked a woman who'd been denied the help she needs to feed her children because you say we need the money to give a tax break to a millionaire or to build a missile we can't even afford to use—maybe then you'd understand. Maybe, Mr. President. But I'm afraid not. Because the truth is, this is how we were warned it would be.

President Reagan told us from the beginning that he believed in a kind of social Darwinism. Survival of the fittest. Government can't do everything, we were told. So it should settle for taking care of the strong and hope that economic ambition and charity will do the rest. Make the rich richer and what falls

Continued

CASE STUDY 3   *Continued*

from their table will be enough for the middle class and those trying to make it into the middle class

The Republicans called it trickle-down when Hoover tried it. Now they call it supply side. It is the same shining city for those relative few who are lucky enough to live in its good neighborhoods. But for the people who are excluded—locked out—all they can do is to stare from a distance at that city's glimmering towers.   9

It's an old story. As old as our history.

The difference between Democrats and Republicans has always been measured in courage and confidence. The Republicans believe the wagon train will not make it to the frontier unless some of our old, some of our young, and some of our weak are left behind by the side of the trail. The strong will inherit the land!   10

We Democrats believe that we can make it all the way with the whole family intact. We have. More than once. Ever since Franklin Roosevelt lifted himself from his wheelchair to lift this nation from its knees. Wagon train after wagon train. To new frontiers of education, housing, peace. The whole family aboard. Constantly reaching out to extend and enlarge that family. Lifting them up into the wagon on the way. Blacks and Hispanics, people of every ethnic group, and native Americans—all those struggling to build their families claim some share of America.   11

For nearly 50 years we carried them to new levels of comfort, security, dignity, even affluence. Some of us are in this room today only because this nation had that confidence. It would be wrong to forget that. So, we are at this convention to remind ourselves where we come from and to claim the future for ourselves and for our children.   12

Today, our great Democratic Party, which has saved this nation from depression, from fascism, from racism, from corruption, is called upon to do it again—this time to save the nation from confusion and division, most of all from fear of a nuclear holocaust.   13

In order to succeed, we must answer our opponent's polished and appealing rhetoric with a more telling reasonableness and rationality. We must win this case on the merits. We must get the American public to look past the glitter, beyond the showmanship, to reality, to the hard substance of things. And we will do that not so much with speeches that sound good as with speeches that are good and sound. Not so much with speeches that bring people to their feet as with speeches that bring people to their senses.   14

We must make the American people hear our "tale of two cities." We must convince them that we don't have one city, indivisible, shining for all its people. We will have no chance to do that if what comes out of this convention, what is heard throughout the campaign, is a babel of arguing voices.   15

To succeed we will have to surrender small parts of our individual interests, to build a platform we can all stand on, at once, comfortable, proudly singing out the truth for the nation to hear, in chorus, its logic so clear and commanding that no slick commercial, no amount of geniality, no martial music will be able to muffle it. We Democrats must unite so that the entire nation can. Surely the Republicans won't bring the convention together. Their policies divide the nation into the lucky and the left-out, the royalty and the rabble. The Republicans are willing to treat that division as victory. They would cut this nation in half, into those temporarily better off and those worse off than before, and call it recovery.   16

We should not be embarrassed or dismayed if the process of unifying is difficult, even at times wrenching. Unlike any other party, we embrace men and women of every color, every creed, every orientation, every economic class. In our family are gathered everyone from the abject poor of Essex County in New York to the enlightened affluent of the gold coasts of both ends of our nation. And in between is the heart of our constituency. The middle class, the people not rich enough to be worry-free but not poor enough to be on welfare, those who work for a living because they have to: white collar and blue collar, young professionals, men and women in small businesses desperate for capital and contracts they need to prove their worth.   17

We speak for the minorities who have not yet entered the mainstream: for ethnics who want to add their culture to the mosaic that is America; for women indignant that we refuse to etch into our governmental commandments the simple rule "thou shalt not sin against equality," a commandment so obvious it can be spelled in three letters: E.R.A.; for young people demanding an education and a future; for senior citizens terrorized by the idea that their only security, their Social Security, is being threatened; for millions of reasoning people fighting to preserve our environment from greed and stupidity. And fighting to preserve our very existence from a macho intransigence that refuses to make intelligent attempts to discuss the possibility of nuclear holocaust with our enemy. Refusing because they believe we can pile missiles so high that they will pierce the clouds and the sight of them will frighten our enemies into submission.   18

We're proud of this diversity. Grateful we don't have to manufacture its appearance the way the Republicans will next month in Dallas, by propping up mannequin delegates on the convention floor.   19

But we pay a price for it. The different people we represent have many points of view. Sometimes they compete and then we have debates, even arguments. That's what our primaries were.   20

But now the primaries are over, and it is time to lock arms and move into this campaign together. If we need any inspiration to make the effort to put aside our small differences, all we need to do is reflect on the Republican policy of divide and cajole and how it has injured our land since 1980.   21

Continued

CASE STUDY 3   *Continued*

The President has asked us to judge him on whether or not he's fulfilled the   22
promises he made four years ago. I accept that. Just consider what he said and
what he's done.

Inflation is down since 1980. But not because of the supplyside miracle   23
promised by the President. Inflation was reduced the old-fashioned way, with
a recession, the worst since 1932. More than 55,000 bankruptcies. Two years
of massive unemployment. Two hundred thousand farmers and ranchers forced
off the land. More homeless than at any time since the Great Depression. More
hungry, more poor—mostly women—and a nearly $200 billion deficit threat-
ening our future.

The President's deficit is a direct and dramatic repudiation of his promise to   24
balance our budget by 1983. That deficit is the largest in the history of this universe; more than three times larger than the deficit in President Carter's last year.
It is a deficit that, according to the President's own fiscal advisor, could grow as
high as $300 billion a year, stretching "as far as the eye can see." It is a debt so
large that as much as one-half of our revenue from the income tax goes to pay the
interest on it each year. It is a mortgage on our children's futures that can only be
paid in pain and that could eventually bring this nation to its knees.

Don't take my word for it—I'm a Democrat.   25

Ask the Republican investment bankers on Wall Street what they think the   26
chances are this recovery will be permanent. If they're not too embarrassed to
tell you the truth, they'll say they are appalled and frightened by the President's
deficit. Ask them what they think of our economy, now that it has been driven
by the distorted value of the dollar back to its colonial condition, exporting agricultural products and importing manufactured ones.

Ask those Republican investment bankers what they expect the interest rate   27
to be a year from now. And ask them what they predict for the inflation rate
then.

How important is this question of the deficit? Think about it: What chance   28
would the Republican candidate have had in 1980 if he had told the American
people that he intended to pay for his so-called economic recovery with bankruptcies, unemployment and the largest government debt known to human-
kind? Would American voters have signed the loan certificate for him on
election day? Of course not! It was an election won with smoke and mirrors,
with illusion. It is a recovery made of the same stuff.

And what about foreign policy? They said they would make us and the   29
whole world safer. They say they have. By creating the largest defense budget
in history, one even they now admit is excessive. By escalating to a frenzy the
nuclear arms race. By incendiary rhetoric. By refusing to discuss peace with
our enemies. By the loss of 279 young Americans in Lebanon in pursuit of a
plan and a policy no one can find or describe.

We give monies to Latin American governments that murder nuns, and then lie about it.   30

We have been less than zealous in our support of the only real friend we have in the Middle East, the one democracy there, our flesh and blood ally, the state of Israel.   31

Our policy drifts with no real direction, other than a hysterical commitment to an arms race that leads nowhere, if we're lucky. If we're not—could lead us to bankruptcy or war.   32

Of course we must have a strong defense! Of course Democrats believe that there are times when we must stand and fight. And we have. Thousands of us have paid for freedom with our lives. But always, when we've been at our best, our purposes were clear.   33

Now they're not. Now our allies are as confused as our enemies. Now we have no real commitment to our friends or our enemies. Now we have no real commitment to our friends or our ideals to human rights, to the refusenicks, to Sakharov, to Bishop Tutu, and the others struggling for freedom in South Africa. We have spent more than we can afford. We have pounded our chest and made bold speeches. But we lost 279 young Americans in Lebanon and we are forced to live behind sand bags in Washington. How can anyone believe that we are stronger, safer or better? That's the Republican record. That its disastrous quality is not more fully understood by the American people is attributable, I think, to the President's amiability and the failure by some to separate the salesman from the product.   34

It's now up to us to make the case to America. And to remind Americans that if they are not happy with all the President has done so far, they should consider how much worse it will be if he is left to his radical proclivities for another four years unrestrained by the need once again to come before the American people.   35

If July brings back Anne Gorsuch Buford, what can we expect in December? Where would another four years take us? How much larger will the deficit be? How much deeper the cuts in programs for the struggling middle class and the poor to limit that deficit? How high the interest rates? How much more acid rain killing our forests and fouling our lakes?   36

What kind of Supreme Court? What kind of court and country will be fashioned by the man who believes in having government mandate people's religion and morality? The man who believes that trees pollute the environment, that the laws against discrimination go too far. The man who threatens Social Security and Medicaid and help for the disabled.   37

How high will we pile the missiles? How much deeper will be the gulf between us and our enemies? Will we make meaner the spirit of our people?   38

This election will measure the record of the past four years. But more than that, it will answer the question of what kind of people we want to be.   39

Continued

CASE STUDY 3   *Continued*

We Democrats still have a dream. We still believe in this nation's future. 40
And this is our answer—our credo: We believe in only the government we
need, but we insist on all the government we need.

We believe in a government characterized by fairness and reasonableness, a
reasonableness that goes beyond labels, that doesn't distort or promise to do
what it knows it can't do. A government strong enough to use the words "love"
and "compassion" and smart enough to convert our noblest aspirations. 41

We believe in encouraging the talented, but we believe that while survival 42
of the fittest may be a good working description of the process of evolution, a
government of humans should elevate itself to a higher order, one which fills
the gaps left by chance or wisdom we don't understand.

We would rather have laws written by the patron of this great city, the man 43
called the "world's most sincere Democrat," St. Francis of Assisi, than laws
written by Darwin.

We believe, as Democrats, that a society as blessed as ours, the most affluent 44
democracy in the world's history, that can spend trillions on instruments of destruction, ought to be able to help the middle class in its struggle, ought to be
able to find work for all who can do it, room at the table, shelter for the homeless, care for the elderly and infirm, hope for the destitute.

We proclaim as loudly as we can the utter insanity of nuclear proliferation 45
and the need for a nuclear freeze, if only to affirm the simple truth that peace is
better than war because life is better than death.

We believe in firm but fair law and order, in the union movement, in privacy 46
for people, openness by government, civil rights, and human rights.

We believe in a single fundamental idea that describes better than most text- 47
books and any speech what a proper government should be. The idea of family.
Mutuality. The sharing of benefits and burdens for the good of all. Feeling one
another's pain. Sharing one another's blessings. Reasonably, honestly, fairly,
without respect to race, or sex or geography or political affiliation.

We believe we must be the family of America, recognizing that at the heart 48
of the matter we are bound one to another, that the problems of a retired school
teacher in Duluth are our problems. That the future of the child in Buffalo is
our future. The struggle of a disabled man in Boston to survive, to live decently
is our struggle. The hunger of a woman in Little Rock, our hunger. The failure
anywhere to provide what reasonably we might, to avoid pain, is our failure.

For fifty years we Democrats created a better future for our children, using 49
traditional democratic principles as a fixed beacon, giving us direction and purpose, but constantly innovating, adapting to new realities; Roosevelt's alphabet
programs; Truman's NATO and the GI Bill of Rights; Kennedy's intelligent tax
incentives and the Alliance for Progress; Johnson's civil rights; Carter's human
rights and the nearly miraculous Camp David peace accord.

Democrats did it—and Democrats can do it again. 50

We can build a future that deals with our deficit. 51

Remember fifty years of progress never cost us what the last four years of 52
stagnation have. We can deal with that deficit intelligently, by shared sacrifice,
with all parts of the nation's family contributing, building partnerships with the
private sector, providing a sound defense without depriving ourselves of what
we need to feed our children and care for our people.

We can have a future that provides for all the young of the present by mar- 53
rying common sense and compassion.

We know we can, because we did it for nearly fifty years before 1980. 54

We can do it again. If we do not forget. Forget that this entire nation has 55
profited by these progressive principles. That they helped lift up generations to
the middle class and higher: gave us a chance to work, to go to college, to raise
a family, to own a house, to be secure in our old age and, before that, to reach
heights that our own parents would not have dared dream of.

That struggle to live with dignity is the real story of the shining city. It's a 56
story I didn't read in a book, or learn in a classroom. I saw it, and lived it. Like
many of you.

I watched a small man with thick calluses on both hands work 15 and 16 57
hours a day. I saw him once literally bleed from the bottoms of his feet, a man
who came here uneducated, alone, unable to speak the language, who taught
me all I needed to know about faith and hard work by the simple eloquence of
his example. I learned about our kind of democracy from my father. I learned
about our obligation to each other from him and from my mother. They asked
only for a chance to work and to make the world better for their children and to
be protected in those moments when they would not be able to protect themselves. This nation and its government did that for them.

And on January 20th, 1985, it will happen again. Only on a much grander 58
scale. We will have a new president of the United States, a Democrat born not
to the blood of kings but to the blood of immigrants and pioneers.

We will have America's first woman vice president, the child of immigrants, 59
a New Yorker, opening with one magnificent stroke a whole new frontier for
the United States.

It will happen, if we make it happen. I ask you, ladies and gentlemen, broth- 60
ers and sisters—for the good of all us, for the love of this great nation, for the
family of America, for the love of God. Please make this nation remember how
futures are built.

Because Cuomo's speech was delivered to the voting delegates at the DNC, Aristotle
would describe it as a deliberative speech; that is, a political speech addressed to a legislative body.

Continued

CASE STUDY 3   *Continued*

Aristotle argued that a speech has four parts, including the proem, statement, argument, and epilogue. The proem is Paragraph 1. Here, Cuomo makes clear that his purpose is to deal with the questions that should determine this election and that are vital to the American people." In Paragraph 2, Cuomo states his argument: "But the hard truth is that not everyone is sharing in this city's splendor and glory." In Paragraphs 3 through 57, Cuomo presents his argument. He begins by articulating the problems in America and attacking Reagan's idea of social Darwinism in Paragraphs 3 through 9. Next, Cuomo compares the Democrats and the Republicans in Paragraph 10, then proceeds to develop the dominant theme in the speech; that is, family. In Paragraphs 2 through 34, Cuomo attacks the prior four years of Reagan's administration. Beginning in Paragraph 35, he outlines the Democratic credo. Then, in Paragraph 58, Cuomo delivers his epilogue, or conclusion, through to the end of the speech.

Throughout the speech, Cuomo makes use of artistic proofs, including ethos, pathos, and logos. As governor of New York state, Cuomo brings with him a certain amount of ethos as was demonstrated in the short movie immediately prior to the speech. During the speech, Cuomo tells how he learned about dignity and democracy through the plights of his father. Paragraphs 56 and 57 enhance the trustworthiness of the speaker.

> *That struggle to live with dignity is the real story of the shining city. It's a story I didn't read in a book, or learn in a classroom. I saw it, and lived it. Like many of you. I watched a small man with thick calluses on both hands work 15 and 16 hours a day. I saw him once literally bleed from the bottoms of his feet, a man who came here uneducated, alone, unable to speak the language, who taught me all I needed to know about faith and hard work by the simple eloquence of his example.*

Cuomo's speech is replete with emotional appeals; that is, the second artistic proof. One of Cuomo's emotional devices is to make an analogy using *A Tale of Two Cities*. Taken, of course, from the famous Dickens story about the French Revolution, Cuomo sees the current political climate as a dichotomy. Dickens's novel begins with the famous line, "It was the best of times, it was the worst of times."[h] Throughout the speech Cuomo compares incumbent President Reagan's view of the county as a "shining city on a hill" (i.e., the best of times) with a different part of the "city" where people suffer (i.e., the worst of times). In Paragraph 2 following through to Paragraph 5, Cuomo says:

> *Ten days ago, President Reagan admitted that although some people in this country seemed to be doing well nowadays, others were unhappy, and even worried, about themselves, their families and their futures. The President said he didn't understand that fear. He said, "Why, this country is a shining city in a hill." The President is right. In many ways we are "a shining city on a hill." But the hard truth is that not everyone is sharing in this city's splendor and glory.... In fact, Mr. President, this nation is more a "Tale of Two Cities" than*

it is a "Shining City on a Hill." Maybe if you visited more places, Mr. President, you'd understand.

A dominant emotional appeal throughout Cuomo's speech is family (i.e., a warmth appeal). As mentioned earlier, throughout much of its history, the Democratic party has been characterized as a disorganized party of special interests. Cuomo's audience that night was the living manifestation of those special interests. Cuomo attempts to unite the party via the family metaphor, "We believe in a single fundamental idea that describes better than most textbooks and any speech what a proper government should be. The idea of family." After attacking the Republicans as divisive Cuomo says, "We Democrats believe that we can make it all the way with the whole family intact" (Paragraph 11). He continues his allegory of *A Tale of Two Cities* and the family metaphor in Paragraphs 15 and 16. "We Democrats must unite so that the entire nation can. Surely the Republicans won't bring the convention together. Their policies divide the nation into the lucky and the left-out, the royalty and the rabble."

The third artistic proof, logos, refers to the use of rational appeals; that is argument by example (inductive) and enthymeme (deductive). Cuomo makes use of both types of arguments. In Paragraph 2 Cuomo makes his general case that "not everyone is sharing in this city's splendor and glory." In subsequent paragraphs (e.g., Paragraphs 3, 4, 6, and 7) Cuomo presents specific examples that demonstrate the validity of his general claim. These examples also demonstrate "the worst of times." Cuomo's inductive argument begins in Paragraph 39 and continues through to the end of the speech. Here Cuomo cites specific examples of what the Democrats believe (e.g., Paragraphs 40 through 53) with the general conclusion that they can do it again, and in Paragraph 60 he concludes with this is "how futures are built."

Cuomo's delivery that evening was atypical for political speeches. His tone was quiet and conversational. His mode of expression was replete with alliteration (e.g., "in the gutter, where the glitter doesn't show," "Our opponent's polished and appealing rhetoric," "reasonableness and rationality," "the lucky and the left-out," and "the royalty and the rabble"), and urban metaphors (e.g., "all they can do is stare from a distance at that city's glimmering towers"). David Brinkley, who was the lead reporter of the convention for the American Broadcasting Corporation (ABC) said, "As for skill and delivery, effective delivery, I think it's the best I've ever heard."[i] Regarding his gestures, one observer noted:

> *Cuomo gesticulated with his right hand raised in the customary benediction of a priest. With his first two fingers raised and his second two folded against his palm, he distinctly made the sign of the cross, a subliminal gesture impressing itself on the subconscious of millions.*[j]

The audience's response to the speech was overwhelming. There was a "thunderous ovation, far beyond what is to be expected on such an occasion . . . the crowd continued to go wild."[k] Within hours of the speech, "CUOMO IN '88" buttons appeared on the convention floor and quickly sold out.[l]

The speech was a critical success. The television ratings were very high where an estimated eighty million people watched the speech. *U.S. News & World Report* said that the

Continued

CASE STUDY 3 *Continued*

speech was "electrifying."[m] Harrison Donnelly wrote in the *Congressional Quarterly* that Cuomo "electrified delegates," that he gave "an eloquent appeal," and dubbed him "Albany's Great Communicator" (at the time, President Reagan was frequently called "The Great Communicator").[n] Hedrick Smith, writing in the *New York Times,* described Cuomo's speech as "shrewd and forceful."[o] Howell Raines of the *New York Times* said that the speech created a "stirring swell of emotional applause," and "drew a pounding roar of approval," and that Cuomo delivered the speech "in a ringing voice, his eyes glistening."[p] Sidney Blumenthal of *The New Republic* wrote that "all the elements of Cuomo's vision are timeless," that the speech was "evocative rhetoric," and that "Cuomo blessed his audience, his physical movements uniting them in one faith."[q]

Whether or not Cuomo consciously thought of Aristotle's principles in constructing the speech is not important. That Aristotle's prescriptions are still applicable some 2,500 years after they were written serves as a testament of their fundamental place in the field of speech communication. Though the speech had no measurable effect on the outcome of the 1984 election, the speech fulfilled its purpose. The Democratic party was more united than ever. Mondale himself attributed some of that unity to Cuomo and believed that after the convention the party was the most unified in its history.

Mario Cuomo's speech: Copyright © 1984 by Mario Cuomo. Reprinted with permission.
a. Fisher, W. (1969). "Method in Rhetorical Criticism," *Southern Speech Communication Journal, 35,* 101–109.
b. Peterson, O. (Ed.) (1985). "Representative American Speeches 1984–1985," *The Reference Shelf, 57,* (3), New York: H. W. Wilson, (p. 23).
c. McElvaine, R. S. (1988). *Mario Cuomo: A Biography,* New York: Charles Scribner's Sons.
d. Peterson, "Representative American Speeches."
e. Donnelly, H. (1984). "Democrats Launch the Mondale-Ferraro Team," *Congressional Quarterly, 42,* (29), 1729–1738.
f. McElvaine, *Mario Cuomo.*
g. Ibid.
h. Dickens, C. (1970). *A Tale of Two Cities,* New York: Penguin, (p. 1).
i. Peterson, "Representative American Speeches," (p. 23).
j. Blumenthal, S. (1984). "Mondale's Manifesto," *The New Republic,* (August 13 and 20), (p. 10).
k. McElvaine, *Mario Cuomo,* (p. 349).
l. Miringoff, L. M., & Carvalho, B. L. (1986). *The Cuomo Factor: Assessing the Political Appeal of New York's Governor,* Poughkeepsie, NY: Marist Institute for Public Opinion.
m. *U.S. News & World Report,* (July 30, 1984), (p. 7).
n. Donnelly, "Democrats Launch the Mondale-Ferraro Team," (p. 1731).
o. Smith, H. (1984). "Battle Plan for the Fall: Cuomo Would Attack Record, Not Reagan," *New York Times,* (July 17, 1984), p. A1.
p. Raines, H. (1984). "Democrat Calls on Party to Unify and Seek Out 'Family of America,'" *New York Times,* (July 17, 1984), p. A1.
q. Blumenthal, "Mondale's Manifesto," (p. 10).

Beyond Greece: Roman Rhetoric

Aristotle died in 322 B.C. To the best of our knowledge no major rhetorical works survived the following 250 years after the *Rhetoric* was introduced. The three centuries following Aristotle's death are known as the Hellenistic age. During this time Rome became the dominant power over the entire Mediterranean. As Rome expanded her power, the people were becoming familiar with Greeks and their method of education. Greek teachers were beginning to make their way into Rome, especially the rhetoricians.[71] During that time great rewards were offered to those who could speak successfully. Ironically, the Romans had little use for the philosophical theories presented by the Greek teachers. They were more interested in practical matters of which rhetoric seemed to fit. As Cicero noted:

> *At first our countrymen knew nothing of the art and did not realize that there was any value in practice or that there were any rules or system, but they achieved such success as could be attained by talent and reflection. Afterwards however, when they had listened to Greek orators, become acquainted with Greek literature and come into contact with Greek teachers, there was a remarkable burst of enthusiasm among our countrymen for the study of the art of speaking.*[72]

Though speaking was seen as valuable, in 161 B.C. the Roman Senate empowered Rome's rulers to expel both philosophers and rhetoricians. By the end of the century, however, rhetoric was firmly established, though it remained mostly in the hands of the Greeks. The next milestone in the history of Roman classical rhetoric occurs during the first century B.C. with the work of Cicero, who is considered the greatest Roman orator and writer on rhetoric.[73]

Cicero's Rhetoric

Marcus Tullius Cicero was born in Arpinum, a small town about sixty miles from Rome, on January 3, 106 B.C. He moved to Rome while still young and by the age of twenty-five began to plead law cases in the forum. By the age of thirty-six, he was considered the most prominent Roman speaker of the day. At age forty-two he was elected to the consulship, the highest office in Rome. During the first triumvirate he was exiled (in 58 B.C.) but was recalled the very next year. When Caesar was assassinated, Cicero led the opposition to Antony but was murdered in December of 43 B.C.[74]

Much of Cicero's writings survive, including fifty-eight of his speeches, over nine hundred of his letters, a series of works on Greek philosophy, and seven works on rhetoric. Much of his work on rhetoric is based on the writings of Aristotle and Isocrates.[75] Two of his most important works on rhetoric include *De Inventione*, or *On Invention*, which was written when he was approximately fifteen years old, and *De Oratore*, or *On the Orator*, which was written in about 55 B.C. after his return from exile and while he was at the height of his intellectual career.

De Inventione

According to Kennedy, of all of Cicero's writings, *De Inventione* was the most read for over fifteen hundred years.[76] Most scholars agree that *De Inventione* is not a well-written book. In fact, some argue that it may be nothing more than the recorded dictations of his teacher.[77] *De Inventione* consists of two books. In Book I, Cicero begins with what has become a classic statement regarding the nature of rhetoric. He states:

> *For my own part, after long thought, I have been led by reason itself to hold this opinion first and foremost, that wisdom without eloquence does too little good of states, but that eloquence without wisdom is generally highly disadvantageous and is never helpful. Therefore if anyone neglects the study of philosophy and moral conduct, which is the highest and most honourable of pursuits, and devotes his whole energy to the practice of oratory, his civic life is nurtured into something useless to himself and harmful to his country.*[78]

In Book I, Cicero classifies oratory as a part of political science whose function is to speak in such a way as to persuade an audience. As the title implies, the major focus of *De Inventione* is on invention or reasoning from the truth. Cicero defines invention as the discovery of valid arguments in order to support one's case. Cicero focuses on *constitutio;* that is, the question at hand, or the case to be heard. Each *constitutio* has two sides which stem from an initial accusation made by some party. For example, if a murder is committed, someone will be accused. The accused person represents one side of the issue or *constitutio.* The accused will be tried by the accuser, which represents the other side of the *constitutio.* Each side of the *constitutio* must then develop a persuasive case to be heard by a jury or court via oration.

Cicero contends that while presenting one's side of the *constitutio,* the orator must arrange the speech in a proper order, which he defines as the (a) exordium, (b) narrative, (c) partition, (d) confirmation, (e) refutation, and (f) peroration.[79] The exordium is a passage designed to put the audience in a proper frame of mind to hear the rest of the persuasive speech. A successful exordium renders the audience well-disposed, attentive, and receptive. The narrative is the exposition of the events as they occurred or were to supposed to have occurred. The narrative outlines to the audience the reason for the dispute or *constitutio.* The partition specifically outlines points of agreement and disagreement between the two sides of the *constitutio.* The orator's goal here is to turn the subject of agreement between the two sides to the advantage of the speaker. Confirmation, or proof, is the part of the speech that supports or lends credit or authority to the arguments already presented. In discussing confirmation, Cicero spends a considerable amount of time outlining arguments by induction and deduction (i.e., the syllogism). The refutation is the part of the speech where arguments are presented to disprove the opponent's case. The same kinds of arguments that are used in confirmation are used in refutation. Finally, the peroration is the conclusion of the speech in which the narrative, partition, confirmation, and refutation are summarized.

Cicero devotes almost all of Book II of *De Inventione* to providing examples of the topics discussed in Book I with particular emphasis on confirmation and refutation. He presents hypothetical *constitutios* and then presents possible arguments of confirmation and refutation based on their definitions presented in Book I.

De Oratore

Many scholars argue that Cicero's greatest contribution to rhetoric was his book titled *De Oratore,* or literally, *On the Orator. De Oratore* was written in 55 B.C. after Cicero's return from exile. Apparently, Cicero was very pleased with this work, as are critics. Kennedy, for example, likens *De Oratore* with Aristotle's *Rhetoric*.[80] Unlike his earlier books, *De Oratore* is written as a dialogue similar to Plato's work, although Cicero calls the method Aristotelian. In fact, many scholars agree that Cicero was consciously rivaling the ancient Greeks with this "new" style.[81]

De Oratore consists of three books. Book I deals with Cicero's ideal picture of an orator. Book II focuses on *inventio,* and Book III outlines style. The principle speakers are Crassus and Antonius, two orators who influenced Cicero in his early years as a student and who were two of the foremost orators of their day. In addition to Crassus and Antonius, Cicero introduces two of their most distinguished followers, Rufus and Cotta.

The fundamental thesis of *De Oratore* is that oratory is a noble and respectful profession that is difficult to learn and requires much training. Because of the great difficulty of the art, truly great orators are rare. To be an orator requires a liberal education, particularly in philosophy; command of the language; pathos; a sense of humor and wit; good delivery; and good memory.[82] *De Oratore* is much more than a treatise on rhetoric, however; the three books represent Cicero's basic philosophy on educational reform.[83]

Book I

In Book I of *De Oratore,* Crassus engages in a discussion about the nature of oratory. He praises it as of primary importance to the society. After some discussion about the proper role of the orator, Crassus describes his own method of rhetorical training in seven stages. First, he argues that the duty of an orator is to speak in a style that is designed to convince an audience. Next, the orator's speech must focus on some general problem or on a problem that is concerned with specific individuals and times. Third, the orator must specify the exact issue to debate; that is, whether some deed was done and the character of that deed. Fourth, certain deeds lend themselves to three types of oratory, including forensic, judicial, and deliberative. Fifth, the activity and ability of an orator falls into five divisions (i.e., canons) including (a) invention, (b) arrangement, (c) style, (d) memory, and (e) delivery. Sixth, the speech should proceed in a certain order by which the orator (a) secures the good will of the audience, (b) states the case, (c) defines the dispute, (d) establishes one's own side of the case, (e) refutes the opposition, and (f) summarizes by reinforcing one's case while further weakening the opposition. Seventh, the rules of diction for the orator include the embellishment of the discourse through pure and correct Latin, grace and eloquence, and in a manner befitting the topic.[84] Book I ends with an elaborate discussion between Crassus and Antonius regarding Crassus's method.

Book II

Book II of *De Oratore* emphasizes *inventio* with a discussion of the role of practical experience. Antonius states that while rhetoric is not a science, the orator can make use of his own observations and experiences. To him, oratory covers all good speaking and all subjects. The facts of any case are established by evidence and practice.[85]

A considerable portion of Book II covers the use of humor and wit; a topic not typically associated with classical rhetoric. Although the topic had been covered by the Greeks before him, Cicero was the first to offer a full treatment of it as it relates to rhetoric.[86] Through the character of C. Julius Caesar Strabo Vopiscus, of which not much is known, humor is considered under five topics, including its nature, its source, whether its use is becoming of an orator, its limits, and a classification of things laughable.[87]

Admitting that he knows very little about the nature of humor, Vopiscus moves on to the second topic, the source of humor, which he states is limited to that which is unseemly or ugly. He says that "for the chief, if not the only, objects of laughter are those sayings which remark upon and point out something unseemly in no unseemly manner."[88] Regarding its appropriateness, Vopiscus contends that it clearly becomes an orator to use humor:

> *Merriment naturally wins goodwill for its author; and everyone admires acuteness, which is often concentrated in a single word, uttered generally in repelling, though sometimes in delivering an attack; and it shatters or obstructs or makes light of an opponent, or alarms or repulses him; and it shows the orator himself to be a man of finish, accomplishment and taste; and best of all, it relieves dullness and tones down austerity, and, by a jest or a laugh, often dispels distasteful suggestions not easily weakened by reasoning.[89]*

In outlining the limits of its use, Vopiscus asserts that restraint must be practiced in humor. Orators should avoid using humor about those topics which are disgusting and/or arouse sympathy. In addition, the orator should avoid buffoonery and mere mimicking. In classifying its objects, Vopiscus indicates that there are two kinds of it; that is, wit of matter, or fact, and wit of form, or words. Wittiness of matter comes in many varieties, especially in comparison, caricatures, understatement, irony, farcical jests, assumed simplicity, hinted ridicule, unexpected turns, and personal retorts. Verbal witticisms can be classified into seven categories, including the (a) the ambiguous; (b) the unexpected; (c) play on words or names; (d) quotations; (e) words taken literally; (f) allegory, metaphor and irony; and (g) antithetical expressions.[90]

Book III

Book III of *De Oratore* is devoted to style. Because Cicero was considered the greatest orator of his time, many scholars and students alike have shown a keen interest in his discussion of style. Kennedy, for example, argues that Cicero's greatest legacy is his own oratory. Petersson asserts that "it can not be stated too strongly that in the case of Cicero the style is the man."[91]

The discussion of style in Book III is professed through Crassus who describes his own exercises in style, which are interpreted by scholars to be those of Cicero. Crassus begins by stating that style is not separable from matter, meaning that the issue at hand and the style by which it is addressed are interdependent. Crassus argues that the human senses differ, but each gives pleasure in its own way. The eyes, ears, nose, tongue, and skin all provide a different way of seeing the world. Likewise, the arts come in many shapes and forms. Hence, the orator may adopt a variety of styles in presenting his speech.

Crassus then pronounces that the job of the orator is to argue the issue and to express it in a particular style. He articulates four primary requisites of style for oratory, including the use of correct, lucid, ornate, and appropriate language. To Cicero, pronunciation was key. Through Crassus, Cicero advocates correct, but not overly excessive or rustic, pronunciation of letters. At this point in Book III, Crassus diverts into a lengthy discussion of the relationship of oratory to philosophy.

The final half of Book III discusses embellishment or ornamentation. Through the voice of Crassus, Cicero explains that embellishment consists of flowery language that avoids extravagance and is spread evenly throughout the speech. Of particular importance is the choice of words, their combination, and the order and rhythm in which they are spoken. Crassus promotes the use of rare words, new coinages, and words used metaphorically. Book III ends with a discussion of delivery, including the use of gestures and voice. Crassus argues that:

> *the effect of all of these oratorical devices depends on how they are delivered. Delivery, I assert, is the dominant factor in oratory; without delivery the best speaker cannot be of any account at all, and a moderate speaker with a trained delivery can often outdo the rest of them.*[92]

The influence of Cicero on the development of rhetoric cannot be overstated. He contributed not only technique but theory to the art of oratory. He gave status to what was considered by many to be a simple skill or vocation. Much of what Cicero pronounced guided the study of rhetoric for over a thousand years and even today serves as the core of contemporary public speaking courses across the country.

Quintilian

Upon the death of Cicero in 43 B.C., it is said that the great tradition of Roman oratory came to an end.[93] Though Cicero was not forgotten, the high status accorded rhetoric during his time experienced a steady decline. This decline was attributed to the luxury of the age, the lack of rewards, and a new law of nature indicating that decline always follows from high achievement.[94] One rhetorician stood out during this time, however, and his name was Quintilian.

Marcus Fabius Quintilanus was born in A.D. 40 and lived to the age of 55, although scholars debate the exact date of his birth. He was a Spaniard and of his early life virtually nothing is known. It is thought that he was born in Calagurris in northern Spain.[95] Quintilian is an important figure in classical rhetorical theory because he is the author of the largest rhetorical composition that survived his time—*Institutio Oratoria,* or *Education of the Orator.*

Rhetoric during Quintilian's time was divided into three areas, including theoretical, educational, and practical rhetoric.[96] Quintilian wrote mostly about theoretical and educational rhetoric and was not considered a great political orator. His chief aim was the education of the perfect orator and his reputation was built on his teaching. He wrote that the perfect orator "should be a good man, and consequently we demand of him not merely the possession of exceptional gifts of speech, but of all the excellence of character as well."[97]

Quintilian's major work, a twelve-book rhetorical treatise titled *Institutio Oratoria,* borrows from Isocrates, Plato, and Aristotle but Quintilian's most notable influence was Cicero.[98] *Institutio Oratoria* focuses primarily on the same issues as Cicero's work; that is, invention, arrangement, style, memory, and delivery. In so doing, Quintilian emphasizes the moral goodness of the orator and spends considerable time outlining his method for educating the young orator. In addition, Quintilian departs from some of his mentors by disavowing their focus on the rules of oratory. He writes:

> *Let no one however demand from me a rigid code of rules such as most authors of textbooks have laid down, or ask me to impose on students of rhetoric a system of laws immutable as fate . . . if the whole of rhetoric could thus be embodied in one compact code, it would be an easy task of little compass . . . the all-important gift for an orator is a wise adaptability since he is called upon to meet the most varied emergencies.[99]*

Institutio Oratoria outlines an entire educational program for the study of rhetoric and serves as an excellent synthesis of traditional Greek and Roman rhetoric. In addition the treatise was a key influence on the study of rhetoric during the Middle Ages.[100]

Beyond Classical Rhetoric

Toward the end of the first century and at about the time of Quintilian's death, democracy was on the decline in Rome. Emperors ruled autocratically and the courts of law operating during the times of Aristotle, Cicero, and Quintilian became a thing of the past. Hence, the role of the orator changed as well. Rather than focusing on civic affairs, oratory regressed back into the study of style and delivery almost void of any relevant content and similar to that of the early Sophists. Hence, this period from approximately A.D. 100 to A.D. 400 is called the Second Sophistic. Virtually no major rhetorical treatises appeared during this time.[101]

The Second Sophistic: St. Augustine

The Second Sophistic and the Middle Ages are linked by the writings of Augustine, who lived from A.D. 354 to A.D. 430 and is regarded as the most important Christian rhetorical theorist of that time.[102] During this period in history, Christianity became a powerful influence and Christian leaders denounced rhetoric as a heathen art form. The main issue was whether the Church should adopt the culture which Rome had taken over from Greece. Religious leaders believed that the ideas of the ancient Greeks and Romans were ungodly and should not be taught. Augustine, however, who did not become a Christian until the age of thirty, had been trained in rhetoric as a young man with a particular emphasis on Cicero. Urged by his followers, Augustine attempted the marriage of rhetoric and Christianity in a major four-book treatise titled *De Doctrina Christiana* or *On Christian Doctrine,* which he composed between 396 and 426.[103] His goal was to provide for the preacher the substance and form for sermons. The first three books outline how the Scripture may be interpreted and understood. The fourth book strongly advocates the use of *eloquentia* (eloquence) in Christian oratory. Augustine argued that rhetoric (i.e., *eloquentia*) should not be rejected simply because it is associated with paganism and/or as a tool of the immoral. He professed Aristotle's notion that rhetoric can be practiced to promote both truth and falsehood.[104]

In the work, Augustine argued that the role of the clergy was to discover Christian knowledge and expound on it to unconverted and ignorant audiences. He was also quite interested in rhetoric as a means of persuading people, particularly Christians, to pursue a holy life. His method followed closely the works of Plato, Aristotle, and especially Cicero and is called Christian Rhetoric. Although Augustine emphasized the importance of style in interpreting and expressing Christian doctrine, he rejected the Sophists' emphasis on style and was much more interested in Cicero's "comprehensive" rhetoric.[105] Augustine compared the Christian preacher to the orator. The preacher should be able to move both the illiterate and the sophisticated and should work to discover truth and the meaning of the Scripture through dialectic. In his work, he focused on the biblical texts of St. Paul. Ironically, Augustine rejected Quintilian's idea that the orator must be a morally good man. In understanding the power of rhetoric, Augustine recognized that even an amoral preacher could persuade his audience to follow Christian doctrine if he was a skillful rhetor. In *De Doctrina Christiana* Augustine makes an outspoken plea for the use of *eloquentia,* or eloquence. Eventually rhetoric would be regarded as a critical part of Scripture.[106] Augustine's work provided the foundation for what is known as the rhetoric of the sermon. Today, that area of study is called homiletics.[107]

The Middle Ages

The Middle Ages, also called the medieval period, is the period from approximately A.D. 400 to 1400. During this time the study of rhetoric progressed through three stages. In the early medieval period from about A.D. 400 to 700 classical rhetoric barely survived through the works of Martianus Capella, Cassidorus, and Boethius. Capella, for example, was responsible for reviving rhetoric as one of the liberal arts. During the second period, from the ninth to twelfth centuries, Cicero's rhetoric dominated the liberal arts in Italy and France. Finally, during the third period, from the twelfth to the thirteenth centuries, the focus of rhetorical training was on preaching, and Augustine's work was again very influential.[108]

The Renaissance

The period of time between A.D. 1400 to 1600 is generally known as the Renaissance, one of the most significant eras in European history because it effected a change in the way human existence was viewed. The word *renaissance,* which was not used to describe the movement until the middle 1800s, means rebirth or renewal.[109] The word has been applied to the revival of ancient learning, the reformation of religion, and the reception of Roman law during the fifteenth, sixteenth, and midway through the seventeenth centuries.[110]

During the Renaissance a philosophical and literary movement known as humanism originated in Italy and was professed by individuals known as Italian humanists, who taught grammar, rhetoric, history, poetry, and moral philosophy. Humanism was basically the study of those sciences that advanced the happiness and perfection of the human race.[111] The humanists felt that through the classics the human spirit, lost during the Middle Ages, could be reborn. Hence, the humanists had great enthusiasm for the literature of the classic Greek and Roman rhetoricians. During this "return to antiquity" many important Latin texts were rediscovered and translated. Some of the earliest versions of Cicero and Quintilian, for example, were printed during this time. As Kennedy notes of this period:

The humanists were intoxicated with the language and literature of antiquity and sought to recover all possible knowledge of it and to make that knowledge the basis of the twin ideals of wisdom and eloquence in the culture of their times, which they regarded as awakening from a long sleep.[112]

Many dominant figures emerged during the Renaissance, including Francesco Patrarcha, known as the founder of the humanist movement. He sought to bridge knowledge and oral expression in the civil and academic environments. In approximately 1433 George Trebizond published *Rhetoricorum Libri V,* or *Five Books of Rhetoric,* which is considered a classic rhetorical treatise that draws on the work of Cicero and Quintilian and introduces their work to the West.[113]

Another movement that began during the Renaissance was called rationalism, which is the philosophical viewpoint that emphasizes the importance of human reasoning in understanding truth about the world. Rationalists were interested primarily in seeking absolute truth through scientific means. An important leader in this movement was Francis Bacon, who lived from 1561 to 1626. He achieved distinction in politics, law, literature, and philosophy of science and is known as the founding father of science in England. Although his interests lie in many areas, one of his greatest works, *The Advancement of Learning,* discusses the role of rhetoric. The function of rhetoric is the application of reason to imagination. "The duty and office of rhetoric," wrote Bacon, "is to apply reason to imagination for the better moving of the will."[114] He believed that rhetoric is the only art that uses imagination to articulate reason. Although he did not hold Plato or Aristotle in high regard, Bacon viewed the art of oratory, including written communication, as did many classical rhetoricians.[115] Bacon wrote about invention and logical proof and distinguished between the reasoning processes of individuals and their emotional and affective states. In addition, he wrote about style, composition, ethos and pathos, memory, and delivery. Bacon was the first to articulate the function of rhetoric within rational science.

Neoclassical Rhetoric

In the seventeenth and eighteenth centuries rhetoric was studied from both a classical and neoclassical perspective. The classical side emphasized a more complete and thorough understanding of ancient Greek rhetoric. In the meantime, other scholars attempted a departure from the classics into new theoretical ideas and positions about rhetoric as they related to the new science of rationalism and empiricism.[116] Of those rhetoricians extending beyond classical rhetoric three names are important, George Campbell, Hugh Blair, and Richard Whately. Throughout much of the 1800s these three were most often studied in British and American schools where rhetoric continued to be taught.

George Campbell

George Campbell, who lived from 1719 to 1796, wrote a book titled *The Philosophy of Rhetoric,* which has been called the most important work on rhetoric produced in the eighteenth century. Unlike its predecessors, which were mainly textbooks on the art and practice of public speaking, Campbell's book offered a "philosophy" of rhetoric, hence its title.[117] Campbell divided rhetoric into two parts—the practical and the philosophical. Practical rhetoric included much of what had been written by the ancient Greeks (e.g., Aristotle, Cicero, etc.) regarding invention, disposition, style, delivery, and so forth. But Campbell was more interested in philosophical rhetoric. One of his main goals was to elevate rhetoric into the realm of other scholarly disciplines such as mathematics and logic. Some disciplines, such as mathematics, have their fundamental principles in the abstract sciences and others have their foundations in the medical arts, such as anatomy and biology. Then there are those like poetry that are based in the elegant arts. Regarding rhetoric, he stated:

> *But there is no art whatever that hath so close a connexion with all the faculties and powers of the mind, as eloquence, or the art of speaking, in the extensive sense in which I employ the term. For in the first place, that it ought to be ranked among the polite or fine arts, is manifest from this, that in all its exertions, with little or no exception, (as will appear afterwards,) it requires the aid of the imagination. Thereby it not only pleases, but by pleasing commands attention, rouses the passions, and often at last subdues the most stubborn resolution. It is also a useful art. This is certainly the case if the power of speech be a useful faculty, as it professedly teaches us how to employ that faculty with the greatest probability of success. Further, if the logical art, and the ethical, be useful, eloquence is useful, as it instructs us how these arts must be applied for the conviction and the persuasion of others. It is indeed the grand art of communication, not of ideas only, but of sentiments, passions, dispositions, and purposes. Nay, without this, the greatest talents, even wisdom itself, lose much of their lustre, and still more of their usefulness.[118]*

Campbell argued that rhetoric could have an end other than to persuade. In Chapter I of Book I of *The Philosophy of Rhetoric*, he contends that "all the ends of speaking are reducible to four; every speech being intended to enlighten the understanding, to please the imagination, to move the passions, or to influence the will." [119]

Central to Campbell's philosophy of rhetoric was his theory of human nature and especially the human mind. He argued that people only know their own mental contents and that sensation is subjective. Our mental entities (i.e., seeing, hearing, touching, etc.) do not reveal to us the "real" external world. Campbell divides the mental capacities into three categories. Sensations, the first category, reveal to us what appears to be the external world, but is subjective (e.g., pain, pleasure, color). Memories, the second category, are the result of sensation; that is, impressions. The third class of sensation includes ideas of imagination which are based on sensation and memory but go beyond to include things that have never been seen or heard. It is through eloquence, or the art of speaking, that we communicate our perceptions to others. Thus, eloquence (i.e., rhetoric) has as its major function the expression of how we see reality. Campbell argued that sensations cannot be communicated directly because they too quickly become memories. Though memories are sometimes communicated by speakers, it is the imagination that is the dominant focus of the rhetor. Hence, rhetorical discourse is characteristically imaginative.[120]

Hugh Blair

The second of the three neoclassical rhetoricians to be discussed here is Hugh Blair. Blair, who was born in 1718 and died in 1800, was known as an innovator of the belles lettres movement. Belles lettres, which means "fine letters," refers to literature that is valued primarily for its aesthetic quality. Blair believed that rhetoric, poetry, drama, and music could be subjected to certain critical standards, especially those regarding taste, beauty, and sublimity. His work served as the foundation for much of what has become modern rhetorical criticism. His most famous book, titled *Lectures on Rhetoric and Belles-Lettres,* contains forty-seven lectures, and by 1835 had been reprinted at least fifty times. George Kennedy refers to Blair as the British Quintilian because of his emphasis on the rhetor as a man of character. Blair asserted that to compose and deliver a speech that amuses an audience is not a difficult task. The true rhetor, however, "demands a great exertion of the human powers."[121] Eloquence, to Blair, is the art of being persuasive and commanding, to seize an audience and leave them with a strong impression. The rhetor must have a strong and lively imagination, a sensible heart, solid judgment, and presence of mind.[122]

Richard Whately

Richard Whately was a preacher and coupled much of his views of rhetoric with religious dogma. For Whately, rhetoric combined with the use of the syllogism and the truths espoused through religion could determine demonstrated conclusions.[123] Whately called rhetoric "the" art rather than "an" art of persuasion. His writings were heavily influenced by Aristotle. He agreed, for example, that rhetoric was the counterpart to logic. He focused much of his writings on the ideas of probability and argumentative fallacies. Whately also introduced ideas as they related to the burden of proof.

All three neoclassical rhetoricians departed from classic rhetoric in a number of ways. None of them, for example, discussed rhetoric in terms of the five canons of rhetoric (i.e., invention, disposition, style, memory, delivery). None of the three classified speeches in terms of their persuasive effect as did the classics. Instead, speeches were classified according to the end or aim with which the orator has been speaking; that is, to inform, to stimulate the imagination, or to move the passions or the will. In addition, contrary to the classical view that ethos, pathos, and logos are independent aspects of persuasion, all three treated them as interdependent. A speaker must convince through reasoning and passion.[124]

Summary

How humans have constructed speeches to persuade others has been the focus of over twenty-five hundred years of study. The impact of Socrates, Plato, and Aristotle cannot be overstated. The entire Western civilization as we know it has been influenced by ancient Greek life and culture and at the core of that culture was human speech. As mentioned before, as a student of contemporary communication theory, it is critical that you have at least an introduction to the history of your field. For whatever reasons, many students lack such an introduction and may have no sense of where and when their discipline began. This chapter has been designed to offer you that introduction by outlining classical rhetorical theory with a special emphasis on ancient Greece and Rome. In the beginning there were the Sophists and their relativistic "ends justify the means" mentality. Then came Socrates with his belief that truth could be known through the Socratic method. His teachings were further advanced by Plato who taught Aristotle. Aristotle produced the first systematic treatment of the persuasive speech. Following him years later were Cicero and Quintilian who took the Greek tradition into Rome. Finally, through the second Sophistic, the Middle Ages, the Renaissance, and the neoclassical period classical rhetorical theory was further developed and refined.

Classical rhetorical theory is still taught at most major universities and colleges, although more emphasis is now placed on contemporary rhetorical theory, which is the focus of the next chapter.

Glossary

Aristotle: Student of Plato in ancient Greece. Aristotle's treatise on rhetoric is the first known systematic treatment on how to construct a speech and remains one of the most important books in the field of communication.

Hugh Blair: Eighteenth-century rhetorician accredited with the innovation of the belles lettres movement.

George Campbell: Eighteenth-century rhetorician who wrote *The Philosophy of Rhetoric,* which attempted to elevate the role of rhetoric to the stature of other academic disciplines.

Cicero: Roman orator and writer on rhetoric. He is best known for his five canons of rhetoric, including invention, arrangement, style, memory, and delivery.

Plato: Student of Socrates and Aristotle's teacher. Plato believed that absolute truth should be sought. He rejected the form of rhetoric taught by the Sophists.

Quintilian: Roman orator and writer. Quintilian emphasized the character of the speaker.

Rhetoric: To discover the available means of persuasion. The study of classical rhetoric involved the study of the public speech. Contemporary rhetoricians study symbolic influence in a variety of contexts.

Second Sophistic: Time period around A.D. 100 to 400 when few major rhetorical works were produced and oratory regressed back to a focus on style and delivery.

Socrates: Plato's teacher. Socrates believed in a philosophical rhetoric and rejected the type of relativistic rhetoric espoused by the Sophists.

Sophists: Teachers of a particular kind of rhetoric in ancient Greek society. They were hired for money to teach a brand of rhetoric where truth was relative.

St. Augustine: An important Christian rhetorical theorist who wrote a major treatise titled *De Doctrina Christiana.* The book was designed to teach the preacher how to use rhetoric.

Richard Whately: Combined Aristotelian rhetoric with religious dogma in an effort to demonstrate truth.

References

1. Crocker, L., & Carmack, P. A. (1965). "Preface," in L. Crocker & P. A. Carmack, (Eds.), *Readings in Rhetoric,* (p. vii), Springfield, IL: Charles C. Thomas.

2. *Merriam Webster's Collegiate Dictionary,* (10th Ed.), (1994). Springfield, MA: Merriam-Webster.

3. Corbett, E. P. A. (1971). *Classical Rhetoric for the Modern Student,* New York: Oxford University Press, (p. 31).

4. Ibid., (p. 32).

5. Cooper, L. (1932). *The Rhetoric of Aristotle,* Englewood Cliffs, NJ: Prentice-Hall, (p. 6).

6. Cooper, *The Rhetoric of Aristotle.*

7. Foss, S. K., Foss, K. A., & Trapp, R. (1991). *Contemporary Perspectives on Rhetoric,* (2nd Ed.), Prospect Heights, IL: Waveland, (p. 14).

8. Smith, B. (1965). "Corax and Probability," in Crocker and Carmack, *Readings in Rhetoric,* (pp. 38–67); Kennedy, G. A. (1963). *The Art of Persuasion in*

Greece, Princeton, NJ: Princeton University Press; Foss, Foss, & Trapp, *Contemporary Perspectives on Rhetoric.*

9. Smith, "Corax and Probability," (pp. 38–67).

10. Ibid.

11. Ibid.

12. Foss, Foss, & Trapp, *Contemporary Perspectives on Rhetoric.*

13. Rankin, H. D. (1983). *Sophists, Socratics, and Cynics,* Totowa, NJ: Barnes & Noble; Stacks, D., Hickson, M., III, & Hill, S. R., Jr. (1991). *Introduction to Communication Theory,* Fort Worth, TX: Holt, Rinehart and Winston.

14. Kennedy, *The Art of Persuasion in Greece.*

15. Guthrie, W. K. C. (1971). *The Sophists,* Cambridge: Cambridge University Press.

16. Ibid, (p. 27).

17. Rankin, *Sophists, Socratics, and Cynics.*

18. Guthrie, *The Sophists,* (p. 50).

19. Ibid., (p. 51).

20. Guthrie, *The Sophists.*

21. Foss, Foss, & Trapp, *Contemporary Perspectives on Rhetoric.*

22. *Merriam Webster's Collegiate Dictionary.*

23. Kennedy, G. A. (1980). *Classical Rhetoric and Its Christian and Secular Tradition from Ancient to Modern Times,* Chapel Hill, NC: The University of North Carolina Press, (p. 41).

24. Vickers, B. (1988). *In Defense of Rhetoric,* Oxford: Clarendon Press; Kennedy, *The Art of Persuasion in Greece.*

25. Kennedy, *Classical Rhetoric and Its Christian and Secular Tradition from Ancient to Modern Times,* (p. 42).

26. Hare, R. M. (1982). *Plato,* Oxford: University of Oxford Press, (p. 42).

27. Vickers, *In Defense of Rhetoric.*

28. Hare, *Plato,* (p. v).

29. Ibid, (p. 24).

30. Black, E. (1965). "Plato's View on Rhetoric," in Crocker and Carmack, *Readings in Rhetoric,* (pp. 68–88).

31. Ibid.

32. Kennedy, *Classical Rhetoric.*

33. West, T. G. (1979). *Plato's Apology of Socrates,* Ithaca: Cornell University Press.

34. Ibid., (p. 21).

35. Ibid., (p. 21).

36. Ibid., (p. 21).

37. Ibid., (p. 21).

38. Ibid., (p. 45).

39. Jowett, B. (1892). *The Dialogues of Plato,* New York: Macmillan, (p. 508).

40. Ibid, (p. 512).

41. Ibid, (p. 513).

42. Ibid, (p. 517).

43. Reprinted by permission of the publishers and the Loeb Classical Library from Fowler, H. N. (1914). *Plato,* (Vol. 1), Cambridge, MA: Harvard University Press, (p. 509).

44. Ibid., (pp. 514–515).

45. Ibid., (p. 517).

46. Ibid., (p. 518).

47. Ibid., (p. 533).

48. Ibid., (p. 525).

49. Ibid., (p. 529).

50. Ibid., (p. 537).

51. Ibid., (p. 537).

52. Ibid., (p. 571).

53. Foss, Foss, & Trapp, *Contemporary Perspectives on Rhetoric.*

54. Cooper, L. (1932). *The Rhetoric of Aristotle,* Englewood Cliffs, NJ: Prentice-Hall, (p. vii).

55. Ibid., (p. xii).

56. Edel, A. (1982). *Aristotle and His Philosophy,* Chapel Hill, NC: The University of North Carolina Press, (p. 4).

57. Edel, *Aristotle and His Philosophy.* Chapel Hill, NC: The University of North Carolina Press.

58. Kennedy, *Classical Rhetoric.*

59. Edel, *Aristotle and his Philosophy.*

60. Kennedy, *Classical Rhetoric.*

61. Cooper, *The Rhetoric of Aristotle,* (p. xvii).

62. Cooper, *The Rhetoric of Aristotle.*

63. Ibid., (p. 7).

64. Ibid., (pp. 8–9).

65. Ibid., (p. 9).

66. Ibid.

67. Ibid., (p. 91).

68. Ibid., (p. xlii).

69. Ibid., (p. 182).

70. Griffin, E. (1994). *A First Look at Communication Theory,* (2nd Ed.), New York: McGraw-Hill, (p. 305).

71. Clarke, M. L. (1953). *Rhetoric at Rome: A Historical Survey,* London: Cohen & West.

72. Clarke, *Rhetoric at Rome,* (p. 10).

73. Kennedy, *Classical Rhetoric.*

74. Petersson, T. (1963). *Cicero: A Biography,* New York: Biblo and Tannen.

75. Sattler, W. M. (1965). "Some Platonic Influences in the Rhetorical Works of Cicero," in Crocker and Carmack, *Readings in Rhetoric,* (pp. 184–192).

76. Kennedy, *Classical Rhetoric.*

77. Hubbell, H. M. (1949). *Cicero: De Inventione De Optimo Genere Oratorium Topica,* Cambridge, MA: Harvard University Press.

78. Ibid., (p. 41).

79. Ibid.

80. Sutton, E. W., & Rackham, H. (1959). *Cicero: De Oratore,* Cambridge, MA: Harvard University Press; Kennedy, *Classical Rhetoric.*

81. Petersson, *Cicero,* (p. 415).

82. Sutton, & Rackham, *Cicero.*

83. Gwynn, A. (1926). *Roman Education: From Cicero to Quintilian,* Oxford: Clarendon Press.

84. Sutton, & Rackham, *Cicero.*

85. Ibid.

86. Clarke, *Rhetoric at Rome.*

87. Sutton, & Rackham, *Cicero.*

88. Ibid., (p. 373).

89. Ibid., (p. 375).

90. Sutton, & Rackham, *Cicero.*

91. Petersson, *Cicero,* (p. 429).

92. Rackham, H. (1960). *Cicero: De Oratore,* Cambridge, MA: Harvard University Press, (p. 169).

93. Clarke, *Rhetoric at Rome.*

94. Ibid.

95. Gwynn, *Roman Education.*

96. Clarke, *Rhetoric at Rome.*

97. Butler, H. E. (1933). *The Institutio Oratoria of Quintilian,* London: Heinemann, (p. 11).

98. Clarke, *Rhetoric at Rome.*

99. Butler, *The Institutio Oratoria of Quintilian,* (p. 291).

100. Foss, Foss, & Trapp, *Contemporary Perspectives on Rhetoric.*

101. Ibid.

102. Infante, D. A., Rancer, A. S., & Womack, D. F. (1993). *Building Communication Theory,* (2nd Ed.), Prospect Heights, IL: Waveland.

103. Murphy, J. J. (1974). *Rhetoric in the Middle Ages: A History of Rhetorical Theory from Saint Augustine to the Renaissance,* Berkeley, CA: University of California Press; Kennedy, *Classical Rhetoric.*

104. Murphy, *Rhetoric in the Middle Ages.*

105. Corbett, E. P. J. (1971). *Classical Rhetoric for the Modern Student,* New York: Oxford.

106. Murphy, *Rhetoric in the Middle Ages;* Kennedy, *Classical Rhetoric.*

107. Corbett, *Classical Rhetoric for the Modern Student.*

108. Kennedy, *Classical Rhetoric.*

109. Green, V. H. H. (1952). *Renaissance and Reformation: A Survey of European History between 1450 and 1660,* London: Edward Arnold.

110. Ibid.

111. Funck-Brentano, F. (1936). *The Renaissance,* New York: Macmillan.

112. Kennedy, *Classical Rhetoric,* (p. 196).

113. Ibid.

114. Wallace, K. R. (1943). *Francis Bacon on Communication and Rhetoric,* Chapel Hill, NC: The University of North Carolina Press, (p. 27).

115. Wallace, *Francis Bacon.*

116. Kennedy, *Classical Rhetoric.*

117. Bitzer, L. F. (1963). "Editor's Introduction," in L. F. Bitzer, (Ed.), *The Philosophy of Rhetoric by George Campbell,* Carbondale, IL: Southern Illinois University Press.

118. Campbell, G. (1850). "Introduction," in *The Philosophy of Rhetoric,* (p. xlix), London: William Tegg & Co.

119. Campbell, *The Philosophy of Rhetoric,* (p. 1).

120. Campbell, *The Philosophy of Rhetoric.*

121. Kennedy, *Classical Rhetoric,* (p. 236).

122. Foss, Foss, & Trapp, *Contemporary Perspectives on Rhetoric.*

123. Ehninger, D. (1965). "Campbell, Blair, and Whately Revisited," in Crocker & Carmack, *Readings in Rhetoric,* (pp. 359–373).

124. Ibid.

Chapter 5

Contemporary Rhetorical Theory

Is there a contemporary theory of rhetoric? Certainly not in the sense of a single, unified, complete, generally accepted body of precepts.[1]—RICHARD L. JOHANNESEN

The roots of contemporary rhetorical theory can be found at the beginning of the twentieth century. Communication as a modern discipline began with the emergence of departments of speech in the early 1900s. During this time, teachers of rhetoric taught in departments of English and many belonged to a professional organization called the National Council of Teachers of English (NCTE). Teachers of English and teachers of rhetoric often quarreled over their respective subjects. Speech teachers (i.e., rhetoricians) often felt as if they were relegated to second-class status. Rhetoric, or public speaking, was not accorded the same level of status as those subjects taught by English professors. Led by James A. Winans (author of the book *Notes on Public Speaking,* which was regarded by historians as *the* textbook of the first half of the twentieth century) and others, a group of rhetoricians separated from the NCTE and formed the National Association of Academic Teachers of Public Speaking (NAATPS). In 1914 this group changed its name to the Speech Association of America and is now called the Speech Communication Association (SCA). Today, SCA's membership includes not only rhetoricians but also those teachers who teach communication from a scientific perspective.[2]

Contemporary rhetorical theory is also called the new rhetoric. Although some contemporary rhetorical theorists focus on the same topic as classical rhetorical theorists—that is, public speaking—many other contemporary theorists focus on a vast array of communication-oriented topics. Foss, Foss, and Trapp argue that

[contemporary] rhetoric is fundamentally the same today as it was in the time of Corax. In one sense this statement is utter nonsense; during the time of Corax,

> *rhetoric was characterized primarily by public speaking, while today, the mass media have changed the process drastically. Other such shifts abound. The ancient rhetoricians, for example, did not deal with interpersonal or organizational communication as we do today. Still, we believe that rhetoric then and now is characterized by the uniquely human ability to use symbols to communicate with one another and that this definition encompasses all formats and contexts.[3]*

Many contemporary rhetorical theorists have shifted focus from public speaking to the general topic of language and how humans use symbols to communicate within many contexts. In his seminal book on the foundations of the new rhetoric, Fogarty contends that contemporary rhetorical theorists

> *all agree upon the newly recognized importance of language as the key to man's understanding of himself and his control of his own progress. They agree fairly consistently that it is in his use of language that he functions with his specific nature, that it is language that makes a man human.[4]*

Contemporary rhetorical theorists are especially interested in how the cultural, economic, political, and social climate influences how humans use and interpret language. Contemporary rhetorical theorists come from a variety of disciplines, including biology, communication, linguistics, philosophy, and sociology. Many of these scholars, who probably would not consider themselves "rhetorical" theorists in the traditional sense, examine language in a variety of contexts, including interpersonal, organizational, and public speaking. Indeed, many focus on mediated language such as television and the interpretation of ancient and contemporary texts. Some of these theorists focus on many topics, not only communication; thus, their theories may apply to a number of disciplines.

Contemporary rhetorical theorists, like their classical counterparts, practice humanistic scholarship. They do not rely on scientific means for discovery. Hence, two contemporary theorists might view the very same language event but interpret it very differently. In fact, many contemporary rhetorical theorists have a clear social or political agenda that guides their scholarship. For example, a recent trend in the field examines feminist issues and how language, used in various contexts, has shaped the evolution of women in society. The focus of this feminist scholarship is to advocate a change in society to further advance women's rights.

No single chapter in a textbook can do historical justice to the topic of contemporary rhetorical theory since entire books and volumes have been written on this subject. This chapter, which is divided into two sections, will simply offer an overview. In the first section, individual rhetoricians are profiled with particular attention to Kenneth Burke, Ivor Armstrong Richards, and Stephen Toulmin. (The reader is encouraged to examine the works of other important theorists who have had an impact on contemporary rhetorical theory, including Richard Weaver and Chaim Perelman.)[5]

The second part of the chapter deals with a body of work linked to contemporary rhetorical theory called critical theory. Critical theory applies value orientations to the use of symbols within various social and cultural contexts. The origins of critical theory are outlined, highlighting the work of Karl Marx and Jurgen Habermas, and feminist critical theory is discussed, including the muted group theory and the work of feminist author and peace activist Starhawk.

Kenneth Burke

Kenneth Burke is one of this century's most prolific writers on the subject of rhetoric. Burke's work is regarded as a "master theory that functions virtually hegemonically in the study of rhetoric."[6] Indeed, his influence is so great that a "Kenneth Burke Society" has formed with accompanying newsletters and conferences. In fact, the society has labeled Burke's work as the "sacred texts."[7] Although he never earned a college degree, Burke taught at such esteemed schools as Bennington College, Harvard, Princeton, and Northwestern University.[8] He wrote several books dealing directly or indirectly with rhetoric, two of his most important include *A Grammar of Motives,* first published in 1945, and *A Rhetoric of Motives,* published in 1950.

Burke asserts that humans are symbol-using and misusing animals and it is their use of symbols that differentiates them from other animals. He defines humans as follows:

> *Man is the symbol-using (symbol-making, symbol-misusing) animal inventor of the negative (or moralized by the negative) separated from his natural condition by instruments of his own making goaded by the spirit of hierarchy (or moved by the sense of order) and rotten with perfection.[9]*

Of particular importance to Burke is his theory of the negative. The highest kind of symbol-using activity of which humans are capable is to symbolize about symbols; that is, the conscious use of words to talk about words. He uses the instance of the negative to demonstrate his point. The idea of "no" or "not" is purely symbolic; it has no empirical substance. The negative cannot exist in nature. For example, the absence of a tree or dog is an idea that can only exist symbolically.[10] In *A Rhetoric of Motives,* Burke discusses the nature of rhetoric. He states:

> *Now, the basic function of rhetoric, the use of words by human agents to form attitudes or to induce actions in other human agents, is certainly not "magical." If you are in trouble, and call for help, you are no practitioner of primitive magic. You are using the primary resource of human speech in a thoroughly realistic way.[11]*

To Burke, rhetoric can be defined as "the use of language as a symbolic means of inducing cooperation in beings that by nature respond to symbols."[12] This definition seems consistent with traditional classical views. Burke was heavily influenced by classical rhetoricians, particularly Aristotle and Cicero. In addition, however, he introduced several new ideas in his rhetorical theory, including the concept of identification and dramatism.

Identification

Central to Burke's new rhetoric is the concept of identification. Burke argues that people are naturally physically divided from one another; every person is a distinct being. Although differentiated from one another, people also have commonalities with others. An artist, for example, is physically distinct from other artists but has the same occupation. This sameness in occupation creates an identification among artists. Identification (which

Burke uses synonymously with "consubstantiality") refers to those things people have in common with other people; that is, what Burke calls their common or shared "substance." Shared substance might include physical objects, occupations, friends, attitudes, beliefs, and values. Person A is identified with Person B to the extent that they share "substance."

Rhetoric is the means by which people achieve identification. Burke refers to this as the "motive" for rhetoric; that is, to bridge the natural division between people. Thus, when people communicate, they are motivated to identify with others. In a sense, Burke uses the terms identification, rhetoric, persuasion, and communication interchangeably. In addition, however, he extends the traditional definition of rhetoric to include other aspects. He states:

> *So, there is no chance of our keeping apart the meanings of persuasion, identification ('consubstantiality') and communication. But, in given circumstances, one or another of these elements may serve best for extending a line of analysis in some particular direction.*[13]

In attempting to eliminate their natural division, people communicate with each other intentionally, unintentionally, verbally, and nonverbally. Here is where Burke departs from traditional rhetoric. For example, Burke asserts that some rhetoric goes beyond the deliberate, intentional public speech to include subtle, perhaps even unconscious, identification. The advertiser who uses a celebrity to endorse a product is explicitly trying to identify that product with an audience. Similarly, the politician intentionally tries to identify with voters. On the other hand, however, people may unconsciously identify with others. For example, when maintaining a relationship people might change their manner of dress or style of speech to identify with their relational partners. Identification is accomplished in a variety of ways in a variety of contexts, including the public speech, sales, education, works of art, literature, and painting. The speaker identifies with the audience, the salesperson identifies with the buyer, the teacher identifies with the student, the artist identifies with the critic, and the writer identifies with the reader—each through their conscious and unconscious use of symbols.[14]

Dramatism

In the opening paragraphs of *A Grammar of Motives* Burke outlines what is called the dramatistic pentad, a practical instrument for the application of his new rhetoric and a tool for studying motivation.[15] Burke's methodology is called dramatism because, as Griffin notes: "For Burke, life is not like drama. Life is drama."[16]

Rooted in Burke's dramatistic notion of rhetoric is the distinction between motion and action. Action refers to the voluntary goal-driven symbol-using behavior of humans. Motion refers to simple reflexes or reactions to external stimuli, such as blinking, etc. Humans are capable of both action and motion whereas animals are only capable of motion.

The pentad is a tool to help understand the rhetorical action of people motivated toward identification with others. Burke describes the pentad:

> *In a rounded statement about motives, you must have one word that names the act (names what took place, in thought or deed), and another that names the scene*

(the background of the act, the situation in which it occurred); also, you must in-dicate what person or kind of person (agent) performed the act, what means or instruments he used (agency), and the purpose.[17]

The pentad represents five ways to analyze a communication event in order to fully understand the rhetorical motive. The act is the actual communicative message; that is, the symbols used. This could be a speech, a commercial, a letter to a loved one, or even a political rally or march by the Ku Klux Klan.

The scene, also called the situation, represents the historical context in which the act is performed including the economic, political, and social factors present during the act. When he was inaugurated as president of the United States in 1960, John F. Kennedy said, "Ask not what your country can do for you—ask what you can do for your country." During that time the country was experiencing vast economic prosperity, had recently won a world war, and was considered a superpower. These aspects of scene are important in determining Kennedy's motive for the act.[18]

The agent is the source of the communicative act; the speaker, the one who acts. In the above example, the agent is John F. Kennedy. The agency is the means or tools the agent uses to accomplish the act. Typically the agency is symbols, as in the case of Kennedy's speech. The agency could be something physical that is symbolic of an idea, however. For example, during the Vietnam War protests, some men burned their draft cards as a symbolic gesture of their opposition to the war. In their strife for equal rights some women stopped wearing their bras.

Finally, the purpose is the goal of the act. For Burke, this is typically identification or persuasion. The purpose is to remove whatever it is that divides the agent from the audience. In Kennedy's speech, he was trying to persuade Americans to work harder for the country.

Burke was careful to point out that the five elements of the pentad operate interdependently in what he calls "ratios." There are at least ten ratios, including scene-act, scene-agent, scene-purpose, act-purpose, act-agent, act-agency, agent-purpose, agent-agency, and agency-purpose.[19]

Regarding the scene-act ratio, according to Burke, the scene contains the act and the act should be consistent with the scene. Hence, to a certain degree the scene determines what kind of act will be performed. A theater with a stage and a set with an audience usually calls for a play. The act-agent ratio refers to the relationship between the symbols and the symbol-user. To a certain extent, the symbols create the identity of the symbol-user. President Ronald Reagan, for example, developed a reputation as "The Great Communicator" because of his symbol-using skill. The agency-purpose ratio looks at how the means used to perform the act are influenced by the purpose. For example, if the purpose of the act is to demonstrate the horrific results of war, then the agency may include graphic pictures of wounded and/or dying soldiers.

According to Nichols, "Burke is difficult and often confusing."[20] To summarize Burke's work, according to Foss, Foss, and Trapp, is to "delve into paradox and antithesis."[21] As Stacks, Hickson, and Hill assert, perhaps for the undergraduate student of communication and rhetoric, Burke's pentad offers a useful method for analyzing many types of rhetorical events. They contend that the pentad "serves as a reminder that effective communication must go far beyond the mere composition of the words of a message."[22] Indeed, Burke offers an extended view of rhetoric by focusing not only on the public speech but also on the more subtle forms of persuasion that are probably the ones most frequently used but least frequently studied from a rhetorical perspective.

CASE STUDY 4   A Pentadic Analysis of President Bush's Operation Desert Storm Speech

Key Terms

Identification

Scene

Agent

Act

Agency

Purpose

This case study applies the fundamental concepts of Kenneth Burke's rhetorical criticism— that is, the pentad—to a speech given by former President George Bush. On January 16, 1991, President Bush delivered a nationally televised address from the Oval Office of the White House to announce that the United States had begun air attacks on military targets in Iraq. In essence, the United States was at war with Iraq. The announcement came five months after Iraqi forces invaded the country of Kuwait on August 2, 1990. Kuwait is a small undemocratic kingdom in the Persian Gulf with vast oil reserves. In Bush's address the following pentadic elements can be identified:

The Scene: Iraq's invasion of Kuwait, failed negotiations.

The Agent: President George Bush.

The Act: Commencement of air attacks on Iraq.

The Agency: Oval Office, prime-time national television.

The Purpose: To inform the citizens of the attack, to provide a rationale for the attacks, and to garner support.

The Scene: At the time of the speech, Iraqi military forces had been inside Kuwait for almost five months. Iraq's invasion of Kuwait began in the early morning hours of August 2, 1990. Within seven hours of crossing the Kuwaiti border, Iraqi troops, known as the Republican Guards, occupied Kuwait City, the capital of Kuwait. Iraqi President Saddam Hussein stated that he would turn Kuwait into a "graveyard" if any outside powers (i.e., the United States and its allies) intervened.[a] President Hussein argued that his decision to attack Kuwait was based on a series of grievances Iraq had against Kuwait, including (a) historical and territorial claims, (b) Kuwait's refusal to lease two strategic islands to Iraq, (c) Iraq's anger over Kuwait's pumping of oil from an oil field that lie underneath both countries, (d) Kuwait's refusal to forgive Iraqi debts incurred during Iraq's long war with Iran, and (e) Iraq's accusation that Kuwait was waging an economic war with Iraq.[b]

Middle East experts also contend that Hussein himself, and his quest for power, was a major factor in the attack against Kuwait. Hussein viewed himself as one of the great leaders in history, comparing himself with the likes of Fidel Castro, Ho Chi Minh, Tito (Josip Broz), and Mao Zedong. Many experts argue that Hussein could have settled his grievances with Iraq without going to war.[c]

On the same day as the attack, the United Nations (UN) Security Council passed Resolution 660, which condemned the invasion and called for Iraq to withdraw its troops. On August 6, the UN Security Council passed Resolution 661 which imposed economic sanctions against Iraq. During this time, the Iraqi army was poised on the border between Iraq and Saudia Arabia. On August 7, Saudi Arabia requested that the United States send in military forces to secure its border with Iraq. By the next day, U.S. troops were in Saudia Arabia. On that same day, August 8, 1990, the Iraqi government formally announced its annexation of Kuwait. The UN Security Council immediately passed Resolution 662 which declared the annexation void. On August 12, President Bush ordered U.S. warships to block all Iraqi oil imports and exports. By August 18, U.S. warships fired shots at, but intentionally missed, two Iraqi oil tankers. On August 25, the UN Security Council passed Resolution 665 which allowed the United States to implement force against Iraq. Slowly but surely, the United States reinforced its military presence in Saudia Arabia and by the first week in September had over one hundred thousand troops stationed there.[d]

In the months to follow the Bush administration orchestrated a huge international coalition against Iraq and especially its leader Saddam Hussein. Countries such as Britain, France, the Soviet Union, Japan, West Germany, and several Middle East countries were behind the U.S. backed coalition against Iraq.

By October, President Bush authorized a troop increase to two hundred thousand. By this time demonstrations against the military buildup were taking place in several major cities in the United States. By the end of November, however, the United States received a near unanimous UN resolution authorizing military action against Iraq.[e]

In the meantime negotiations with Iraq continued. Throughout the negotiations, Iraq continued to make unacceptable demands on the United States. For example, in one of their first offers, Iraq agreed to leave Kuwait if Israel would agree to end its occupation of the West Bank, Gaza, and the Golan Heights. The United States immediately rejected the offer "linking" any negotiations with other countries.

With negotiations reaching a standoff, the U.S. Congress passed the Solarz-Michael Resolution which effectively gave President Bush the authorization to use military force against Iraq. Bush gave Iraq one last deadline to remove its troops—January 15.[f]

The Agent: The agent is President George Bush. The president of the United States is widely regarded as the most powerful man in the world. Prior to being elected president, Bush

Continued

CASE STUDY 4   *Continued*

was a member of the U.S. Congress, U.S. ambassador to the UN, chief liaison to the People's Republic of China, director of the Central Intelligence Agency, and two-time vice president of the United States. At the time of his speech, his approval rating was 53 percent.[g] On the day after the speech, January 17, 1991, a Gallup poll indicated that 79 percent of those surveyed approved of the president's action, 15 percent disapproved, and 6 percent had no opinion. Few could have predicted that by March of the next year, Bush would receive an 87 percent approval rating, matched only once in history by Harry Truman after World War II.[h]

The Act: Presented below is a transcript of the president's speech. Each paragraph has been numbered for reference. The speech was delivered at 9:00 P.M. from the Oval Office of the White House on January 16, 1991. According to the *New York Times,* the speech drew the largest television audience in the history of American television with an estimated 79 percent of American households watching.[i] During the speech, the nation was at a virtual standstill.

Five months ago, Saddam Hussein started this cruel war against Kuwait; tonight the battle has been joined. This military action, taken in accord with United Nations resolutions and with the consent of the United States Congress, follows months of constant and virtually endless diplomatic activity on the part of the United Nations, the United States and many, many other countries.   1

Arab leaders sought what became known as an Arab solution, only to conclude that Saddam Hussein was unwilling to leave Kuwait. Others travelled to Baghdad in a variety of efforts to restore peace and justice. Our Secretary of State James Baker held an historic meeting in Geneva only to be totally rebuffed.   2

This past weekend, in a last ditch effort, the Secretary General of the United Nations went to the Middle East with peace in his heart, his second such mission, and he came back from Baghdad with no progress at all in getting Saddam Hussein to withdraw from Kuwait.   3

Now, the 28 countries with forces in the Gulf area have exhausted all reasonable efforts to reach a peaceful resolution, have no choice but to drive Saddam from Kuwait by force. We will not fail.   4

As I report to you, air attacks are under way against military targets in Iraq. We are determined to knock out Saddam Hussein's nuclear bomb potential. We will also destroy his chemical weapons facilities. Much of Saddam's artillery and tanks will be destroyed.   5

Our operations are designed to best protect the lives of all the coalition forces by targeting Saddam's vast military arsenal.   6

Initial reports from General Schwarzkopf are that our operations are proceeding according to plan.   7

Our objectives are clear. Saddam Hussein's forces will leave Kuwait. The legitimate government of Kuwait will be restored to its rightful place and Kuwait will once again be free.   8

Iraq will eventually comply with all relevant United Nations resolutions and then when peace is restored, it is our hope that Iraq will live as a peaceful and cooperative member of the family of nations, thus enhancing the security and stability of the Gulf.   9

Some may ask, "Why act now? Why not wait?" The answer is clear. The world could wait no longer.   10

Sanctions, though having some effect, showed no signs of accomplishing their objective. Sanctions were tried for well over five months and we and our allies concluded that sanctions alone would not force Saddam from Kuwait.   11

While the world waited, Saddam Hussein systematically raped, pillaged and plundered a tiny nation—no threat to his own. He subjected the people of Kuwait to unspeakable atrocities, and among those maimed and murdered—innocent children. While the world waited Saddam sought to add to the chemical weapons arsenal he now possesses an infinitely more dangerous weapon of mass destruction, a nuclear weapon.   12

And while the world waited, while the world talked peace and withdrawal, Saddam Hussein dug in and moved massive forces into Kuwait. While the world waited, while Saddam stalled, more damage was being done to the fragile economies of the Third World, the emerging democracies of Eastern Europe, to the entire world, including to our own economy.   13

The United States, together with the United Nations, exhausted every means at our disposal to bring this crisis to a peaceful end.   14

However, Saddam clearly felt that by stalling and threatening and defying the United Nations he could weaken the forces arrayed against him.   15

While the world waited Saddam Hussein met every overture of peace with open contempt. While the world prayed for peace Saddam prepared for war.   16

I had hoped that when the United States Congress, in historic debate, took its resolute action Saddam would realize he could not prevail and would move out of Kuwait in accord with the United Nations resolutions. He did not do that.   17

Instead, he remained intransigent, certain that time was on his side. Saddam was warned over and over again to comply with the will of the United Nations—leave Kuwait or be driven out. Saddam has arrogantly rejected all warnings. Instead, he tried to make this a dispute between Iraq and the United States of America.   18

Well, he failed. Tonight, 28 nations, countries from five continents—Europe and Asia, Africa and the Arab League—have forces in the Gulf area standing shoulder-to-shoulder against Saddam Hussein. These countries had hoped the use of force could be avoided. Regrettably, we now believe that only force will make him leave.   19

Continued

CASE STUDY 4   *Continued*

Prior to ordering our forces into battle, I instructed our military commanders   20
to take every necessary step to prevail as quickly as possible, and with the
greatest degree of protection possible for American and allied service men and
women. I've told the American people before that this will not be another Vietnam, and I repeat this here tonight.

Our troops will have the best possible support in the entire world. And they   21
will not be asked to fight with one hand tied behind their back.

I'm hopeful that this fighting will not go on for long and that casualties will   22
be held to an absolute minimum. This is an historic moment. We have in this
past year made great progress in ending the long era of conflict and Cold War.
We have before us the opportunity to forge for ourselves and for future generations a new world order, a world where the rule of law, not the law of the jungle, governs the conduct of nations. When we are successful, and we will be,
we have a real chance at this new world order, an order in which a credible
United Nations can use its peacekeeping role to fulfill the promise and vision
of the U.N.'s founders.

We have no argument with the people of Iraq. Indeed, for the innocents   23
caught in this conflict, I pray for their safety. Our goal is not the conquest of
Iraq. It is the liberation of Kuwait.

It is my hope that somehow the Iraqi people can even now convince their   24
dictator that he must lay down his arms, leave Kuwait and let Iraq itself rejoin
the family of peace-loving nations.

Thomas Paine wrote many years ago: "These are the times that try men's   25
souls." Those well-known words are so very true today.

But even as planes of the multinational forces attack Iraq, I prefer to think   26
of peace, not war. I am convinced not only that we will prevail, but that out of
the horror of combat will come the recognition that no nation can stand against
a world united, no nation will be permitted to brutally assault its neighbor.

No president can easily commit our sons and daughters to war.   27

They are the nation's finest. Ours is an all-volunteer force, magnificently   28
trained, highly motivated. The troops know why they're there. And listen to
what they say, for they've said it better than any president or prime minister
ever could. Listen to Hollywood Huddleston, Marine lance corporal.

He says, "Let's free these people so we can go home and be free again." And   29
he's right. The terrible crimes and tortures committed by Saddam's henchmen
against the innocent people of Kuwait are an affront to mankind and a challenge to the freedom of all.

Listen to one of our great officers out there, Marine Lieutenant General   30
Walter Boomer. He said, "There are things worth fighting for. A world in which
brutality and lawlessness are allowed to go unchecked isn't the kind of world
we're going to want to live in."

Listen to Master Sergeant J. K. Kendall of the 82nd Airborne. "We're here   31
for more than just the price of a gallon of gas. What we're doing is going to
chart the future of the world for the next 100 years. It's better to deal with this
guy now than five years from now."

And finally, we should all sit up and listen to Jackie Jones, an Army lieuten-   32
ant, when she says, "If we let him get away with this, who knows what's going
to be next?" I've called upon Hollywood and Walter and J. P. and Jackie and all
their courageous comrades in arms to do what must be done.

Tonight America and the world are deeply grateful to them and to their fam-   33
ilies.

And let me say to everyone listening or watching tonight: When the troops   34
we've sent in finish their work, I'm determined to bring them home as soon as
possible. Tonight, as our forces fight, they and their families are in our prayers.

May God bless each and every one of them and the coalition forces at our   35
side in the Gulf, and may He continue to bless our nation, the United States of
America.

The Agency: Bush uses several rhetorical mechanisms in his speech to the nation. As mentioned, the speech was televised live from the White House by all of the major television
networks. Bush sat by himself at his desk in the Oval Office and portrayed a very somber
and serious mood. He looked directly at the camera and provided much direct eye contact
throughout the speech. Using television helped the president communicate to millions of
people simultaneously. Television can be a critical tool for a president. As Cronin argues,
"A president who is knowledgeable of its use can use it to shape public opinion, to gain
support for his policies, and to boost his chances for political survival. . . . Television fixes
on a president and makes him the prime symbolic agent of government."[j] With much of the
nation watching, President Bush tried to persuade the public to support his decision to attack. In Paragraphs 1 through 3, Bush briefly outlines a history of the problem. Note that in
these paragraphs, Bush refers to the Iraqi leader as Saddam Hussein. In Paragraphs 4
through 9 Bush presents a status report on the attack and what he hopes to achieve. At this
point the country is now informed about the attack and has its first combat report from the
president himself. Notice that in Paragraph 6 Bush refers to Saddam Hussein as "Saddam."

In paragraphs 10 through 19 Bush outlines his rationale for acting at this particular time.
Here Bush tries to persuade the public that waiting any longer would be futile. Bush's strategy here is to place blame not on Iraq, but on its leader, Saddam Hussein. He personalizes
the issue by referring to the Iraqi leader by his first name at least five times; an unusual form
of address between world leaders. He also uses alliteration by combining the words "world"
and "wait" several times.

In Paragraphs 20 through 27 Bush assures the public that the war can be won, that it will
be short, and that the United States is strong. He makes reference to the Vietnam syndrome
in Paragraph 21 when he says (referring to the troops) that "they will not be asked to fight
with one hand tied behind their back."

Continued

CASE STUDY 4   *Continued*

In Paragraphs 28 through 32 Bush uses the testimony of the troops themselves in garnering support for the effort. This informs the public that the men and women fighting the battle understand their role and support the president's decision. Finally, Bush ends his speech by reassuring the public that the troops will be brought home as soon as possible.

The Purpose: As Burke contends, the purpose of any rhetorical act is to bring about identification. In addition to informing the U.S. public of the factual events surrounding the attack, one of Bush's foremost goals was to garner support for the war; that is, to identify with the American public.

Certainly, many Americans would easily identify with Bush and his decision to attack Iraq. As Senator Patrick Moynihan told a group of Arab leaders just one month after Iraq's invasion, "You must understand that Americans are a warrior nation."[k] For many other Americans, however, Bush would have to make a compelling case if consubstantiality was to be achieved. As Elbaum argues:

> Bush had to contend with major sections of the country's political and economic elite who held an alternative vision of the U.S. role in the post-Cold War world. In contrast to Bush and his "geo-strategists," these "geo-economists" saw maintaining U.S. super-power status as principally dependent upon rebuilding economic dynamism relative to Japan and Western Europe. They feared the political consequences of waging war and worried that bloated sums poured into the military-industrial complex would weaken U.S. capacity to compete with its capitalist rivals.[1]

In addition to political pressure, Bush was up against popular reluctance to go to war. Since the Vietnam War public opinion regarding U.S. military involvement in foreign countries has undergone what experts call the "Vietnam syndrome," which refers to declining popular support for wars because of the tragic consequences of the Vietnam War. Families of people in the military as well as military personnel and veterans of previous wars actively opposed U.S. involvement in Kuwait. Specifically, for example, on November 8, 1990, after President Bush announced his decision to double the number of troops in Saudia Arabia, public support for his action dropped. A November 19, 1990, *New York Times*/CBS poll indicated that more than half of those polled said that Bush had not offered a convincing explanation of the reasons for the U.S. military buildup in Saudia Arabia. Only 21 percent of those surveyed favored a quick military action.[m] Indeed, both liberal and conservative congressional leaders actively spoke out against Bush's plan. Grass-roots protests were staged throughout the nation in major metropolitan areas and small towns. The antiwar movement was unusual in that is was politically heterogeneous. In his speech, Bush needed to bring these groups together if his action was to succeed.

a. Niva, S. (1991). "The Battle is Joined," in P. Bennis & M. Moushabeck, (Eds.), *Beyond the Storm: A Gulf Crisis Reader,* (pp. 55–74), New York: Olive Branch Press.
b. Bahhah, B. A. (1991). "The Crisis in the Gulf: Why Iraq Invaded Kuwait," in Bennis & Moushabeck, *Beyond the Storm,* (pp. 50–54).
c. Ibid.

d. Niva, "The Battle Is Joined," (pp. 55–74).

e. Ibid.

f. Ibid.

g. Lacayo, R. (1991). "Back to Reality," *Time*, (April 27, 1991), (pp. 28–29).

h. "Bush Wins Early Support," *New York Times*, (January 18, 1991), p. A11.

i. Carter, B. (1991). "Giant TV Audience for Bush's Speech," *New York Times*, (January 18, 1991), p. A14.

j. Cronin, T. (1980). *The State of the Presidency*, Boston: Little, Brown, (pp. 95–96).

k. Ehrenreich, B. (1991). "The Warrior Culture," in Bennis & Moushabeck, *Beyond the Storm*, (pp. 129–131).

l. Elbaum, M. (1991). "The Storm at Home: The U.S. Anti-War Movement," in Bennis & Moushabeck, *Beyond the Storm*, (pp. 142–149).

m. Ibid.

I. A. Richards

The contributions of I. A. Richards to the new rhetoric present a unique departure from classical rhetorical theory. Ivor Armstrong Richards was born in England in 1893 and died in 1979. He was educated at Cambridge and taught there for several years after receiving his degree. The author of many books on rhetoric, two of his most important works include *The Meaning of Meaning*, published in 1923 and coauthored with C. K. Ogden, and *The Philosophy of Rhetoric* published in 1936.

Richards is well known for his disdain for traditional rhetorical theory. In *The Philosophy of Rhetoric*, for example, he writes:

> *I need spend no time, I think, in describing the present state of Rhetoric. Today it is the dreariest and least profitable part of the waste that the unfortunate travel through in Freshman English! So low has Rhetoric sunk that we would do better just to dismiss it to Limbo than to trouble ourselves with it—unless we can find reason for believing that it can become a study that will minister successfully to important needs.*[23]

Viewing classical rhetoric as "just a set of dodges that will be found to work sometimes,"[24] Richards departs from traditional rhetoric in at least two ways, including (a) his use of modern biology and psychology to explain meaning, and (b) his approach to rhetoric not only within the public speaking arena but also emphasizing the importance of other communication processes, including reading, writing, listening, and speaking.[25]

The focal point of his book *The Meaning of Meaning* is how symbols take on meaning. Borrowing terminology and concepts from biology and psychology, Richards examines the relationship between thoughts, symbols, and referents (i.e., what he called "Things"). He states:

> *Symbols direct and organize, record and communicate. In stating what they direct and organize, record and communicate, we have to distinguish as always between Thought and Things. It is Thought (or, as we shall usually say, reference) which is directed and organized, and it is also Thought which is recorded and communicated. But just as we say that the gardener mows the lawn when we know that it is the lawn-mower which actually does the cutting, so, though we know that the di-*

rect relation of symbols is with thought, we also say that symbols record events and communicate facts.[26]

Richards argued that symbols have no meaning other than those given to them by a person or group of people (e.g., society or culture). With the exception of those symbols that are essentially equivalent with their referent (e.g., "buzz" or the nonverbal shaking of the fist to express anger), there is no natural connection between any symbol and that which it represents. The relationship between a symbol and its referent is arbitrary and learned—that is, indirect. As Richards states, "It is only when a thinker makes use of them that they stand for anything, or in one sense, have meaning."[27] For example, there is nothing "cat-like" about the symbols *c, a,* and *t*. The only thing that connects "cat" to the fuzzy little animal is the person who thinks it.[28] Unlike the indirect relationship between the symbol and the referent, there is, however, a direct causal relationship between the thought and the symbol, and between the referent (i.e., the Thing) and the thinker. In *The Meaning of Meaning* Ogden and Richards present their "semantic triangle" to illustrate these relationships (see Figure 5.1).[29]

At the top of the triangle is the thought or what Richards calls a reference. He defines a reference as a "set of external and psychological contexts linking a mental process to a referent."[30] At the lower left is the symbol, defined as "arrangements of words, images, gestures, and such representations as drawings or mimetic sounds."[31] At the lower right is the referent, or thing, which is defined as "entity, ens, or object."[32] Things can be either physical or mental. These three elements work together to create meaning whenever people communicate.

The reference, or thought, is based on a person's past experiences with an object or thing and the symbols he or she uses to represent the experience. For example, when people encounter a cat, their past experience with the same or other cats will influence their current experience with the cat (i.e., what it means). Past experiences leave "engrams, residual traces which help determine what the mental processes will be."[33] These residual traces occur in nerve tissue or in some other psychological area and are remembered, thus reinforcing the links between the thought and the symbol and the thought and the referent.

Richards argues that many of the problems with meaning are rooted in the fallacious assumption that symbols and their referents are directly related; that is, that the communi-

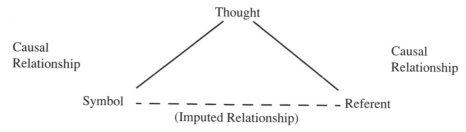

FIGURE 5.1
The Semantic Triangle

cated content of a symbol is the same as the content of the referent it represents.[34] Having disproved this assumption, Richards's theory demonstrates how a symbol can mean different things to different people.

Richards was also careful to address the influence of the psychological context on the relationship between the thought, symbol, and referent. The contexts refers to all of the past experiences one has had with some object. A psychological context refers to the mental processes of a person making the link between their past experiences, the current experience, and the symbols. Because people will have different experiences with objects, they may derive slightly different meanings. Thus the word *cat* may mean different things to different people. To Person A it may mean "cute fuzzy little animal" whereas to Person B it may mean "stinky animal to which I am allergic."

The work of I. A. Richards should not be underestimated. Today his work may seem rather conventional, but given the fact that he was writing in the early part of the century, his work has served to advance contemporary rhetorical theory into the spotlight. Three of his most important contributions include his shift from the public speech to "everyday" communication as the unit of analysis, his articulation of how words derive their meaning, and his skillful integration of social scientific language and concepts into his theory.

Stephen Toulmin

One of the most widely recognized models of argumentation was created by Stephen Toulmin. Foss, Foss, and Trapp assert that most scholars in speech communication would classify Toulmin among the most influential in the field of rhetoric in this century.[35] Toulmin was born and educated in England. Though he earned his doctorate of philosophy from Cambridge University and taught philosophy at several universities, his bachelor of arts degree is in mathematics.[36] Toulmin has spent much of his career as a philosopher trying to understand the relationship between formal logic and its practical use. Though he has authored several books, he is most well known for his book published in 1958 titled *The Uses of Argument*. In that book, Toulmin outlined his famous model of argumentation.

Argumentation, from a philosophical and/or rhetorical perspective, is the process of communication whereby reasoned propositions or statements (usually called "proofs") are spoken or written for the purpose of influencing and persuading. Argumentative proofs are based on logic. In the process of argumentation, one reaches a conclusion (i.e., a claim) about some topic or issue and supports it with reasons.

Toulmin's goal is to present a system of argumentation that offers a practical solution to argumentation rather than a strict adherence to formal logic. Toulmin argued that people do not use formal logic when they engage in arguments. Anyone who has ever taken an introductory course in logic probably agrees with Toulmin's assertion. He was quite critical of his colleagues in philosophy for their lack of attention to the practical and functional use of logic. He wrote:

> *in science and philosophy alike, an exclusive preoccupation with logical systematicity has been destructive of both historical understanding and rational criti-*

cism. Men demonstrate their rationality, not by ordering their concepts and beliefs in tidy formal structures, but by their preparedness to respond to novel situations with open minds.[37]

In an effort to resolve the problem of formal logic, Toulmin offered his model of argumentation based on what is called "practical logic." Practical logic differs from formal logic in at least two important ways. Arguments in formal logic are based on inference. To infer is to proactively conclude something based on the available data. For example, if a person hears a window break, then observes two children nearby, one with a baseball bat and the other wearing a baseball glove, the person may infer that the window was broken by a baseball. Chronologically, one (a) takes the available information (i.e., the two children) and then (b) infers the claim (i.e., that the children broke the window). Practical logic, on the other hand, is based on the justification of claims. To justify a claim involves producing reasons only after having reached the claim. In this case, the person begins with the claim and then retrospectively produces the information supporting it. This process allows one to critically test the soundness of the justification.[38]

Another important contribution to practical logic involves Toulmin's idea of field dependence. Field dependence refers to the influence of context and situation on how one justifies a claim. The structure of formal logic is such that certain claims can be proven formally regardless of the context or topic in which the argument is made. Practical logic recognizes that the claims and arguments may be sensitive to the field in which they are proposed. The justification for the claim that "Jim is a good cook" may not follow the same practical logic as the claim "Abraham Lincoln was a good president," because two very different fields are being discussed. Using formal logic to prove these two claims would involve very similar if not identical inductive inferences. In using practical logic, however, very different justifications may be produced.[39]

Toulmin structures his model in a way that corresponds to the rational process people use in making decisions. According to Toulmin, people "move" through the parts of an argument. To Toulmin, an argument is a movement from: (a) accepted data, through (b) a warrant, to (c) some claim. Graphically the model looks like this:

Actually, argumentation begins when someone makes a claim. Claims are explicit appeals, like propositions of a controversial nature, and require justification.[40] The entire process of argumentation centers around the claim. Claims require proof for a rational person to accept them as true or false.

There are four types of claims, including factual, definitional, value, and policy claims. Factual claims are statements of fact that can be verified usually through observation. The claim "The cat weighs fifteen pounds" is a factual claim. Definitional claims focus on how something is to be defined, classified, or categorized. The statement "JoJo is a domestic short-haired feline" is a definitional claim. Value claims assert an evaluation or judgment about something, as in the statement "Jim is a good cook." Policy claims prescribe action as in the statement "You should eat Jim's good cooking."[41]

Claims are supported by the grounds, or what is typically called data or evidence. Grounds are the factual evidence upon which the "proof" is based. Grounds, which must be believable to be accepted as evidence, come in the form of testimony from experts, observations or witnesses, historical accounts, or even the proven claim from an earlier proof.

Warrants provide the means by which the proof is "carried" from the data to the claim and point out the relationship between the data and claim. Warrants may be found in things generally regarded as true, such as common sense, common knowledge, customs, and societal norms.[42]

Together the grounds, warrant, and claim make up what Toulmin called the primary triad of argumentation. Figure 5.2 presents an application of the primary triad.

In addition to the three primary components of the model, Toulmin created a second triad consisting of backing, rebuttal, and qualifier. Toulmin noted that any or all of these components may, but need not necessarily, be present during an argument. Graphically, the model looks like:

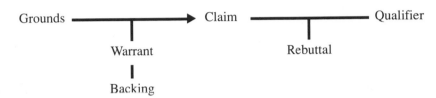

Backing supplies additional justification for the claim. This may be needed if the warrant is insufficient. In some cases, the backing may simply be an additional statement of fact. In other cases the backing may be a complete proof consisting of its own primary triad. Sometimes the backing is called the support.[43] The rebuttal performs the function of a safety valve or escape hatch by recognizing certain conditions under which the claim will not hold. Sometimes the rebuttal is called the reservation.[44]

The qualifier indicates the strength or force of the argument. Not all arguments have the same strength and may require some qualification. Qualifiers take the form of adverbs, adverbial phrases, or prepositional phrases that modify the action made in the claim. Words and phrases such as *presumably, necessarily, certainly, perhaps, maybe, in certain cases, at this point in time, with the exception that,* and *in all probability* represent types of qualifiers.[45] Figure 5.3 presents an application of the complete model of argumentation, including the primary and secondary triads.

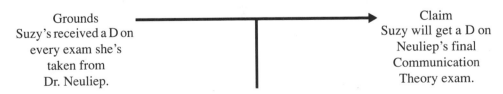

FIGURE 5.2   Toulmin's Primary Triad with Examples

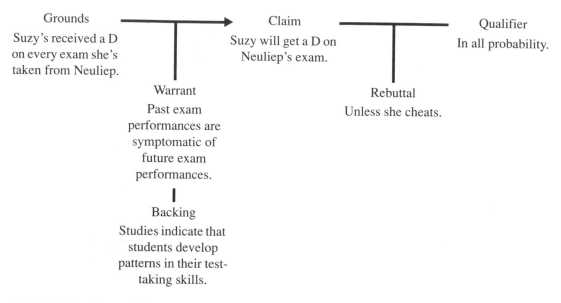

FIGURE 5.3   Primary and Secondary Triads of Toulmin's Model of Argumentation

Ironically, Toulmin's model of argumentation was rejected by most of his British colleagues in philosophy. Some reports indicate that even his graduate advisor barely spoke to him for some twenty years after it was published.[46] Their reaction was based on their adherence to formal logic, which was the primary topic for philosophers at the time the book was published. Scholars in rhetoric and communication applauded the work, however, and it has become a widely used model in the field. Several books on argumentation use the model as their primary focus and it has become the generally accepted way of teaching argumentation in many communication programs. As Brockriede and Ehninger note:

> *Toulmin's analysis and terminology are important to the rhetorician for two different but related reasons. First, they provide an appropriate structural model by means of which rhetorical arguments may be laid out for analysis and criticism; and second, they suggest a system for classifying artistic proofs which employs argument as a central and unifying construct.*[47]

CASE STUDY 5   Toulmin's Model of Argumentation and *Roe v. Wade*

Key Terms

Grounds

Warrant

Claim

Backing

Reservation

Rebuttal

On January 22, 1973, the U.S. Supreme Court announced what was to become one its most controversial decisions of this century. On that day, Justice Harry Blackmun delivered the opinion of the court in the case of *Roe v. Wade*. The Court ruled that existing abortion laws were unconstitutional. The essence of that decision legalized abortions in all fifty states, ending nearly a century of antiabortion statutes.[a] The well-known *Roe v. Wade* decision empowered pregnant mothers of unborn babies with the right to choose abortion as a means to terminate their pregnancies. This case study centers on the *Roe v. Wade* decision and applies Toulmin's model of argumentation to the arguments advanced by the Supreme Court in announcing its decision.

In Texas in 1969, Norma McCorvey became pregnant. She was unmarried and wanted to terminate her pregnancy by abortion. At the time, she could not afford to keep the baby nor did she secure the means to travel to California to obtain a legal abortion. She made the decision to carry the baby but to give it up for adoption. Perhaps ironically, her adoption lawyer knew of two other lawyers who were searching for someone to contest the existing antiabortion laws in Texas.[b]

In March of 1970, McCorvey (now using the pseudonym "Jane Roe") brought action in the District Court for the Northern District of Texas against Henry Wade, the district attorney of Dallas County, Texas. Roe's attorneys sought what is called a "declaratory judgment" (i.e., a binding conclusion by the court) that the existing Texas abortion statutes, which render abortions illegal, were unconstitutional. Roe's attorneys also sought an "injunctive relief" (i.e., an order from the court) preventing the district attorney (i.e., Wade) from enforcing the statutes. The court heard arguments on May 22, 1970, and filed its decision on June 17, 1970. The three-judge court agreed with Roe and entered a judgment declaring the laws unconstitutional.[c]

Continued

CASE STUDY 5 *Continued*

Immediately following the district court ruling, an appeal was made to the U.S. Supreme Court. The Supreme Court heard arguments on December 13, 1971, heard rearguments on October 11, 1972, and rendered its decision on January 22, 1973. The Supreme Court basically upheld the ruling of the lower court with some qualifications. Justice Harry Blackmun delivered the opinion of the court. Chief Justice Warren Burger and Justices William Douglas and Potter Stewart issued concurring opinions. Justices William Rehnquist and Byron White issued dissenting opinions. A rehearing was denied on February 26, 1973.[d]

Toulmin's model of argumentation can be applied to the opinion delivered by the Supreme Court in *Roe v. Wade*. Recall that Toulmin's primary triad consists of grounds, warrant, and claim.

Claim: The claim is the conclusion of the argument that needs justification. In *Roe v. Wade* the claim was that the Texas criminal abortion statutes prohibiting abortions at any stage of pregnancy, except to save the life of the mother, were unconstitutional. This is a definitional claim.

Grounds: The grounds provide the evidence upon which the claim is based. The principal grounds for the attack on the Texas statutes are that they improperly invade the right of the pregnant woman to choose to terminate her pregnancy.[e]

Warrant: Warrants connect the grounds with the claim. Here the warrant is that the U.S. Constitution recognizes the right and guarantee of certain areas or zones of personal privacy. In the Court's opinion, the right to privacy is broad enough to include a woman's decision to terminate her pregnancy.[f]

Backing: Additional support for the warrant can be found in past Supreme Court decisions where issues of personal privacy were confirmed, including the First, Fourth, Fifth, and Ninth Amendments and the Due Process clause of the Fourteenth Amendment to the Constitution. Justice Blackmun cited such cases in his statement.[g]

Qualifier: The qualifier indicates the strength or force of the argument. Although the Court agreed that the right to privacy included the decision to have an abortion they also stipulated that "the right is not unqualified and must be considered against important state interests in regulation."[h] Such regulations may include maintaining health and medical standards.

Reservation: The reservation, or rebuttal, outlines the boundary conditions under which the argument is not valid or warranted. In *Roe v. Wade*, the Court ruled that its decision that the Texas statutes were unconstitutional was limited to the first trimester of pregnancy. States may, if they so choose, regulate abortion in those cases where the mother is into the second and/or third trimester of pregnancy.[i]

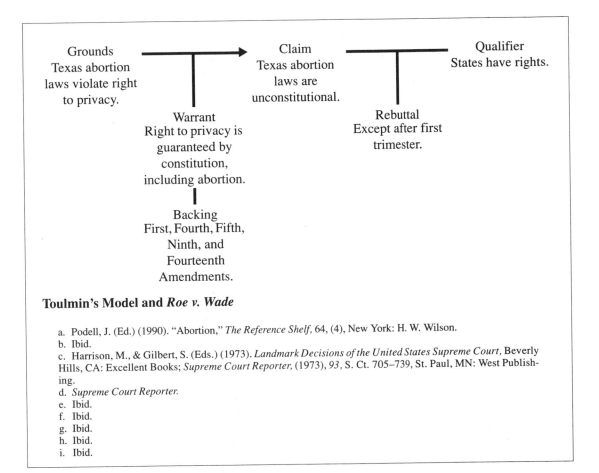

Toulmin's Model and *Roe v. Wade*

a. Podell, J. (Ed.) (1990). "Abortion," *The Reference Shelf*, 64, (4), New York: H. W. Wilson.
b. Ibid.
c. Harrison, M., & Gilbert, S. (Eds.) (1973). *Landmark Decisions of the United States Supreme Court*, Beverly Hills, CA: Excellent Books; *Supreme Court Reporter*, (1973), *93*, S. Ct. 705–739, St. Paul, MN: West Publishing.
d. *Supreme Court Reporter*.
e. Ibid.
f. Ibid.
g. Ibid.
h. Ibid.
i. Ibid.

Critical Theory: Marxist and Feminist Critique

David Ingram, an associate professor of philosophy at Loyola University and noted scholar on critical theory, writes that "critical theory offers a distinctive approach to understanding the social and political life of modern societies."[48] Unlike "scientific" theories where the primary goal is to explain and predict, critical theories are concerned with "evaluating" the justice and happiness of modern societies and are more like philosophy than science. Recall from Chapter 1 and the discussion of science that scientists seek to discover order, find patterns, and explain and predict phenomena. The scientist's efforts are generally regarded as value neutral and objective.

Like scientists, critical theorists also define and describe phenomena. Critical theorists generally focus on whole societies or political institutions such as democracy and socialism. In addition, critical theorists, like philosophers, seek to discover the most universal, most basic, and innermost features of their subject. Unlike either scientists or philosophers, however, critical theorists go beyond description and move toward "prescription." The goal of critical theorists is to prescribe "a norm or ideal to which the activity or thing being defined must conform in order for it to be truly what it is."[49] In other words, critical theorists observe phenomena, attempt to fully describe and define their essential and ideal qualities, then prescribe criteria to which the phenomena must adhere in order to fully realize their potential (i.e., their ideal form). The job of the critical theorist, then, is to evaluate whether the observed phenomena meet the prescribed standards. By definition, to be critical is to offer evaluation. The primary aim of critical theory is "the proffering of critical enlightenment regarding the justness and goodness of social and political institutions."[50] To be sure, critical theory is not a communication theory per se, but some critical theorists see communication as central in their "critique" and/or evaluation of modern society.

Critical theory goes by many names, including "radical social theory" and "cultural criticism." Some have even referred to it as "philosophical speculation."[51] The tradition of critical theory begins around 1920 in Frankfurt, Germany, at the Institute of Social Research. Although the institute was formally affiliated with the University of Frankfurt, it operated with considerable autonomy through private funding. Carl Grünberg was its first director and was the first avowed Marxist to hold a teaching position at a German university. Though the Institute claimed political neutrality, members of the Institute adhered to various political and social dogma especially Marxism, which inspired the theoretical foundations of critical theory. In its early years, for example, there was frequent interaction between the Institute and the Marx-Engels Institute in Russia. Indeed, many of Grünberg's associates in the Institute were members of the Communist Party.[52]

The Institute's second director, and one who had considerable influence on its development, was Max Horkheimer. Horkheimer led the Institute during its most active years from 1930 to 1944. He was strongly influenced by the critical philosophy of Immanuel Kant and the political-economy philosophy of Karl Marx. Under Horkheimer, the Institute became formally known as "critical theory" or simply "The Frankfurt School." During Horkheimer's reign, the main task of the Institute was "to critique scientific knowledge and rationality from the standpoint of a social theory proffering 'moral' enlightenment and to critique capitalist society as a crisis-laden system frustrating human freedom and fulfillment."[53]

During Horkheimer's tenure at the Institute, the rise of Nazism in Europe forced many members to flee Germany and emigrate to other countries, such as the United States. With most of its members dislocated many of the Institute's programs were never finished. By the 1950s many of the members resettled in West Germany while others remained in America. For a period of about thirty years, relatively little was accomplished. Then, during the 1960s and 1970s, with the birth of the New Left, critical theory underwent a revitalization.

From its beginnings, the philosophical roots driving the Institute was Marxism. Although a complete treatise on Marxism is beyond the scope of this chapter, a few central tenets can be presented. Marxist thought should not necessarily be associated with societies created in his name (e.g., the former Soviet Union, Cuba, China). One can be a Marxist without being a Communist, for example. Remember that Marxism is a critique of society; that is, Marx is offering his evaluation of the political and social system of capitalism.[54]

Marx argued that human ideas are based on economic forces operating within societies. To Marx, the course of human history is fueled by material production, including production forces and production relations. Production forces include human labor and production relations include ownership of the means of production and the distribution of wealth.[55]

At the basis of Marxist thought is materialism. Here materialism does not refer to a desire to make money, drive expensive cars, or own expensive homes. Marx conceptualized materialism as the way in which a society organizes itself and he theorized that when people interact and develop relationships with others, they do so on the basis of their material powers of production. Social production (i.e., the development of relationships with others) is guided by material production (i.e., economic relationships). Society is shaped by its economic system which, in turn, affects the political, social, and spiritual life.

Marx is critical of capitalism. He views capitalism as not only an economic system, but a driving force that shapes a society's attitudes, values, and belief systems.[56] Marx was critical of capitalism because material is produced for its value and profit, not for the happiness and justness of the people. To Marx, capitalism does not produce a harmonious social whole. The products of human labor are seen as distinct from those who produce them. Workers become "alienated" from their product and lose their sense of identity. In addition, workers lose their control over their own laboring activity. The conditions under which workers produce are determined by those who have ownership in the mode of production. Marx argued that these working conditions are often simple repetitive movements (i.e., assembly-line type of work) that dehumanize the worker. Workers eventually see themselves as just another commodity. To Marx, workers should be "liberated" and "emancipated" from a political-economic system that fosters such dehumanization.[57]

In capitalist societies there is a tendency toward capital-intensive industry and increased concentration of capital, which tends to create a class distinction. First there is the ruling class—the dominant material force in society, which Marx called the bourgeois. Beneath them is the working class—the mass of workers, which Marx called the proletariat. The problem is that the dominant material class is simultaneously the dominant intellectual class. This means that the class who controls the material production also controls mental production (i.e., the establishment of social knowledge and social relationships). The ideas of the ruling class are the ideal expression of the dominant material relationships. Communication systems are important here because the ruling class creates the messages which sustain their material dominance. Because media are important vehicles by which the ruling class sends its messages, they have a central place in a Marxist critique of capitalism.[58]

Marx was convinced, as are other critical theorists, that knowledge of the truth emancipates. Critical theorists recognize two kinds of knowledge, scientific knowledge and philosophical moral principles. In sum, scientific and moral knowledge allow society and its members to be free. Marx, and others, believed that each human possesses the necessary mental attributes—reason and common sense—by which to attain universal truth.[59]

With their Marxist critique of capitalism in modern society, critical theorists are left with some rather daunting problems. For example, critical theory must explain how societies move from capitalism to emancipation; that is, the creation of the ideal society. Critical theorists must also grapple with the question of what constitutes an ideal society. Finally, critical theorists are also very concerned with the role of science in their critique of society;

that is, what is the relationship between scientific and moral knowledge? One contemporary critical theorist who addresses these concerns with a unique perspective on communication is Jurgen Habermas.

Jurgen Habermas: Critical Theory and Communicative Action

Jurgen Habermas is said to be "unquestionably the most influential exponent of critical theory living today."[60] Born in Dusseldorf, Germany, in 1929, Habermas was raised in Nazi Germany and was a member of the Hitler Youth, though his parents were not members of the Nazi Party. The end of the war was particularly important to him because he realized that he had been living in a criminal political system. Habermas was educated in philosophy, history, psychology, German literature, and economics. He received his doctorate from the University of Bonn in 1954. Since then he has authored numerous books and been the recipient of many distinguished awards for his scholarship.[61]

Habermas is a prolific writer in many areas of the humanities and social sciences. Because of his vast knowledge on so many topics, he is sometimes very difficult to understand. As Foss, Foss, and Trapp assert: "Habermas's knowledge is encyclopedic, and he assumes that his readers are also familiar with a range of disciplines, philosophic traditions, and approaches. His dense writing style, combined with the difficulties of translation, also hinders understanding."[62]

Like other critical theorists, the ultimate goal of Habermas's critical theory is the emancipation of the people from capitalist domination. Like the others, Habermas believes that knowledge of the truth is emancipatory and that communication plays a key role in realizing truth.

The idea of knowing truth poses some knotty problems for critical theorists. Some critical theorists believe that objective truth may not exist, particularly that which comes from science. A rather substantial body of work from Habermas and other critical theorists attacks the methodology of natural science, particularly the notion of logical positivism and the covering laws approach. Some critical theorists argue that the truth of scientific statements is determined by their usefulness to society, not through objective empirical observation. Recall Marx's notion of how the ruling class determines the intellectual production of knowledge. Facts are not value neutral nor are they independent of the observer, because the observer interprets what has been observed. Habermas contends that the "truth" of any fact is based on the number of observers who agree on its content, what he calls "intersubjective agreement." Again, recalling Marx's idea of how ideas are formulated, Habermas continues to argue that since the observer influences the observation, even a large group of observers who have reached intersubjective agreement may be influenced by some societal ideology (e.g., capitalism). The truth of any scientific claim can only be validated through "universal consensus," which can only be achieved through "rational communication."[63]

Habermas's theory of communication is called the theory of communicative action, though Habermas refers to it as universal pragmatics. The goal of the theory is to "identify and reconstruct universal conditions of possible understanding."[64] The crux of the theory is that there are universal conditions, regardless of language or culture, under which people can reach understanding. Habermas asserts that many forms of social action (i.e., conflict, competition) stem from communicative action designed to reach understanding.

Habermas reasons that whenever people communicate, or what he calls perform "a speech action," they make, perhaps unconsciously, several "validity claims" about their action. The speaker claims to be:

> a. *Uttering something understandably;*
> b. *Giving (the hearer) something to understand;*
> c. *Making himself thereby understandable; and*
> d. *Coming to an understanding with another person.*[65]

In communicative action, speakers know (implicitly) that they must satisfy the four validity claims. Speakers also understand that they may have to justify their validity claims if they are questioned. Unfortunately, many times these claims are violated, particularly when the speaker is incomprehensible and/or intentionally or unintentionally untruthful. Coming to an understanding, then, is the process of agreeing on the four validity claims. When people disagree on the validity claims, however, communicative action stops and alternative forms of action take over, including breaking off communication or argumentative speech.

Habermas's universal pragmatics is based on the fundamental assumptions of speech act theory but diverges in several important ways. First, Habermas outlines what he calls the "double structure of speech" and distinguishes between illocutionary and perlocutionary acts. He states:

> By means of an illocutionary act a speaker lets a hearer know that he wants what
> he says to be understood as a greeting, command, warning, explanation, and so
> forth. His communicative intent does not go beyond wanting the hearer to under-
> stand the manifest content of the speech act.[66]

Through illocutionary acts the speaker performs an action in saying something. Thus saying "Hello" has the illocutionary force of a greeting. To say "I promise I'll pay you back tomorrow" has the illocutionary force of a promise. The speech itself performs the act. On the other hand, perlocutionary acts produce some effect upon the hearer. Habermas states that "the perlocutionary act aim of the speaker, like the ends pursued with goal-directed actions generally does not follow from the manifest content of the speech act; this aim can be identified only through the agent's intention."[67]

Another divergence from speech act theory is Habermas's contention that speech acts serve as a medium for understanding because they: (a) establish and renew interpersonal relations, (b) represent states and events in the world, and (c) represent one's subjective experiences. In other words, when one performs a speech act, the act itself is a commentary on the relationship between the speaker and the hearer. This is very similar to the notion of content and relational levels of messages articulated by systems theorists. Second, speech acts also serve as the medium for people to express what they believe is the true state of the world as they see it. For example, the statement "It is cold out today" represents one's understanding of the world. Third, speech acts also allow people to express their internal states. For example, the speech act "I feel tired" represents one's understanding of his emotional or physical state.

Understanding is achieved through three specific types of speech acts, including constatives, expressives, and regulatives. Constative speech acts are assertions of truth that serve to describe the world as the speaker sees it. For example, the statement "The door is closed" is a constative. Expressive speech acts convey the internal state of the speaker, emotions, feelings, etc. Regulative speech acts manage the relationship between the speaker and hearer as in the case of a command or promise.[68]

A third departure from speech act theory is the idea of communication competence. Habermas emphasizes that if truth and understanding are to be achieved speakers must communicate in ways that satisfy the four validity claims mentioned above. He argues that all people have the capacity to reach understanding but may fail at times. His theory parallels Noam Chomksy's notion of language competence and language performance. Language competence refers to the knowledge of language rules. Chomsky argued that all humans have an innate ability for language and the underlying rules for its use. He referred to this as the "blueprint" for language. Language performance, on the other hand, is the actual use of the language. When people produce ungrammatical sentences, for example, their language performance does not coincide with their language competence.

Analogously, Habermas argued that speakers have the capacity to communicate in ways that satisfy the four validity claims, through the use of constatives, expressives, and regulatives. Speakers are competent users of speech acts. This competence is based on a set of universal rules that are known by all speakers, regardless of language or culture.[69] To be sure, however, speech performance may not always achieve understanding or truth. As Huspek notes:

> *Just as it is for Chomsky that all speakers possess an ideal capacity to produce grammatical sentences but can fail to be fully grammatical in their actual performances, so it is for Habermas that all speakers possess an ideal capacity to represent the world truthfully (in ways that satisfy consensually agreed upon truth statements), to appeal to norms (in ways that satisfy consensually agreed upon normative standards), and to express freely (as society understands freedom), intentional states, personal needs and desires. (He has termed these ideals, respectively, truth, justice, and freedom.) If speakers' ideal capacities are not fully realized, it is because society constrains speakers in ideological or other ways that produce systematically distorted communication.[70]*

The ideal speech situation is one where speakers achieve understanding through the expression of truth (i.e., constatives), management of their relations with others (regulatives), and the expression of freedom (expressives). If the ideal speech situation is not realized in performance, it is because the communicative means necessary are distorted by the ideological constraints of the society. In other words, the speakers are not emancipated from the constraints of the dominant ideology.[71] Again it is important to remember Marx's notion of the influence of the economic system on how people think and relate to others and how the dominant ruling class determines the social structure of the society.

Though Habermas has outlined his theory of communicative action and why truth and understanding may not always be achieved, he has not adequately provided a practical solution for how people can "liberate" themselves from the dominant ideology that restricts and constrains their ability to emancipate themselves. In addition, many scholars harshly criticize Habermas's dense and often ambiguous writing style. Hence the final chapter on Habermas has yet to be written.

Feminist Rhetoric and Critique

In most cultures and societies a hierarchy of power and status exists. At the top of the hierarchy are those with the most power and influence—the dominant group. At the bottom are those with little or no power or status, or the subordinate group. Exactly who occupies the top of the hierarchy depends on one's theoretical perspective. According to Marx, for example, at the top of the hierarchy are those with the most capital. According to some African Americans, whites occupy the top. Many women, some who call themselves feminists, maintain that biological sex (i.e., gender) affects one's hierarchical place. Scholars working from a feminist perspective have developed a group of theories and critiques that examines women's issues in contemporary society. The fundamental assumption guiding most of these theories is that culture, particularly in the United States, is androcentric (i.e., having a male-oriented bias) and patriarchal (i.e., from the Greek word meaning "rule of the father"). Androcentrism affects virtually every aspect of human behavior and culture, including language, dress, literature, religion, law, school, professions, and sports. The goal of feminism is to liberate women from androcentric patriarchal societies.

Feminism, defined as "an analysis of women's subordination for the purpose of figuring out how to change it,"[72] is a political theory; that is, a critical theory with some added ingredients. Many people think the feminist movement is a relatively recent phenomena emerging from the counterculture in the 1960s. The roots of feminism, however, can be traced back to at least the 1400s.[73]

Hester Eisenstein argues that feminism evolved from liberalism and draws upon at least three streams of political and philosophical thought.[74] The first is the "liberal" philosophy and political theory of the seventeenth and eighteenth centuries. During this time writers and philosophers such as John Locke and Jean-Jacques Rousseau contested the divine rights of kings and wealthy landowners and argued for democratic egalitarianism (i.e., a belief in human equality). Liberal theorists sought equal rights for all, especially the right to vote and to hold public office. Rousseau argued that citizens should only obey those laws which represent the true rational interests of everyone.[75] Though the specific arguments generally applied to men, these ideas brought forth similar claims for equal rights for women.

The second stream influencing feminist thought is Marxism. Recall that Marx defines society as people in relation to one another based on their production. Humans develop their identity through their labor. Work is seen as a social process that creates people as social beings as they create material value. Alison Jaggar writes that:

> *On the Classical Marxist view, the oppression of women is, historically and currently, a direct result of the institution of private property; therefore, it can only be ended by the abolition of that institution . . . everyone is oppressed by living in a society where a small class of individuals owns the means of production and hence*

is enabled to dominate the lives of the majority who are forced to sell their labor power in order to survive.[76]

Though Marxists do not believe that capitalism is the sole cause of women's oppression, strict Marxists believe that women are subject to special forms of oppression to which men are not. They believe that women's oppression is rooted on the notion of family. Families, they contend, exclude women from public life. Indeed, marriage allows for the concentration of wealth to men. In 1884, Frederick Engels wrote that "he is the bourgeois and the wife represents the proletariat."[77] Whereas Marx sees society divided into two classes—the bourgeois and the proletariat—feminists see society as a division of two sexes, of course, men and women. Sexual division determines social relations. According to MacKinnon:

Sexuality is that social process which creates, organizes, expresses, and directs desire, creating the social beings we know as women and men, their relations create society. As work is to marxism, sexuality to feminism is socially constructed.... As the organized expropriation of the work of some for the benefit of others define class—workers—the organized expropriation of the sexuality of some for the use of others defines sex, woman.... Marxism and feminism are theories of power and its distribution: inequality.... In marxism to be deprived of one's work, in feminism of one's sexuality, defines each one's conception of lack of power.[78]

The third stream of thought begins during the late nineteenth century. Here, the focus is on the relationship between sexuality and society. Writers such as Freud are typical of this period. Though not a feminist, Freud was one of the first to analyze relations within the family unit. Many of his ideas about the roles of men and women within families and especially how infants develop into adults remain an important aspect of feminist theory.[79]

Within the last thirty years or so, feminism has made its way into contemporary rhetorical theory. To be sure, not much is said about women in classical rhetoric. In fact Aristotle wrote that "we should look upon the female state as being as if it were a deformity, though one which occurs in the ordinary course of nature."[80] Now, however, theory and research about women is gaining increased attention within communication. According to Foss and Griffen, the primary goal of feminist scholarship is to "discover whether existing rhetorical theories account for women's experiences and perspectives and to construct alternative theories that acknowledge and explain women's practices in the construction and use of rhetoric."[81]

Spitzack and Carter describe five conceptualizations of women in communication research, including (a) womanless communication, (b) great women communicators, (c) woman as other, (d) the politics of woman as other, and (e) women as communicators. Womanless communication research simply ignores women. As mentioned earlier, most of the classical rhetorical theory described in Chapter 4 pays no attention to women. Spitzack and Carter cite a study whereby forty-five speech anthologies, covering thousands of speeches, were surveyed and only fifty-two speeches were by women. The second area, great women speakers, is most closely related to rhetoric. In this area women thought of as influential in public speaking contexts are analyzed according to the style and themes of their public address. Some studies examine the unique rhetorical strategies adopted by women. The third category, woman as other, has a scientific bent to it by focusing on the role of women not only in public contexts but also in small group settings, organizational structures, and interpersonal relationships. Much of this seeks to identify differences in the way men and women interact within the various settings. The fourth type, the politics of woman as other, is the critical approach to women's studies. Here the point is to critique the androcentric view that women's speech is devalued by emphasizing the inherent value of women's communication. This type of research requires novel conceptualizations of women and their communication situations (e.g., childbirth). In this category, female communication is studied on its own terms. Finally, the fifth conceptualization is women as communicators. In this area, research is directed at seeing women as a part of the process rather than as some unusual subgroup that is "different" from everything else. Here, women are seen as inherent in the development of culture, not as an external group with little or no influence.[82] The body of scholarship about women in communication is developing and there have been some important contributions, two of which include the muted group theory and Starhawk's rhetoric of inherent value and rhetoric of domination, among others.

Muted Group Theory

The muted group theory is not a communication theory per se but offers a heuristic framework from which communication scholars can explain and critique women's communication in contemporary society. The theory was first articulated by sociologists Shirley and Edwin Ardener and has since been applied to communication by Cheris Kramarae and others.[83]

The muted group theory is an explanation of how language functions to subordinate certain societal groups into a muted state; that is, unable to express themselves. The underlying assumptions of muted group theory, which are outlined in the following list, are a combination of the work of Shirley and Edwin Ardener and Cheris Kramarae. Generally the phrase *subordinate cultural group* refers to women, but it could equally apply to others such as racial groups.

Assumptions of the Muted Group Theory

1. The experiences and perceptions of subordinate cultural groups are different than those of the dominant cultural group. They experience life differently primarily because of their domination.

2. Subordinate cultural groups (e.g., race, sex) are not as free or as able as the dominant cultural group (e.g., white males) to say what they wish, when and where they wish.

3. Subordinate cultural groups contribute little, if any, to the formulation of the language in their culture.

4. The language of a particular culture does not serve all its members equally, for not all speakers contribute in an equal fashion to its formulation. The language may not provide the words and symbols representative of the subordinate group's perceptions and experiences.

5. Because subordinate groups are forced to express themselves (i.e., speak, write) within the dominant mode of expression they may not be able to communicate and become "muted."

6. Because subordinate groups are muted it is difficult if not impossible to emancipate themselves without the appropriate symbols. Thus, the language of the dominant cultural group actually keeps subordinate groups subordinate.[84]

The manifestations of the muted group theory are dramatic. Since they experience difficulty expressing themselves fluently within the dominant mode of expression, subordinate cultural groups' speech and writing are devalued. For example, until recently and the emergence of the female comic, women were not thought of as having a sense of humor. The stereotype was that they cannot tell jokes. When they were funny, it was usually because they were in some self-compromising situation, like Lucy Ball or Phyllis Diller often were. Moreover, men's sense of humor is targeted toward women and other subordinate groups and typically serves to denigrate them. As a result, interaction between members of the dominant and subordinate groups is difficult and hinders the establishment of interpersonal relationships. In fact, the dominant cultural group experiences more difficulty than the subordinate group in understanding that group.

Subordinate groups may respond to the dominant mode of expression in two ways. Some will refuse to live by the standards set forth by the dominant group and will try to change the dominant mode of expression. In the United States, for example, the replacement of such words as *chairman* with simply *chair* or *mailman* with *mail carrier* is demonstrative of this phenomena. Another way subordinate group members may respond is with the creation of their own "private" language. Drug cultures, for example, rarely refer to drugs by their formal technical names but instead create jargon and slang that allows them to interact. In essence the private language serves as a medium for expression and also as a boundary separating them from others. The African American form of "playin' the dozens" and "rappin'" serves to maintain blacks' unique identity and to bond them as a distinct sociocultural group.[85]

The muted group theory offers an important critique of contemporary society, especially as it relates to the function of language in an androcentric patriarchal society. The theory articulates the idea that the language of a culture is value-laden and not an objective representation of the society and its members. The theory stresses that changes in language are central to the emancipation of subordinate cultural groups, particularly women.

Starhawk's Rhetoric of Immanent Value and Psychology of Liberation

Starhawk, a peace activist and leader of several feminist causes, is the author of the best-selling books *Spiral Dance* and *Dreaming the Dark*. She teaches at several San Francisco colleges and travels widely conducting workshops on the topic of witchcraft. Most of her rhetorical theory is presented in her third book, *Truth or Dare*.

Starhawk's birth name was Miriam Simos, which she changed because she believes that "naming affirms value" that can "affirm a new beginning or a transition."[86] Her rhetorical theory emphasizes the inherent value of things on earth and that no one thing has more power than another. She contends the contemporary notion of power is based on androcentric and patriarchal ideals. In her theory she points out the importance language plays in the power structure and how it should be changed to liberate people.[87] Some of the ideas that characterize her theory include magic, immanent value, power, authority and obedience, and the psychology of liberation.

Central to Starhawk's rhetorical theory is the notion of magic and power. She sees magic as "the art of liberation, the act that releases the mysteries, that ruptures the fabric of our beliefs and lets us look into the heart of deep space where dwell the immeasurable, life-generating powers."[88] To practice magic is to uncover the source and essence of power. Power is ubiquitous, difficult to define, and impossible to quantify. Starhawk asserts: "The forces that push blood cells through our veins are the same forces that spun the universe out of the primal ball of fire We do not know what those forces are. We can invoke them, but we cannot control them, nor can we disconnect from them. They are our life. . . .[89]

Power exists in all people, but because it takes many shapes and forms, many of which are not fully comprehensible to human beings, it is mysterious. Magic, then, attempts to solve the mystery. The problem, as Starhawk sees it, is that the culture has been created in which the mysteries of power have been denied such that power is distorted and defined as domination and control.[90]

Starhawk defines three types of power, including power-over, power-from-within, and power-with. Power-over, which is most closely related to dominance and control, is a human conception that stems from the perspective that the world is made up of individual parts mechanistically interacting, not unlike Descartes's view of the world or the logical positivist notion of reality. According to Starhawk, we are born into this type of structure. Power-over is represented by such things as the police force, guns, or anything that is backed by coercion and force, or it could be in the form of money, food, or even love. Power-over affects every institution of society, including the workplace, relationships with others, law courts, schools, etc. Starhawk asserts that people in the culture are so accustomed to power-over that they only become aware of it when it is used in extreme forms (e.g., police action, crime, etc.). In societies characterized by power-over, humans have no inherent value. Instead, human worth must be earned. Power-over creates false divisions between people because they have different amounts of power.[91]

Power-from-within is the "sense of mastery" felt when one accomplishes something such as running fast, growing a plant, writing a book, or making love. Power-from-within stems from the sense of connection and bonding that people have with other humans and other aspects of the world. Humans are integrally connected with the stars, animals, plants, and rocks. Within the perspective of power-from-within all things have inherent or immanent value that does not have to be earned. One cannot lose it or have more of it than another. Starhawk is careful to point out that immanent value does not mean that everyone is innately good or that nothing should be destroyed. What is valued is the pattern of connections between all things. Rhetorically, power-from-within is expressed through poetry, metaphor, symbols, rituals, myth, and especially action.[92]

The third type of power, power-with, is most closely related to persuasion or rhetoric and is represented in our relationships with other humans. Starhawk contends that the dominant culture commonly confuses power-over as power-with. Power-with is exercised through respect for others and is "the power not to command, but to suggest and be listened to."[93] Power-with is also related to gaining influence with others. For women, power-with is difficult to maintain because they have been taught that their ideas and contributions are not as highly valued as are men's.

The goal of Starhawk's rhetoric is to liberate people from the power-over androcentric patriarchal society. As she states, "given a world based on power-over, we must remake the world."[94] Though her liberation psychology is not restricted to women, it emphasizes a patriarchal dominant group. Her liberation psychology is designed to "free us from the domination of the all-male God who has so strongly legitimized male rule, and by extension, all systems of domination."[95]

Language plays an important role in the psychology of liberation. Echoing muted group theory, Starhawk asserts that "language is political."[96] Language is structured so that people with power can maintain power and make power inaccessible to those without it. Language communicates power, knowledge, and value. People with a command of the language are more valuable because they have enough knowledge to exercise language against others which, in turn, makes them more powerful. To liberate people, especially women, from power-over, a language is needed that "is concrete, a language of poetry, not jargon; of metaphors that clearly are metaphors; a language that refers back to the material world, that is sensual, that speaks of things that we can see and touch and feel. It is a vocabulary not of the elite but of the common, and its concepts can be tested by experience."[97] Such a language will empower the oppressed to resist compliance to the dominant group and challenge their power-over.

Feminists understand that there is not a single theory of communication. They reject many theories as inadequate and misleading because they either ignore or distort women's communication. Like the general topic of critical theory, feminist critique looks at the contemporary society, sees an inherent problem, and comments on how to change it. In this case, the feminists see the dominant group comprised of men. As Kramarae asserts, theories that expose the male bias and examine the importance of women's issues "offer a more diversified, holistic understanding of communication."[98]

Summary

Although contemporary rhetorical theory started with the beginning of the twentieth century, its roots are in classical rhetorical theory which began some twenty-five hundred years ago. Certainly many changes have occurred since its inception. Perhaps the major departure for contemporary rhetorical theory is its focus on other modes of communication than just public speaking. Contemporary rhetorical theory's theme is symbol using of humans in many contexts. Another sharp distinction between the two theories—and perhaps the most exciting area of contemporary rhetorical theory today—is the introduction of the critical approach to symbol use. Scholars have moved beyond simply describing the way symbols are used toward prescription and interpretation. In so doing, these scholars employ a humanistic method, which certainly distinguishes rhetorical theorists from scientists.

Although a complete treatise on contemporary rhetorical theory is not possible here, you should now have a decent introduction to the nature of contemporary rhetorical theory and how it functions within the discipline. An undergraduate degree in communication is incomplete without such an introduction.

Glossary

Kenneth Burke: Contemporary rhetorical theorist who emphasized the role of language in rhetoric and developed the pentad for analyzing rhetorical situations.

Critical Theory: School of thought stemming from Frankfurt, Germany, and strongly influenced by Marx. The goal of critical theory is to evaluate and critique modern society, especially modes of communication.

Dramatism: A rhetorical approach to communication using drama as a metaphor for social interaction. People are seen as actors acting out social roles.

Feminist Critique/Theory: School of thought influenced by Marxism focusing on women's subordination and androcentric society.

Jurgen Habermas: Critical theorist who developed the theory of communicative action. Habermas argues that all people have the ideal capacity for truthful communication but may not fully realize it because society constrains them via the predominant ideology.

Identification: Term defined by Burke as the motive for rhetoric. People are naturally divided and identify with one another through rhetoric.

Muted Group Theory: Developed by Shirley and Edwin Ardener, this approach contends that the language of a particular culture actually mutes certain groups within it. Language serves the dominant group and keeps subordinate groups subordinate.

Pentad: Tool developed by Burke for analyzing rhetorical situations via their scene, act, agent, agency, and purpose.

I. A. Richards: Contemporary rhetorical theorist who rejected classical rhetorical theory's emphasis on the public speech in favor of an emphasis on other communication processes, including reading, writing, listening, and speaking. Richards was especially interested in the relationship between people, symbols, and referents.

Stephen Toulmin: British philosopher and contemporary rhetorical theorist responsible for the model of argumentation. Toulmin's primary model consists of grounds, warrant, and claim. Secondary elements of the model include backing, reservation, and qualification.

Starhawk: Feminist theorist and peace activist, author of several books advocating her rhetoric of immanent value and the psychology of liberation.

References

1. Johannesen, R. L. (1971). "Editor's Introduction: Some Trends in Contemporary Rhetorical Theory," in R. L. Johannesen, (Ed.), *Contemporary Theories of Rhetoric: Selected Readings,* (pp. 1–6), New York: Harper & Row.

2. Infante, D. A., Rancer, A. S., & Womack, D. F. (1993). *Building Communication Theory,* (2nd Ed.), Prospect Heights, IL: Waveland Press.

3. Foss, S. K., Foss, K. A., & Trapp, R. (1985). *Contemporary Perspectives on Rhetoric,* Prospect Heights, IL: Waveland Press, (p. 13).

4. Fogarty, D. (1968). *Roots for a New Rhetoric,* New York: Russell & Russell, (p. 144).

5. For an excellent discussion of contemporary rhetorical theory and individual theorists, see Foss, Foss, & Trapp. *Contemporary Perspectives on Rhetoric,* (2nd Ed.), Prospect Heights, IL: Waveland Press.

6. Foss, S. K., & Griffen, C. L. (1992). "A Feminist Perspective on Rhetorical Theory: Toward a Classification of Boundaries," *Western Journal of Communication, 56,* 330–349, (p. 331).

7. Ibid.

8. Griffin, E. (1994). *A First Look at Communication Theory,* (2nd Ed.), New York: McGraw-Hill.

9. Rueckert, W. H. (1989). "Kenneth Burke," in E. Barnouw, (Ed.), *International Encyclopedia of Communications,* (Vol. 1), (pp. 218–219), New York: Oxford University Press.

10. Fogarty, *Roots for a New Rhetoric.*

11. Burke, K. (1969). *A Rhetoric of Motives,* Berkeley: University of California Press, (p. 41).

12. Ibid., (p. 43).

13. Ibid., (p. 46).

14. Foss, Foss, & Trapp, *Contemporary Perspectives on Rhetoric.*

15. Fogarty, *Roots for a New Rhetoric.*

16. Griffin, *A First Look at Communication Theory,* (p. 276).

17. Burke, K. (1955). *A Grammar of Motives,* New York: George Braziller, (p. x).

18. Stacks, D., Hickson, M., III, & Hill, S. R., Jr. (1991). *Introduction to Communication Theory,* Fort Worth, TX: Holt, Rinehart and Winston.

19. Burke, *A Grammar of Motives,* (p. 15).

20. Nichols, M. H. (1965). "Kenneth Burke and the 'New Rhetoric'," in L. Crocker & P. A. Carmack, (Eds.), *Readings in Rhetoric,* (pp. 556–575), Springfield, IL: Charles C. Thomas.

21. Foss, Foss, & Trapp, *Contemporary Perspectives on Rhetoric,* (p. 199).

22. Stacks, Hickson & Hill, *Introduction to Communication Theory,* (p. 122).

23. Richards, I. A. (1936). *The Philosophy of Rhetoric,* New York: Oxford University Press, (p. 3).

24. Ibid.

25. Fogarty, *Roots for a New Rhetoric.* New York: Russell & Russell.

26. Ogden C. K., & Richards, I. A. (1946). *The Meaning of Meaning: A Study of the Influence of Language upon Thought and the Science of Symbolism,* (8th Ed.), New York: Harcourt, Brace, & World, (p. 3).

27. Ibid.

28. Foss, Foss, & Trapp, *Contemporary Perspectives on Rhetoric.*

29. Ogden, & Richards, *The Meaning of Meaning,* (p. 11).

30. Ibid., (p. 90).

31. Ibid., (p. 23).

32. Ibid., (p. 9).

33. Ibid., (p. 52).

34. Fogarty, *Roots for a New Rhetoric.*

35. Foss, Foss, & Trapp, *Contemporary Perspectives on Rhetoric.*

36. Ibid.

37. Toulmin, S. (1972). *Human Understanding,* (Vol. 1), Princeton, NJ: Princeton University Press, (pp. vii–viii).

38. Foss, Foss, & Trapp, *Contemporary Perspectives on Rhetoric.*

39. Ibid.

40. Brockreide, W. E., & Ehninger, D. (1971). "Toulmin on Argumentation: An Interpretation and Application," in Johannesen, *Contemporary Theories of Rhetoric,* (pp. 241–255).

41. Rybacki, K. C., & Rybacki, D. J. (1986). *Advocacy and Opposition: An Introduction to Argumentation,* Englewoods Cliffs, NJ: Prentice-Hall.

42. Ibid.

43. Brockreide, & Ehninger, "Toulmin on Argumentation," (pp. 241–255).

44. Ibid.

45. Rybacki, & Rybacki, *Advocacy and Opposition.*

46. Foss, Foss, & Trapp, *Contemporary Perspectives on Rhetoric.*

47. Brockreide, & Ehninger, "Toulmin on Argumentation," (p. 242).

48. Ingram, D. (1990). *Critical Theory and Philosophy,* New York: Paragon House, (p. xix).

49. Ibid., (p. xx).

50. Ibid., (p. xxi).

51. Ibid., (p. 1).

52. Held, D. (1980). *Introduction to Critical Theory: Horkheimer to Habermas,* Berkeley: University of California Press.

53. Ingram, *Critical Theory and Philosophy,* (p. 29).

54. Brummett, B. (1994). *Rhetoric in Popular Culture,* New York: St. Martin's Press.

55. Ibid.

56. Ibid.

57. Ingram, *Critical Theory and Philosophy.*

58. Brummett, *Rhetoric in Popular Culture.* Foss, Foss, & Trapp. *Contemporary Perspectives on Rhetoric.* Held, *Introduction to Critical Theory.*

59. Ingram, *Critical Theory and Philosophy.*

60. Ibid., (p. 106).

61. Foss, Foss, & Trapp, *Contemporary Perspectives on Rhetoric.*

62. Ibid., (p. 241).

63. Ingram, *Critical Theory and Philosophy.*

64. Habermas, J. (1979). *Communication and the Evolution of Society,* (translated by Thomas McCarthy), Boston: Beacon Press, (p. 1).

65. Ibid., (p. 2).

66. Habermas, J. (1981). *The Theory of Communicative Action (Vol. 1): Reason and the Rationalization of Society,* (translated by Thomas McCarthy), Boston: Beacon Press, (p. 290).

67. Ibid.

68. Ibid.

69. Foss, Foss, & Trapp, *Contemporary Perspectives on Rhetoric.*

70. Huspek, M. (1991). "Taking Aim on Habermas' Critical Theory: On the Road Toward a Critical Hermeneutics," *Communication Monographs, 58,* 225–233, (p. 227).

71. Ibid., (p. 225–233).

72. Gordon, L. (1979). "The Struggle for Reproductive Freedom: Three Stages of Feminism," in Z. R. Eisenstein, (Ed.), *Capitalist Patriarchy and the Case for Socialist Feminism,* (p. 107), New York: Monthly Review Press. See also Eisenstein, H. (1983). *Contemporary Feminist Thought,* Boston: G. K. Hall, (p. xii).

73. Kelly, J. (1982). "Early Feminist Theory and the 'Querelle des Femmes', 1400–1789," *Signs: Journal of Women in Culture and Society, 8,* 4–28. See also Eisenstein, *Contemporary Feminist Thought,* (p. xiii).

74. Eisenstein, *Contemporary Feminist Thought.*

75. Ingram, *Critical Theory and Philosophy.*

76. Jaggar, A. (1977). "Political Philosophies of Women's Liberation," in M. Vetterling-Braggin, F. A. Elliston, & J. English, (Eds.), *Feminism and Philosophy,* (pp. 5–21), Totowa, NJ: Littlefield, Adams.

77. Donovan, J. (1985). *Feminist Theory,* New York: Ungar, (p. 65).

78. MacKinnon, A. (1982). "Feminism, Marxism, Method, and the State: An Agenda for Theory," in N. O. Keohane, M. Z. Rosaldo, & B. C. Gelpi, (Eds.), *Feminist Theory: A Critique of Ideology,* (pp. 1–30), Chicago: University of Chicago Press.

79. Eisenstein, *Contemporary Feminist Thought;* Donovan, *Feminist Theory.*

80. Boxer, M. J. (1985). "Are Women Human Beings? Androcentricity as a Barrier to Intercultural Communication," in L. A. Samovar & R. E. Porter, (Eds.), *Intercultural Communication: A Reader,* (4th Ed.), (pp. 141–149), Belmont, CA: Wadsworth, (p. 143).

81. Foss, & Griffen, "A Feminist Perspective on Rhetorical Theory," (p. 331).

82. Spitzack, C., & Carter, K., (1987). "Women in Communication Studies: A Typology for Review," *The Quarterly Journal of Speech, 73,* 410–423.

83. Kramarae, C. (1981). *Women and Men Speaking,* Rowley, MA: Newbury House; Ardener, S. (Ed.) (1975). *Perceiving Women,* London: Malaby Press.

84. Kramarae, *Women and Men Speaking.*

85. Weber, S. N. (1991). "The Need to Be: The Socio-cultural Significance of Black Language," in L. A. Samovar & R. E. Porter, (Eds.), *Intercultural Communication: A Reader,* (6th Ed.), (pp. 277–283), Belmont, CA: Wadsworth.

86. Starhawk, (1987). *Truth or Dare: Encounters with Power, Authority, and Mystery,* Cambridge: Harper & Row, (p. 212); Foss, & Griffen, "A Feminist Perspective on Rhetorical Theory," 330–349

87. Ibid.

88. Starhawk, *Truth or Dare,* (p. 6).

89. Ibid.

90. Starhawk, *Truth or Dare.*

91. Ibid.

92. Ibid.

93. Ibid., (p. 10).

94. Ibid., (p. 8).

95. Ibid., (p. 21).

96. Ibid., (p. 20).

97. Ibid., (p. 21).

98. Kramarae, C. (1989). "Feminist Theories of Communication," in E. Barnouw, (Ed.), *International Encyclopedia of Communications,* (Vol. 2), (pp. 157–160), New York: Oxford University Press, (p. 160).

Chapter 6

Causal Process Theories

I think that all adequate scientific explanations and their everyday
counterparts claim or presuppose at least implicitly the deductive
or inductive subsumability of whatever is to be explained under
general laws.[1]—CARL G. HEMPEL

The world view and value system that lie at the base of Western civilization began in the sixteenth century when Copernicus hypothesized that the earth was not at the center of the universe but was merely a planet, from among many, that revolved around the sun. Following Copernicus was Johannes Kepler, who was responsible for the empirical laws of planetary motion which supported Copernicus's hypothesis. During this same period of history, Galileo Galilei, considered the father of modern science, became famous for his discovery of the laws of falling bodies. Later, Isaac Newton combined the discoveries of Kepler and Galileo by formulating the general laws of motion that govern all objects in the solar system. These laws were considered very important because of their universal application; that is, they were found to be valid throughout the solar system. The Newtonian theory, now called Newtonian mechanics, operated according to exact mathematical laws and remained the foundation of scientific thought into the seventeenth century and thus completed the scientific revolution. Newton's work influenced Einstein and other great scientists and even today influences how scientists conduct their work.[2]

What all of the great scientific achievements mentioned above share is their emphasis on laws and the idea of causality. Galileo, Kepler, and Newton, three of the greatest thinkers in the history of the world, constructed theories employing causal, rather than teleological, explanations. In Aristotle's theories all natural and human phenomena were explained in terms of the purposes or goals served by the behavior. Such explanations, which are called teleological (i.e., the study of ends), assert that the future state of a thing explains its earlier, past state. For example, say a theorist wanted to know why two people greeted each other when they passed in a hallway. From a teleological perspective, the theorist might posit that people desire to create a positive image of themselves to others. This goal (i.e., to create a desired image) explains their greeting behavior. The difficulty of such an explanation is easy to see; that is, the future event cannot cause the past. In order to make predictions about human behaviors, theorists would have to know the motives and/or goals of people. Even if theorists know the goals, they still cannot tell how a particular individual will attain them. There are many ways a person might create a desired image of themselves of which greeting behavior is only one.[3]

Newton was able to demonstrate that the motion of objects could be explained and predicted without any reference to what purposes such motions might have served. He looked to the position and momentum of the objects themselves. This all started, according to legend, when Newton witnessed an apple fall from a tree, and in a sudden flash of inspiration, deduced that the apple was pulled to the earth by gravity; the same force that pulled the planets toward the sun. Newton argued that the force of gravity caused the apple to fall.[4]

Causation

A cause is generally thought of as the source, origin, or that which produces something else. That which is produced is the effect of the cause. The effect might be a new substance or simply a change in the state of a substance that already exists. For example, the effect of combining two parts hydrogen with one part oxygen produces a completely different substance called water. The effect of lowering the temperature of water to 32 degrees Fahrenheit changes water from a liquid to a solid. The solid substance remains two parts hydrogen and one part oxygen, however.[5]

Generally, nothing but a state or a change of an object can be called a cause or effect. Causes and effects can be thought of as changes: the heating of the ice (cause) caused it to melt (effect). Causes and effects can be thought of as states: this door will not open (effect) because it is locked (cause). Thus, regarding causes, a state or change in some object A is said to have been the cause of a state of change of another object B if the presence of A (i.e., the persistence of A, if A is a state, or the occurrence of A, if A is a change) was sufficient to produce the occurrence of B. Regarding effects, a state or change of object B is said to be the effect of a state or change of object A if the occurrence of B was necessitated by the occurrence of A.[6]

Universal and Uniform Causes

Throughout the history of philosophy the universality of causation was thought to be obvious; that is, every event has its cause. The problem here is, of course, that some events are experienced or observed that do not appear to have any cause—they just seem to happen. Many theorists operate under the assumption that the cause of some event does indeed exist whether or not it has been experienced. In fact, many theorists spend much of their lives trying to uncover the causes of certain events.

To assert that causation is uniform is to affirm that similar causes produce similar effects and may be the result of some law. The belief that causation is uniform allows the theorist to make predictions. Causal process theorists maintain that the future will resemble the past. To identify the causal mechanism for some event then allows the theorist to make accurate predictions about the future. The problem here is, of course, that some causes may produce several effects and that some effect may have multiple causes. Weather, for example, may be the cause of many effects. A thunderstorm may cause a roof to leak, a plant to grow, and a person to get wet. A roof may leak not only because of a thunderstorm but also because of a hole. The job of the theorist is to ascertain the conditions under which similar causes produce similar effects.[7]

Necessary Causes

The above discussion implies that a cause and its subsequent effect are generally not thought of as accidental but that there is a necessary or inherent relationship between them. Recall from Chapter 2 that the concept of causal necessity was introduced. A cause is something that upon its presence or occurrence, produces an effect that must follow. For example, when water is heated to 212 degrees Fahrenheit it must boil. Water does not choose not to boil.

There is considerable disagreement among theorists and philosophers about the power of a cause to produce an effect. The well-known and oft-cited philosopher David Hume said that there are three essential characteristics between a cause and effect, including (a) contiguity, (b) succession in time, and (c) constant conjunction. Hume means that (a) causes and their effects are adjacent in time and space, (b) causes precede their effects temporally, and (c) causes are followed by their effects in a constant fashion.[8]

Hume argued that there is no necessary connection between causes and effects. He asserted that humans can only observe that a certain event follows another event, and that it does so regularly. Indeed, humans learn from observation that such things happen in a certain order. For example, some Event B regularly follows some Event A. Humans cannot observe, however, any connection or tie between events. Hence, they can observe ice melting when it is heated but they cannot observe any necessary connection between heat and melting ice. Humans cannot observe the heat "forcing" the ice to melt; they can only observe the regularity of the occurrence.

Causal process theorists generally agree that a cause does not extend to events in the past. Causes cannot occur after their effects. Events in the past are unchangeable. Events in the present, however, are sometimes changeable and can be changed in any number of ways depending on what causes act on them. Hence, A is the cause of B provided that A was immediately followed by B.[9]

The Structure of Causal Process Theories

Causal process theories, like other theories, are made up of descriptive theoretical statements about theoretical concepts, which, you will recall from Chapter 2, represent the foundation of any theory. Gravity, for example, is the theoretical concept driving Newtonian mechanics. Arthur Stinchcombe argues that most theoretical concepts vary; that is, they have various values. For example, temperature is a theoretical concept in thermodynamics, and we know that temperature can vary. Causal process theorists refer to varying theoretical concepts as variables.

A theoretical concept might vary in several ways. The simplest kind of variable is dichotomous; that is, has only two possible values that are mutually exclusive. Biological sex, for example, is a natural dichotomous variable. Socially created dichotomous variables include employed/unemployed. Sometimes socially created variables are created by people other than theorists. For example, governments may classify people as citizens or noncitizens. Even theorists create their own dichotomous variables. For example, communication theorists often refer to people as having either high or low communication apprehension. Theorists classify people or things into such categories for the purpose of designating subgroups that represent unique characteristics.[10]

Another kind of categorical variable has multiple values. Like dichotomous variables, these values are mutually exclusive but have more than two designations. For example, one's marital status could be classified according to four possibilities, including single, married, divorced, or widowed.

A third kind, called an ordinal variable, has as many values associated with it as there are members of the classification. For example, the rank order of finishers in a race (i.e., first, second, third, etc.) represents an ordinal classification. There are unspecified and unequal intervals between ordinal rankings. For example, the difference between the first and second finisher may be a fraction of a second whereas the difference between second and third may be three seconds.

A fourth kind of variable, called a continuous variable, classifies concepts into equal intervals. Natural continuous variables such as one's weight, height, and age are classified continuously, as are socially created continuous variables such as IQ and income. With continuous variables, unlike ordinal variables, the magnitude between intervals is equal. The difference between two people, one who is thirty-five years old and the other who is thirty-seven years old, is equal to the difference between two people, one who is three years old and the other who is five years old. Sometimes researchers will use continuous variables to create dichotomous variables. For example, persons under the age of thirty-five may be classified as "young," whereas persons over the age of thirty-five may be classified as "old."

Descriptive theoretical statements of causal process theories identify a connection between two or more variables; that is, the two variables seem to vary together regularly. Such statements assert that the value of Variable A (i.e., the cause) is associated with the value of a subsequent Variable B (i.e., an effect) and produces this change without changing other variables in the environment. Variable A is thought of as the causal mechanism of the change in Variable B if the following conditions are met:

1. A change in Variable A is associated with a change in Variable B. For example, when people with communication apprehension (Variable A) present public speeches, they gesture less (Variable B) than those without communication apprehension.

2. A change in Variable A produces a change in Variable B, but a change in Variable B does not produce a change in Variable A. For example, differing levels of communication apprehension produce changes in the frequency of one's gestures, but the frequency of one's gestures does not change one's level of communication apprehension. One's frequency of gestures depends on the presence of communication apprehension. Communication apprehension is not dependent on the presence or frequency of gestures.

3. Variations of other variables may also produce variation in the caused variable. For example, the frequency of gestures may also be caused by other factors, such as the speaker's familiarity with the audience, or his or her preparation of speech, etc. This does not invalidate the assertion that communication apprehension is a causal mechanism for the frequency of gesturing.[11]

Verification of Causal Mechanisms

Once causal mechanisms have been identified, causal process theorists need to derive observations to support or refute their theoretical statements. Stinchcombe contends that theorists need to create observations of four kinds, including those that (a) reveal differing values of the causal variable, (b) demonstrate covariation, (c) establish causal direction, and (d) confirm nonspuriousness.[12]

Unless there is variation in the causal variable, covariation and causality cannot be established. For example, to assert that communication apprehension causes speakers to gesture less requires that speakers without communication apprehension be observed. To observe only those speakers with such apprehension does not allow theorists to claim any causal link between communication apprehension and gesturing. Theorists must compare the frequency of gesturing of speakers with and speakers without communication apprehension.

In addition to observing different levels of the causal variable, theorists must also observe different levels of the effect that covary with the different levels. Such observations demonstrate the principle of covariation. For example, to assert that communication apprehension causes the frequency of gesturing, the theorist would have to observe different levels of communication apprehension (e.g., high/low) covarying with different frequency rates of gesturing. If the theorist observed no difference between the frequency of gestures between high and low communication apprehensive speakers, then covariation could not be claimed. The communication theorist might set up an experiment where speakers are assessed for their level of communication apprehension. Those with high levels are placed into one group and those without it in another. The theorist could then have members of both groups give speeches and simply count the number of gestures. A comparison can then be made between the two groups.

If covariation is observed, the theorist must then demonstrate the direction of the covariation. Causal variables are antecedent to their effect. Hence the theorist must observe that it is not possible to change the value of the causal variable by changing the value of the effect, or that it is possible to change the value of the effect by changing the value of the causal variable. For example, a communication theorist could, in some way, ask speakers without communication apprehension to gesture at high frequencies to ascertain if such gesturing changes their level of communication apprehension. If it does not, then directional covariation has been demonstrated. In addition, if theorists know of other causes of the effect unrelated to the causal variable of interest, then causal direction can be established. The theorist would have to observe the effect (due to the other causes) without variation in the variable of interest.

Finally, causal theorists must observe that there are not other variables in the environment that might cause changes in the effect that are equal to and simultaneous with the causal variable. This does not rule out multiple causation, however. To demonstrate nonspuriousness requires theorists to create controlled experiments that remove other possible causes of the effect from the environment. For example, a communication theorist might suspect that low frequencies of gestures may also be caused by poor preparation by the speaker. To control for preparation the theorist could require a certain amount of preparation (which would be monitored) prior to observing the speeches. If the speakers continued to gesture at low frequency rates the spuriousness factor has been removed.

The goal of the causal process theorist is to derive empirically verifiable theoretical statements which identify covariation, causal direction, and nonspuriousness. Such theoretical statements are sometimes called laws, axioms, or postulates. These statements, which express a causal relationship between theoretical concepts, serve as the starting point for the theorist who uses them to deduce predictions. Many of the great thinkers of history conducted their theoretic activity within the realm of laws. Laws have been at the foundation of theory for centuries and continue to influence theorists today, even communication theorists. Though communication probably has no pure laws, many communication scholars are interested in the idea of causality and lawlike statements of communication behavior.

Theoretical Foundations of the Laws Perspective

As earlier chapters in this book have argued, the basic task of the theorist is to explain phenomena in nature and to predict their occurrence. This tradition goes back at least as far as Aristotle and probably farther. As mentioned above, throughout history many great achievements have been based on the discovery of laws. Though a theorist need not adhere to any particular philosophic school in order to understand the importance of laws in scientific explanation, one group of theorists and philosophers, called the logical positivists, championed what is known as the covering law model of scientific explanation.[13] The term *covering law* was first introduced in 1957 by William Dray who, at the time, was a professor of philosophy at the University of Toronto. Dray argued that:

> *explanation is achieved, and only achieved, by subsuming what is to be explained under a general law. Such an account of the basic structure of all explanation is sometimes referred to as 'the regularity analysis'; but because it makes use of the notion of bringing a case under a law, i.e. 'covering' it with a law, I shall often speak of it hereafter as 'the covering law model'.[14]*

Logical positivism, also known as logical empiricism or sometimes called just positivism or empiricism, was a revolutionary philosophic movement that began in the 1920s among a group of philosophers known as the "Vienna Circle."[15] This group consisted of such scholars as Rudolf Carnap, Moritz Schlick, A. J. Ayer, Herbert Feigl, and Otto Neurath. Later, Carl Hempel also joined the group and has since become a leading proponent of the positivist movement.[16] The term *logical* was indicative of the Circle's reliance on logic or its special attention to language and scientific explanation. The term *positivism* was used by nineteenth-century philosopher Auguste Comte to refer to his view that all knowledge is derived from observable phenomena.[17] Perhaps you can recall from Chapter 1 that empiricism was defined as the branch of philosophy and science that adheres to the notion that all knowable reality is gained via observation, that all knowable reality is sensible and gained via experience. In this sense positivism and empiricism are used interchangeably.

A fundamental question in philosophy has always been "How do I know?" Empiricists have always maintained that our knowledge comes from sensations (i.e., what we can see, hear, touch, smell, and taste). In adhering to this philosophy, the logical positivists rejected the idea that any knowledge can be gained via metaphysics, or via transcendent, supersensible, or supernatural means. Descartes, for example, held that certain aspects of knowledge are innate, that we gain them without the use of our senses.[18] In vehemently rejecting that any knowledge can be gained through metaphysical means, the positivists developed their own covering law model of scientific explanation which maintains that a scientific explanation of Event A consists of deriving three types of statements, including (a) a statement describing Event A, (b) statements of scientific laws that include the types of phenomena described in Statement a and, (c) statements describing antecedently known empirical facts, called initial conditions.[19] Two important ingredients for this model are the use of laws and deduction. The rest of this chapter attempts to spell out how this covering law model works according to the logical positivists.

Definitions of Laws

In theoretical terms, a law is a statement that expresses a universally invariant relationship between two or more objects and/or events. For example, the statement "Whenever A occurs, B follows" is a law that expresses a relationship between A and B. A universally invariant relationship is one that occurs everywhere, at all times, and does not change or vary. Theoretically, laws transcend time and space. Carl Hempel, a leading laws philosopher, defines a law as "a statement of universal conditional form which is capable of being confirmed or disconfirmed by suitable empirical findings."[20] Recall from your introductory logic class that a conditional statement is one expressed in "if-then" form. For example, "*If* A occurs, *then* B will follow" is a law stated in conditional form. Though theoretically defined as universally invariant, laws only apply under certain boundary conditions; that is, sometimes they operate and sometimes they do not. This is a widely misunderstood notion about laws. For example, a classical lesson learned very early in school is the law "Water boils at 212 degrees Fahrenheit." Though expressed as a law and widely considered universal, not all water boils at 212 degrees. In Denver, Colorado, for example, where the altitude is almost six thousand feet, water boils at a slightly lower temperature, at about 192 degrees. Hence, in Denver, you need to boil your macaroni a little longer than you would have to in Chicago. Another misconception about laws is that they come in only one type of format. In fact, contrary to popular opinion, there are several different types and forms of laws. Table 6.1 on page 152 distinguishes between the different types, forms, and domains of laws.

TABLE 6.1 Types, Forms, and Domains of Laws

Types	Forms	Domain Of Laws
Determination:	**Qualitative:**	**Laws of Succession:**
Laws that express precise and rigid relationships between objects and events.	Laws that express universal generalizations without specifying any exact numerical magnitudes of the object or event.	Laws that concern temporal changes in a system. These laws express relationships between objects or events by referencing the sequence between antecedent causes and subsequent effects.
1. If A, then B. 2. Water boils at 212°. 3. Every body near the earth freely falling towards the earth falls with an acceleration of 32 feet per second squared.	1. Rubbing produces heat. 2. Rubber does not conduct electricity.	1. When heated to 212° at sea level, water will boil. 2. When exposed to heat, mercury will expand and rise upward in a thermometer.
Statistical:	**Semiquantitative:**	**Laws of Coexistence:**
Laws that express probabilistic relationships between objects and events based on laws governing frequency ratios.	Laws that express relationships between objects and events with the relational and logical operators "greater than," "less than," or "equal to."	Laws that express universal generalizations co-occurring at one and the same time.
1. If a two-sided coin is flipped ten times, it will land on Side 1 approximately five times. 2. When high and low pressure systems collide, it usually produces precipitation. 3. If the telephone rings, and Jan is capable of hearing the ring, she will probably answer it.	1. The greater the pressure exerted on a balloon, the more likely it is to burst. 2. The greater the distance between magnets, the smaller the force.	1. Male cardinals are red. 2. Water—2 parts hydrogen + 1 part oxygen.
	Fully Quantitative:	
	Laws that express relationships between objects and events with mathematically exact degrees of magnitude.	
	1. Every body near the earth freely falling towards the earth falls with an acceleration of 32 feet per second squared. 2. At sea level, water boils at 212°.	

Types of Laws

Most natural and social scientists distinguish between two types of laws, including (a) deterministic laws and (b) statistical laws.[21] Deterministic laws are very exact and specify strict and precise predictability between two or more events. The law stating that water boils at 212 degrees is a deterministic law. Deterministic laws usually reflect occurrences in nature and typically express how nature changes. For example, the law "Water boils at 212 degrees" specifies how water changes when heated to a certain temperature. These laws are deterministic in the sense that given a particular physical system (e.g., water) at any one time they determine its state at any other, earlier or later, time (e.g., boiling).[22] For example, assume that we are going to observe water at two different time intervals. During

Time Period 1, the temperature of water is 200 degrees. We know, based on the law that water boils at 212 degrees, what kind of state water is in; that is, it is certainly not boiling. However, assume that in Time Period 2, the temperature of water is 212 degrees. Given the law "Water boils at 212 degrees" we can determine that the state of water in Time Period 2 will be different than in Time Period 1; that is, it is now in the state of boiling.

Statistical laws are not as exact and precise as deterministic laws. Statistical laws specify predictions on the basis of stable frequency ratios or according to laws governing frequency distributions. These laws specify the probability of two or more events being related. For example, if your flip a coin, what is the probability of the coin landing on heads or tails? No deterministic law can precisely predict on which exact side the coin will land. We can, however, determine the probability of which side the coin will land on. The probability of any outcome can be calculated by dividing the specific number of outcomes (e.g., heads = 1 outcome) by the total number of potential outcomes (e.g., heads and tails = 2 possible outcomes). Thus the probability of a coin landing on heads with a single toss is $\frac{1}{2}$ or 50 percent. Given this formula, you can predict how many times a coin will land on heads with ten flips. For example, if you flip a coin ten times it will land on heads approximately five times, or 50 percent of the time. Be careful to note, however, that it is possible that it will land on heads only four times. Statistically, the coin should land on heads five times based on what we know about the frequency distribution of flipping a coin. Although statistical laws are theoretically no less precise in their predictions than are deterministic laws, they are clearly less reliable. Most theoretical statements in causal process communication theories are statistical.

Forms of Laws

Some laws express precise mathematical relationships between events or happenings whereas other laws only express generalizations about the relationships between things. In fact, laws can be expressed qualitatively, semiquantitatively, or fully quantitatively.[23] For example, the law "Friction produces heat" is stated qualitatively. Since any amount of friction, regardless of quantity, will produce heat, to specify exact quantities is not necessary. Semiquantitatively stated laws include the qualifiers "greater than," "less than," or "equal to." For example, the law "The higher the temperature the greater the speed of chemical reactions" is stated in the semiquantitative mode. Fully quantitative laws express nearly exact magnitudes. The law "Water boils at 212 degrees" is a fully quantitatively expressed law.[24] Many of the laws in the natural sciences can be stated with exact mathematical precision. In contrast, many of the laws in the social sciences are stated qualitatively. Most theoretical statements in communication theory are qualitative or semiquantitative. There are probably no fully quantitative statements in communication theory.

Domain of Laws

In addition to the different types and forms of laws, most laws describe a temporal or sequential succession. For example, the law "If A occurs, then B follows" describes a particular sequence of events. If B is observed, then we must conclude that A has preceded it temporally; that is, in time. Other laws express the regular coexistence of certain dimensions in objects or events without reference to any time order. The law "All ravens are black" expresses the co-occurrence between black and ravens. There is no succession of events here. To state "If black, then raven" makes little sense. Indeed, even the statement "If raven, then black" is not logical since a raven cannot exist prior to the presence of black, whereas in the case of the law "If A, then B," A must occur prior to B.[25]

The Function of Laws: Explanation

The discovery of laws probably dates back to prehistory but we know that almost five hundred years ago the scientific revolution was stimulated by the discovery and formulation of Kepler's laws of planetary motion, Galileo's laws of falling bodies, and Newton's general laws of motion. Laws have played a key role in the advancement of science, particularly the natural sciences.[26] The major function of a lawlike statement is to enable explanations, especially causal explanations, to be made of specific events, happenings, or observations.[27] The general goal of the theorist is to go beyond the "what" of explanation to the "why." Events, happenings, or relationships that are explained with laws are said to have causal explanations; they are based on causal necessity.

Types of Explanations

Recall from earlier chapters in this book that a major goal of theory to is explain; to go beyond the question What? and answer the question Why? Advocates of the laws perspective believe that they have the best method of explaining the Why question. Explanations of the laws perspective are based on causal necessity. Thus, when the theorist asks "Why?" the answer is found in determining the cause and discovering the law. In his classic treatment of the role of laws in scientific explanation, Carl Hempel argues that the laws theorist has three types of explanations at his or her disposal in answering the Why question. These three types of explanations have rather technical sounding labels, including (a) deductive-nomological, (b) deductive-statistical, and (c) inductive-statistical.[28] Try not to let these labels hinder your understanding of these methods of explanation.

Deductive-Nomological

This first type of explanation available to the laws theorist is the deductive-nomological explanation, or the D-N explanation for short.[29] It is called deductive because it requires the theorist to engage in deductive reasoning. Deductive reasoning, or deduction, is when we move from general principles to less general principles or to individual events.[30] Recall from earlier chapters the classic form of deductive logic represented in the syllogism:

> *All men are mortal. (general principle)*
> *Socrates is a man. (individual judgment)*
> *Socrates is mortal. (conclusion based on deductive inference)*

In addition to making a deduction, the theorist using the D-N explanation is also required to have some knowledge of applicable laws. The D-N explanation is called nomological because of its reliance on the use of lawlike statements to do the explaining. By definition, nomology is the science of physical and logical laws. Thus, to use this method of explaining you will have to use a law and engage in deductive logic. The D-N method of explanation accounts for any particular happening by subsuming it under general laws.[31] Hempel provides the following example of how a theorist might use the D-N explanation:

> *In a beaker filled to the brim with water at room temperature, there floats a chunk of ice which partly extends above the surface. As the ice gradually melts, one might expect the water in the beaker to overflow. Actually the water level remains unchanged. How is this to be explained?*[32]

At this point, the theorist knows two things: (a) the initial conditions he or she is facing (i.e., the beaker filled with ice and water), and (b) the law of physics which states that a body of ice turns into a body of water having the same weight, and that amounts of water that are equal in weight are equal in volume. Knowing these things, the theorist now engages in the process of deduction. The following list presents how this argument might look.

Deductive-Nomological Explanation

General Principles/Law

1. A body of ice that turns into a body of water has the same weight.
2. Amounts of water that are equal in weight are equal in volume.

Initial Conditions/Judgment

1. This particular beaker has a piece of ice extending above the surface.

Conclusion Based on Deductive Inference

1. This particular beaker will not overflow because a body of ice that turns into a body of water has the same weight and amounts of water that are equal in volume.

The explanation of why this particular beaker did not overflow was to be expected in view of the initial conditions and the general laws. The law states that a body of ice turns into a body of water having the same weight and that amounts of water that are equal in weight are equal in volume. In front of the theorist is a beaker with an amount of ice that has turned into water. We can now explain why the beaker did not overflow; ice turned into water has the same volume and weight. Note that this explanation has the same logical structure as the syllogism regarding the mortality of Socrates.

You should know two additional technical terms of the D-N explanation, including (a) the explanans and (b) the explanandum. The explanans is composed of the initial conditions observed by the scientist and the general laws known. In the above example, the explanans is the beaker of water *and* ice observed and the laws of weight and volume that apply to water and ice. The particular laws expressed here are known as Archimedes' principle.[33] The explanandum is that which is to be explained. In the above example the explanandum is the end of the process, the beaker contains *only* water. The explanandum is the statement describing that which is to be explained. The explanans is the statements that are forwarded to provide an explanation.[34]

Deductive-Statistical

The deductive-statistical explanation, called the D-S explanation for short, has the same basic components as the D-N explanation with the exception that instead of universally invariant laws, the explanans contains statistical laws. Statistical laws, though very much like universal laws, are different in that they express the probability of a relationship between two events rather than some certain or deterministic relationship. For example, it is a universal law that a body of ice turns into a body of water having the same weight and that amounts of water that are equal in weight are equal in volume. The theorist can be certain, 100 percent of the time, that given a certain temperature and atmospheric pressure, this will occur. Many events in nature, and especially those in the social sciences, cannot be subsumed under general laws, however. For example, when we flip a coin we cannot predict with 100 percent accuracy upon which side the coin will land. We know for certain, however, the probability of the coin landing on either side is 50 percent. This kind of certainty is based on the laws governing frequency ratios, statistical laws.

Essentially statistical laws are statements that express the statistical probability of an event being related to another event. Statistical and universal laws are similar in that they both make claims concerning a class of events that may be said to be infinite. For example, we know that *whenever* we flip *any* two-sided coin, the exact probability of it landing on either side is .50. This same prediction can be made for an infinite number of two-sided coins. We cannot, however, predict the outcome of any particular coin flip. Statistical laws only allow us to predict particular collections of events, while universal deterministic laws allow us to predict particular events.[35] For example, we can predict with a certain probability the likelihood of being dealt four aces from a deck of cards. However, we are not in a position to predict the makeup of a particular hand of cards. Charles Berger contends that we can predict with a certain probability that if males and females with certain eye colors have large numbers of children, a certain proportion of those children will have a certain eye color. However, we are not in a position to predict the eye color of a particular child.[36] Although statistical laws are regarded as less stringent than universal laws, essentially the basic explanatory process remains deductive and is composed of the same two components as in the D-N explanation; that is, the explanans and the explanandum. In the case of the S-N explanation the explanans contains a statistical law based on laws governing frequency distributions rather than a universal law.[37]

Inductive-Statistical

The third type of explanation, called the inductive-statistical explanation or I-S explanation for short, accounts for a given event by reference to general statistical laws but does not rely on deductive inference and instead employs inductive logic. Induction is the process by which we move from knowledge of individual instances to knowledge of universals.[38] Through repeated observations of some event, we believe that the same event will recur because it has done so in the past. Our faith in the sun rising tomorrow is based on our inductive logic; we believe the sun will rise tomorrow because it has done so in the past. Through such repeated observations of some event, we can establish statistical probabilities of its recurrence. We then use these probabilities to explain, inductively, why some event occurred. Like in the D-N and D-S explanations, we still have the two basic components, the explanans and the explanandum. Here is an example of how this explanation might look.

Inductive-Statistical Explanation

Explanans

Jon has red hair and is a communist.
Jim has red hair and is a communist.
Jan has red hair and is a communist.

Joe has red hair.

Explanandum

Joe is a communist.

Inductively derived explanations are problematic for some theorists because some argue that simply because an event has occurred in the past is no reason to expect that it will occur in the future, thus cannot provide an explanation of its occurrence. This is unlike deductively based explanations wherein if the premises, including a general or statistical law, are held to be true, then the conclusions must also be true.

The Search for Laws: The Hypothetico-Deductive Method

Regardless of which of the three types of explanations theorists may use, they must have a keen awareness and knowledge of the applicable laws in their field. The question now becomes: "Where do laws come from?" The positivists call the procedure for developing laws the "Hypothetico-Deductive" method, sometimes called the H-D method.[39] Upon the observation of some new event or happening, the theorist is faced with the task of developing an explanation. In some cases, the event or happening may have never before been observed and therefore there are no laws that "cover" it. In this case, the theorist develops a hypothesis and his or her task now is to test whether the hypothesis is true. The positivists weren't interested in exactly how the theorist creates the hypothesis so they didn't propose a system of logic for explaining it. We know however, that given the name of the model—that is, the hypothetico-deductive model—the theorist somehow deduces the hypothesis from observing the surroundings in which the event or happening took place.

For example, upon the observation that a particular pot of water is boiling, the theorist, never having before seen this happening, might posit that the heat surrounding the pot had something to do with the quality of the boiling water. The next step for the theorist is to test the hypothesis, usually several times. In our earlier example, the theorist may observe the water while raising the temperature while also observing a different pot of water while holding its temperature constant. If the hypothesis is found to be true, it might provide the law needed to explain the new observation. Interestingly, if the repeated tests of the hypothesis convinces the theorist that he or she has found the cause or the law, then the theorist has used induction to establish the validity of the law. If the theorist observes over and over that raising the temperature of the water co-occurs with the water boiling, then he or she induces that the temperature causes the water to boil and can now state the law of temperature and boiling point of water. As Bertrand Russell, a leading empiricist, argues, "Induction raises perhaps the most difficult problem for the whole theory of knowledge. Every scientific law is established by its means, and yet it is difficult to see why we should believe it to be a valid logical process."[40]

CASE STUDY 6   The Overthrow of Phlogiston Theory

The study of causes and effects is not unique to the study of human communication. Scholars in a variety of academic disciplines, especially in the natural sciences, are constantly in search of causes. To establish causation can be difficult, however. Some philosophers and theorists argue that absolute causality can never be attained.

Throughout the history of science, scientists and philosophers have made incorrect attributions about causes and effects. One of the most noteworthy examples of mistaken causality is related to the overthrow of phlogiston theory and the beginnings of the chemical revolution.[a] For centuries, physicists and chemists explained the principle of inflammability—or that by which bodies and substances become combustible or capable of burning—through a process by which air is charged with large quantities of phlogiston. Chemists often spoke of fire and phlogiston as being the same thing, or signifying the same element. In the eighteenth century, German physician and chemist Georg Ernest Stahl coined the term *phlogiston* from a Greek word meaning "to set on fire."[b] According to Stahl, combustible substances were rich in phlogiston and the process of burning involved the loss of phlogiston to the air. Substances such as wood were particularly rich in phlogiston whereas substances such as rock or ash were not. In addition, Stahl argued that the rusting of metals was analogous to the burning of wood. Metal substances, according to Stahl, possessed phlogiston while their rust did not. Air was considered important in the process because it served as a carrier of phlogiston as it left the wood or metal substance.

Joseph Priestley, a chemist who would later discover a gas he called dephlogisticated air, argued that Stahl's discovery was one of the greatest discoveries ever made in science. Other chemists and physicists disagreed with Stahl, arguing that combustion and fire were too different (i.e., one process has a flame and the other does not) to be caused by the same substance. Stahl responded that in certain substances phlogiston left so fast as to heat the substance and produce a flame. In other substances, such as metal, the release of phlogiston was slow and thus did not create heat. A major problem with Stahl's analysis was that combustible substances were lighter in weight after burning whereas other substances, such as metals, were heavier. Though there were other problems with Stahl's phlogiston theory, most chemists accepted it as valid.

Chemists of the last part of the eighteenth century were forced to deal with the unanswered questions from phlogiston theory. Their answers would lie in the study of gases. At the time many were afraid of gas because of its elusive nature. It was hard to control and confine, and hence quite difficult to observe. After a series of advancements in the confinement and measurement of gases, several important discoveries were made. One such discovery was made by Joseph Priestley, a minister by trade and a chemist by hobby. In a series of experiments with mercury, Priestley found that when heated, mercury formed a reddish substance called calx. He also found that when the calx was heated it became mercury. During this process the calx gave off a peculiar gas which caused other combustibles to burn more rapidly. Using phlogiston theory as his base (a theory he never abandoned) Priestley argued that this new gas enabled substances to give off more phlogiston than usual. He reasoned that the new gas was a sample of air from which the usual amount of phlogiston had been drained such that it accepted a new supply with special eagerness. Priestley called this gas "dephlogisticated air." Later the gas would become known as oxygen.[c]

Priestley communicated his discoveries to the French chemist Antoine Lavoisier, who is credited with synthesizing the discoveries into a coherent, and radically different, explanation for combustion. In a series of experiments of his own, Lavoisier discovered that some substances did not lose weight upon burning but actually gained in weight. He reasoned that the increase in weight was the result of large quantities of air that are fixed during combustion and combine with the vapors of the substance. Lavoisier argued that:

> *This discovery, which I have established by experiments, that I regard as decisive, has led me to believe that what is observed in the combustion of sulphur and phosphorus may well take place in the case of all substances that gain in weight by combustion and calcination; and I am persuaded that the increase in weight of metallic calxes is due to the same cause.[d]*

The major point here is that something is consumed from the atmosphere during combustion and calcination rather than released into the atmosphere as explained in phlogiston theory. Lavoisier believed that air was a mixture of two gases; what he called *oxygen,* from the Greek word for "acid producer," and *azote,* from the Greek word for "no life."[e] Azote was later renamed nitrogen. Lavoisier believed that life was supported by processes similar to combustion; that is, life forms breathe in air heavy in oxygen but exhale air low in it. Lavoisier would later coin the name for hydrogen as well. Though at the time not all of his theories were accepted, Lavoisier is universally remembered as the father of the chemical revolution and modern chemistry. Ironically, the term *phlogiston* is now used as an analogy to describe theories or explanations erroneously attributed to an imaginary cause.[f]

a. Conant, J. B. (Ed.) (1967). The Overthrow of the Phlogiston Theory, Cambridge, MA: Harvard University Press; Kuhn, T. S. (1970). The Structure of Scientific Revolutions, Chicago: University of Chicago Press.
b. Asimov, I. (1965). A Short History of Chemistry: An Introduction to the Ideas and Concepts of Chemistry, Garden City, NY: Anchor Books.
c. Conant, The Overthrow of the Phlogiston Theory; Asimov, A Short History of Chemistry.
d. Conant, The Overthrow of the Phlogiston Theory, (p. 31).
e. Asimov, A Short History of Chemistry.
f. Fisher, B. A. (1978). Perspectives on Human Communication, New York: Macmillan.

Summary

This chapter profiled causal process theories and the covering laws model of explanation. The logical positivism view offers a systematic method of explanation by providing an account that uses deduction to demonstrate how events or happenings can be explained by subsuming them or covering them by laws. In addition, the positivists have also forwarded an account of how particular events or happenings provide evidence for how laws can be developed. In the following chapter, we will see how this philosophic and theoretic viewpoint has been espoused in the communication field.

Glossary

Causal Necessity: Principle stating that effects are not produced accidentally, but are the necessary or inherent product of some cause.

Causation: The source, origin, or that which produces something else.

Covariation: Differing levels of a causal variable produce simultaneous differing values in some other variable.

Deductive-Nomological Explanation: Explanations that rely on deductive reasoning and laws for methods of explanation.

Deductive-Statistical Explanation: Explanations that express the probability of something occurring.

Determinant Laws: Laws that express precise and rigid relationships between objects and/or events.

Effect: That which is produced or is the result of some cause. The effect can be a change in something or a state of something.

Fully Quantitative Laws: Laws that express relationships between objects and events with mathematically exact degrees of magnitude.

Inductive-Statistical Explanation: Accounts for a given event by reference to general statistical laws and employs inductive logic.

Law: A theoretical statement that expresses a universally invariant relationship between concepts.

Logical Positivism: Philosophical perspective that contends that all knowledge is knowable through sensation and the use of laws.

Semiquantitative Laws: Laws that express relationships between objects and events with the relational and logical operators "greater than," "less than," or "equal to."

Statistical Laws: Laws expressing probabilistic relationships between objects and/or events.

Qualitative Laws: Laws that express universal generalizations without specifying any exact numerical magnitudes.

Variable: A theoretical concept that varies; that is, can have more than one value.

References

1. Hempel, C. G. (1968). "Explanatory Incompleteness," in M. Brodbeck, (Ed.), *Readings in the Philosophy of the Social Sciences,* (pp. 398–411), New York: Macmillan, (p. 411).

2. Capra, F. (1988). *The Turning Point: Science, Society, and the Rising Culture,* Toronto: Bantam.

3. Rosenberg, A. (1988). *Philosophy of Social Science,* Boulder, CO: Westview.

4. Capra, *The Turning Point.*

5. Taylor, R. (1967). "Causation," in P. Edwards, (Ed.), *The Encyclopedia of Philosophy,* (pp. 56–66), New York: Macmillan & The Free Press.

6. Ducasse, C. J. (1969). *Causation and the Types of Necessity,* New York: Dover.

7. Taylor, "Causation," (Vol. 2), (pp. 56–66).

8. Suppes, P. (1970). *A Probabilistic Theory of Causality,* Amsterdam: North-Holland.

9. Taylor, "Causation," (pp. 56–66).

10. Stinchcombe, A. L. (1968). *Constructing Social Theories,* New York: Harcourt, Brace, & World.

11. Ibid.

12. Ibid.

13. Bechtel, W. (1988). *Philosophy of Science: An Overview for Cognitive Science,* Hillsdale, NJ: Erlbaum.

14. Dray, W. (1957). *Laws and Explanation in History,* London: Oxford University Press, (p. 1).

15. Hanfling, O. (1981). *Logical Positivism,* New York: Columbia University Press.

16. Ayer, A. J. (1959). "Editor's Introduction," in A. J. Ayer, (Ed.), *Logical Positivism,* (pp. 3–30), Glencoe, IL: Free Press.

17. Hanfling, *Logical Positivism.*

18. Ibid.

19. Bechtel, *Philosophy of Science.*

20. Hempel, C. G. (1965). *Aspects of Scientific Explanation and Other Essays in the Philosophy of Science,* New York: Free Press, (p. 231).

21. Feigl, H. (1953). "Notes on Causality," in H. Feigl & M. Brodbeck, (Eds.), *Readings in the Philosophy of Science,* (pp. 408–418), New York: Appleton-Century-Crofts.

22. Hempel, *Aspects of Scientific Explanation.*

23. Feigl, "Notes on Causality," (pp. 408–418).

24. Ibid.

25. Ibid.

26. Capra, *The Turning Point.*

27. Walters, R. S. (1967). "Laws of Science and Lawlike Statements," in P. Edwards, (Ed.), *The Encyclopedia of Philosophy,* (Vol. 4), (pp. 410–414), New York: Macmillan.

28. Hempel, *Aspects of Scientific Explanation.*

29. Berger, C. R. (1977). "The Covering Law Perspective as a Theoretical Basis for the Study of Human Communication," *Communication Quarterly, 25,* 7–18; Hempel, *Aspects of Scientific Explanation.*

30. Henle, R. J. (1983). *Theory of Knowledge,* Chicago: Loyola University Press.

31. Hempel, *Aspects of Scientific Explanation.*

32. Ibid., (p. 298).

33. Hempel, *Aspects of Scientific Explanation.*

34. Ibid.

35. Berger, "The Covering Law Perspective," 7–18.

36. Ibid.

37. Hempel, *Aspects of Scientific Explanation.*

38. Henle, *Theory of Knowledge.*

39. Bechtel, *Philosophy of Science.*

40. Russell, B. (1961). *An Outline of Philosophy,* London, Allen & Unwin, (p. 14).

Chapter 7

Causal Process Theories in Communication

[A] strange and incongruous phenomenon exists in the social sciences. Explanations do not admit of causal relationships. Yet such explanations seem somehow to appear to be causal.[1]
—B. AUBREY FISHER

Throughout their history, the social and behavioral sciences have followed in the footsteps of their natural science counterparts. Many of their research methods are modeled after those used in the natural sciences. The social sciences have spent a considerable amount of time searching for causal mechanisms that pertain to social phenomena. In fact, some scholars argue that this approach is perhaps the oldest and most frequently employed perspective in communication, but it is not without controversy because many scholars within the communication field eschew the causal mechanism approach and logical positivism.[2]

This chapter will outline the causal process perspective as it relates to communication. In doing so, this chapter is divided into two major sections, including an outline of the basic assumptions of the approach as they apply to communication, and a discussion of several representative causal process theories in communication, including (a) The Yale studies of attitude change, (b) Byrne's attraction paradigm, (c) uncertainty reduction theory, (d) nonverbal expectancy violation theory, (e) trait approaches, and (f) the biosocial approach.

Assumptions of Causal Process Theories in Communication

In Chapter 6 a law was conceptually defined as a statement that expresses a universally invariant relationship between two or more objects and/or events. Theoretically, laws transcend time and space. If one strictly adheres to the notion that a law prescribes absolute universal invariant phenomena then there are probably no pure laws in the social sciences

163

or communication.[3] Instead, most communication theorists seek to find causal mechanisms in communication processes and behavior. Causal mechanisms, unlike pure laws, prescribe with some degree of probability, rather than absolute certainty, that given a certain set of conditions some communicative behavior will recur on a regular basis.

Although the set of laws in communication may be empty for now, not too long ago Gerald Miller formulated his own definition of a law specifically for communication theorists. He defined a law as a statement that describes the "ways in which specified objects will behave in specified environments."[4] This definition deserves close examination. The key phrases are: (a) "specified objects," (b) "specified environments," and (c) "will behave." Because social communicative phenomena are so much more dynamic than natural phenomena, communication theorists must be very careful and precise in formulating law-like statements. In order to accurately outline the boundary conditions under which laws operate, communication laws will have to be much more specific than natural laws. In some cases, communication laws may have to be so detailed and specific as to lose their generalizability, and hence their utility to the scientist. This is one reason why communication theorists try to identify causal mechanisms rather than laws.

To illustrate this point Gerald Miller compared a well-known natural law, "If water is heated to a temperature of 212 degrees Fahrenheit, it will boil," with a hypothetical communication law, "If a source receives immediate feedback from a receiver then the source will transmit an accurate message." In this comparison, the specified object under examination for the natural scientist is "water." Note that this poses no significant problem for the natural scientist. Water is composed of two parts hydrogen and one part oxygen. Few theorists would quarrel over this definition. For the communication theorist, the specified object is "source." In communication, a source is typically defined as a person sending a message. Few communication theorists would disagree over this general definition, but some might. Sources can differ in many ways; some of which could invalidate the hypothetical law. For example, not just any source receiving immediate feedback from a receiver will transmit an accurate message. Some sources may have conditions (e.g., deafness or blindness) that may prohibit their ability to process immediate feedback. In such cases the communication law might not apply.

Another problem faced by both the natural and social scientist is to specify the environment in which the law operates. With the natural law, "at 212 degrees Fahrenheit" represents a precise environmental condition. Not only is this environmental condition easy to satisfy, but natural scientists have at their disposal standardized instrumentation (i.e., thermometers) to accurately assess environmental conditions. In the communication example, the specified environment is "immediate feedback." Exactly how a communication theorist might measure "immediate feedback" is uncertain. There are no standardized instruments analogous to the thermometer to measure or quantify "immediate feedback." For example, just how fast is immediate? Two seconds after the message has been sent? Three, four, or five seconds? Many communication scholars maintain that in any communicative exchange feedback occurs spontaneously; that is, people send and receive messages simultaneously. Hence, it appears that the communication law may be subject to individual interpretations as to what constitutes "immediate feedback."

Finally, the notion of "will behave" must be considered. In the case of the well-known natural law, "boiling" designates the water's reaction to a temperature of 212 degrees. Few scientists quarrel over whether water is or is not boiling. The process of liquid transforming to gas is called vaporization. With the communication law, the behavior is "transmit an accurate message." Again, the communication theorist is faced with the problem of defining and measuring "accuracy." A rather famous cliché in the communication field is that "the message sent is not the message received." This seemingly axiomatic statement illustrates the difficulty confronting the communication scientist who attempts to somehow quantify "accuracy."

The problems articulated in the above comparison of natural and social laws are minor in scope to the fact that by definition, communication itself is dynamic. Recall from Chapter 1 that a dynamic process is one that continually develops; that is, it is in a constant state of development and is never the same from one moment to the next. When one person sends a message to another person both are forever changed. Communication is irreversible. In some respects this means that any law, however accurate and specific, may only apply once. The natural scientist need not worry about the dynamic state of water. Water remains relatively stable; that is, two parts hydrogen and one part oxygen. Even after the theorist boils the water and allows it to cool down, the water remains essentially unchanged.

Advocates of the causal process perspective understand that social phenomena are not universally invariant and that the underlying structure of a causal mechanism must be stated in probabilistic rather than absolute conditional terms. For example, rather than stating "If a source receives immediate feedback from a receiver then the source will transmit an accurate message" a causal mechanism could be stated such that "given Boundary Condition 1, Boundary Condition 2, and Boundary Condition 3, if a particular source of Kind Y receives immediate feedback of Type X from a receiver, then the source is more likely to transmit a message that is more accurate than if the immediate feedback is not sent." Note the probabilistic terminology used in the statement; that is, the words "more likely" and "more accurate." The communication theorist must specify the conditions and the frequency with which the causal mechanism applies.

Although communication theorists might find it difficult to specify the exact conditions under which a causal mechanism operates, this does not render the lawlike statement theoretically useless. Hence the statement "If a source receives immediate feedback from a receiver then the source will transmit an accurate message" is no less useful because it lacks empirical verification. The fundamental principles underlying the causal mechanism are theoretically valid. Causal mechanisms in the natural sciences are subject to the same kinds of problems. Newton's law of gravitational force and inert mass, for example, was dramatically confirmed hundreds of years after its conception when astronauts landed on the moon and empirically tested the law under ideal naturally occurring environmental conditions (i.e., a pure vacuum). Although it took a very long time to verify, theorists used the laws and applied the principles under which it operated for hundreds of years.

That the causal process approach poses some problems for the communication theorist is not reason enough to abandon it. Through repeated observations via the hypothetico-deductive method described in Chapter 6, the theorist will eventually be able to determine the probability of a certain event's outcome and be able to explain and predict it. Thus, in the communication example presented above, we can explain why certain messages are more accurate than others; that is, because the source has received immediate feedback. The causal process theorist must always be conscious, however, of the fact that there may be other factors influencing the accuracy of a message.

Causal Process Based Communication Theories

When looking through communication textbooks and journals, very rarely will you come across a study or theory labeled as a logical positivist or a covering law theory. Communication theorists are often reluctant to identify themselves as logical positivists in search of covering laws or causal mechanisms because there is a stigma attached to anyone conducting research within those approaches.[5] Ironically, however, some of the most productive research programs in contemporary communication theory are founded in a logical positivist, covering law, or causal mechanism based perspective. The following sections outline several of these approaches.

The Yale Studies of Attitude Change

In their classic book titled *Communication and Persuasion,* Carl Hovland, Irving Janis, and Harold Kelley presented one of the first contemporary approaches to communication phenomena that can be classified as a causal mechanism approach using the logical positivist hypothetico-deductive method.[6] Ironically, none of these scholars were trained in communication. They were teaching in the psychology department at Yale University.

Hovland and his associates were interested in uncovering the conditions under which individuals are most susceptible to the persuasive messages of others. They deduced specific hypotheses (i.e., hypothetico-deductive) regarding communication and persuasion. They then tested their predictions within strictly controlled experimental conditions. They write:

> *The first experiment to test a general hypothesis is capable only of showing that the hypothesis holds true under the conditions represented in the experiment. It is necessary to carry out further investigations of the same hypothesis under carefully selected conditions, assigning different values to the supposedly irrelevant factors. Only in this way can one ultimately determine whether or not the hypothesis is a valid generalization and, if so, whether it requires specifications of limiting conditions.*[7]

Sometimes called the Yale chain of response model, this theory argued that a response to a persuasive message can be conceived as a chain of responses: (a) attention to the persuasive message, (b) comprehension of the message, (c) acceptance of, or yielding to what is comprehended, (d) retention, or memory of the message, and (e) action, consistent with that recommended in the message.[8] Attention, comprehension, acceptance, and memory serve as antecedent conditions to action.

The Yale theorists focused much of their attention on factors that affected the acceptance of the message rather than the other four areas. In their subsequent investigations, Hovland and his associates focused on "Who says what to whom with what effect?"[9] They argued that many variables influence the acceptance of a persuasive message including (a) the source of the persuasive message, (b) the content of the persuasive message, (c) the channels used to send the persuasive message, and (d) the receiver of the persuasive message.

The Source: Who Says It

The source of a particular persuasive message is a very important determinant in whether or not a persuasive message is effective. Most of the research in this area has focused on source credibility.[10] Aristotle viewed ethos as the most important source characteristic in persuasion.[11] Credibility is typically defined as the attitudes or perceptions held by receivers about sources.

Dozens of studies have been conducted in the area of credibility and most conclude that the two fundamental components of credibility include expertise and trustworthiness. In other words, a source is perceived as credible to the extent that he or she is perceived as an expert and trustworthy. The general conclusion regarding credibility and persuasion is that messages are more persuasive if sent by credible sources.[12] Subsequent work on credibility by Hovland and Weiss indicated that credibility has little effect on the immediate comprehension or delayed retention of message information but has a large effect on acceptance and attitude change.[13] In another study, Kelman and Hovland found that the effects of high credibility on attitude change are very short-lived. They report that, over time, receivers dissociate a message from its source. Hence, credibility seems to effect attitude change but only for a limited time.[14] Though the Yale theorists never expressed their theory in lawlike statements, credibility can be seen as one causal mechanism by which receivers become persuaded.

Since the early work of the Yale theorists, many studies have been done that investigate other factors associated with sources. Though the researchers conducting these studies may not necessarily consider themselves proponents of logical positivism, their research certainly follows in the footsteps of Hovland and his associates. For example, several studies have found that source similarity enhances persuasion.[15] Cody and Bettinghaus argue that sources of higher status are more persuasive.[16] Finally, many researchers have found a positive relationship between physical attractiveness and persuasiveness.[17]

The Message: What Is Said

The content of a persuasive message is a critical component in the Yale chain of response model. The Yale theorists focused specifically on rational and emotional appeals within messages. Rational appeals are statements that appeal to logic and reasoning and they might include the number of arguments presented, the amount of evidence included, and the frequency of exposure. Emotional appeals are those message aspects that arouse the affective state of the receiver such as humor, guilt, or fear.

Much of the early work of Hovland and the Yale theorists focused on fear as a drive to attitude change. Fear appeals are messages that literally try to scare a receiver into compliance. A typical fear appeal attempts to scare people by threatening harmful consequences for failing to adopt a persuader's recommendation. Antidrug commercials, for example, frequently use fear appeals in their attempt to stop people from abusing drugs (e.g., "If you use drugs you will die; don't use drugs"). Fear acts as an emotional drive that motivates people to act in order to reduce the unpleasant side effects brought on by fear. The reduction of unpleasant side effects, not the fear itself, leads to attitude or behavior change. The behaviors in which one engages become learned responses to the fear appeal. Hence, if people are fearful of dying, then they will develop a behavioral pattern that avoids drug abuse. The acceptance of the persuasive message occurs when fear is aroused and subsequently reduced. Fear must not get too high, however, because people tend to develop defensive reactions and avoid the message since it creates too much discomfort.[18]

Based on the work of Hovland and his associates, other researchers focused their attention on rational rather than emotional responses to fear appeals. Leventhal in his "parallel process model" argued that learned behaviors associated with fear appeals originate from cognitive attempts to control the danger, not from emotional attempts to control the fear. He asserted that if people think about the threatening message and enact behaviors to avoid the danger they are engaging in "danger control processes." On the other hand, if people react to their feelings of fear and engage in denial behaviors, they are engaging in "fear control processes."[19]

Rogers extended Leventhal's work and advocated a theory called the protection motivation theory in which he argued that behaviors designed to control the danger of a fear appeal are a result of (a) one's perceived vulnerability to the danger, (b) the magnitude of the noxiousness in the appeal, (c) the perception that the recommended actions to alleviate the danger are effective, and (d) the perception that one has the ability to engage in the prescribed behavior.[20]

Although fear appeals and their explanations have been the focus of hundreds of studies over the past forty years, the results have been inconsistent and generally contradictory. Some studies indicate that as threat or fear arousal increase so does message acceptance; that is, there is a positive linear relationship between fear and persuasion. Other scholars have found that threat or fear arousal interacted with other variables (e.g., self-esteem, anxiety, etc.) to positively influence one's acceptance of the persuasive message. For example, individuals with high self-esteem seem to be more susceptible to fear appeals than individuals with moderate or low self-esteem. A third group of scholars found that as threat increased, the acceptance of the persuasive message decreased. In these studies, individuals exposed to threats did the opposite of what was advocated. This is typically called a "boomerang" effect.[21]

Subsequent research on fear appeals indicates that moderate levels of fear produce the greatest attitude or behavioral change. High fear appeals tend to produce an avoidance effect on the part of the receiver; that is, the threat is so real and terrifying that the receiver avoids thinking about it. Low fear appeals, on the other hand, do not produce enough emotional tension.[22] Given the results of these studies one could posit that moderate fear appeals are a causal mechanism that increases the persuasiveness of a message.

Message Organization.   The effectiveness of a persuasive message depends not only on motivational appeals but also on the organization of the arguments presented. For example, what are the effects of explicitly stating one's conclusion or leaving the conclusion implicit? Should a persuasive speaker present only those arguments favoring the recommended conclusion or should arguments opposed to the position be advocated? If both sides are presented, which side should be presented first?

An experiment by Hovland and Mandell systematically studied the relative effectiveness of persuasive communications that were identical in every way except that in one instance the receiver drew his or her own conclusion and in the other case the conclusion was explicit. Their findings revealed that almost twice as many receivers changed their opinions in the direction advocated by the communicator when the conclusion was explicitly drawn as when it was left to the audience.[23] The causal mechanism here is that explicitly drawn conclusions are more persuasive than implicitly drawn conclusions.

Message Sidedness.　One of the first questions investigated by Hovland and his Yale associates was the comparative effectiveness of one- versus two-sided messages. A one-sided message occurs when persuaders present arguments favoring their position without reference to any opposing viewpoints. A two-sided message occurs when persuaders present arguments in favor of their viewpoint and the opposition. Hovland, Lumsdaine, and Sheffield conducted the first test of one-sided and two-sided messages and found that in some cases, a one-sided approach was preferable to a two-sided approach, especially in cases where the audience was favorable to the persuader's position. In cases where the audience is hostile toward the persuader, a two-sided approach is preferable. In addition, they found that two-sided messages are preferable for intelligent or well-educated audiences and that one-sided messages are preferable for less intelligent or less educated audiences.[24]

Recently there has been an upsurge in the amount of research examining the persuasiveness of one- versus two-sided approaches. Much of this research indicates that two-sided messages with counterarguments are more effective than one-sided messages, both in immediate effects on persuasion and in immunizing the audience against future arguments favoring the opposition.[25] Hence, in most cases, two-sided messages are causal mechanisms.

The Channel: How the Message Is Sent
The third link in the Yale response chain is the channel of the persuasive message. Communication channels refer to the human senses that enable humans to send and receive messages; that is, via sight, sound, touch, taste, and smell. The two most frequently used channels in human communication are sight and sound.[26] Hovland and his associates did little work with channel variables themselves but work by other researchers indicates that noise in the channel and the choice of medium affect the processing of persuasive messages.

Channel Noise.　Noise is typically referred to as any distraction that competes with a message. Television or radio static are good examples of channel noise. Research in this area indicates that while noise accompanying a persuasive message generally decreases comprehension of the message, it increases the attention paid to the message. In addition, noise often increases immediate acceptance of the message because it inhibits counterarguments.[27] One should be careful with noise, however, because it may also decrease the generation of supportive arguments and generally has little effect on long-term change. Given these contradictory findings, it is too early to formulate any causal mechanism regarding noise and persuasiveness.

Choice of Medium.　The choice of medium has an important impact on the acceptance of a persuasive message. For the most part, research shows that the use of multiple channels produces more attitude change than the use of single channels. Specifically, persuasive messages that implement sight and sound are more persuasive than messages implementing only sound. Yet, auditory messages seem to be more persuasive than printed ones. Research also indicates that message content and audience characteristics are key factors related to the use of multiple channels. Variables such as message complexity, redundancy, and length interact with the effect of multiple channels. Audience characteristics such as size, education, interest, and initial attitude and familiarity with the topic also interact with the acceptance of persuasive messages.[28]

The Receiver: To Whom What Is Said

The fourth critical ingredient in the Yale chain of response model is the receiver of the persuasive message. As Smith argues, "The individual characteristics of message recipients exert a profound influence on how they process information."[29] The two receiver characteristics studied by Hovland and his Yale associates were group membership and personality.

Group Membership.   People belong to many groups and tend to use groups as a guide for their attitudes and behaviors. The underlying assumption of the Yale theorists was that there is a positive association between group membership and the development of attitudes and behaviors that are normative or characteristic of that group.[30]

Their findings indicate that those group members who place a high value upon the group are less influenced by a persuasive communication that is contrary to the group's norms than those group members who place a low value on group membership. In addition, they found that group members with high status within the group are highly resistant to persuasive messages contrary to the norms of the groups.

Personality.   The Yale theorists recognized that while individuals are influenced by their group membership, reality can be experienced in different ways by different people and hence the effects of a persuasive message are somewhat dependent upon unique characteristics of the individual—that is, one's personality. Hovland and his associates focused specifically on those personality dispositions independent of the subject matter of the communication. These variables included intelligence, measures of self-esteem (i.e., social inadequacy, inhibition of aggression, and depression), aggressiveness, social withdrawal, and indices of acute psychoneuroses (i.e., anxiety, obsessional symptoms). Their results are mixed. They found persons of high intelligence to be more influenced than persons of low intelligence when exposed to logical arguments but less influenced than persons of low intelligence when exposed to messages with unsupported generalities or false illogical arguments. They found feelings of social inadequacy, inhibition of aggression, and depression to be associated with high persuasibility (i.e., people with high self-esteem are less susceptible to persuasion). They found individuals with persistent aggressiveness towards others to be more resistant than those with less than average amounts of aggressiveness. They found individuals with social withdrawal tendencies to be resistant to persuasion. Finally, they found that anxiety-ridden individuals were more susceptible as were those with obsessional symptoms (i.e., inability to get rid of some unimportant idea which comes to mind over and over again and a constant need to make up rules of self-control so as to be sure to do the right things at the right time).[31]

Subsequent work related to personality has investigated many other personality traits with mixed results, including dogmatism, Machiavellianism, authoritarianism, ego-involvement, communication apprehension, and cognitive complexity.

CASE STUDY 7   Advertising and the Yale Studies of Attitude Change

Key Term

Fear Appeals

The results of the Yale Studies of Attitude Change can be very useful for persons or organizations whose purpose is to create persuasive messages. The survival of advertising agencies, for example, depends on their ability to invent messages so appealing that consumers will be persuaded to buy the product they advertise. Advertisers are well advised to take stock in the Yale Studies. In this case study, we will see how advertisements apply some of the variables studied by Hovland and his associates, in this case, fear appeals.

Fear Appeals

Fear appeals are those messages that attempt to frighten people by describing the noxious things that will happen to them if they do not comply with the messages' recommendation. One conclusion from the Yale Studies is that moderate fear appeals are more persuasive than either high or low fear appeals. Too high a fear produces an avoidance reaction whereas too low a fear garners little attention. The ad below has a moderate fear appeal.

If you *don't* have a Will...	If you *do* have a Will
Read this:	*Read this:*
Accidents and death can strike any of us at any time regardless of our age. And should it happen before we've written a Will or living trust our loved ones will inherit a big financial mess—regardless of how little our estate may be. First, the courts will step in to take control of your savings, property, all your assets and debts. Probate can slice up to 10% or so from your estate. Next, the court will appoint an administrator to manage affairs and pay off creditors. They generally get up to 5% of your estate in fees a year! Finally, after months or years, the court decides who shares and gets your home, car, bank account and everything else in your estate—according to their formulas rather than your wishes. Sound horrible? It's a living nightmare for your family. All because you put off writing a simple legal document. What can the average wage earner do to avoid such a disaster? Plenty! We have shown hundreds of thousands of people just like you how to avoid huge probate settlement fees by setting up their own legal living trust. It's simple.	Did you know that having only a Will may be one of the biggest finanacial mistakes we can make? It's true. Because a Will doesn't protect our loved ones against paying huge fees to probate even the smallest estate. Probating a Will can slice away up to 10% from your estate and take months or years before your heirs get one penny. Never forget that probate lawyer and executor fees—usually 4% to 6% are paid before your heirs receive their inheritance. That can take a huge amount out of even the smallest estate when attorneys charge from $60.00 to $150.00 an hour or more. Look what happened to Simon Morris's $77,500 estate. Before his widow could receive it, the probate process grabbed $9,375. The pity of it is that the Morris's could have avoided the high cost of sharing their estate by using a revocable living trust. Unlike a Will, a living trust passes every cent on to your loved ones without delay—and without going through the courts or attorneys. We have shown hundreds of thousands of people just like you how to set up your own legal living trust. Read on to save thousands.

CASE STUDY 7   *Continued*

How a Living Trust Saves You Thousands

A living trust has been praised by our nation's leading financial planners and reported in publications such as The Wall Street Journal, Money Magazine, Business Week, Kiplinger's Changing Times and others because:

• It eliminates costly, time-consuming probate and legal fees. The estate goes at once to whomever you name.

• You can name yourself as trustee in most cases, and your spouse or someone else as co-trustee. And you can change trustees at any time.

• A living trust is revocable. You can change your mind at any time about who shares your estate.

• Unlike a Will where your estate is a public record for anyone to see, a living trust is secret.

• Your family suffers no settlement delays—assets are transferred at once without going through court.

If you think a living trust is only for the rich you couldn't be more wrong. It's not only for millionaires. Actually, the small estate saves more on a percentage basis than the large one.

And you can save even more because we have shown hundreds of thousands of people just like you how to set up a living trust. You can do it with the DSA Living Trust Kit.

The DSA Trust Kit was developed after much research with a team of legal scholars and practicing attorneys. Using easy-to-understand English and easy-to-follow illustrated forms it shows you how to set up your own legal living trust.

You can custom-tailor a legal trust to meet all your special personal wishes to heirs and bequests to charities, etc. As Dale Eklund of Virginia writes: "If my father-in-law had only taken the time to look into a living trust we could have saved time and money."

Though DSA's exlusive Living Trust Kit will save your heirs thousands of dollars later on—we have kept the price especially low so everyone can benefit from it. You will find it so invaluable that we insist you use it on a 90-Day No Risk Trial.

To get your complete Kit simply print your name and address and the words "living trust" on a plain piece of paper. Send it along with your check or money order in the amount of $9.95 plus $2 handling or charge to your VISA/MasterCard by including account number and expiration date to: DSA Financial Publishing Corp., 708 - 12th Street N.W., Dept. W0000, Canton, Ohio 44703. For even faster service, VISA/MasterCard or C.O.D., call toll free 1-800-757-7444, Ext. W0000.

Want to save even more? Do a favor for a relative or close friend and order a second Kit. That's 2 for only $20 postpaid. Use your Kit for 90 risk-free days. Show it to your lawyer or advisor. If not 100% delighted—don't keep it. Simply tear off the cover and send half of it back for a full refund. Fair enough?

A living trust is too important to put off another day... For your family's future well-being order the DSA Kit by phone or mail now!

The fear appeal in the DSA Living Trust Kit advertisement appears early. The facts following the statements "If you *don't* have a Will..." and "If you *do* have a Will..." outline the negative consequences that may confront those persons without living trusts. For example, without a will the courts will intrude and take control of your savings, property, and all of your assets. With a will lawyers and executors may take as much as 4 to 6 percent. As the ad states, "Sound horrible? It's a living nightmare...." Of course, to prevent these horrible outcomes, one should adopt the message's recommendation of buying a kit designed to teach you how to compose a living trust. By doing so, receivers can eliminate the fear of all of the horrible things happening to them. As the ad states, "A Living Trust Saves You Thousands."

Interpersonal Attraction

Issues of interpersonal attraction permeate the human condition, particularly as they relate to the development and maintenance of human relationships. The importance of who is attracted to whom cannot be exaggerated since each of us owes our very existence to the attraction that once existed between a man and a woman.[32] Scholars in communication have long been interested in the mysteries surrounding our feelings of attraction to others. As Berscheid notes:

> *an understanding of attraction processes has been vital because human life is conceived, lived, and terminated within social relationships, and thus most human behavior takes place within a social context. The ultimate understanding of human behavior requires, therefore, recognition and understanding of the role of this context, which, in turn, is saturated with the causes and consequences of interpersonal attraction. Accordingly, attempts to identify the laws of attraction are as old as psychology itself.[33]*

Theories of interpersonal attraction are very important for the communication scholar because judgments about another person's attractiveness are made continuously throughout the initiation, maintenance, and termination of relationships.[34] Why we initiate or terminate communication with others is, in many cases, strongly influenced, perhaps even determined, by how attracted we are to that other person. A simple law here is that we tend to interact more frequently with those to whom we are attracted and less frequently with those to whom we are not attracted.

Many communication scholars who study attraction base their work on the pioneering work of Donn Byrne and his associates. Byrne's goal was to discover the interpersonal determinants of attraction and to conduct experimental research to establish a causal relationship between attitudinal similarity and interpersonal attraction. Byrne's basic premise was that as attitudinal similarity increases, attraction increases.[35]

Byrne and his associates were careful to point out that it is not the sheer number of similar attitudes between people that determines attraction but the proportion of similar attitudes. For example, you should like, or be attracted to, the person who agrees with you on four issues and disagrees on none ($\frac{4}{4}$ = 100 percent similar) more than the person who agrees on eight issues but disagrees on four ($\frac{8}{12}$ = 67 percent similar) because the proportion of similar attitudes is higher in the first case. Through their research they formulated a tentative law of attraction, which states that attraction toward another is a positive linear function of proportion of similar attitudes. This linear function has been demonstrated numerous times and is so consistent that the degree of attraction can be calculated. Figure 7.1 on page 174 presents a graph demonstrating the linear function and the formula for calculating attraction.

In using the above formula, Byrne argued that attraction scores can range from 2 to 14. Thus, if you know that two strangers, Tom and Bill, agree on eight out of ten issues (80 percent similar), then using the above formula, you would calculate $.80 \times 5.44 + 6.62 = 10.97$ or rounded to 11. On a scale of 2 to 14, this would probably be considered a rather high attraction score. Hence, you could predict that Tom and Bill would be attracted to each other.

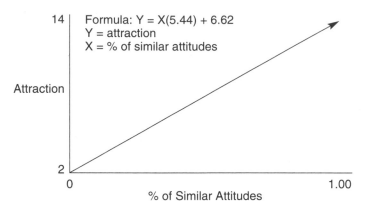

FIGURE 7.1 Byrne's Law of Attraction

Byrne, D., & Nelson, D. (1965). "Attraction as a Linear Function of a Proportion of Positive Reinforcements," *Journal of Personality and Social Psychology, 1,* 659–663.

Though Byrne's law of attraction is very useful in predicting how attracted people will be towards each other, some cautions need to be presented. First, knowledge of similarity on a limited number of topics does not always predict attraction because any two people may disagree on hundreds of other issues. Second, besides attitudinal similarity, there are many other factors associated with attraction, including proximity, appearance, and the number of personal rewards we perceive as available from another person. Third, Byrne's research was conducted in carefully controlled laboratory settings which may not be 100 percent representative of the real world.

Uncertainty Reduction Theory

One of the most representative theories of the hypothetico-deductive, causal process approach is Berger and Calabrese's theory of initial interactions or what has become known as uncertainty reduction theory (URT).[36] This theory, in which uncertainty is the causal mechanism for communication behaviors, focuses on the initial phases of interaction between strangers and is guided by the assumption that relationships develop through a series of three stages. The first stage is called the entry stage, during which the communication behaviors of the interactants are determined by a set of communication rules or norms. For example, strangers typically engage in more polite forms of communication during initial interactions (e.g., saying "please"). The second phase is called the personal phase, during which the interactants communicate about their attitudes, dispositions, motives, and values. This phase is typically reserved for those people who have had repeated interactions with one another. The final phase is called the exit phase, during which the interactants discuss whether the relationship will continue or dissolve. Theoretically, some couples will never reach this phase.

Although Berger and Calabrese outline three phases of relational development, their initial theory focuses specifically on the entry phase. The major premise guiding this theory is that when strangers meet, their primary goal is to reduce uncertainty and/or to increase the predictability about the behavior of both themselves and the other.

Uncertainty is conceptualized as both a proactive and retroactive process. Individuals proactively reduce uncertainty when they weigh alternative behavioral options prior to interacting with another. That is, they attempt to figure out ways the other might interact and then select their own behavioral alternatives based on this prediction. Retroactively, uncertainty is reduced by attempting to explain behavior after it has been enacted.

Based on the assumptions outlined above, Berger and Calabrese originally posited seven axioms and twenty-one theorems. Recall that an axiom is a statement generally accepted as valid; that is, an established principle or law of science, art, etc. The logic of the hypothetico-deductive approach begins with axiomatic statements. In the case of Berger and Calabrese's theory, the axioms represent assumed causal relationships between uncertainty and communication. The following list outlines the original seven axioms of the theory.[37]

Seven Axioms of Uncertainty Reduction Theory

Axiom 1: Given the high level of uncertainty present at the onset of the entry phase, as the amount of verbal communication between strangers increases, the level of uncertainty for each interactant in the relationship will decrease. As uncertainty is further reduced, the amount of verbal communication will increase.

Axiom 2: As nonverbal affiliative expressiveness increases, uncertainty levels will decrease in an initial interaction situation. In addition, decreases in uncertainty level will cause increases in nonverbal affiliative expressiveness.

Axiom 3: High levels of uncertainty cause increases in information-seeking behavior. As uncertainty levels decline, information-seeking behavior decreases.

Axiom 4: High levels of uncertainty in a relationship cause decreases in the intimacy level of communication content. Low levels of uncertainty produce high levels of intimacy.

Axiom 5: High levels of uncertainty produce high rates of reciprocity. Low levels of uncertainty produce low reciprocity rates.

Axiom 6: Similarities between persons reduce uncertainty, while dissimilarities produce increases in uncertainty.

Axiom 7: Increases in uncertainty level produce decreases in liking; decreases in uncertainty level produce increases in liking.

Axioms 1 and 2 deal with the quantity of verbal and nonverbal communication and its effect on uncertainty; that is, as communication increases, uncertainty decreases. Nonverbal affiliative expressiveness refers to one's duration of eye contact, pleasantness of vocal expressions, head nods per minute, head and arm gestures per minute, and closer physical distance between interactants. Axiom 3 is closely related to the first two insofar as information-seeking behavior is defined as the number of questions asked by each interactant.

Axiom 4 refers not to the quantity of communication, as in the case of the preceding axioms, but the quality of communication. In this case, the lower the level of uncertainty the more intimate the communication. Intimate communication might be defined as interaction based on issues related to the interactants' attitudes, beliefs, motivations, and dispositions.

Axioms 5, 6, and 7 each deal with separate concepts and uncertainty. Axiom 5 deals with the concept of communication reciprocity, or the mutual exchange of information between interactants. Berger and Calabrese contend that at early stages in a relationship, the interactants are compelled to ask for and give the same kinds of information at the same rate in order that neither person gains information power over the other. As the relationship develops, and uncertainty is reduced, there is less felt need to reciprocate since the interactants are more comfortable with the relationship. To be sure, however, symmetrical reciprocity is essential if the relationship is to remain healthy, it just need not be immediate.

Axiom 6 centers around the notion of similarity. As demonstrated by Bryne and his law of attraction, similarity leads to interpersonal attraction. Berger and Calabrese argue that as similarity increases, uncertainty decreases and vice versa. As Berger and Calabrese state, "Why do disagreements along attitude dimensions tend to raise uncertainty? After all, if a person holds an opinion opposed to mine, does that not reduce my uncertainty about him?" Their answer is that knowledge of dissimilar attitudes leads to a greater number of attributions about why another may hold such attitudes, thus increasing uncertainty about the other.

Finally, Axiom 7 focuses on the concept of liking. This axiom is based on research that indicates a positive relationship between similarity and liking; that is, the more similar two people are, the more they tend to like each other. Thus, as similarity decreases uncertainty, then it is likely to increase liking simultaneously.

Based on the theory's seven axioms, Berger and Calabrese deduced twenty-one theorems. Theorems are statements of covariation between the variables specified in the axioms. Unlike an axiom, a theorem does not postulate causal links between variables and hence it is not stated in the conditional "if-then" form of a lawlike statement. The following list presents the twenty-one theorems of the theory.[38]

Twenty-One Theorems of Uncertainty Reduction Theory

Theorem 1: Amount of verbal communication and nonverbal affiliative expressiveness are positively related.

Theorem 2: Amount of communication and intimacy level of communication are positively related.

Theorem 3: Amount of communication and information-seeking behavior are inversely related.

Theorem 4: Amount of communication and reciprocity rate are inversely related.

Theorem 5: Amount of communication and liking are positively related.

Theorem 6: Amount of communication and similarity are positively related.

Theorem 7: Nonverbal affilitative expressiveness and intimacy level of communication content are positively related.

Theorem 8: Nonverbal affilitative expressiveness and information seeking are inversely related.

Theorem 9: Nonverbal affilitative expressiveness and reciprocity rate are inversely related.

Theorem 10: Nonverbal affilitative expressiveness and liking are positively related.

Theorem 11: Nonverbal affilitative expressiveness and similarity are positively related.

Theorem 12: Intimacy level of communication content and information seeking are inversely related.

Theorem 13: Intimacy level of communication content and reciprocity rate are inversely related.

Theorem 14: Intimacy level of communication content and liking are positively related.

Theorem 15: Intimacy level of communication content and similarity are positively related.

Theorem 16: Information-seeking and reciprocity rate are positively related.

Theorem 17: Information-seeking and liking are negatively related.

Theorem 18: Information-seeking and similarity are negatively related.

Theorem 19: Reciprocity rate and liking are negatively related.

Theorem 20: Reciprocity rate and similarity are negatively related.

Theorem 21: Similarity and liking are positively related.

As the list shows, Theorems 1 through 6 focus on the quantity of communication and its relationship with nonverbal affiliative expressiveness, intimacy level of communication, information-seeking behavior, reciprocity rate, liking, and similarity. Except for information-seeking behavior and reciprocity rate, amount of communication is said to covary positively with nonverbal affiliative expressiveness, intimacy level of communication, liking, and similarity. Positive covariation simply means that as the amount of communication increases, nonverbal affiliative expressiveness, intimacy level of communication, liking, and similarity increase also. In the case of Theorems 3 and 4, reciprocity rate and information-seeking behavior are said to be inversely related. In other words, they covary negatively. This means that as the amount of communication increases, reciprocity rate and information-seeking behavior decrease.

Theorems 7 through 11 deal specifically with nonverbal affiliative expressiveness and its relationship with intimacy level of communication, information-seeking behavior, reciprocity rate, liking, and similarity. The theory posits that as nonverbal affiliative expressiveness increases, so does the intimacy level of communication, liking, and similarity. Conversely, as duration of eye contact, pleasantness of vocal expressions, head nods per minute, head and arm gestures per minute, and closer physical distance increase, reciprocity rate and information-seeking behavior decrease.

Theorems 12 through 15 center on the quality of communication, or, as Berger and Calabrese call it, the level of intimacy of communication. Here they indicate that as interactants communicate on a more intimate level, the information-seeking behavior and reciprocity rate decrease. In addition, as the intimacy level of communication increases, so does liking and similarity.

Theorems 16, 17, and 18 all deal with information-seeking behavior and its positive relationship with reciprocity rate and its negative relationship with liking and similarity. Theorems 19 and 20 indicate that reciprocity rate is negatively related to liking and similarity. Finally, Theorem 21 predicts that similarity and liking are positively related.

Uncertainty Reduction Strategies

In his further work with URT, Berger and some of his colleagues outline several communicative strategies that people use to increase knowledge of another thereby reducing uncertainty. These strategies include (a) passive strategies whereby an individual unobtrusively observes the other in social contexts, (b) active strategies whereby an individual may ask others about the target person or somehow manipulate some aspect of the target's physical or social environment in order to observe how the target responds, and (c) interactive strategies in which the individual interrogates the target, self-discloses to the target, and attempts to detect deception.[39]

Extensions of URT

Since its original inception as an initial interaction theory, Berger and others have modified and refined URT and extended the theory to developed relationships. In addition, several researchers have focused on specific strategies to reduce uncertainty. Still others have examined the relationship between uncertainty and attraction. Most recently, URT has been explored in interethnic, intercultural, small group, and organizational communication contexts.

Based on related research, Berger and Gudykunst added an eighth axiom and seven new theorems to complement the original seven axioms and twenty-one theorems. Axiom 8 reads: "Shared communication networks reduce uncertainty, while lack of shared networks increases uncertainty."[40] This axiom is based on research that indicates that romantic partners who interact more often with their partner's family and friend network experience less uncertainty about their partner than those who do not. Based on this new axiom, seven new theorems were posited and are presented below:[41]

Theorem 22: Shared communication networks and the amount of verbal communication are related positively.

Theorem 23: Shared communication networks and nonverbal affiliative expressiveness are related positively.

Theorem 24: Shared communication networks and information seeking are related inversely.

Theorem 25: Shared communication networks and intimacy level of communication are related positively.

Theorem 26: Shared communication networks and reciprocity rates are related positively.

Theorem 27: Shared communication networks and similarities are related positively.

Theorem 28: Shared communication networks and liking are related positively.

Along with the new axiom and theorems, URT has generated literally dozens of studies. The following list presents a typology of some of the research associated with URT.[42] Not all of the research cited in the list directly supports URT, but much of it does.

Research in Uncertainty Reduction Theory

Initial Formulation and Conceptualization

Berger & Calabrese (1975): First publication of the thirteen Axioms and twenty-one Theorems.

Theory Extensions and Refinements

Berger (1979): Extends URT beyond initial interaction into developed relationships.

Berger (1986): Answers criticism related to URT and extends theory.

Berger & Bradac (1982): Major extension of URT focusing on the nature of language and the acquisition of social knowledge in reducing uncertainty.

Kellermann & Reynolds (1990): Integrates the notion of motivation to reduce uncertainty into the axioms of URT.

Sunnafrank (1986): Challenges the assumptions of URT and argues that positive relational outcomes are the primary concern during initial interactions. Posits alternative predicted outcome value (POV) theory.

Sunnafrank (1990): Tests several competing hypotheses from URT and POV and offers support for POV that uncertainty reduction processes are subservient to outcome maximization goals.

Douglas (1991): Introduces global uncertainty; the concept that strangers' interaction is influenced by their separate conversational histories as well as events and judgments that occur during an initial meeting.

Uncertainty Reduction and Initial Interactions

Clatterback (1979): Develops CLUES scale designed to measure persons' subjective feelings about uncertainty.

Douglas (1984): Presents results that support the proposition that uncertainty is high at the beginning of relationships and is reduced during the entry phase.

Douglas (1990): Supports URT propositions that uncertainty is reduced by disclosure and that attraction increases as uncertainty decreases.

Gardner (1976): Focuses on reciprocity during initial interaction.

Kellermann (1986): Amount of uncertainty experienced is not related to anticipation of future interaction.

Sherbloom & Van Rheenan (1984): Examines the effects of uncertainty on language use.

Uncertainty Reduction in Developed Relationships

Harvey, Wells, & Alverez (1978): Uncertainty is examined as a contributor to relational disintegration.

Parks & Adelman (1983): Focuses on communication networks and uncertainty with romantic partners. Challenges some of the fundamental axioms of URT which leads to major extension of URT and the eighth axiom.

Planalp & Honeycutt (1985): Increased uncertainty produces negative relational consequences.

Planalp, Rutherford, & Honeycutt (1988): Extends earlier study by Planalp & Honeycutt and finds that increases in uncertainty in developed relationships were temporary.

Prisbell & Anderson (1980): Supports axioms related to similarity and uncertainty.

Strategies to Reduce Uncertainty

Berger & Bradac (1982): Outlines active, interactive, and passive strategies for reducing uncertainty.

Berger & Douglas (1981): Investigates self-monitoring and uncertainty reduction.

Douglas (1985): Results reveal that the effects of anticipated interaction are limited.

Douglas (1987): Concludes that anticipated interaction does not affect question-asking strategies.

Berger & Kellermann (1983): Results indicate that about 50 percent of questions asked during initial interaction inquired about demographic and attitudinal information.

Berger, Gardner, Parks, Schulman, & Miller (1976): Outlines three strategies for knowledge generation, including interrogation, self-disclosure, and deception detection.

Uncertainty Reduction in Small Groups

Booth-Butterfield, Booth-Butterfield, & Koester (1988): Study indicates that reducing uncertainty alleviates group tension.

Uncertainty Reduction and Attraction

VanLear & Trujillo (1986): Concludes that uncertainty reduction is a necessary but not sufficient condition for liking.

Douglas (1990): Argues that social attraction and uncertainty are related as predicted by URT.

Uncertainty Reducation and Organizations

Lester (1987): Presents thirteen new axioms of URT as related to organizations.

Kramer (1993): Applies URT to job transfer within organizations.

Uncertainty Reduction and Cultural Differences

Gudykunst (1983): One of the first studies to compare uncertainty reduction between cultures.

Gudykunst (1985): This study reveals that cultural similarity and type of relationship influence uncertainty reduction processes.

Gudykunst, Chua, & Gray (1987): This study focuses on cultural dissimilarity and uncertainty reduction processes.

Gudykunst & Nishida (1984): Reports that frequency of communication predicts uncertainty reduction in individualistic cultures but not in collectivistic cultures.

Gudykunst, Nishida, & Schmidt (1989): Found that cultural variability in individualism-collectivism influences uncertainty reduction in ingroup and outgroup relationships.

Gudykunst, Yang, & Nishida (1985): Tests a model of URT that is generalizable across relationships and cultures.

Sanders, Wiseman, & Matz (1991): Examines uncertainty reduction processes in America and Ghana.

Uncertainty Reduction and Interethnic Relationships

Gudykunst & Hammer (1988): Investigates the impact of relational intimacy in interethnic relationships on uncertainty reduction processes.

Gudykunst, Sodetani, & Sonoda (1987): Suggests that question-asking as a form of uncertainty reduction may be limited to whites.

Sanders & Wiseman (1991): Study reveals that positive nonverbal expressiveness predicts uncertainty reduction for whites, Hispanics, and Asian Americans.

URT remains one of the most representative theories of the laws approach and one of the most researched theories of interpersonal communication. The strength of the theory lies in its clearly articulated axioms and theorems, which allow researchers to easily deduce testable hypotheses. Many of the tests have supported the general axioms of the theory but some have not.

Another strength of the theory is its heuristic value in the scores of studies it has generated. Theorists continue to refine the theory, including Berger himself, in an effort to more fully understand how people interact to reduce uncertainty. URT is a classic example of the dynamic process of theory building.

CASE STUDY 8   Beginning Relationships and Uncertainty Reduction Theory

Key Terms

Uncertainty Reduction

Information-Seeking

Reciprocity

Similarity

Intimacy Level

This case study is an application of uncertainty reduction theory (URT). The case involves a young man and woman who meet for the first time. The young man, Brian Tomus, and woman, Laurie Kohn, are each students attending the same college. Although they may have seen each other before, they have never actually interacted. The scene is

Continued

CASE STUDY 8 *Continued*

a Friday night party given at the residence of a mutual friend. Brian and Laurie are about to interact for the first time. Theoretically, uncertainty is very high. Notice that during the initial phases of their interaction there is a great deal of information-seeking behavior (Axiom 3), reciprocity (Axiom 5), and nonverbal affiliative expressiveness (Axiom 2). Also notice that as the interaction progresses, similarities are revealed that reduce uncertainty (Axiom 6). Toward the end of their interaction the intimacy level of the communication increases (Axiom 4). At the close of their interaction note how much they know about each other (Axiom 1).

Scene: A college party. The room in which the interaction occurs is moderately crowded. Most of the attendees are students at the same college. Music is playing and people seem to be enjoying themselves. Brian and his friend Rob are interacting together as Laurie approaches.

BRIAN: So you think Jim will be suspended? (Laurie approaches)	1
ROB: Yeah. (Notices Laurie approaching) Hey Laurie, what's up?	2
LAURIE: (Smiles) Hi Rob, how ya doin?	3
ROB: Good. Hey Laurie, have you ever met my friend Brian?	4
LAURIE: (Makes eye contact with Brian and smiles) Ah, no, I don't think so. Hi Brian.	5
BRIAN: (Returns the eye contact and smiles) Hi.	6
ROB: (Seems to notice something across the room) Oh—I gotta go. (Exits)	7
BRIAN: (Moves a little closer to Laurie) So, do you go here?	8
LAURIE: (Leans toward Brian) Yeah, do you?	9
BRIAN: Yeah.	10
LAURIE: Are you a senior?	11
BRIAN: Sophomore.	12
LAURIE: Me too. What's your major?	13
BRIAN: Poly sci, what's yours?	14
LAURIE: Psychology.	15
BRIAN: Oh yeah? I was thinking about minoring in psychology. I think it's really cool. (Smiles)	16
LAURIE: Wow, me too. (Smiles) Have you ever had any classes in psych?	17
BRIAN: Yeah, I had 101.	18
LAURIE: Me too! (Touches Brian on his forearm) Did you have Dr. Korkhaven?	19
BRIAN: Yeah, wow, (Laughs) he's sorta weird.	20
LAURIE: I know. He's funny with that way he talks. (Both laughing)	21
BRIAN: Right. (Imitating the psychology professor) "Let's settle down people and begin today's discussion." (Laughs)	22
LAURIE: That's great—it sounds just like him! (Laughs)	23

BRIAN: Thanks (Slight pause)—So where you from? 24

LAURIE: I'm from a suburb outside of Milwaukee, Brookfield, have you ever heard 25
of it? (At this point some other people pass by Brian and Laurie. Brian moves
closer to Laurie.)

BRIAN: I think so. Is it on the west side? 26

LAURIE: Yeah. Where are you from? 27

BRIAN: Chicago area. 28

LAURIE: A lot of people from there go here. 29

BRIAN: Yeah, that makes it easy to get a ride home on breaks and stuff. 30

LAURIE: I'll bet. So . . . what do you like to do? (Smiles inquisitively) I'll bet you 31
study a lot—you seem pretty smart.

BRIAN: I put my time in. But I like to go to parties like this one. Rob and I have 32
known each other for a few years now. I like to snow and water ski. I scuba dive
too. Not around here of course.

LAURIE: Wow, cool. Since you're a poly sci major, what did you think of the pres- 33
ident's speech?

BRIAN: Man, what a jerk he is. 34

LAURIE: Oh, I can't believe it! (Big smile) 35

BRIAN: What? (Looks concerned) 36

LAURIE: You're the first person I've met who thinks that. (Holds his arm) I do too! 37
Are we the only two on campus who know what's going on?

BRIAN: Must be. Wow, so you think he's a jerk, too. That's great. 38

LAURIE: I totally disagree with his policies. 39

BRIAN: Me, too. It just doesn't make sense. 40

LAURIE: Really. 41

Several of the axioms from URT directly apply to the interaction between Laurie and
Brian. Lines 8, 9, 11, 13, 14, 17, 19, 24, 25, 26, 27, 31, 33, 36, and 37 demonstrate information-seeking behavior. As Axiom 3 states, high levels of uncertainty cause increases in information-seeking behavior. If either Laurie or Brian had been interacting with one of their
close friends, the same kind of questions would not be expected. Lines 8, 9, 13, 14, and 24
through 28 represent reciprocity (Axiom 5). Here Laurie and Brian ask each other the very
same questions and respond similarly. In lines 15 through 23 and in lines 33 through 41,
Laurie and Brian discover similarities (Axiom 6) about each other which clearly reduces uncertainty since by the end of their conversation they discuss more intimate topics in lines
31, 32, 37, 39, and 40 (Axiom 4). Nonverbal affiliative behaviors (Axiom 2) increase as
Brian and Laurie discover more about each other. For example, in lines 8 and 9 they move
closer to each other. In lines 16 and 17 and throughout much of the interaction they smile at
each other. In line 19, Laurie actually touches Brian and by line 37 she holds his arm. By
the end of the conversation Brian and Laurie know each other's year in school, major, hometown, hobbies, and even some political beliefs, thereby reducing uncertainty to a certain degree (Axiom 1).

Nonverbal Expectancy Violation Theory

Judee Burgoon and her associates have formalized one of the few theories of nonverbal communication called nonverbal expectancies violation (NEV) theory.[43] This theory, like Berger's uncertainty reduction theory, is rooted in the hypothetico-deductive, logical positivist tradition.

The basic premise of the theory is that people hold expectancies about the nonverbal behaviors of others. Expectancies include cognitive, affective, and instinctive judgments about communicative behaviors that are feasible and appropriate for the particular context and set of interactants. Many expectations are learned and culturally driven. Violations of these expectations produce arousal, which heightens the salience of cognitions about the communicator and behavior. Arousal mediates the violation of the expectation and the subsequent communication behavior. Arousal can be physiological or cognitive and possesses a valence (i.e., positive/negative) and intensity (i.e., low/high) dimension. Following heightened arousal, recipients of violations pay greater attention to those communicative messages pertaining to the nature of the relationship. Arousal also diverts attention away from the ostensive purpose of the interaction and redirects it toward the source of the violation. Burgoon and her colleagues maintain that once a violation has been perceived and arousal is triggered, the recipient evaluates the violation and the violator. Violations initiated by highly attractive sources may be evaluated positively while those initiated by unattractive sources may be negatively evaluated.[44]

Expectancy violations and subsequent arousal are the causal mechanism for communicative behaviors. For example, students have certain expectations about the way their professors behave nonverbally (e.g., dress, gestures, stance). If the professors violate the expectations by dressing unusually or inappropriately, students become aroused (either positively or negatively) and react. The evaluation of the violation can be either positive or negative depending on (a) the evaluation of the communicator (in this case, the teacher), (b) implicit messages associated with the violation, and (c) evaluations of the act itself.

NEV Axioms

In presenting the theory, Burgoon and her colleagues follow the logical positivist, hypothetico-deductive model by (a) outlining several key axioms, (b) deriving a set of propositions, and (c) deducing hypotheses. The axioms of the NEV are presented in the following list.[45]

Axioms of the Nonverbal Expectancies Violation Theory

Axiom 1: Humans have two competing needs, a need for affiliation and a need for personal space (or distance). These two needs cannot be satisfied at once.

Axiom 2: The desire for affiliation may be elicited or magnified by the presence of rewards in the communication context. The rewards may be biological or social.

Axiom 3: The greater the degree to which a person or situation is defined as rewarding, the greater the tendency for others to approach that person or situation; the greater the degree to which a person or situation is defined as punishing, the greater the tendency for others to avoid that person or situation.

Axiom 4: Humans are able to perceive gradations in distance.

Axiom 5: Human interaction patterns including personal space or distance patterns are normative.

Axiom 6: Humans may develop idiosyncratic behavior patterns that differ from the social norms.

Axiom 7: In any communication context, the norms are a function of three classes of factors: (a) characteristics of the interactants, (b) features of the interaction itself, and (c) features of the immediate physical environment.

Axiom 8: Interactants develop expectations about the communication behavior of others. Consequently, they are able to recognize or at least respond differently to normative versus deviant behaviors on the part of others.

Axiom 9: Deviations from expectations have arousal value.

Axiom 10: Interactants make evaluations of others.

Axiom 11: Evaluations are influenced by the degree to which the other is perceived as rewarding such that a positively valued message is only rewarding if the source is highly regarded and a negatively valued message is only punishing if the source is highly regarded.

Burgoon bases Axiom 1 on the literature from anthropology, sociology, and psychology that indicates that humans are a social species that have a biological/survival instinct to be with others of the same kind. Conversely, humans cannot tolerate extended physical contact with or excessive closeness with others; that is, humans have a basic need to insulate themselves from others and a need for privacy. Axiom 2 indicates that affiliation for others is triggered by rewards within a social communicative context. These rewards may be biological (e.g., food, sex, safety) or social (e.g., belonging, esteem, status). Axiom 3 extends Axiom 2 by stating that humans are attracted to rewarding situations and repelled by punishing situations. Axiom 4 simply says that humans have the perceptual ability to discern differences in spatial relationships. We can tell when someone is standing close to or far away from us. Axiom 5 deals with the establishment of normative nonverbal behaviors. Normative behavior, either verbal or nonverbal, is that which follows a regular pattern. For example, the lecture style of your professor is probably consistent day after day; that is, he or she has established a normative way of delivering the material. Many normative behaviors are established by society. In our culture, for example, saying "good-bye" is a normative way of terminating a telephone conversation. Axiom 6 recognizes that even though most of us follow the same normative rules and regulations regarding our verbal and nonverbal behavior, we can develop our own personal style that is different from others'.

Axiom 7 states that norms operate as a function of the interactants, the interaction, and the environment. Characteristics of the interactants might include their sex, age, personality, and race. Characteristics of the interaction itself might include the level of dominance or intimacy. Finally, characteristics of the environment may include the physical features of the setting such as furniture arrangement, lighting, or even the temperature. Axiom 8 deals with the notion of expectancies, a key element of the theory. Burgoon and others argue that during interaction, interactants develop expectancies and preferences about the behaviors of others. These expectancies are anticipations of others' behavior which is perceived to be, at the time, possible, probable, and appropriate for the situation. Typically, expectancies are based on a combination of societal norms and idiosyncrasies of the interactants. For example, students expect that their professors will behave in an appropriate and consistent manner. In certain cases, however, students might expect idiosyncratic deviations from the norms for particular professors (e.g., a certain professor that frequently tells jokes in class). Axiom 9 focuses on two other key ingredients in the theory, violation of expectancies and arousal. Burgoon ascribes to the notion that ostensibly deviant behavior by a source/communicator stimulates arousal in the receiver/communicator. The violation tends to stimulate the receiver/communicator's attention and arouse either adaptive or defensive reactions. If, during one of his or her lectures, for example, your professor were to suddenly barrage the class with profanities, this would serve as a violation of expectancy whereby the class might respond negatively or defensively. If, on the other hand, the same professor were to jump off of the podium and do a series of acrobatic maneuvers, the class may find this violation rather humorous and respond by laughing and applauding (positive adaptive mechanism).

Axiom 10 simply states that people make value judgments about others. Axiom 11, however, extends this notion by specifying how evaluations are made. Burgoon and her associates contend that the first factor influencing the valencing (i.e., the positive or negative evaluation) of a violation is the "communicator reward valence." This refers to how much the violator is perceived as someone with whom it is desirable to interact. Thus, communicator reward valence is based on communicator and relationship characteristics (e.g., age, sex, personality, status, reputation, anticipated future interaction) and interactional behaviors (style, positive feedback).

Communicator reward valence influences how one will evaluate the violation. NEV theory holds that more favorable evaluations will be given when the violation is committed by a high reward person than a low reward person. For example, if someone to whom you are attracted stands very close to you at a party, much closer than is normative, you may interpret this violation positively as a sign of mutual attraction or affiliation. Conversely, however, if someone to whom you are repulsed stands really close to you at a party you may evaluate this violation quite negatively.

Burgoon asserts that positively evaluated violations produce favorable communication patterns and consequences whereas negatively evaluated violations produce unfavorable communication patterns. In addition, Burgoon contends that even extreme violations, if committed by a high reward person, can be evaluated positively and produce reciprocal communication patterns.

Derived from the eleven axioms, Burgoon also outlines thirteen propositions that can be used to posit specific hypotheses. The following list presents these propositions.[46]

Propositions of the Nonverbal Expectancy Violation Theory

Proposition 1: Distancing and personal space expectations are a function of the social norms and the known idiosyncrasies of the interactants.

Proposition 2: The communication outcome of an interaction is a function of the reward value of the initiator, the direction of deviation from expectations, and the amount of deviation.

Proposition 3: Distance can be interpreted as a statement of threat or evaluation from the initiator, such that (a) when distance is equated with the initiator's evaluation of the reactant, closer distances are perceived as more positive regard and farther distances as more negative regard (for distance farther than the threat threshold); (b) when distance is equated with threat, closer distances are perceived as more threatening and farther distances as less threatening (for distances farther than the threat threshold).

Proposition 4: Distances closer than the threat threshold are perceived as punishing because they produce discomfort.

Proposition 5: The size of the threat threshold differs according to the nature of the initiator such that the threat distance becomes smaller as the initiator becomes more rewarding and the threshold may temporarily be nonexistent for highly rewarding interactions.

Proposition 6: Positive communication outcomes result when an interaction is perceived as rewarding and negative when an interaction is perceived as punishing.

Proposition 7: Distances closer than the threat threshold produce negative communication outcomes.

Proposition 8: Rewarding initiators produce positive communication outcomes at closer distances than punishing initiators.

Proposition 9: The closer the deviation from expectations, the more positive the communication outcome when the deviation is committed by a rewarding initiator, up to the point of the threat threshold.

Proposition 10: The farther the deviation from expectations, the more negative the communication outcome when the deviation is committed by a rewarding initiator.

Proposition 11: The closer the deviation, the more negative the communication outcome when the deviation is committed by a punishing initiator.

Proposition 12: A punishing initiator will produce the most positive communication outcome by observing expectations or deviating slightly farther than expectations.

Proposition 13: Extreme far deviations from expectations by a punishing source will produce negative communication outcomes.

Support for NEV Theory

Virtually dozens of studies have been prompted by NEV theory. The propositions outlined above have led Burgoon and others to deduce many specific hypotheses, too numerous to mention here. There are, however, several general conclusions that can be drawn from the accumulated research findings as they relate to the thirteen propositions.[47]

Communicator Rewards Mediate Communication Outcomes

Consistent with Propositions 2 and 6, communicator characteristics such as positive and negative feedback, physical attractiveness, smiling, head nods, task competence, socioeconomic status, purchasing power, and attitudinal similarity have been shown to affect communication outcomes.

Conversational Distance

Consistent with Propositions 3, 5, and 8, many studies have demonstrated that rewarding communicators produce favorable communication outcomes by violating rather than conforming to distance expectancies. In addition, not only does the violation benefit the rewarding communicator alone but also in comparison with other nonviolating communicators. Consistent with Propositions 11, 12, and 13, punishing communicators produce the most favorable communication outcomes with which they conform to others' distance expectancies. Nonrewarding violators are perceived as less attractive, less credible, and less influential than their nonviolating peers.

Violations and Arousal

Consistent with Propositions 4 and 7, distance expectancy violations have been shown to produce physical reactions of discomfort and have been shown to shift attention from the task or topic of conversation. NEV theory was initially designed with an emphasis on nonverbal proxemic violations. Recently the theory has been extended to account for other types of expectancy violations, including conversational involvement, eye gaze, reciprocity and compensation, and interaction outcomes. The most current research refers to this theory as simply expectancy violation theory.[48]

NEV theory, like URT, is a classic representation of the logical positivist, covering laws based approach to nonverbal communication. The strength of the theory lies in its clearly presented axioms and propositions. Many of the hypotheses deduced from the axioms and propositions have been supported empirically by dozens of studies. Please note that while these studies are tests of the theory, their authors may or may not consider themselves laws theorists. To be sure, however, their research stems from a laws-based theory and must be considered as either verifying or falsifying lawlike statements about nonverbal expectancies and communication. NEV theory continues today, nearly twenty years since its original inception, to generate research. To be sure, this represents its heuristic value as well as its stamina as a communication theory.

CASE STUDY 9 Intercultural Relationships and Nonverbal Expectancy Violation Theory

Key Terms

Expectancy

Spatial Violations

Personal Space

Deviation

This case study, an application of nonverbal expectancy violation (NEV) theory, occurs in an intercultural communication context, which involves the same communication dimensions discussed in Chapter 1 but includes the added dimension of cultural differences between the interactants. Communication scholars agree that communication is culture bound and that verbal and nonverbal codes differ significantly from culture to culture. Gudykunst and Kim define intercultural communication as "a transactional, symbolic process involving the attribution of meaning between people from different cultures."[a]

In this case study, Jim and Akira are interacting. Akira, an exchange student from Japan who is spending a semester studying at an American college, was born and raised in Tokyo, Japan. Jim is also a student at the same college and was born and raised in Milwaukee, Wisconsin. We will witness Jim and Akira in two different scenarios. But first, some background information about the nature of Japan and the United States.

Case Study Background Report

The Japanese and U.S. cultures differ significantly. Japan is regarded as a collectivistic, high context culture, while the United States is viewed as an individualistic, low context culture. Collectivistic cultures de-emphasize the role of the individual in society and focus on one's position within social groups—in Japan, individuals are almost exclusively defined that way. Individualistic cultures stress the importance of each person's unique identity and emphasize the individual's goals over group goals with values that serve the self by making the self feel good, distinguished, and independent. Each person is viewed as having a unique set of talents and/or potentials and the translation of potentials into reality is the main purpose in life.[b]

Such an orientation is easily seen in the United States, where, from an early age, children are taught that they are individuals with unique abilities and talents. People are rewarded for being "the best," "the one and only," and "number one" in whatever they do Americans desire to be "outstanding in their field." A well-known cliché in the United States is that "the squeaky wheel gets the grease," meaning that in order to get attention or have your needs met, you must draw attention to yourself.

Unlike individualistic cultural orientations, collectivistic cultures place precedence on group goals and emphasize values that subordinate personal goals for the sake of preserving in-group integrity, interdependence of members, and harmonious relationships. These cultures do not view people as isolated individuals. Group activities are dominant and pervasive. Responsibility is shared and accountability is collective.[c]

Japan has an unofficial motto that reads "Deru kugi wa utareru," or "The protruding nail gets hammered down," which is truly reflective of a collectivistic culture. Children are taught at a young age that their identity is based on their relationship within the group (family or business). Group leadership rather than individual initiative is valued. A new sense of individualism is growing in Japan, however, especially among Japanese youth.[d]

That one or another culture may be more or less "individualistic" or "collectivistic" does not mean that they cannot share similar values related to other things. For example, many cultures value such things as wisdom, broadmindedness, and inner harmony that serve both personal and in-group interests. Cultures that are considered "collectivist" may have values that are collective but that are not those of the *in*-group. For example, equality for all, social justice, preserving the natural environment, and a world at peace are values that serve the larger collectivity beyond the in-group. Hence, individualistic and collectivistic cultures should not be viewed in polar opposition to each other.[e] As mentioned earlier, the United States is considered a low context culture where Japan is regarded as high con-

Continued

CASE STUDY 9 *Continued*

text. Recall that the context is the physical, social, and psychological setting and/or environment in which communication occurs. For example, in your college classroom, the physical context includes the actual geographical location of the room, as well as the walls, desks, color, temperature, and size. The social context of the college classroom includes the role relationships between the interactants, in this case the roles are student and teacher. The psychological context includes the attitudes, dispositions, values, beliefs, and motivations held by the interactants. For example, your dislike for the teacher is a part of the psychological context, as is your teacher's attitude toward you. Context strongly influences communication. Although different cultures may share similar contexts—that is, there are classrooms in Japan and the United States—their interpretation of the context certainly differs.

Cultures can be categorized as high context or low context. A high context culture is one where its members are highly sensitive to the physical, social, and psychological environment. For example, a high context communication or message is one in which most of the information is either in the physical context or internalized in the person, while very little is in the coded, explicit, transmitted part of the message. High context cultures have a restricted code system (language) and are very aware of their surroundings. Members rely on silence and nonverbal behavior, rather than verbal communication, as their main source of information. In high context cultures such as Japan, statements of affection are very rare. Members are quite adept at decoding nonverbal behavior. Japanese, for example, expect others (i.e., Japanese) to understand the unarticulated communication. Cultural members are expected to know how to perform in various situations where the guidelines are implicit.[f]

Members of a low context culture are less sensitive to the physical, social, and psychological environment. That is not to say that they ignore the environment, they are simply less aware of it than are members of a high context culture. For example, a low context communication is one in which the mass of information is vested in the explicit code. Hence low context cultures have an elaborated code system. Verbal messages are extremely important where information to be shared with others is coded in the verbal message. Members of low context cultures do not perceive the environment for information. Guidelines and expectations are frequently explained explicitly.[g]

In addition to his high-low context distinctions, Hall also distinguishes between high and low contact cultures.[h] Hall contends that cultures can be categorized according to the degree of physical contact preferred by their members. Cultures where the members prefer to stand close to one another and touch frequently are called high contact cultures and those cultures where people prefer to stand apart and tend not to touch very much are called low contact cultures. Persons in high contact cultures positively evaluate close distances and touch from others. People in low contact cultures do the reverse. Japan is considered a low contact culture. Gudykunst and Kim designate the United States as a "moderate" contact culture.[i]

Many of the communicative behaviors of high-low context, individualistic-collectivistic, and high-low contact cultures vary. When individuals from different cultures communicate, they frequently use different verbal and nonverbal behaviors and there probably is a high level of uncertainty. In addition, the interactants will inevitably violate each others' expectations regarding appropriate nonverbal behavior. Here is where Burgoon's NEV theory can be applied. In the following two scenarios, Jim and Akira interact. Notice how each violates the others' expectations without the other knowing they have made the deviation. As Gudykunst and Kim note, we will probably notice when others violate our expectations, but the violators may not realize it unless we tell them, and vice versa. Perhaps even more importantly, we may not even notice our expectations are violated if the violation is not major. In such cases we may negatively interpret the other's behavior unconsciously. In situations like these, misunderstandings may occur.[j]

The following two scenarios depict Akira and Jim interacting and violating each others' nonverbal expectations. When reading the scenes, keep in mind the different cultural orientations and the axioms of NEV.

Scene One: Jim and Akira are eating dinner together in a local restaurant.

JIM: (Talking loudly with food in his mouth) This is absolutely the best steak. I love   1
it! How's your dinner there—big guy?

AKIRA: (Shocked at how loudly Jim is talking in a restaurant slightly smiles, then   2
softly says—) Very good . . . thank you, Jim.

JIM: Huh? Didn't hear ya.   3

AKIRA: (Uncomfortable speaking any louder) It's good, Jim.   4

JIM: I can tell a good restaurant when I see one—eh? Whoa—check out that waitress!   5
(Watches the waitress walk by the table) She's your type—eh—stud boy!

AKIRA: Oh . . . yes, Jim . . . this is a very nice place. (Doesn't comment on Jim's re-   6
mark about the waitress nor does he look at her.)

JIM: Yes sireee, I am stuffed. Well . . . I've got to pee, I'll be right back. (Pats Akira   7
on the back as he passes.)

AKIRA: (Startled) Oh! Hmmm . . . Yes . . . OK.   8

Scene Two: Jim and Akira are at a party.

JIM: (Slapping Akira on the back) Great party eh? Give me five! (Holds up his hand)   9

AKIRA: (Is startled—stands back—trying to put some distance between him and Jim   10
and does not slap Jim's hand) Yes . . . thank you.

JIM: (Annoyed) If you want to meet some girls just go up and sorta nudge them as   11
you walk by—that'll get their attention. Especially if you're wearing cologne.
Then give them a big smile and say "Hi." Here like this. (Demonstrates by bump-
ing his shoulder against Akira's) "Hi." Could you smell my new cologne?

AKIRA: (Backs away) But I don't know them. They might be upset.   12

JIM: But that's the way you meet them. Here—watch me . . .   13

AKIRA: (Thinks to himself *It isn't polite to bump into people. I can't smile like that*   14
to someone I don't know, why does he smell like that? This is terrible.)

(Mitsuko, another Japanese exchange student, approaches Jim and Akira. She knows Akira but not Jim.)

Continued

CASE STUDY 9   *Continued*

MITSUKO: Hello, Akira. (Bows slightly and looks down)   15
AKIRA: Ah, Mitsuko, this is my friend Jim.   16
JIM: Hi!   17
MITSUKO: Hi, Jim. (Bows slightly and does not make direct eye contact)   18
JIM: Are you two friends? (Wonders why she won't look at him—thinks to himself,   19
    Well, I'm not one of them, she probably thinks I'm ugly.)
AKIRA: Yes, we know each other.   20

(A long pause ensues.)

JIM: (Thinks to himself *This is going nowhere—I've got to think of something to say.*   21
    He says rather loudly—) Great party hey guys?

(Akira and Mitsuko both jump back.)

AKIRA: Yeah, we think it's fun.   22

Several of the axioms and propositions from Burgoon's NEV theory can be applied to the above interaction between Akira and Jim. Specifically, Axioms 4 through 6 and 8 through 11 will be discussed. According to Axiom 4, people are able to perceive gradations in distance. Notice in lines 10 and 12 that Akira perceives that Jim is standing too close and backs away. In line 5 Jim notices the approach of the waitress. According to Axiom 5, personal space and/or distance patterns are normative. Normative behavior is that which occurs on average and conforms with some norm. A norm is a standard shared by members of a social group of which the members of the group are expected to conform. In the United States, for example, the act of shaking hands during a greeting is normative behavior. Though some cultures may share some norms, many differ from culture to culture. In the above scenes, where Jim and Akira stand, their physical proximity to each other, the loudness of their voices, and the eye contact between Jim, Akira, and Mitsuko are all based on cultural norms regarding nonverbal behavior. According to Axiom 6, however, people may develop behaviors that differ from the social norms. This becomes especially relevant in intercultural situations where the interactants do not share the same norms. Obviously, based on the above examples, Jim perceives Akira's behavior differing from the norms as does Akira about Jim.

According to Axiom 8, people respond differently to normative versus deviant behaviors. If Akira were an American he would not have responded as he did to Jim's nonverbal "violations." Jim violated Akira's "expectations" of how one should act. Likewise, if Jim were Japanese, he would not have acted as he did nor responded to Akira's "violations" of his "expectations." Throughout the two scenes are various violations of expectations. From Akira's point of view Jim violated his expectations in lines 1, 5, 7, 9, 11, and 21. Jim violated Akira's nonverbal expectations regarding vocal volume, personal distance, touch, and eye contact. From Jim's vantage point, Akira violated his expectations in lines 2, 6, 10, 18, and during the long pause toward the end of Scene 2. For example, Jim probably does not understand why Akira speaks so softly, does not look at the waitress, or does not want to attract the attention of women at the party. To Jim, Akira is violating social norma-tive "expectations."

According to NEV theory, violations have arousal value (Axiom 9). In lines 2, 4, 8, 10, 11, 14, and 19 we can see how Akira and Jim became aroused (e.g., shocked, uncomfort-able, startled) by each others' violations. Both Mitsuko and Akira jumped when Jim yells "Great party eh guys?" in line 21.

In lines 14, 19, and 21 we can see how Axiom 10 applies in that the arousal leads to evaluations (e.g., "This is terrible," "This is going nowhere"). In this case, the evaluations are negative. According to the theory, the greater the degree a person is perceived as re-warding, the greater the tendency for others to approach that person. Likewise, the greater the degree a person is perceived as punishing, the greater the tendency for others to avoid that person. As Gudykunst and Kim argue, we tend to avoid dissimilar others more than we do similar others.[k] One reason for this is the high levels of uncertainty. Unless we are attracted to those who are dissimilar, such persons will have lower reward value than sim-ilar others (Axiom 11). The costs of interacting with dissimilar others are greater than the rewards. Hence when dissimilar others violate our expectations, our evaluations of the vi-olations are likely to be negative. Unfortunately for Akira, since he is in a "foreign" coun-try he will be the more likely of the two to change his behavior to conform to the expectations of others.

a. Gudykunst, W. B., & Kim, Y. Y. (1992). *Communicating with Strangers: An Approach to Intercultural Commu-nication,* New York: McGraw-Hill, (pp. 13–14).
b. Schwartz, S. H. (1990). "Individualism-Collectivism: Critique and Proposed Refinements," *Journal of Cross-Cultural Psychology,* 21, 139–157.
c. Ibid.
d. Harris, P. R., & Moran, R. T. (1991). *Managing Cultural Differences,* Houston, Gulf Publishing.
e. Schwartz, "Individualism-Collectivism," 139–157.
f. Hall, E. T. (1976). *Beyond Culture,* Garden City, NY: Anchor.
g. Gudykunst, W. B. (Ed.) (1983). *Intercultural Communication Theory: Current Perspectives,* Beverly Hills: Sage.
h. Hall, *Beyond Culture;* Hall, E. T. (1966). *The Hidden Dimension,* Garden City, NY: Anchor.
i. Gudykunst & Kim, *Communication with Strangers.*
j. Ibid.
k. Ibid.

Trait Approaches

A great deal of research in communication focuses on traits, or relatively enduring person-ality characteristics that determine behavior. The concept stems from psychology. Psychol-ogists have long been interested in traits because they predict behavior. Raymond Cattell, a noteworthy psychologist, has spent decades studying this area. He defines a trait as that "which permits a prediction of what a person will do in a given situation."[49] Maddi defines a trait as a "stable set of characteristics and tendencies that determine those commonalities and differences in psychological behavior."[50] Communication scholars are interested in a subset of personality traits that deal with communication. Infante, Rancer, and Womack de-fine a communication trait as a characteristic that "accounts for certain kinds of communicative behaviors."[51] As these three definitions imply, traits are precursors to behavior; that is, traits serve as the causal mechanism for behavior. Cattell's definition states that a trait "permits a prediction," Maddi argues that traits "determine" behavior, and Infante et al. say that traits "account" for communication. From a causal process approach view, if people possess a certain trait, then they will behave in a certain way; that is, if *trait,* then *behavior.* Three communication traits that have received a substantial amount of interest include (a) communication apprehension, (b) symbolic aggression, and (c) cognitive complexity.

Communication Apprehension

Imagine that it is the night before you are to give a speech in the most difficult course you're taking this semester. You lie awake tossing and turning thinking about the speech, trying to memorize your lines, imagining how horrible it will be. Now imagine that it is the next day, you are in the class listening to the speaker immediately before your turn. The speaker is finished, the professor calls your name, and you walk up to the front of the class and see your professor and twenty-five of your classmates looking directly at you waiting for you to begin. How do you feel? The nervousness, sweaty palms, shaking hands, loss of memory, and general anxiety you may be feeling is common; most people experience some form of discomfort when delivering a public speech. For others, however, the anxiety may be extreme and occurs not only in public speaking situations but in almost all communication situations. These people may suffer from what is called *communication apprehension.*

In the past three decades, a substantial body of literature has accumulated regarding the nature and prevalence of communication apprehension (hereafter referred to as CA). By most accounts, CA is the most widely examined variable in social scientific communication research. Virtually hundreds of studies have been done on this subject.

James C. McCroskey, professor and chair of the Department of Communication at West Virginia University, is regarded as the foremost scholar in the area of CA. He defines it as "an individual's level of fear or anxiety associated with either real or anticipated communication with another person or persons." McCroskey contends that approximately 20 percent of all adults experience CA.[52]

Types of CA

There are generally four types of CA and just about everyone experiences one type at some point. The first type is trait CA. A trait is an enduring personality characteristic that influences behavior. Individuals with trait CA tend to either experience high CA in almost all interactive situations or experience virtually no CA in any interactions. Estimates indicate that approximately 15 percent to 20 percent of the population is high trait CA. The second type of CA occurs in generalized situations and is called context-based CA. People in this group experience CA in some contexts but not in others. Here, the situation seems to arouse CA, as in the case of a public speech. Many individuals experience CA prior to and during public speaking but have little to no CA in other types of communicative events such as a small group meeting or a conversation.[53]

The third type of CA, called audience-based CA, occurs with a given person or group of people across situations. Here, the person or persons with whom one interacts arouses

CA. For example, people may experience CA when they interact with their boss regardless of the context. Whether interaction is at work, at a party, or in the grocery store, people simply become anxious when talking with their boss.

The final type of CA, called situational CA, is a combination of the second and third types. Here, CA is experienced with a specific person or persons in a specific context. The combination of the person and situation arouses anxiety. For example, some people may experience CA with their boss at work but are perfectly comfortable interacting with the boss at a social gathering.

Sources of CA

Although the causes of CA are not fully understood, many children enter kindergarten with high CA already firmly established. CA alters the development of basic speech skills and the social learning environment, which subsequently leads to a future of severe anxiety while engaged in communication situations. In fact, CA may be one of the most pervasive handicaps confronting children in American schools.[54] Relevant literature has focused on four general causes of CA, including heredity, reinforcement, skill deficiency, and modeling.[55] Research investigating inherited CA indicates that there may be a genetic link between parent and children's levels of CA.[56] Most researchers believe, however, that any genetic component to CA is mediated by the child's home and school environment.

Perhaps the most commonly attributable cause of CA is reinforcement.[57] Individuals become high or low CA individuals on the basis of reinforced behavior. Individuals finding interaction unrewarding and/or painful tend to develop high CA. In comparison, individuals finding communication rewarding and pleasurable become low CA individuals. For example, children who are scolded by their parents or teachers for talking may develop a fear of talking. Some parents and teachers may still believe in the old cliché "Children are meant to be seen, not heard" and subsequently punish their children when they talk. Conversely, children who are encouraged and rewarded for talking are less likely to develop CA.[58]

Some people simply lack the essential skills for interacting which can lead to CA. Children who stutter or speak with a lisp, for example, may fear communication with others. Unfortunately, many children with speech impediments are ridiculed by their peers which serves as a kind of negative reinforcement. Generally, once children develop the necessary skills, their levels of CA decrease.[59]

Modeling is another possible source of CA. Here, it is suggested that children develop CA by imitating others in their environment such as parents, siblings, teachers, or peers. For example, children with talkative parents may try to model their behavior and become talkative themselves. Children may also imitate celebrities.[60]

The Effects of CA

The debilitating effects experienced by high CA individuals are dramatic. For example, those with high CA claim to withdraw from and avoid communication whenever possible, are perceived less positively than their low CA peers, and claim to experience negative consequences in their academic, professional, and social careers.[61] Academically, high CA individuals receive lower grades in elementary school, junior high school, and college, and are predicted to have less career success by teachers, produce lower scores on standardized tests, and are perceived as less competent and less intelligent than talkative people.[62] Those with high CA experience similar negative effects in the business world. For example, they take less satisfying jobs and are perceived as less competent by their employers. They accept positions of lower pay and status and are less likely to be offered an interview or a job.[63]

Finally, those with high CA are negatively affected in their social lives. For example, those with high CA are perceived as less socially and interpersonally attractive; less credible; less physically attractive; less friendly, attentive, and relaxed; more tense; less trustworthy; and less of a leader than those with low CA. In addition, college students with high CA interact less with peer strangers, are less likely to accept a blind date, have fewer dates, and have fewer close relationships than individuals with low CA.[64]

In addition to heredity, reinforcement, skill deficiency, and modeling, some research suggests that parental attitudes toward communication, ethnicity, and community size also influence the development of CA in children. For example, if parents use communication as a weapon against each other and/or against their children, the children may begin to avoid communication to escape negative feelings. Infrequent or antagonistic communication exhibited between parents may be observed, conditioned into, or modeled by a child.

In addition to parental attitudes toward communication, ethnicity may foster the development of CA. In one study a significantly disproportionate number of high CA college students were from first- and second-generation ethnic families.[65]

Another possible predictor of CA is community size. Higher levels of CA are found in elementary, secondary, and college students from rural versus urban communities. Perhaps small populations present more demands on the child for personal communication, increasing opportunities for success or failure, and thus increasing the chances children will discover their inadequacies in communication early and develop CA.[66]

Symbolic Aggressiveness

Remember the last time you and your close friend argued over some trivial subject such as whose turn it was to wash the dishes. Perhaps at some point in the argument you resorted to name-calling and screamed at your friend, "You're such a lazy jerk—do the damn dishes!" Most people are guilty of making such statements from time to time, but some individuals actually engage in such behavior regularly. These individuals are considered "symbolically aggressive."

Symbolic aggressiveness is a topic in which many scholars in the communication field are interested. Dominic A. Infante, professor of communication at Kent State University, is the primary researcher in this area and is well known for his work. Like communication apprehension, symbolic forms of aggression are regarded as traits. For ex-ample, Infante defines verbal aggressiveness, one form of symbolic aggression, as a personality trait whereby an individual attacks the self-concept of another person instead of, or in addition to, the person's position on a topic of communication.[67] Infante also describes verbal aggressiveness as a form of symbolic aggression involving the use of verbal and nonverbal communication to dominate and damage and/or to defeat and destroy another person's position on a topic of communication and/or that person's self-concept. Verbally aggressive messages come in the form of character attacks, competence attacks, insults, profanity, harmful teasing, ridicule, and nonverbal emblems (e.g., giving someone "the finger").[68]

Sources of Aggression

Verbal aggression is only one form of the generic trait of aggression. As a general trait, aggression has been studied extensively. Much of this literature focuses on aggression as an instinct, the result of frustration, or a learned behavior.

Researchers believe that some aggression is based on the instinct to survive. In prehistoric times the most aggressive individual, usually a male, mated the most and continued his blood line. Primitive groups relied on their aggressive instincts in fighting for their territorial grounds.[69]

Some scholars argue that aggressive behaviors are the result of built-up frustrations. People become frustrated when their goals are blocked or thwarted and may resort to aggression in trying to achieve them. Upon its release aggression produces a cathartic effect; after people react aggressively they "feel" better.[70]

From a social learning perspective, aggression is a conditioned response. For example, if people are reinforced for their aggressive behavior, they may develop or learn to behave aggressively on a frequent basis. For example, many professional athletes (e.g., boxers, football players) are reinforced for their aggressive behavior in the ring or on the field. Many athletes are paid millions of dollars to act aggressively. These same athletes may have difficulty withholding their aggressive traits outside the athletic arena. They may quickly resort to aggression in otherwise nonaggressive contexts. Likewise, a young man might model the aggressiveness of a professional athlete or that of his father or an aggressive television character.[71]

Though aggression has been studied by social scientists as a general trait, communication scholars are interested in symbolic aggressiveness as a specific form of aggression that occurs in interpersonal relationships as a form of interpersonal communication. Communication scholars agree that symbolic aggression may be the result of frustration and social learning but assert that two other reasons may include psychopathology and argumentative skill deficiency. From a psychopathological perspective, people become communicatively aggressive with others who symbolize unresolved conflict. For example, some teenagers may be verbally aggressive with adults because of unresolved conflicts with their parents. To the teenagers, adults symbolize parents.

Argumentative skill deficiency as a cause of symbolic aggression, particularly verbal aggressiveness, is a useful avenue for communication scholars to pursue. Here it is posited that people become verbally aggressive because they lack the essential communicative skills for dealing with everyday frustrations and conflict with others. Because they lack the tools for constructing a reasonable argument, they resort to symbolic violence in the form of verbal aggressiveness (VA).[72]

Types of Symbolic Aggression

Infante contends that there are four distinct types of symbolic aggression, two of which are constructive and two of which are destructive. The two constructive forms include assertiveness and argumentativeness and the two destructive types include hostility and verbal aggressiveness.[73]

Symbolic aggression is considered constructive if it facilitates interpersonal relations. Infante understands that it may be difficult to see aggression as constructive but contends that given the right circumstances aggression can foster the development of relationships in positive ways. For example, if during an argument a husband and wife resort to name-calling and profanity, it may shock them into seeking a marriage counselor which could lead to a better marriage. In all four aggression traits—assertiveness, argumentativeness, hostility, and verbal aggression—are possible constructive results.

Most aggression is destructive, with damage to the other's self-concept being the most frequent outcome, and one that may have longer lasting consequences than the results of physical aggression. The old cliché "Sticks and stones may break my bones but names will never hurt me" is one of the most misleading lessons a child learns. To tease a child about a physical or mental deformity could last a lifetime, especially if done by a parent or a significant other such as a teacher or older sibling.

In addition to damage to one's self-concept, other destructive results of symbolic aggression include hurt feelings, embarrassment, and relational deterioration and termination. Unfortunately, a common result of VA is physical violence. As Infante asserts, "The effects of verbally aggressive messages in interpersonal communication provide sufficient and compelling justification for studying verbal aggression in order to gain control over its occurrence."[74]

Assertiveness.   Defined as a "person's general tendency to be interpersonally dominant, ascendant and forceful," assertiveness is a constructive form of aggression. Assertiveness involves communicating expressively and is negative related to shyness and loneliness. Assertive people express their rights without denying others' rights, are direct, independent, and refuse to be intimidated. One study found that assertive people make more speech errors than nonassertive people. The researchers speculate that assertive people may take more risks in speech situations which produces arousal and thus more errors.[75]

Argumentativeness.   Argumentativeness is another form of constructive aggression and is regarded as a subset of assertiveness. Defined as "a predisposition to defend positions on controversial issues while attempting to refute others' positions," people high in argumentativeness perceive arguing as an exciting competitive event that results in a sense of accomplishment. They are verbose, willing to attack and defend their positions, generally expert in the topics of their arguments, and set in their positions. Men are typically higher in argumentativeness than women. An important line of research regarding argumentativeness focuses on marriage. Here, happily married couples tend to argue constructively while unhappily married couples argued destructively (i.e., verbally aggressive).[76]

Hostility.   Defined as a "broad tendency to be angry," hostility is a destructive form of symbolic aggression. Hostile people have quick tempers, are perceived negatively, have little patience, are rude and inconsiderate of others, refuse to cooperate, are antagonistic, and are generally suspicious of others. Hostile people are not persistently angry but have been conditioned to be aggressive whenever they become frustrated.[77]

Verbal Aggressiveness.   VA is a subset of hostility. As mentioned before, VA is defined as a trait in which the other's self-concept is attacked instead of, or in addition to, the topic of communication. VA is a form of destructive aggression. Research on VA, married couples, and depression indicates that the more verbally aggressive women were, the more their husbands reported symptoms of depression. In contrast, however, husbands' VA showed no correlation with their wives' level of depression. In another study, Infante, Chandler, and Rudd found that VA is a catalyst for interspousal violence. They contend that "unless aroused by verbal aggression, a hostile disposition remains latent in the form of unexpressed anger." Persons in violent marriages were more verbally aggressive than other people. They also found that violent spouses were actually less argumentative than people in nonviolent marriages.[78]

Because of the severe consequences associated with symbolic aggression, this topic remains a central theme in communication research. Infante and Wigley recommend that such research should be extended into international contexts:

> *When two nations stoop to name-calling from across an ocean, are the causes basically the same as when two neighbors engage in name-calling across a backyard fence? A central issue here would be whether the likelihood of war or other military of even economic action is increased when certain types of verbal aggression are exchanged between nations. The ability to predict such actions would be valuable.*[79]

Clearly, this line of research is ripe for extension and development in communication.

Cognitive Complexity

In the last twenty years or so, a fairly large body of literature has accumulated regarding a personality trait called cognitive complexity. Sometimes called interpersonal cognitive complexity, this refers to the way in which people gather, process, and interpret information about their social environment. Many scholars interested in cognitive complexity approach it from a perspective called constructivism. Foremost among the constructivists are Jesse Delia and Daniel O'Keefe of the University of Illinois and Brant R. Burleson of Purdue University.

Central to the constructivist theory is the principle that human behavior is guided and directed by cognitive (i.e., mental) processes called interpretative schemes. An interpretive scheme is an individual's mental organization of thoughts and impressions of other people and their social environment. Interpretive schemes are composed of personal constructs. According to the theory, people do not directly experience reality but perceive and filter it through personal constructs. Constructs are defined as patterns or templates created to facilitate the interpretation of reality.

Constructivists believe that people give structure and meaning to their world by grouping places, events, and other people together on the basis of their perceived similarities and differences. For example, tall people would be grouped in one category and short people in another. Personal constructs are those that people create when grouping places, events, and other people. For example, if Maria described her dorm room as "small, messy, and uncomfortable," she would have used three personal constructs. Impressions of reality, then, are filtered and interpreted through personal constructs.[80]

In addition to personal constructs, constructivists argue that individuals possess a special class of constructs used for forming impressions about other persons. These constructs, called interpersonal constructs, form the basis for making decisions and inferring attributes about other people.[81] For example, if you were to describe your roommate as "fat, greasy, and gross" you have used three interpersonal constructs. Hence, whenever you interact with your roommate, your impressions are filtered through your interpersonal constructs. As one of the leading scholars in cognitive complexity, Walter Crockett, maintains: "The impression that one person forms from observing the appearance and behavior of another is affected by an extensive array of factors. Among these determinants are the attributes that characterize the other person as a stimulus object."[82] These "attributes" are the constructs that make up the cognitive interpretive scheme. Moreover, constructivists argue that individual interpretive schemes, or cognitive systems, differ from person to person. As Crockett indicates: "individual differences in the impressions formed from a standard set of stimulus information reflect systematic differences in the cognitive processes of the perceivers."[83]

Specifically, cognitive systems vary from simple to complex. Cognitively complex systems, which contain relatively large amounts of interpersonal constructs, are called highly differentiated. These constructs help individuals to discriminate among a wide variety of person-oriented information and aid in construct organization. Complex cognitive systems also contain relatively abstract interpersonal constructs. For example, the interpersonal construct "short" is less abstract than the construct "honest." In comparison to complex cognitive systems, cognitively simple systems contain relatively few and less abstract interpersonal constructs. Highly abstract constructs enable people to better mentally represent personality dynamics and psychological aspects of other people.[84]

Individual levels of cognitive complexity are determined by asking people to describe in writing and in great detail two people—someone with whom they are intimate and someone who they dislike. In the typical experiment, subjects are given four to five minutes to complete each description. The descriptions are then coded for the number of and abstractness of constructs. Below are two descriptions, one representing a cognitively complex system and the other a cognitively simple system.

Simple Impression

My friend is twenty-one years old, tall, with blond hair. He is a sophomore in college. He is majoring in biology. He likes to watch sports, especially football.

Complex Impression

My friend is a junior in college and is very smart. He is honest, sincere, and cares about other people. He tries to do his best at whatever he does. He likes just about everyone he meets and is very accepting of different ideas and lifestyles. Some might call him a perfectionist. Probably the only negative thing about him is that sometimes he comes down on himself too hard.

The simple impression has six interpersonal constructs, including (a) twenty-one years old, (b) tall, (c) blond, (d) sophomore, (e) biology major, and (f) watches sports. Notice also that these constructs are relatively concrete and simple. They describe the person's physical appearance and social demographics. In the complex impression there are at least ten interpersonal constructs, including (a) junior, (b) smart, (c) honest, (d) sincere, (e) caring, (f) does his best, (g) likes others, (h) accepting, (i) perfectionist, and (j) is hard on himself. Notice the relative abstractness of these constructs. For example, to say that someone is caring is much more abstract than saying that he has blond hair. In the complex impression the constructs reflect general affective and psychologically centered constructs that refer to general traits, dispositions, and motivations that have implications for the other's conduct and character across a wide range of situations and relationships. Keep in mind that according to constructivism, social reality is interpreted through the cognitive system of constructs.[85]

The transition from a simple cognitive system to a complex system is developmental. Initially, one's cognitive system is simple, where conceptions of the environment are broad and general. Typically, constructs in a simple system are unrelated and unorganized. Children's cognitive systems, for example, are considered simple. As they grow older and mature, their systems develop and become more differentiated and abstract. Construct systems develop in adults, also. Adults who meet others for the first time may have a simple scheme representing those others. As adults learn more about their new acquaintances, their construct systems become more differentiated and abstract.

Construct system development is important in interpersonal relationships because the way people perceive others influences their behavior with those others. For example, people whose construct systems toward others are relatively simple might be more cautious about what they say than if they know a lot about the other person; that is, have a complex set of interpersonal constructs. O'Keefe and Sypher argue that cognitive complexity is a "determinant of sophisticated communicative conduct in situations requiring differentiated understandings of other's perspectives and motivational dynamics." Many constructivists believe that interpersonal constructs underlie all social perception processes. Research in this area reveals that levels of cognitive complexity are linearly associated with age and that high complex persons are better able to represent the perspectives of others. Cognitive complexity is also related to a number of communication variables.[86]

Cognitive Complexity and Communication

A substantial amount of empirical research indicates that individual levels of cognitive complexity affect a wide range of social functioning, especially communication. The general theme among these studies is that individuals possessing high levels of cognitive complexity are generally disposed positively to communication, more so than their cognitively simple peers. Most of the research focuses on the relationship between cognitive complexity and person-centered communication. Person-centered communication is that which reflects an awareness of and adaptation to the needs, feelings, and interests of others. The ability to construct person-centered messages is dependent on one's ability to represent the psychological characteristics of the listener. As Burleson notes, "Interpersonal constructs constitute the fundamental cognitive mechanisms through which features of another's thoughts, behaviors, and communicatively relevant characteristics are inferred and represented."[87]

Cognitive complexity is related to persuasive message generation. Individuals high in cognitive complexity create more effective persuasive messages than cognitively simple individuals. In addition, cognitively complex people generally create more appeals within their persuasive messages than do cognitively simple people. Another study found that children with cognitively complex interpretive schemes created persuasive messages that accommodate the perspective of the target more so than children with simple systems.[88]

Cognitive complexity is also related to informal interaction. Highly complex people are more likely to include individual characteristics and personality judgments of participants as the focus of their interaction than are low complex people. In related research, highly complex people were found to be better at giving instructions to others than low complex people. In addition, high cognitive complexity was shown to be positively associated with listener-adapted communication. Listener-adapted communication is the ability to construct messages based on the viewpoints of others.[89]

Burleson and his associates have found consistent relationships between cognitive complexity and comforting communication. Defined as messages intended to alleviate, moderate, or salve the distressed emotional states of others, studies indicate that persons with high levels of cognitive complexity are more likely to construct comforting messages than cognitively simple persons.

Other extant research on cognitive complexity has found that it is negatively related to communication apprehension; that is, as levels of cognitive complexity increase, communication apprehension decreases. Finally, some research indicates that cognitively complex individuals have better recall of conversations than cognitively simple persons and that cognitively complex persons are less susceptible to interference than cognitively simple persons.[90]

The Biosocial Approach

A relatively new approach emerging in communication, the biosocial approach, is being advanced by Don Stacks, professor of communication at the University of Miami, and Mark Hickson III, professor of communication at the University of Alabama. The central thrust of this approach is that biological factors and sociopsychological factors interact to trigger behavior and communication.[91] This approach borrows heavily from the work of Charles Darwin and his arguments regarding evolution. In his classic book *The Origin of the Species,* Darwin articulated several assumptions about how humans came into existence and the means by which they survive. Central to Darwin's thesis is that (a) humans evolved from single-celled animals, and (b) through natural selection only the strongest individuals of a species survive. Stacks and Hickson contend that if biological factors evolved then social factors, such as communication behaviors, also evolve. They argue: "Using Darwin's general approach and applying it to social variables, it would appear that social adaptation is also necessary for survival. Only those behaviors which society views as useful remain."[92]

Human communication, both verbal and nonverbal, is seen as a particular evolutionary variation that has allowed humans to survive. This ability to use symbols renders the human species the "strongest." Just as larger ground-feeding birds that seldom take flight have developed a nearly wingless condition, humans have developed communication, beginning with rudimentary nonverbal signals and symbols that eventually developed into complex purely abstract symbolic language forms.

Adherents of the biosocial approach place great importance on how the brain functions. These theorists believe that the brain is responsible for our ability to communicate and that humans exist within an exoskeleton device (i.e., the physical body) that, through evolution, houses the brain. The brain controls the mind, the body, and the interaction between the mind and body. Assumptions of the biosocial approach include:[93]

1. Humans have no control over their births or deaths (except through suicide).
2. The activities of life are both biological and social.
3. Humans are biologically similar to animals.
4. Humans are socially superior to other animals.
5. The human body is one dimensional.
6. The brain is multidimensional. The brain creates social reality through biological functions.
7. The brain and the body interact to produce communication patterns. The interaction of the brain and the body creates the concept of "mind" which yields reality.

Philosophers have long been interested in the relationship between the mind and the body. John Searle, a highly regarded philosopher and developer of speech act theory presented in Chapter 9, has recently written about the mind and its relationship to the physical body. Searle writes:

The famous mind-body problem, the source of so much controversy over the past two millennia, has a simple solution. . . . Here it is: mental phenomena are caused by neurophysiological process in the brain and are themselves features of the brain. . . . Mental events and processes are as much part of our biological natural history as digestion, mitosis, meioses, or enzyme secretion.[94]

Searle continues:

Causally we know that brain processes are sufficient for any mental state and that the connection between those brain processes and the motor nervous system is a contingent neurophysiological connection like any other.[95]

Searle contends that behavior is neurophysiologically based. Humans are constrained by evolution. Consciousness itself is a neurophysiological process. This does not mean that humans do have not choices, but that the choices are biologically determined by the neurophysiological structure of the brain which controls the human body. Tone of voice, hand and arm gestures, and even verbal language is contingent upon the physical being controlled by the brain. In this sense the neurophysiological processes are the causal mechanism for behavior.

Biosocial theorists maintain that the brain is responsible for our communicative behavior. The brain contains some ten to fourteen billion cells called neurons. These neurons are the smallest unit in the nervous system and transmit electrical-chemical information throughout the brain. Neurons are connected to each other creating a very complex network that serves as the mechanism for consciousness, language, and interaction with others.[96]

The brain has two sides called hemispheres. This two-sidedness is called cerebral lateralization. Many communication researchers believe that the left side of the brain controls verbal language functions and the right side controls nonverbal language functions. Andersen, Garrison, and Andersen contend that perception of spatial, proxemic, tactile, kinesic, artifactual, and nonlinguistic environmental sounds are processed in the right brain hemisphere. Other scholars believe that language processing occurs in both hemispheres, with each side processing different styles of language. For example, the left hemisphere processes analytical, syntactical, and deliberate language whereas the right hemisphere is more instinctive and affective.[97]

The basic assumption of the biosocial approach is that at least some of our social behavior is determined physiologically, and the implications are quite serious. People generally do not like to think that their behavior is determined by forces beyond their control. To be sure, human beings are physically different. People are tall, short, male, female, dark-skinned, light-skinned, thin, and fat. Biosocial theorists are looking into how social behavior may actually produce changes physiologically. Stacks and Hickson maintain that the process is interactive; that is, the brain determines behavior and behavior may determine the chemical structure of the brain. Many other disciplines such as anthropology, philosophy, psychology, and sociology are interested in how much of our behavior is determined by our physical makeup. The nineties should prove very exciting in this area.

Summary

Causal process theorists in communication have generated some of the most productive research programs in the discipline. These theories have offered a great deal of insight into the communication process. Many scholars in communication eschew the very idea of causality and do not like the idea that human behavior is caused by anything. Many believe that humans choose to act rather than react. Perhaps there is always some slippage between reality and fantasy.

Glossary

Biosocial Approach: Theoretical approach positing that communicative behaviors are caused by biological factors in the human body and brain.

Cognitive Complexity: Communication trait referring to the way in which people gather, process, and interpret information about their social environment.

Communication Apprehension: Communication trait where people experience fear or anxiety about communicating with others.

Fear Appeal: A persuasive message that is designed to frighten a receiver into compliance.

Interpersonal Attraction: A positive linear function of proportion of similar attitudes with another person.

Nonverbal Expectancy Violation Theory: A causal process theory that posits that people hold expectations about the nonverbal behaviors of others. When these expectations are violated, people evaluate the violation positively or negatively depending on the source of the violation.

One-Sided Message: A persuasive message that presents only those arguments in favor of its position on an issue or topic.

Source Credibility: The degree to which the sender of a persuasive message is perceived as possessing expertise and trustworthiness.

Trait: A relatively enduring personality characteristic that serves as a causal mechanism for communication behavior.

Two-Sided Message: A persuasive message that presents arguments favoring both sides of an issue.

Uncertainty Reduction Theory: Theory that posits that uncertainty is a causal mechanism for communication behavior during initial interactions with people.

Verbal Aggressiveness: Communication trait whereby the self-concept of another is attacked instead of, or in addition to, the topic of communication.

Yale Chain of Response: A persuasive message can be conceived as a chain of responses, including, attention, comprehension, acceptance, retention, and action.

References

1. Fisher, B. A. (1978). *Perspectives on Human Communication,* New York: Macmillan, (p. 34).

2. Infante, D. A., Rancer, A. S., & Womack, D. F. (1993). *Building Communication Theory,* (2nd Ed.), Prospect Heights, IL: Waveland; O'Keefe, D. J. (1975). "Logical Empiricism and the Study of Human Communication," *Speech Monographs, 42,* 169–183.

3. Miller, G. R. (1978). "The Current Status of Theory and Research in Interpersonal Communication," *Human Communication Research, 4,* 164–178.

4. Ibid, (p. 171).

5. Miller, G. R., & Berger, C. R. (1978). "On Keeping the Faith in Matters Scientific," *Western Journal of Speech Communication, 42,* 44–57.

6. Infante, Rancer, & Womack, *Building Communication Theory;* Hovland, C. I., Janis, I. L., & Kelley, H. H. (1953). *Communication and Persuasion,* New Haven: Yale University Press.

7. Hovland, Janis, & Kelley, *Communication and Persuasion,* (pp. 5–6).

8. Ibid.; Smith, M. J. (1982). *Persuasion and Human Action: A Review and Critique of Social Influence Theories,* Belmont, CA: Wadsworth.

9. Smith, *Persuasion and Human Action,* (p. 215).

10. McCroskey, J. C., & Young, T. (1981). "Ethos and Credibility: The Construct and Its Measurement after Three Decades," *Central States Speech Journal, 32,* 24–34.

11. Ibid.

12. Bettinghaus, E. P., & Cody, M. J. (1994). *Persuasive Communication,* (5th Ed.), Fort Worth, TX: Harcourt Brace.

13. Hovland, C. I., & Weiss, W. (1951). "The Influence of Source Credibility on Communication Effectiveness," *Public Opinion Quarterly, 15,* 635–650.

14. Kelman, H. C., & Hovland, C. I. (1953). "'Reinstatement' of the Communicator in Delayed Measurement of Opinion Change," *Journal of Abnormal Social Psychology, 48,* 327–335.

15. Bettinghaus, & Cody, *Persuasive Communication.*

16. Ibid.

17. Smith, *Persuasion and Human Action,* (p. 223).

18. Witte, K. (1992). "Putting the Fear Back into Fear Appeals: The Extended Parallel Process Model," *Communication Monographs, 59,* 329–349.

19. Ibid.

20. Ibid.

21. Ibid.

22. Ibid.

23. Hovland, C. I., & Mandell, W. (1952). "An Experimental Comparison of Conclusion-Drawing by the Communicator and by the Audience," *Journal of Abnormal Social Psychology, 47,* 581–588.

24. Hovland, C. I., Lumsdaine, A. A., & Sheffield, F. D. (1949). "The Effects of Presenting 'One Side' Versus 'Both Sides' in Changing Opinions on a Controversial Subject," in C. I. Hovland, A. A. Lumsdaine, & F. D. Sheffield, (Eds.), *Experiments on Mass Communication: Studies in Social Psychology in World War II,* Princeton, NJ: Princeton University Press.

25. Allen, M., Hale, J., Mongeau, P., Berkowitz-Strafford, S., Stafford, S., Shanahan, W., Agee, P., Dillon, K., Jackson, R., & Ray, C. (1990). "Testing a Model of Message-Sideness: Three Replications," *Communication Monographs, 57,* 275–291.

26. Smith, *Persuasion and Human Action.*

27. Ibid.

28. Ibid.; Bettinghaus, & Cody, *Persuasive Communication.*

29. Smith, *Persuasion and Human Action,* (p. 233).

30. Hovland, Janis, & Kelley, *Communication and Persuasion.*

31. Ibid.

32. Berscheid, E. (1985). "Interpersonal Attraction," in L. Gardner and E. Aronson, (Eds.), *The Handbook of Social Psychology,* (Vol. II), (pp. 413–484), Hillsdale, NJ: Erlbaum.

33. Ibid., (p. 414).

34. Knapp, M. L., & Vangelisti, A. L. (1992). *Interpersonal Communication and Human Relationships,* Boston: Allyn & Bacon.

35. Baron, R. A., & Byrne, D. (1977). *Social Psychology: Understanding Human Interaction,* Boston: Allyn & Bacon.

36. Berger, C. R., & Calabrese, R. J. (1975). "Some Explorations in Initial Interaction and Beyond: Toward a Developmental Theory of Interpersonal Communication," *Human Communication Research, 1,* 99–112.

37. Ibid. Copyright © 1975, International Communication Association. Reprinted by permission from the International Communication Association and Charles R. Berger.

38. Ibid. Copyright © 1975, International Communication Association. Reprinted by permission from the International Communication Association and Charles R. Berger.

39. Berger, C. R., & Bradac, J. J. (1982). *Language and Social Psychology: Uncertainty in Interpersonal Relations.* London: Arnold.

40. Berger, C. R., & Gudykunst, W. B. (1991). "Uncertainty and Communication," in B. Dervin & M. J. Voight, (Eds.), *Progress in Communication Sciences, (Vol. 10),* (pp. 21–66), Norwood, NJ: Ablex.

41. Ibid.

42. The following references are cited in this list. They are presented here in alphabetical order.

Berger, C. R. (1979). "Beyond Initial Interaction: Uncertainty, Understanding, and the Development of Interpersonal Relationships," in H. Giles & R. N. St. Clair, (Eds.), *Language and Social Psychology,* (pp. 122–144). Oxford: Basil Blackwell.

Berger, C. R. (1986). "Uncertain Outcome Values in Predicted Relationships: Uncertainty Reduction Theory Then and Now," *Human Communication Research, 13,* 34–35.

Berger & Bradac, *Language and Social Psychology,* (pp. 18–28).

Berger & Calabrese, "Some Explorations in Initial Interaction and Beyond," 99–112.

Berger, C. R., & Douglas, W. (1981). "Studies in Interpersonal Epistemology III. Anticipated Interaction, Self-Monitoring, and Observational Context Selection," *Communication Monographs, 48,* 183–196.

Berger, C. R., Gardner, R. R., Parks, M. R., Schulman, L., & Miller, G. R. (1976). "Interpersonal Epistemology and Interpersonal Communication," in G. R. Miller, (Ed.), *Explorations in Interpersonal Communication,* (pp. 149–171), Beverly Hills, CA: Sage.

Berger, & Gudykunst, "Uncertainty and Communication," (pp. 21–66).

Berger, C. R., & Kellermann, K. A. (1985). "To Ask or Not to Ask: Is That a Question?" in R. N. Bostrom, (Ed.), *Communication Yearbook 7,* (pp. 342–368), Beverly Hills, CA: Sage.

Booth-Butterfield, M., Booth-Butterfield, S., & Koester, J. (1988). "The Function of Uncertainty Reduction in Alleviating Primary Tension in Small Groups," *Communication Research Reports, 2,* 146–153.

Clatterback, G. W. (1979). "Attributional Confidence and Uncertainty in Initial Interaction," *Human Communication Research, 5,* 147–157.

Douglas, W. (1984). "Initial Interaction Scripts: When Knowing Is Behaving," *Human Communication Research, 11,* 203–219.

Douglas, W. (1985). "Anticipated Interaction and Information Seeking," *Human Communication Research, 12,* 243–258.

Douglas, W. (1987). "Question-Asking in Same- and Opposite-Sex Initial Interactions: The Effects of Anticipated Future Interaction," *Human Communication Research, 14,* 230–245.

Douglas, W. (1990). "Uncertainty, Information-Seeking, and Liking During Initial Interaction," *Western Journal of Speech Communication, 54,* 66–81.

Douglas, W. (1991). "Expectations About Initial Interaction: An Examination of the Effects of Global Uncertainty," *Human Communication Research, 17,* 355–384.

Gardner, R. R. (1976). *Information Sequencing, Background Information, and Reciprocity in Initial Interaction.* Unpublished doctoral dissertation, Northwestern University.

Gudykunst, W. B. (1983). "Uncertainty Reduction and Predictability of Behavior in Low- and High-Context Cultures," *Communication Quarterly, 31,* 49–55.

Gudykunst, W. B. (1985). "The Influence of Cultural Similarity, Type of Relationship, and Monitoring on Uncertainty Reduction Processes," *Communication Monographs, 52,* 203–217.

Gudykunst, W. B., Chua, E., & Gray, A. (1987). "Cultural Dissimilarities and Uncertainty Reduction Processes," in M. McLaughlin, (Ed.), *Communication Yearbook 10,* (pp. 456–469), Newbury Park, CA: Sage.

Gudykunst, W. B., & Hammer, M. (1988). "The Influence of Social Identity and Intimacy of Interethnic Relationships on Uncertainty Reduction Processes," *Human Communication Research, 14,* 569–601.

Gudykunst, W. B., & Nishida, T. (1984). "Individual and Cultural Influences on Uncertainty Reduction," *Communication Monographs, 51,* 23–36.

Gudykunst, W. B., Nishida, T., & Schmidt, K. (1989). "Cultural, Relational, and Personality Influences on Uncertainty Reduction Processes," *Western Journal of Speech Communication, 53,* 13–29.

Gudykunst, W. B., Sodetani, L. L., & Sonoda, K. T. (1987). "Uncertainty Reduction in Japanese-American-Caucasian Relationships in Hawaii," *Western Journal of Speech Communication, 51,* 256–278.

Gudykunst, W. B., Yang, S. M., & Nishida, T. (1985). "A Cross-Cultural Test of Uncertainty Reduction Theory," *Human Communication Research, 11,* 407–454.

Harvey, J. H., Wells, G. L., & Alvarez, M. D. (1978). "Attribution in the Context of Conflict and Separation in Close Relationships," in J. H. Harvey, W. Ickes, & R. F. Kidd, (Eds.), *New Directions in Attribution Research 2*, (pp. 235–260), Hillsdale, NJ: Erlbaum.

Kellermann, K. (1986). "Anticipation of Future Interaction and Information Exchange in Initial Interaction," *Human Communication Research, 13*, 41–75.

Kellermann K., & Reynolds, R. (1990). "When Ignorance Is Bliss: The Role of Motivation to Reduce Uncertainty in Uncertainty Reduction Theory," *Human Communication Research, 17*, 5–75.

Kramer, M. W. (1993). "Communication and Uncertainty Reduction During Job Transfers: Leaving and Joining Processes," *Communication Monographs, 60*, 178–198.

Lester, R. E. (1987). "Organizational Culture, Uncertainty Reduction, and the Socialization of New Organizational Members," in S. Thomas, (Ed.), *Studies in Communication: Culture and Communication*, (pp. 105–113), Norwood, NJ: Ablex.

Parks, M. R., & Adelman, M. B. (1983). "Communication Networks and the Development of Romantic Relationships: An Expansion of Uncertainty Reduction Theory," *Human Communication Research, 10*, 55–79.

Planalp, S., & Honeycutt, J. M. (1985). "Events That Increase Uncertainty in Personal Relationships," *Human Communication Research, 11*, 221–230.

Planalp, S., Rutherford, D. K., & Honeycutt, J. M. (1988). "Events That Increase Uncertainty in Personal Relationships II: Replication and Extension," *Human Communication Research, 14*, 516–547.

Prisbell, M., & Anderson, J. F. (1980). "The Importance of Perceived Homophily, Level of Uncertainty, Feeling Good, Safety, and Self-Disclosure in Interpersonal Relationships," *Communication Quarterly, 28*, 22–33.

Sanders, J., & Wiseman, R. (1991). *Uncertainty Reduction among Ethnicities in the United States*. Paper presented at the International Communication Association, Chicago, IL.

Sanders, J., Wiseman, R., & Matz, I. (1991). "Uncertainty Reduction Processes in Acquaintance Relationships in Ghana and the United States," in S. Ting-Toomey & F. Korzenny, (Eds.), *Cross-Cultural Interpersonal Communication*, (pp.79–88), Newbury Park, CA: Sage.

Sherbloom, J., & Van Rheenan, D. D. (1984). "Spoken Language Indices of Uncertainty," *Human Communication Research, 11*, 221–230.

Sunnafrank, M. (1986). "Predicted Outcome Value during Initial Interactions: A Reformulation of Uncertainty Reduction Theory," *Human Communication Research, 13*, 3–33.

Sunnafrank, M. (1990). "Predicted Outcome Value and Uncertainty Reduction Theories: A Test of Competing Perspectives," *Human Communication Research, 17*, 76–103.

VanLear, C. A., Jr., & Trujillo, N. (1986). "On Becoming Acquainted: A Longitudinal Study of Social Judgement Processes," *Journal of Social and Personal Relationships, 3*, 375–392.

43. Burgoon, J. K. (1978). "A Communication Model of Personal Space Violations: Explication and an Initial Test," *Human Communication Research, 4*, 129–142.; Burgoon, J. K., & Jones, S. B. (1976). "Toward a Theory of Personal Space Expectations and Their Violations." *Human Communication Research, 2*, 131–146.

44. The following article presents an excellent review of research associated with NEV. Burgoon, J. K., & Hale, J. L. (1988). "Nonverbal Expectancy Violations: Model Elaboration and Application to Immediacy Behaviors," *Communication Monographs, 55*, 58–79.

45. Burgoon, J. K. (1978). "A Communication Model of Personal Space Violations: Explication and an Initial Test," *Human Communication Research, 4*, 129–142. Copyright © 1978, International Communication Association. Reprinted by permission from the International Communication Association and Judee Burgoon.

46. Ibid. Copyright © 1978, International Communication Association. Reprinted by permission from the International Communication Association and Judee Burgoon.

47. Burgoon, & Hale, "Nonverbal Expectancy Violations," 58–79.

48. LePoire, B. A., & Burgoon, J. K. (1994). "Two Contrasting Explanations of Involvement Violations: Expectancy Violations Theory Versus Discrepancy Arousal Theory," *Human Communication Research, 20*, 560–591; Burgoon, J. K., Newton, D. A., Walther, J. A., & Baesler, E. J. (1991). "Nonverbal Expectancy Violations and Conversational Involvement," *Journal of Nonverbal Behavior, 13*, 97–120; Burgoon, J. K. (1992). "Relational Message Interpretations of Touch, Conversational Distance, and Posture," *Journal of Nonverbal Behavior, 15*,

233–259; Burgoon, J. K., Dillman, L., & Stern, L. (1993). "Adaptation in Dyadic Interaction: Defining and Operationalizing Patterns of Reciprocity and Compensation," *Communication Theory, 3,* 295–316.

49. Cattell, R. (1950). *Personality: A Systematic, Theoretical, and Factual Study,* New York: McGraw-Hill, (p. 2).

50. Maddi, S. R. (1972). *Personality Theories: A Comparative Analysis,* Homewood, IL: Dorsey Press, (p. 9).

51. Infante, Rancer, & Womack, *Building Communication Theory,* (p. 140).

52. McCroskey, J. C. (1977). "Oral Communication Apprehension: A Summary of Recent Theory and Research," *Human Communication Research, 4,* 78–96.

53. McCroskey, J. C., Richmond, V. P., & Stewart, R. A. (1986). *One on One: The Foundations of Interpersonal Communication,* Englewood Cliffs, NJ: Prentice-Hall.

54. Garrison, K. R., & Garrison, J. P. (1977). *Measurement of Communication Apprehension among Children.* Paper presented at the annual meeting of the International Communication Association, Berlin, West Germany; Garrison, K. R., & Garrison, J. P. (1979). "Measurement of Communication Apprehension Among Children: A Factor in the Development of Basic Speech Skills," *Communication Education, 28,* 119–128; McCroskey, Richmond, & Stewart, *One on One;* McCroskey, J. C. (1977). "Classroom Consequences of Communication Apprehension," *Communication Education, 26,* 27–33.

55. Daly, J. A., & Friedrich, G. (1981). "The Development of Communication Apprehension: A Retrospective Analysis of Contributing Correlates," *Communication Quarterly, 29,* 243–255.

56. Ibid.

57. McCroskey, "Oral Communication Apprehension," 78–96.

58. Beatty, M. J., Plax, T. G., & Kearney, P. (1985). "Reinforcement Versus Modeling in the Development of Communication Apprehension," *Communication Research Reports, 2,* (pp. 80–85); Daly & Friedrich, "The Development of Communication Apprehension," 243–255.

59. Daly, & Friedrich, "The Development of Communication Apprehension," 243–255.

60. Hutchinson, K. L., & Neuliep, J. W. (1993). "The Influence of Parent and Peer Modeling on the Development of Communication Apprehension in Elementary School Children," *Communication Quarterly, 41,* 16–25.

61. McCroskey, "Oral Communication Apprehension," 78–96.

62. McCroskey, Richmond, & Stewart, *One on One;* McCroskey, J. C., & Anderson, J. (1976). "The Relationship Between Communication Apprehension and Academic Achievement Among College Students," *Human Communication Research, 3,* 73–81; Smythe, M. J., & Powers, W. G. (1978). "When Galatea Is Apprehensive: Effects of Communication Apprehension on Teacher Expectations," in B. D. Ruben, (Ed.), *Communication Yearbook II,* (pp. 487–494), New Brunswick, NJ: Transaction Books; Davis, D., & Scott, M. D. (1978). "Communication Apprehension, Intelligence, and Achievement Among Secondary School Students," in Ruben, *Communication Yearbook II,* (pp. 457–472).

63. Daly, J. A., & Leth, S. (1976). *Communication Apprehension and the Personnel Selection Decision.* Paper presented to the International Communication Association, Portland, Oregon; Daly, J. A., & McCroskey, J. C. (1975). "Occupational Choice and Desirability as a Function of Communication Apprehension," *Journal of Counseling Psychology, 22,* 309–313.

64. McCroskey, Richmond, & Stewart, *One on One;* Burgoon, J. K., & Koper, R. S. (1983). *Communication Reticence and Relational Message Behavior.* Paper presented to the International Communication Association, Dallas, Texas; Arnston, P., Mortenson, D., &. Lustig, M. (1980). "Predisposition Toward Verbal Behavior in Task Oriented Interaction," *Human Communication Research, 6,* 239–252; Fenton, R. S., & Hopf, T. S. (1976). *A Conceptual Explanation of Three Common Approaches to Communication Apprehension.* Paper presented to the Western States Speech Communication Association, Phoenix, Arizona; McCroskey, J. C., & Sheahan, M. (1978). "Communication Apprehension, Social Preference, and Social Behavior in a College Environment," *Communication Quarterly, 26,* 41–50; Mulac, A., & Sherman, A. R. (1975). "Relationships Among Four Parameters of Speaker Evaluation: Speech Skill, Source Credibility, Subjective Speech Anxiety, and Behavioral Speech Anxiety," *Speech Monographs, 42,* 302–310; Pilkonis, P. (1977). "The Behavioral Consequences of Shyness," *Journal of Personality, 45,* 596–611; Porter, D. T. (1982). "Communicator Style Perceptions as a Function of Communication Apprehension," *Communication Quarterly, 30,* 237–244.

65. Phillips, G. M., & Butt, D. (1966). "Reticence Revisited," *Pennsylvania Speech Annual, 23,* 40–57.

66. McCroskey, J. C., & Richmond, V. P. (1980). *The Quiet Ones: Communication Apprehension and Shyness,* Dubuque: Gorsuch-Scarisbrick.

67. Infante, D. A., & Wigley, C. J., III, (1986). "Verbal Aggressiveness: An Interpersonal Model and Measure," *Communication Monographs, 53,* 61–69.

68. Infante, D. A. (1987). "Aggressiveness," in J. C. McCroskey & J. A. Daly, (Eds.), *Personality and Interpersonal Communication,* (pp. 157–194). Newbury Park, CA: Sage.

69. Ibid.; Lorenz, K. (1966). *On Aggression,* New York: Harcourt, Brace.

70. Infante, "Aggressiveness," (pp. 157–194).

71. Ibid.; Infante, & Wigley, "Verbal Aggressiveness," 61–69.

72. Infante, "Aggressiveness," (pp. 157–194).

73. Ibid.

74. Ibid.

75. Tucker, R. K., Weaver, R. L., & Redden, E. M. (1983). "Differentiating Assertiveness, Aggressiveness, and Shyness: A Factor Analysis," *Psychological Reports, 53,* 607–611; Bell, R. A., & Daly, J. A. (1985). "Some Communicator Correlates of Loneliness," *Southern Speech Communication Journal, 50,* 121–142.

76. Infante, "Aggressiveness," (pp. 157–194); Infante, D. A. (1981). "Trait Argumentativeness as a Predictor of Communicative Behavior in Situations Requiring Argument," *Central States Speech Journal, 32,* 265–272; Infante, D. A. (1982). "The Argumentative Student in Speech Communication Classrooms: An Investigation and Implications," *Communication Education, 31,* 141–148; Gottman, J. M. (1979). *Marital Interaction: Experimental Investigations,* New York: Academic Press.

77. Infante, "Aggressiveness," (pp. 157–194); Infante, Rancer, & Womack, *Building Communication Theory,* (p. 165); Berkowitz, L. (1962). *Aggression: A Social Psychological Analysis,* New York: McGraw-Hill; Berkowitz, L. (1983). "The Experience of Anger as a Parallel Process in the Display of Impulsive, 'Angry' Aggression," in R. G. Green & E. I. Connerstein, (Eds.), *Aggression: Theoretical and Empirical Reviews,* (pp. 103–133), New York: Academic Press.

78. Segrin, C., & Fitzpatrick, M. A. (1992). "Depression and Verbal Aggressiveness in Different Marital Types," *Communication Studies, 43,* 79–91; Infante, D. A., Chandler, T. A., & Rudd, J. E. (1989). "Test of

Argumentative Skill Deficiency Model of Interspousal Violence," *Communication Monographs, 56,* 163–177.

79. Infante, & Wigley, "Verbal Aggressiveness," (p. 67).

80. Delia, J. G., & Grossberg, L. (1977). "Interpretation and Evidence," *Western Journal of Speech Communication, 41,* 32–42; Burleson, B. R. (1982). *Developmental and Individual Differences in Comforting Communication Skills.* Unpublished Doctoral Dissertation, University of Illinois at Urbana-Champaign.

81. Delia, J. G., O'Keefe, B. J., &. O'Keefe, D. J. (1982). "The Constructivist Approach to Communication," in F. E. X. Dance, (Ed.), *Human Communication Theory: Comparative Essays,* (pp. 147–191), New York: Harper & Row.

82. Crockett, W. H. (1965). "Cognitive Complexity and Impression Formation," in B. A. Maher, (Ed.), *Progress in Experimental Personality Research,* (Vol. 2), (pp. 47–89), New York: Academic Press, (p. 47).

83. Ibid., (p. 48).

84. Burleson, *Developmental and Individual Differences in Comforting Communication Skills.*

85. Burleson, B. R. (1984). "Age, Social-Cognitive Development, and the Use of Comforting Strategies," *Communication Monographs, 51,* 140–153.

86. O'Keefe, D. J., & Sypher, H. E. (1981). "Cognitive Complexity Measures and the Relationship of Cognitive Complexity to Communication," *Human Communication Research, 8,* 72–92.

87. Burleson, B. R. (1987). "Cognitive Complexity," in McCroskey & Daly, *Personality and Interpersonal Communication,* (p. 320).

88. Applegate, J. L. (1982). "The Impact of Construct System Development on Communication and Impression Formation in Persuasive Contexts," *Communication Monographs, 49,* 277–289; Clark, R. A., & Delia, J. G. (1977). "Cognitive Complexity, Social Perspective Taking, and Functional Persuasive Skills in Second- to Ninth-Grade Children," *Human Communication Research, 3,* 128–134; O'Keefe, B. J., & Delia, J. G. (1979). "Construct Comprehensiveness and Cognitive Complexity as Predictors of the Number and Strategic Adaptation of Arguments and Appeals in a Persuasive Message," *Communication Monograph, 46,* 231–240; Delia, J. G, Kline, S. L., & Burleson, B. R. (1979). "The Development of Persuasive Communication Strategies in Kindergartners through Twelfth-Graders," *Communication Monographs, 46,* 241–256.

89. Delia, J. G., Clark, R. A., & Switzer, D. E. (1974). "Cognitive Complexity and Impression Formation in Informal Social Interaction," *Speech Monographs, 41,* 299–308; Delia, J. G., Clark, R. A., & Switzer, D. E. (1979). "The Content of Informal Conversations as a Function of Interactants' Interpersonal Cognitive Complexity," *Communication Monographs, 46,* 274–281; Hale, C. L. (1980). "Cognitive Complexity-Simplicity as a Determinant of Communicative Effectiveness," *Communication Monographs, 47,* 304–311; Hale, C. L. (1982). "An Investigation of the Relationship between Cognitive Complexity and Listener-Adapted Communication," *Central States Speech Journal, 33,* 339–344.

90. Burleson, "Age, Social-Cognitive Development, and the Use of Comforting Strategies," 140–153; Burleson, B. R., & Samter, W. (1985). "Consistencies in Theoretical and Naive Evaluations of Comforting Messages," *Communication Monographs, 52,* 103–123; Samter, W., & Burleson, B. R. (1984). "Cognitive and Motivational Influences on Spontaneous Comforting Behavior," *Human Communication Research, 11,* 231–260; Neuliep, J. W., & Hazleton, V. (1985). "Cognitive Complexity and Apprehension About Communication: A Preliminary Report," *Psychological Reports, 57,* 1224–1227; Neuliep, J. W., & Hazleton, V. (1986). "Enhanced Conversational Recall and Reduced Conversational Interference as a Function of Cognitive Complexity," *Human Communication Research, 13,* 211–224.

91. Stacks, D., Hickson, M., III, & Hill, S. R., Jr. (1991). *Introduction to Communication Theory,* New York: Holt, Rinehart, & Winston.

92. Stacks, D., & Hickson, M., III (1994). "An Evolutionary, Bio-Social Approach to Intrapersonal Communication." Unpublished manuscript.

93. Stacks, Hickson, & Hill, *Introduction to Communication Theory.*

94. Searle, J. (1992). *The Rediscovery of the Mind,* Cambridge, MA: MIT Press, (p. 1).

95. Ibid, (p. 23).

96. Goss, B. (1989). *The Psychology of Human Communication,* Prospect Heights, IL: Waveland.

97. Andersen, P., Garrison, J. P., & Andersen, J. F. (1979). "Implications of a Neurophysiological Approach for the Study of Nonverbal Communication," *Human Communication Research, 6,* 74–89.

Chapter *8*

The Human
Action Approach:
Historical Roots

*The common behaviour of mankind is the system of reference by
means of which we interpret an unknown language.[1]*
—LUDWIG WITTGENSTEIN

Imagine someone driving a car on the highway at fifteen miles an hour above the speed limit. A police officer pulls the person over and issues a citation. Imagine two elderly gentlemen sitting under a shade tree quietly playing a game of chess. Each man intently watches the other's move. Imagine a surgeon removing the damaged heart of a patient and replacing it with a healthy one. Surgeries such as these can take as long as seven or eight hours. Finally, imagine yourself chatting with a few friends in the hallway of your dormitory. One of your friends comments that his or her communication class is really boring. You respond that yours is quite interesting.

Each of the above four situations has much in common with the others. Each is dependent on the knowledge and application of socially shared rules. The driver of the car is violating the rules associated with speed limits that are posted all along the highway. The driver may pay a heavy fine for violating the rule. The two elderly gentlemen pay close attention to the rules and regulations for playing chess. Moving one's king or queen can only be done according to strictly prescribed rules. The one who applies the rules most strategically will win the game. In the third situation, the physician must apply very precise medical rules for heart transplants. Certain kinds of instruments and procedures must be used to complete the operation successfully. The surgeon and staff went to school for many years to learn the rules. Finally, in the fourth situation, as you chat with your friends in the hallway, you apply the rules of conversation, including such things as sentence structure, word choice, and turn taking. The application of these rules was probably done unconsciously.

211

Though the four situations are very different from one another, each is dependent on a certain set of rules. Without the knowledge and application of such rules, none of the situations could have occurred.

The purpose of this chapter is to present the metatheoretical perspective called the human action approach, or the rules approach. This chapter is organized into five major sections. The first section focuses on the historical foundations of the rules approach. The second section outlines the major assumptions guiding rules theorists. The third section establishes the definitional boundaries of a rule. The fourth section discusses how rules explain behavior and the idea of practical necessity. Finally, the last section outlines the relationship between rules and social behavior.

Historical Foundations of the Rules Approach

Philosophers, humanists, and social scientists have been interested in the concept of rules. Whereas the causal process approach can be called upon to explain both natural and social phenomena, the rules approach is strictly tied to human behavior; that is, it does not apply to the natural sciences. In fact, the contemporary rules approach grew out of a dissatisfaction with the laws approach and its mechanistic view of human behavior.

The discussion of rules can be traced back to the writings of Aristotle, who distinguished between the laws of men and those of nature. The laws of nature refer to natural laws such as those discussed in Chapter 6. The laws of men are what contemporary rules theorists call rules.[2] The notion that social phenomena can be explained by rules can also be found in the writings of the German philosopher Immanuel Kant. Writing in the late eighteenth century, Kant observed that humans are active beings who possess goals and the capacity of choice. Similar to Aristotle, Kant distinguished between the physiological and pragmatic study of humans. The physiological approach investigates how nature affects humans. The pragmatic approach emphasizes that humans are free agents with the ability to make choices and examines what humans can and should make of themselves.[3]

Historically, linguists (i.e., scholars who study language) have had keen interest in rules. Wilhelm von Humbolt, for example, writing in the early nineteenth century, and noted as the father of the linguistic relativity hypothesis, argued that language was a system of rules. Similarly, the linguist Ferdinand de Saussure, in the early twentieth century, compared language to a game of chess, arguing that language consists of a finite set of rules that is capable of generating an infinite set of sentences.[4]

Influenced by the writings of Saussure, Ludwig Josef Johann Wittgenstein, a philosopher of mathematics and professor philosophy at Cambridge until his death in 1951, is responsible for the contemporary interest in rules.[5] Perhaps Wittgenstein's most important contribution was the idea that rules are inherently social. Wittgenstein writes:

> *It is not possible that there should have been only one occasion on which someone obeyed a rule. It is not possible that there should have been only one occasion on which a report was made, an order given or understood; and so on.—To obey a rule, to make a report, to give an order, to play a game of chess, are customs. . . . And hence also 'obeying a rule' is a practice. And to think of obeying a rule is not to obey a rule. Hence it is not possible to obey a rule 'privately.'*[6]

Wittgenstein's point is that rules are created by means of convention; that is, that they are initiated, negotiated, and practiced between people. Rules may be created culturally or individually. For example, in American culture, one rule is that people should not burp at the dinner table. In some Far Eastern cultures, however, it is perfectly acceptable, and even polite, to burp out loud after eating. Burping is perceived as a compliment to the cook. The individual rules we create and practice may only apply to ourselves, although we enact them in social contexts. For example, we may dress a certain way or adopt a certain unique style of speech to capture the attention of others. Unlike laws, rules are created by people and thus are not universally invariant nor absolute.

One of the most influential contemporary scholars associated with a rules approach is Noam Chomsky. As a theoretical linguist, Chomsky aims to answer the question "What is language?" To this end, Chomsky developed his famous theory of generative grammar. He argues that, at birth, all humans possess the capacity for language. Although this capacity is universal, it is not detailed enough to dictate exactly what language any specific child will speak. The particular language surfaces when the child hears his or her parents speak and then imitates them. Of particular importance is that children derive the structural regularities—that is, the grammatical rules of the language—from their parents. Armed with the basic rules the child can then "generate" an infinite number of new sentences. Language, then, consists of all of the possible sentences one can generate from the basic structural rules. Chomsky contends that these grammatical rules are innate with any native speaker of the language.[7] In this sense language is like the game of chess. By knowing a finite set of rules for chess, two people will probably never play the exact same game twice. The rules allow for an almost infinite number of plays and strategies.

Currently, scholars in a variety of academic disciplines share an interest in rules, including anthropological linguists, linguists, philosophers, sociologists, and communication scholars.[8] Although these scholars come from a variety of academic backgrounds, they share certain fundamental assumptions about social phenomena.

Basic Assumptions from a Rules Perspective: Action versus Motion

A fundamental assumption shared by rules theorists is that human behavior is not random but is regular and recurs in similar situations. Rules theorists believe that most behavior is intentional, controllable, and the result of free choice rather than the effect of some cause. For example, choosing to go to class today would be considered intentional, controllable, and freely chosen behavior. Like the causal process theorists, rules theorists also believe that some behavior is governed by mechanistic or lawlike forces. For example, slipping on ice is something that one cannot control, is unintentional, and is not the result of free choice.

Rules theorists refer to intentional, goal-related behavior as *action* and call mechanistically determined behavior (i.e., lawlike) *motion*. The action-motion dichotomy is a major departure from either the laws or systems approaches to social phenomena.[9]

In advocating an action approach to human behavior, philosopher Rom Harré and psychologist Paul Secord have developed what they call the anthropomorphic model of man. (Anthropomorphic means to describe something in terms of human form or attributes.) In their anthropomorphic model Harré and Secord firmly reject the mechanistic model espoused by laws theorists and logical positivists. They contend that human beings should be treated as agents acting according to rules. They also argue that the theory of movements (i.e., causally determined behavior) should be separated from any theory of action. Their anthropomorphic model argues that human beings: (a) have the power to initiate change, (b) are capable of being aware of things other than themselves, and (c) have the power of speech.[10]

Like the systems theorists, rules theorists believe that all action is goal driven (i.e., teleological). Harré and Secord write:

> *Social behaviour is meaningful behaviour. It involves an agent with certain intentions and expectations, an agent capable of deliberating and choosing from a variety of courses of action...a central part of this process is communication between people.[11]*

Harré and Secord believe, as do other rules theorists, that behaviors (i.e., actions) can be explained in terms of the ends or goals for which they are performed. For example, you are attending college to achieve some future goal (e.g., gainful employment). This is called a teleological explanation and is a fundamental part of the rules approach. This is also a sharp departure from the causal process perspective that views behavior as the result of some antecedent condition.

Definitions of a Rule

Dictionaries define rules as prescribed guides for conduct or action.[12] Under this definition there are many different kinds of rules, including rules in games, rules of language, moral rules, and rules of law.[13] In order to identify and use rules to explain human behavior, however, rules theorists need a more detailed definition of rule. Susan Shimanoff, a leading rules theorist, provides a very applicable definition. She defines a rule as "a followable prescription that indicates what behavior is obligated, preferred, or prohibited in certain contexts."[14] Mary John Smith, another leading rules theorist, defines rules as "descriptive statements linking human intentions or goals with actions that are goal satisfying."[15] A key term in Shimanoff's definition is the notion of followability.

Followability

That rules are followable means that they may also be broken.[16] A person can choose to follow or violate a rule. For example:

> *R₁: After Mark burped, he did not excuse himself...the slob.*

In this example, Mark chose not to follow the rule that one should excuse oneself upon burping. Followability involves choice, if there was not choice, then it would be a law. Laws describe noncontrollable phenomena (i.e., motion). For example:

> *R₂: Laura should not bleed if she cuts herself.*

Obviously, Laura cannot "decide" whether to bleed. Bleeding is the effect of some cause. Followability also means that rules must refer to empirically possible behavior. For example:

R_3: *Students should not hit the ground after they jump out of trees.*

Students cannot choose whether to hit the ground and even if they could, it is not empirically possible for them to remain in suspended animation after jumping out of a tree.

Although followability involves choice and empirically possible behavior, some rules may prescribe behavior that is almost impossible to perform. For example:

R_4: *Communication students must speak Swahili during class.*

Although this rule prescribes behavior that is practically impossible for students to follow, it is empirically possible and thus a rule. The maker of the rule may not know what is practical when formulating the rule. Because of this, some rules may contradict one another. For example:

R_5: *Communication students should inform their professor if they witness another student cheating on an exam.*

R_6: *Communication students should not "rat" on each other.*

By following one of these rules a communication student automatically breaks the other rule. Hence, rules need not be followed in practice to be rules.

Prescriptiveness

A second defining characteristic of rules is that they prescribe behavior that is preferred, obligated, or prohibited.[17] Preferred and obligated behavior is that which ought or should occur. Prohibited behavior is that which one ought not perform. Preferred behavior is that which is the most desirable for the given context but may not necessarily be obligated. For example:

R_7: *Students should study very hard for their exams.*

Obligated behavior is that which is enacted to satisfy the requirements of some social contract between people as in the fulfillment of a promise or the repayment of debts. For example:

R_8: *After Julie finishes her meal, she should pay the waiter.*

Prohibited behavior is that which is forbidden or not permitted:

R_9: *Communication students should not cheat on examinations.*

Because rules are prescriptive and followable, people who choose not to follow them may be subject to negative evaluation. As Smith and Shimanoff note, laws are not prescriptive. Laws are descriptions of previously observed relationships between two or more events or objects.[18] In most cases, people who knowingly violate a rule are conscious of the possible ramifications. Drivers who speed, students who cheat, customers who shoplift, and children who swear realize that they are accountable and that their behavior is subject to negative sanction. Likewise, individuals who follow the rules are typically thought of as "responsible citizens," "scholarly," "faithful customers," and "good kids." There is a prescriptive or normative force that motivates one to follow the rule.

Situational Constraints

Like causal processes, rules operate under certain boundary conditions; that is, they apply in some situations and not in others.[19] Shimanoff argues that rules prescribe what behavior is appropriate in particular contexts; hence, such behavior recurs in similar contexts. Several "scope conditions" specify what rule to apply, including: (a) the physical surroundings, (b) the episode, (c) the participants, and (d) the medium of interaction.[20] For example, consider all the rules that apply to the act of yelling. The *physical surroundings* might prohibit yelling:

R_{10}: *When in church, Page, you should not yell.*

The *episode* being enacted might indicate that yelling is the preferred behavior:

R_{11}: *One should yell as loudly as possible when their team scores.*

The *actors* themselves may specify with whom one should and should not yell:

R_{12}: *Don't yell at the Dean, Erin.*

Finally, the *medium of communication* will denote what rule to apply:

R_{13}: *Ed, stop yelling at me over the phone.*

The act of engaging in rule-related behavior is based on a series of decisions made by the actor regarding the scope conditions of the situation. These decisions probably occur quite rapidly and may even come unconsciously, especially if the situation is familiar to the actor. Figure 8.1 outlines this process.

Remember that the actor has a goal and uses the rule to inform him or her of the type of behavior most likely to achieve the goal. Thus, the first decision is whether or not the behavior will achieve the desired outcome. If so, then the actor will assess the scope conditions beginning hierarchically with the physical surroundings, the episode, the actors present, and finally the medium of the communication. If at any point the actor perceives that one of the scope conditions renders the behavior in question as inappropriate, the actor will decide not to engage in the behavior. If, however, the scope conditions appear consis-

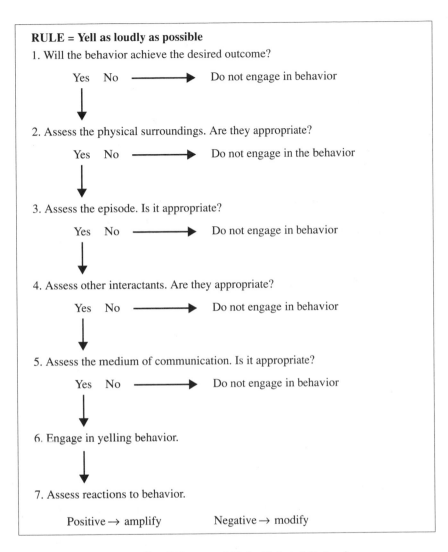

FIGURE 8.1   Scope Conditions and Rule-Related Behavior

tent with the behavior, then the actor will probably engage in the behavior. Important here is the notion of prescriptive force. Upon the completion of the behavior, the actor will monitor the reaction of others who have witnessed it. If it is perceived positively via positive feedback or the lack of negative feedback, the actor will continue to engage in such behavior when similar scope conditions arise; prescriptive force operates. If the actor receives negative feedback, the prescriptive force operates in the opposite direction indicating that the behavior was inappropriate. Prescriptive force also operates at the beginning of the decision-making process. The extent to which the actor believes the behavior achieves the desired outcome determines the rule's prescriptive force. In addition, the force of the rule is contingent upon cultural or societal sanctioning. The actor may not know for sure if the behavior will achieve the goal. It is always possible that it won't.

Types of Rules

Smith contends that there are two types of rules, implicit and explicit.[21] Explicit rules are those that have been stated publicly, either formally or informally. For example, your college or university has a written code of conduct regarding student behavior on and off campus. Many organizations have written constitutions expressing their rules. The Constitution of the United States, for example, may be considered an explicit set of rules specifying how the government is to operate. These examples would be considered formal rules. Rules that your family and groups of friends have developed over time are also considered explicit rules but are considered informal. For example, many families have explicit rules regarding what time children are allowed to go out and come home. Implicit rules are those which are unstated but have as much prescriptive force as explicit rules. For example, one of your friends may have recently engaged in some action that you thought unethical or wrong (e.g., smoked pot, had premarital sex, cheated on an exam, etc.) but you decided not to say anything in order to avoid conflict. Here, your goal was to avoid conflict and your implicit rule was to remain silent.

CASE STUDY 10   Rules for Organizational Communication

Key Terms

  Hierarchical Rules

  Task Rules

  Work-Group Rules

  Individual Rules

Many communication scholars agree that organizational communication, like small group or interpersonal communication, is governed by rules. Within organizations rules are produced via communication and rules govern organizational communication. Because organizational communication operates in a different physical, sociological, and psychological context than either small group or interpersonal communication, the rules that emerge in organizations are different. Tompkins, for example, outlines four kinds of organizational communication rules, including (a) hierarchical, (b) task, (c) work-group, and (d) individual rules.[a] Hierarchical rules are those that may come in the form of official policies from other organizations and are interpreted by the highest level superiors in the organization who communicate them to descending levels. Governmental regulations, for example, are one type of hierarchical rule. Task rules, those rules specific to the particular job within the organization, are learned in professional and/or vocational training or during on-the-job training or internships. Accountants, for example, apply specific rules when performing financial audits. Chemists apply particular rules when conducting their experiments. Work-

---

group rules are generally informal rules produced by the work force for the purpose of group identification and solidarity. Tompkins maintains that these rules are created as a means of self-protection against exploitation from the higher levels in the organizational hierarchy. A committee might, for example, establish its own rules for conducting meetings. A road crew might establish its own rules for who drives the truck and who speaks to the higher levels in the organization. The fourth type, individual rules, are those idiosyncratic rules that apply to individual members of the organization. Such rules might be implicit, as in the case of how much criticism a known employee is willing to take, or explicit, as in the case of contractual agreements regarding salary. An examination and application of these four types of rules will be the the the focus of this case study.

This case study centers on the private accounting firm of Weasel, Weasel, and Gopher (WWG). WWG employs fourteen people, including five certified public accountants, each with their own assistant, and four secretarial staff members. WWG conducts financial audits for various organizations, including the local hardware store, a tool and dye manufacturing company, a small private liberal arts college, and several local charitable organizations. Recently there has been some confusion, at both the local and national level, as to the proper role of the accountant for fraud detection when conducting routine financial audits. Accountants are unsure as to the extent of their legal and professional responsibility to detecting and subsequently reporting fraud. The public perception is that auditors, because of their education, expertise, and public certification, can easily detect fraud when it occurs. Unfortunately, this simply is not accurate. In 1986 the U.S. Congress passed the Financial Fraud Detection and Disclosure Act (the Act) which amends existing federal securities laws to provide reasonable assurance that fraud will be discovered and reported. The Act strengthens the present system and clarifies the role of the accountant by outlining clear standards for the detection and reporting of financial fraud.

In the case of WWG, the Act serves as a set of hierarchical rules. In many ways, the Act governs communication between auditors and their clients and the communication within individual private accounting firms. As the hierarchical rules are interpreted by accounting firms such as WWG, new task, work-group, and individual rules will be created.

In addition to several technicalities, the Act requires that auditors include specific and substantive procedures for detecting financial fraud as a part of the overall routine audit. In the case of WWG, four of the auditors are unfamiliar with such procedures and will have to attend professional seminars to learn the new procedures; that is, they will learn new task rules. The Act requires that the individuals actually responsible for the audit sign it on behalf of the firm conducting the audit. In the case of WWG, the senior member of the firm has agreed to do all of the audits until the other members are more comfortable with the new procedures; that is, a new work-group rule has been established. The Act requires that accountants report known or suspected illegal activities to the appropriate government authorities. This represents a hierarchical rule that will vary from organization to organization because different states have different governing bodies that regulate accounting procedures. This rule also obligates communication between governmental agencies and accounting firms such as WWG. At WWG, a new form has been created specifically for reporting suspected fraud; thus, a new task rule has been created. The five assistants to the auditors are uncomfortable with the new procedures and the general topic of fraud. Informally they have agreed to disassociate themselves, for the time being, with any audit where there is suspected fraud. This represents a work-group rule. Finally, John Weasel, the senior accountant with WWG, has decided to give himself a salary increase based on the new responsibilities he has incurred since the passage of the Act; that is, an individual rule. In addition, Mike Neef, the newest member of WWG, has informally negotiated with WWG that he will typically not conduct such audits; hence another individual rule is enacted.

[a]Tompkins, P. K. (1984). "The Functions of Human Communication in Organization," in C. C. Arnold & J. W. Bowers, (Eds.), *Handbook of Rhetorical and Communication Theory,* (pp. 659–719), Boston: Allyn & Bacon.

Explanation from a Rules Perspective: Practical Necessity

Recall from Chapter 2 that the primary function of theory is to explain. Remember also that phenomena are explained to the extent that (a) regularity is identified, and (b) the force which makes the regularity necessary is identified. From a causal process perspective the force which makes regularity necessary is causal. From a rules perspective the force is practical. Explanations based on practical necessity are called teleological and only apply to action, they are not explanations of, nor can they be applied to, motion. Georg Henrik von Wright, an eminent philosopher and author of many books on the philosophy of science, offers a detailed analysis of teleological explanations and practical necessity. von Wright compares teleology with causality and teleological explanation with causal explanation and argues that in designating the force which makes regularity necessary, causal explanations usually look to some set of antecedent conditions.[22] An effect occurs because of some *prior* cause. The cause precedes the effect. Water boils "because" its temperature reached 212 degrees.[23]

Teleological explanations, on the other hand, point to the future. Something is said to occur "in order" that something else should or will occur. Von Wright presents the following schema:

> *A intends to bring about 'p'*
> *A considers that he cannot bring about 'p' unless he does 'a'*
> *Therefore, A sets himself out to do 'a'*[24]

von Wright calls this schema a practical syllogism. The major premise, "A intends to bring about 'p'" specifies the goal. The minor premise, "A considers that he cannot bring about 'p' unless he does 'a'" indicates what behavior is necessary to achieve the goal. The conclusion "Therefore, A sets himself out to do 'a'" indicates what action occurs. The rule is found in the minor premise. "A" must have knowledge of a set of rules regarding "p" and "a" such that the rule is "In order to have 'p' one should engage in 'a'."

Practical necessity is based on the amount of normative or prescriptive force an actor feels to perform some action. Prescriptive force exerts pressure and/or motivates actors to select certain goals.[25] Rules specify the appropriate actions for achieving those goals and link the intention and the action. For example:

> *John intends to get a job. (Goal based on prescriptive force)*
> *John considers that he cannot get a job unless he has an education. (Rule)*
> *Therefore, John sets out to get an education. (Action)*

The rule here is that in order to get a job, the act of getting an education is necessary. Whether or not John actually goes to college depends on how much prescriptive force there is in the major premise; that is, how badly John wants to get a job. The amount of prescriptive force may stem from personal, societal, or cultural values. In America, for example, a college education is highly valued both socially and culturally.

von Wright contends that John's behavior (i.e., getting an education) has an inner and outer aspect. The inner aspect is his intention or will behind the outer manifestations.[26] The immediate outer aspect is the muscular activity required to achieve the inner aspect. Not all behaviors have inner and outer aspects. Behaviors void of the inner aspects are called reflexes, or motion. Such behaviors, said to be reactions or responses to some stimuli, are lawlike and can be explained using a causal explanation. From a teleological perspective, one's intentions and goals are linked by rules. The following of rules is seen as the force prompting social behavior.[27] Rules explain why people behave the way they do.

The Relationship between Rules and Behavior

As mentioned previously, rules apply to action. They are not used to explain motion. For the communication theorist rules may function in a number of ways. Shimanoff contends that in addition to explaining human action, rules may function to regulate, interpret, evaluate, justify, correct, and predict behavior.[28]

Regulation

Because of their prescriptive force, rules regulate behavior; that is, they manage, direct, or moderate actions.

> R_{14}: *Becky should not refer to police officers as big fat pigs.*

Interpretation

Rules help to define, translate, or decipher the meaning of another's behavior. For example, a wife makes sexual advances to her husband. The husband indicates that he has a headache. The wife interprets his behavior as meaning he is not interested in having sex with her on this particular night though he has not specifically said that.

> R_{15}: *If a spouse has a headache, then the other spouse should not make sexual advances.*

Evaluation

Because rules specify what behavior is preferred, obligated, or prohibited, they can be used to evaluate another's action. For example, Susan exclaims, "I can't stand Jim, he talks too much." Susan's rule is:

R_{16}: *People should not dominate conversations.*

Because Jim has violated the rule, Susan negatively evaluates him.

Justification

People can use rules to justify or excuse their behavior. For example, a coworker wards off the sexual advances of another coworker by saying, "I will not sleep with you because we are not married." The rule here is:

R_{17}: *People who are not married should not sleep with each other.*

Correction

Shimanoff indicates that in addition to using rules to evaluate behavior, rules can be used to correct behavior. For example, if a child says "I want goes swimming," the parent can correct the child by informing him or her of the correct rules (i.e., syntax) of language and sentence structure.

Prediction

Remember from Chapter 2 that a fundamental function of theory is prediction. Because of their explanatory power, rules can also predict the behavior of others. For example, in searching for his friend, Joe predicts, "Well, it's Friday, Smith must be at the bar." The rule here is that on Fridays, Smith goes to the bar.

R_{18}: *If it is Friday, then meet friends at bar.*

Identification of Rules from Behavior

In order to extend and advance rules theory, communication theorists must be able to identify rules. Explicit rules are probably easy to identify. Implicit rules, however, can only be identified by observing behavior. Remember from Shimanoff's definition that a rule is a followable prescription that indicates what behavior is preferred, obligated, or prohibited in certain contexts. Because rules are followable (and breakable), rule-generated behavior is controllable; that is, a person decides whether to engage in the behavior. Remember also that rules refer to that behavior which is empirically possible, hence controllable. Motion, on the other hand, is uncontrollable since it is governed by lawlike forces. As Shimanoff notes, if the behavior in question is not within the actor's physical ability to choose whether or not to perform it, it is meaningless to hold the actor responsible for such behavior.[29]

Because rules prescribe behavior, violations of a rule subjects the violator to negative evaluation from others. Likewise, the appropriate application of a given rule subjects the actor to positive evaluation. Hence, rule-generated behavior is criticizable. For example, if someone laughs out loud in church they have violated the rule that people should be quiet in church. Others are likely to be critical of the behavior. If however, someone suffers a nosebleed during church, their behavior is not controllable and probably would not be criticized. Note that not all compliant or noncompliant behavior will be openly praised or criticized. That someone waits their turn in line is hardly going to draw much attention.

Finally, because the application of rules depends on the scope conditions of the context, rule-generated behavior recurs in similar contexts. This is not to say that the rule will always be followed, but that behavioral patterns will develop that are consistent with the rule. Hence, in observing rule-generated behavior, we expect to see behavioral regularity.

Observing Rule-Generated Behavior

Shimanoff has created a decision-tree that a researcher could follow in identifying rules from observing behavior (see Figure 8.2 on page 224).

In using Shimanoff's decision-tree, the researcher begins by observing behavior and then determines if the behavior recurs in similar contexts; hence multiple observations of the behavior are needed. If the observed behavior does not recur, or appears random or idiosyncratic, then the researcher can conclude that it is not rule-generated behavior. If the behavior is observed to recur in similar contexts, the next step is to determine if the behavior is controllable (i.e., deviation from the behavior is possible). Some behavior may recur in similar contexts but is not controllable. For example, you may witness several people falling on a sheet of ice. While their behavior is contextual, it is not controllable and not rule-generated. If it is determined that the behavior is controllable, the researcher should then determine if it is criticizable. To assess whether behavior is criticizable, Shimanoff recommends that three types of information be sought, including (a) judgments of appropriateness, (b) negative sanction for deviation, and (c) repairs of deviations.[30] In other words, does the behavior appear appropriate, can one impose negative sanctions if deviation from the behavior occurs, and is there any evidence of people trying to repair (i.e., correct) their deviations? If the answer is yes to any one of the three questions, then the behavior is likely rule-generated.

At this point, the researcher has determined that the behavior is contextual, controllable, and criticizable and can now write the hypothetical rule. Shimanoff recommends writing the rule in conditional form (i.e., "if-then"). For example, assume that you have observed two people on your college campus greeting each other as they pass on the sidewalk. Person A says "Hello" and Person B responds with "Hi!" Assume that you observe this kind of behavior multiple times. Whenever someone greets another person, the other person responds in kind. Using the decision-tree you can conclude that the behavior is contextual. Next, you conclude that the behavior was within the control of either person; that is, Person A did not have to greet Person B nor did Person B have to respond. Their behavior was out of choice, thus controllable. Next, you determine that the behavior is criticizable. If Person B, for example, did not respond to Person A, he or she might be thought of as rude

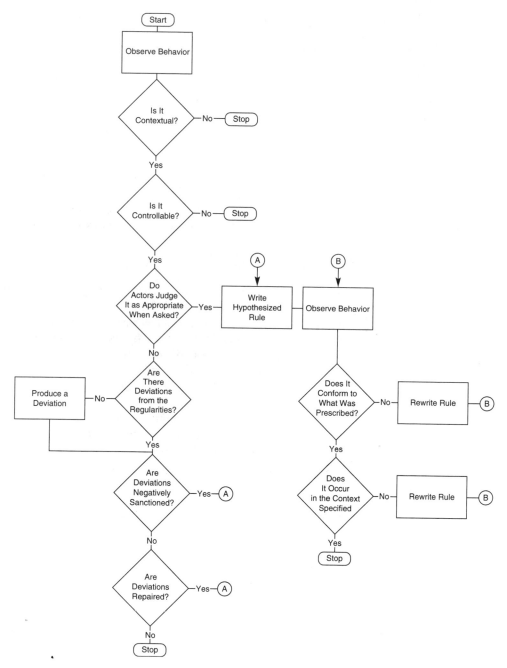

FIGURE 8.2 **Decision-Tree for Inferring Rules**

Decision-Tree for Inferring Rules, from *Communication Rules: Thoery and Research,* by Susan B. Shimanoff, (pp. 106–107), copyright © 1980 by Sage Publications. Reprinted by permission from Sage Publications, Inc.

or inconsiderate. Now you can write the rule. Using conditional form you can write the following rule:

> R_{19}: *If someone greets you, then you should reciprocate their greeting in kind.*

Once the rule has been written it should be tested for its validity. Following the decision-tree, Shimanoff recommends that you go back and observe behavior again, this time to see if it conforms with your rule. If it does not, then rewrite the rule. For example, say you went to your local shopping mall and did not observe the greeting behavior. You might decide that the physical surroundings of the college campus had an influence on the applicability of your rule. Hence, you might rewrite your rule as follows:

> R_{20}: *If a member of the college community greets another member, the other should reciprocate the greeting.*

By specifying the context, your rule has more validity. Now you can test your new rule. You observe the behavior as it was prescribed in the rule and notice that it occurs within the context of the college campus. You have inferred rule-generated behavior and formulated the rule. Armed with this information, you can explain and predict the greeting behaviors of members of the college campus.

Types of Rule-Generated Behavior

Rules theorists distinguish between different types of rule-generated behavior. Stephen E. Toulmin, a philosopher, for example, distinguishes between seven types of rule-related behavior, including (a) behavior that occurs "as a rule," (b) regular behavior, (c) rule-governed behavior, (d) rule-conforming behavior, (e) rule-applying behavior, (f) rule-following behavior, and (g) rule-reflective behavior.[31] Philosopher Joan Ganz lists three types of rule-related behavior, including (a) rule-fulfilling behavior, (b) rule-accordance behavior, and (c) rule-following behavior.[32] Social psychologist Peter Collett identifies three types of rule-related behavior, including (a) rule-fitting behavior, (b) rule-following behavior, and (c) rule-governed behavior.[33]

Combining the works of Toulmin, Ganz, and Collett, Shimanoff has developed a typology (i.e., classification scheme) of nine different types of rule-related behavior, which appears in the following list.[34]

> *Rule-Absent Behavior:* Behavior that is noncontrollable, noncriticizable, or noncontextual. Behavior that fails to meet any of these criteria is rule-absent behavior (physiological phenomena-lawlike). Example: slipping on ice.
>
> *Rule-Fulfilling Behavior:* Behavior that is rule-governed but the actor has no knowledge of the rule. Behavior that is done through imitation, accident, or by design. Example: Students refer to their professors as "Dr." but they know they did not go to medical school.

Rule-Ignorant Behavior: Behavior that fails to fulfill a rule because the actor is unaware of the rule. Example: Freshmen who call their professors by their first names.

Rule-Conforming Behavior: Behavior that conforms with the rule by an actor who does not consciously refer to the rule while performing the behavior. Example: putting on socks before shoes.

Rule-Error Behavior: Behavior that fails to fulfill the rule though the actor has knowledge of the rule. Usually occurs because of carelessness, inattention, or forgetfulness. Example: overdue books in the library.

Rule-Following Behavior: Behavior performed with conscious knowledge and application of the rule. Example: playing a game of chess.

Rule-Violating Behavior: Behavior that intentionally fails to fulfill the rule. Example: Underage person providing false identification to get into a bar.

Rule-Reflective Behavior: Behavior performed with conscious knowledge and application of the rule whereby the actor evaluates the rule itself. The actor may judge the moral or ethical dimensions of the rule either positively or negatively. Example: Doctors performing abortions.

In order to explain and predict behavior via rules, researchers must be able to articulate and observe the relationship between rules and social action. In most cases, communication theorists are interested in rule-following, rule-violating, and positive and negative rule-reflective behavior because the actor is conscious of his or her behavior. These three types of rule-related behavior are more informative than the other types whereby the actor is not aware that he or she is following some rule.

CASE STUDY 11   Small Group Communication and Inferring Rule-Related Behavor

Key Terms

Rule-Error Behavior

Rule-Following Behavior

Rule-Reflective Behavior

Rule-Violating Behavior

This case study focuses on a group of students who are working on a class assignment that requires them to write a term paper and make a formal presentation of the paper to the class. In this case study Shimanoff's decision-tree for inferring rules will be applied to the group's interaction.

Scene: In a college classroom four students are interacting about their upcoming paper and presentation. The group has met several times prior to this and has made some progress on the paper. The purpose of this particular meeting is to discuss the presentation. The members of the group include Mike, Sean, Holly, and Chris.

HOLLY: Where's Chris? She's been late to almost every one of our meetings	1
MIKE: I know, she said she'd be here. I saw her this morning.	2
SEAN: Well, we can't do much until she gets here.	3
HOLLY: This pisses me off, the rest of us are here	4
SEAN: We agreed that we'd meet now, didn't we?	5
MIKE: Yeah, I saw her this morning, she knows.	6
HOLLY: Hmmm...	7
(Chris enters.)	
CHRIS: Hi you guys, I'm really sorry I'm late. I'm sorry.	8
HOLLY: Did you not know what time we're meeting?	9
CHRIS: Yeah I knew, I'm sorry. I just lost track of time.	10
MIKE: Let's get started. Have you got the references?	11
CHRIS: Yeah, I typed them, they're all in order. They go at the back of paper. The paper has to be typed. Is that done?	12
SEAN: Yeah, it's just all typed. I just have to put the page numbers on the pages.	13
CHRIS: We're supposed to have ten references—that's stupid. What's so magical about having ten?	14
SEAN: Really.	15
MIKE: It's dumb.	16
CHRIS: Well, we didn't use ten, so I just looked in the card catalog under our topic and added two more references.	17
HOLLY: What if he looks them up?	18
SEAN: He'll never do that, I bet he doesn't even read them. I do it all the time.	19
MIKE: Yeah, but if he does, we're screwed.	20
CHRIS: No way... I've done it before too.	21
HOLLY: Yeah, just leave 'em on there, who cares?	22
MIKE: By the way, our presentation is worth half our grade.	23
SEAN: That sucks!	24
HOLLY: Well, let's just do it the way he wants so we can get the points.	25
CHRIS: I agree, it's so unfair, but let's do it his way.	26
MIKE: O. K.	27
SEAN: Yeah, that's fine.	28
HOLLY: All I need is a B in this class to up my GPA.	29
CHRIS: I wish I could say the same.	30

At least four types of rule-related behavior are represented in the above interaction, including (a) rule-error, (b) rule-following, (c) rule-violating, and (d) rule-reflective behavior. The rules regarding the behavior can be inferred from Shimanoff's decision-tree model. The first step is to observe behavior. The above transcript represents the observation. There appears to be rule-related behavior in lines 1 through 10. After observing the interaction, the next step is to determine if the behavior is contextual; that is, does it recur in similar contexts? In the beginning of the interaction, Mike, Sean, and Holly appear upset that Chris

Continued

CASE STUDY 11   *Continued*

is late. Holly mentions that Chris has been late for several meetings and Mike concurs. Chris's behavior, then, is contextual. The next step is to determine if the behavior is controllable; that is, does Chris have control over her lateness. After Chris arrives, she mentions that she lost track of time. Hence, her behavior was controllable. The third step is to discern if the behavior is criticizable. Both Holly and Mike react negatively to Chris's tardiness and Chris apologizes; thus, her behavior is criticizable. At this point the rule can be written:

R_1: *Group members should be on time for group meetings.*

Chris's behavior is an example of rule-error behavior; that is, behavior that unintentionally fails to fulfill the rule even though the interactant has knowledge of it. Failing to fulfill the rule is based on carelessness, inattention, or forgetfulness.

The next rule-related behavior occurs in lines 12 and 13. The students know that the paper has to be typed and they have followed the rule. Their behavior is contextual since many professors require papers to be typed. The behavior is controllable—they could turn in an untyped paper if they so choose. Their behavior (i.e., typing the paper) is also criticizable. The professors would probably lower their grade on the paper if it was submitted not typed. Hence a second rule can be hypothesized.

R_2: *All papers submitted in this particular class should be typed.*

That this group decided to type the paper represents rule-following behavior; that is, behavior performed with conscious knowledge and application of the rule.

The third type of rule-related behavior occurs in lines 14 through 22. Here is an example of rule-violating behavior. The group knows that the paper is to have ten references, but because they do not have ten, Chris decides simply add two more to the bibliography even though they were not used. Although the group seems to follow the rule that there are ten references, the group clearly violates the spirit of the rule that the ten references are ones that were actually used in writing the paper. Their behavior is intentional, controllable, and criticizable and is an example of rule-violating behavior.

The fourth instance of rule-related behavior occurs in lines 23 through 28. Here the group discusses the presentation and that it is worth half of their grade on the assignment. Apparently the professor has a rule that indicates that presentations are worth 50 percent of the paper assignment. Although the group disagrees with the rule, they agree to perform the presentation as prescribed by the professor. They indicate that they will do the presentation just as the professor wants, but only because they need the grades; that is, they are following a rule they find unfair. Their behavior is controllable (they do not have to perform the presentation in the way the professor prescribes), contextual (it recurs in the classroom), and criticizable (if they choose not to follow the prescription, they may be negatively evaluated by the professor) and is an example of rule-reflective behavior. This type of behavior is performed with conscious knowledge of the rule whereby the interactants evaluate the utility of the rule.

Summary

This chapter has offered a look at the rules approach by discussing its historical roots, the major assumptions of the theorist using the approach, the definition of a rule, the notion of practical necessity, and the relationship between rules and behavior. The rules approach offers a unique way to theorize about social action. The approach is a clear departure from either the causal process or systems perspectives in that it recognizes the importance of human choice making and goal achievement. In addition, the rules perspective is strictly a theory of social action and is not applicable to natural or lawlike phenomena. The rules approach meets the criteria of any theory in that it allows the theorist a way of explaining and predicting. Because of its emphasis on prescriptive force and practical necessity, the rules approach can offer an explanation of human action that neither the causal process or systems as they are currently conceived can provide.

Glossary

Action: Intentional, goal-related behavior, for example, choosing to go to college.

Anthropomorphic Model of Man: Developed by Rom Harré and Paul Secord, this model rejects the deterministic model of humans proposed by laws theorists in favor of a view that humans have the power to initiate change, are aware of things other than themselves, and have the power of speech.

Explicit Rules: Publicly stated rules indicating appropriate behavior. For example, codes of conduct and the U.S. Constitution are explicit rules. Family rules such as when children may go out and play are also explicit rules.

Implicit Rules: Rules that people follow but are not actually stated, for example, not saying anything to your roommates after they flunked a test in order not to hurt their feelings.

Motion: Mechanistic, lawlike, and unintentional behavior, for example, falling on ice.

Practical Necessity: The normative force an actor feels to perform some behavior. Normative or prescriptive forces exert pressure on actors to behave according to personal, societal, or cultural standards. The force of practical necessity rests on the power of the actor to respond to such pressures.

Rule: A followable prescription that indicates what behavior is preferred, obligated, or prohibited in certain contexts.

Scope Conditions: Situational dimensions that specify when to apply certain rules. Scope conditions include (a) the physical environment, (b) the episode enacted, (c) the actors, and (d) the medium of communication.

Teleological Explanation: A teleological explanation explains behavior by pointing to the future. Behavior is said to have occurred "in order" that something else can occur, typically the achievement of some goal. Behavior that is performed to bring about some future state is said to be action-like.

References

1. Wittgenstein, L. (1953). *Philosophical Investigations* (translated by G. E. M. Anscombe), New York: Macmillan, (p. 81e).

2. Collett, P. (1977). "The Rules of Conduct," in P. Collett, (Ed.), *Social Rules and Social Behaviour,* (pp. 1–27), Totowa, NJ: Rowman and Littlefield.

3. Smith, M. J. (1982). *Persuasion and Human Action: A Critique of Social Influence Theories,* Belmont, CA: Wadsworth, (p. 62); Kant, I. (1974). *Anthropology from a Pragmatic Point of View* (translated by M. J. Gregor), The Hague: Netherlands; Kant, I. *Critique of Pure Reason* (1965) (translated by N. K. Smith), New York: St. Martin's Press.

4. Collett, "The Rules of Conduct," (pp. 1–27).

5. Ibid.

6. Wittgenstein, *Philosophical Investigations,* (p. 81e).

7. Lyons, J. (1970). *Noam Chomsky,* New York: The Viking Press.

8. Shimanoff, S. (1980). *Communication Rules: Theory and Research,* Beverly Hills: Sage.

9. Ibid.; Smith, *Persuasion and Human Action.*

10. Harré, R., & Secord, P. F. (1972). *The Explanation of Social Behaviour,* Totowa, NJ: Rowman and Littlefield.

11. Ibid., (p. 35).

12. *Merriam Webster's Collegiate Dictionary,* (1994), (10th Ed.), Springfield, MA: Merriam-Webster, Inc.

13. Garver, N. (1967). "Rules," in P. Edwards, (Ed.), *The Encyclopedia of Philosophy,* (Vol. 7), (pp. 231–233), New York: Macmillan.

14. Shimanoff, *Communication Rules,* (p. 57).

15. Smith, *Persuasion and Human Action,* (p. 62).

16. Burke, K. (1961). *The Rhetoric of Religion: Studies in Logology,* Boston: Beacon Press; Shimanoff, *Communication Rules;* Smith, *Persuasion and Human Action.* The discussion of followability closely parallels Shimanoff's.

17. Collett, "The Rules of Conduct," (pp. 1–27); Shimanoff, *Communication Rules;* Smith, *Persuasion and Human Action.*

18. Shimanoff, *Communication Rules;* Smith, *Persuasion and Human Action.*

19. Shimanoff, *Communication Rules.*

20. Ibid.

21. Smith, *Persuasion and Human Action.*

22. von Wright, G. H. (1971). *Explanation and Understanding,* Ithaca, NY: Cornell University Press.

23. Ibid.

24. Ibid.

25. Cushman, D. P., & Pearce, W. B. (1978). "Generality and Necessity in Three Types of Theory about Human Communication, with Special Attention to Rules Theory," *Human Communication Research, 4,* 344–353.

26. von Wright, *Explanation and Understanding.*

27. Smith, *Persuasion and Human Action.*

28. Shimanoff, *Communication Rules.*

29. Ibid.

30. Ibid.

31. Toulmin, S. E. (1974). "Rules and Their Relevance for Understanding Human Behavior," in T. Mischel, (Ed.), *Understanding Other People,* (pp. 185–215), Oxford: Blackwell.

32. Ganz, J. S. (1971). *Rules: A Systematic Study,* Paris: Mouton.

33. Collett, "The Rules of Conduct," (pp. 1–27).

34. Shimanoff, Communication Rules.

Chapter 9

=======================================

Human Action Approaches
in Communication

Communication is an activity which gains meaning and significance from consensually shared rules.[1]
—*DONALD CUSHMAN & GORDON C. WHITING*

The human action and/or rules approach to communication functions as a metatheory. Like causal process theories, it is not a communication theory until communication scholars apply the metatheoretical assumptions to communication. Donald Cushman and Gordon Whiting have been credited with introducing the concept of rules to the communication field in the early 1970s. Since then a rather substantial body of research has resulted that continues to grow today.

According to Pearce and Wiseman, the rules perspective caught on quickly in communication for three reasons. First, a number of other approaches to the study of communication were not fulfilling their promise. Second, the metatheoretical assumptions of the rules perspective (e.g., action versus motion) were very attractive to communication theorists. Finally, although new to the field, the rules perspective had a very respectable history beginning with such scholars as Kant and Wittgenstein.[2]

A substantial and varied body of research is associated with the rules perspective. Many communication theorists studying various contexts and topical themes of communication have adopted the rules approach as their metatheoretical foundation. This chapter will outline four of its major theoretical applications including the coordinated management of meaning, Reardon's regulative rule model of persuasion, Smith's contingency rules theory, and conversation analysis. Before describing these four theories, however, the basic assumptions of the rules approach as they apply to communication will be outlined.

Basic Assumptions of Communication Rules Approach

Donald Cushman is one of the foremost advocates of a communication rules approach. Cushman and his associates contend that many kinds of human actions are dependent on rules, including human communication. Rules theorists assert that rules influence human action in two very important ways, including (a) governing and regulating it, and (b) establishing its meaning.[3] Rules that govern and regulate communication are called regulative rules. Rules that establish the meaning of communication are called constitutive rules. Regulative rules guide, direct, and manage human action. For example, rules governing turn taking during a conversation would be considered regulative rules. Constitutive rules define the meaning of a particular action. For example, if someone says to you "Your hair looks nice" you would interpret the remark as a compliment. The constitutive rule here is that the remark functions as a compliment.

According to communication rules theorists, human interaction gains significance and coherence through the following of rules.[4] Four basic assumptions—called propositions by rules theorists—provide the foundation for a rules approach to human communication and are presented in the following list.[5]

Four Propositions of a Rules Approach to Human Communication

Proposition 1: Conjoint, combined, and associated action is characteristic of human behavior.

Proposition 2: The transfer of symbolic information facilitates conjoint, combined, and associated behavior.

Proposition 3: The transfer of symbolic information requires the interaction of sources, messages, and receivers guided and governed by communication rules.

Proposition 4: Communication rules form general and specific patterns which provide the ground for fruitful explanation and description of particular communication transactions.

These four propositions guide communication rules theorists in developing their theories of human interaction. Proposition 1 simply says that a characteristic of human behavior is that it is made up of, or carried on by, two or more persons. This does not mean that all human behavior requires two or more people. Situations in which an actor does not require the cooperation of another to achieve some goal are called information-processing situations. Situations in which goal attainment can only be achieved via the cooperation with others are called coordinated situations. Communication rules theorists are only interested in coordinated situations because it is only within these situations that the transfer of symbolic information is required to attain some goal.[6] Proposition 2 maintains that the exchange of information between people facilitates, or makes easier, the acting out of human behavior.

Propositions 3 and 4 are particularly important for the communication theorist. Proposition 3 says that in order to exchange information between persons, rules are needed. According to Cushman and his colleagues, communication occurs when information is successfully transmitted from person to person.[7] For example, Person A knows something.

When Person A successfully communicates it to Person B, Person B knows it also. This process requires that Person A encodes a message (i.e., puts his or her thoughts into a code) and sends it to Person B. Person B then decodes the message (i.e., takes it out of its code). For understanding to occur Person B must have knowledge of the code used by Person A. Codes are made up of symbols that represent something else. For example, the English alphabet is made up of symbols (e.g., *a, b, c,* etc.). To communicate with others, we select certain symbols, combine them via a set of rules (e.g., grammar), and use them to verbally represent our thoughts. If Person A and Person B have that same knowledge of the symbols, and especially the rules for combining them, then the transfer of information is more likely to be successful.

Rules indicate how to put the symbols together and what the symbols mean. For example, Person A sees a cute little cat and wants to tell Person B about it. Guided by rules, Person A selects three symbols from the code to represent the fuzzy little animal, including the symbols *A, C,* and *T.* Additional rules, sometimes called grammar or syntax, indicate in what order Person A should combine these three symbols. The rules tell Person A to put the *C* first, then the *A,* and then the *T.* Rules also indicate that, in combination, these three symbols represent the fuzzy little animal that Person A wants Person B to see; that is, "CAT." The point here is that without sharing the same rules, Person A might have great difficulty in transferring the information to Person B.

Even though two people share the same rules for combining symbols, they may not share their meaning. Cushman and his associates distinguish between two basic levels of meaning.[8] The first is the "personal level" of meaning. These are unique, idiosyncratic meanings developed out of an individual's direct interaction with the environment. For example, if Person A had been bitten by a cat and thus disliked cats, then Person A's personal meaning and Person B's personal meaning of the symbols "CAT" may be different. The second level is the "interpersonal level." Here, at least two persons agree on the meaning of a symbol or symbols. This level of meaning exists on a continuum moving from dyads, to small groups, to larger groups, to organizations, and eventually to cultural groups. At any or each level, there may be "private" rules for symbols developed by members of the group. Your group of friends, for example, has private meanings for symbols that others around you do not understand. In many ways you use these "private" symbols to define the boundaries of the group and keep others out. You can probably hold a conversation with a friend in front of your parents and they would not be able to understand you. Even whole countries develop "secret codes" during wartime to communicate to each other without the enemy knowing what has been communicated.

When large groups share the same rules for combining symbols and their subsequent meaning, the rules are said to have taken on a "standardized usage." These rules are required for successful communication. Perhaps the largest set of standardized rules are those directing mass communication, or those rules shared by large groups of people that provide information about social institutions and that prescribe communication patterns for a society. Moving down to smaller groups, organizational communication standardized rules function to prescribe those communication patterns necessary for the survival of the organization. Group communication standardized rules regulate human action according to common interests (e.g., women's rights). Finally, interpersonal standardized rules direct human action within the dyad.[9]

Finally, Proposition 4 says that communication rules form general and specific patterns (of symbol use) which provide the basis for explanation. This is also related to the notion of standardized usage. When a particular rule is performed consistently over time it takes on normative and prescriptive force and becomes standardized. To explain why Person A transferred the symbols "CAT" to Person B requires a knowledge of the standardized usages of such symbols. In this case, the word *CAT* is a specific case of the general rule for combining symbols. We can explain Person A's behavior by saying he or she was following the general rule. By knowing the rule, we can also predict that the next time Person A sees a cute fuzzy little animal, the same symbols will be used to communicate to another person. Thus we can explain and predict via rules.

Coordinated Management of Meaning

One of the most prominent oft-cited rules theories in the communication field is the coordinated management of meaning (CMM), developed by Barnett Pearce, Vernon Cronen, and their colleagues. The theory focuses on the ability of two persons to engage in conversation.[10] Pearce and his fellow theorists view communication as a form of social action and as a process of *creating and managing* social reality rather than as a technique for describing objective reality.[11] CMM theorists reject the traditional view of communication where communication is seen as a way to express inner attitudes, purposes, or feelings and serves as a vehicle for describing events and objects of the physical or external world.[12] Instead, CMM theorists contend that as two or more people interact, the interaction itself creates the reality being experienced by the interactants. This creative process is sometimes referred to as the "social construction of reality." Because people create reality there can be no one objective reality. CMM theorists do not deny the existence of external or physical reality but argue that any knowledge of it derives from human perception; that is, to see, hear, feel, taste, or touch. Of perception, Pearce writes:

> *When we wake in the morning and look around, the events and objects around us appear to present themselves as pictures, sounds, smells, and the like. Studies of the process of perception, however, have shown that what we actually perceive is very remote from that which engages our senses. . . . You may think you perceive a tree, but you do not. The event/object you are now perceiving presents itself to you not as a "tree" but as a pattern of light waves/particles and perhaps minute traces of chemicals in the air.[13]*

Anything perceived is filtered through our senses. Thus, our communication is inherently and personally theory-laden and not neutral or objective.

In essence, CMM theorists argue that there are as many possible meanings for objects, events, or happenings as there are people to observe them. Communication is seen as social action; and there cannot be any action without meaning nor meaning without action. A major premise of CMM is that during communication individuals try to *manage and coordinate* their various meanings.

The Dramatistic Metaphor

The theater is frequently used as an analogy of life. Pearce and Cronen use the "undirected theater" as a metaphor for describing communication. They argue that the theater is a mirror of the human experience.[14] They see communication as a play which has no director. Following the metaphor, there are many actors in the play and each has his or her own unique omniscient (i.e., all-knowing, all-seeing) perspective of his or her surroundings, like that of God, a novelist, or a playwright. How actors view the stage is "correct" from their perspective. The other actors enter the stage with their own perspectives. The actors understand that it is important to be a part of the play, but they do not know what play is being performed nor are they certain of their role They could be a leading part, member of the crew, stagehand, etc.

The actors in the play know some lines from some plays but the various actors differ considerably in the specific plays they know. Thus, when one actor reads a line from Shakespeare's *Hamlet* another may respond with a line from Neil Simon's *Plaza Suite*. In some cases, actors will meet with other actors who share the lines from the same play. In these cases communication can proceed. In most cases, however, incoherence dominates the scene.[15]

Basic Propositions of CMM

Pearce and Cronen assert that the undirected play metaphor demonstrates the inherent problems entailing human communication. They contend that people can be analyzed in terms of their individual meanings and the extent to which they coordinate their meanings. CMM describes people as human actors attempting to achieve coordination by managing the ways messages take on meaning. CMM rests on five basic propositions listed below.[16]

Five Propositions of Coordinated Management of Meaning

Proposition 1: Human beings will create systems of meaning and order even when there are none.

Proposition 2: Human beings organize meanings hierarchically.

Proposition 3: Human beings organize meanings temporally.

Proposition 4: Individual's systems of meaning are to some extent idiosyncratic.

Proposition 5: The behavior of individuals is uninterpretable except in the context of larger systems.

Meaning

CMM theorists see people as patterns of organized meanings. As mentioned in Propositions 1 and 2, people create meanings and unconsciously organize them hierarchically. The meaning of a particular object, event, or happening is based on many aspects of our lives, including the culture from which we come, the culmination of our life experiences, the relationships we develop with others, individual events in our lives, specific communications with others, and the language that we speak. In this sense, meanings are quite individual and also context dependent. Hence, when we get together with other people and communicate, we try to manage and coordinate all of these aspects so that the people with whom we are interacting can understand our meaning and we can understand them. The levels of the hierarchy of meaning are depicted in the following list.[17] Generally, higher levels of meaning determine interpretations at the lower levels within the hierarchy.

Hierarchy of Meaning

VI. Cultural Patterns: Sometimes called archetypes, this is the highest level and involves the broader definitions of life scripts, relationships, and episodes that are the result of cultural norms and values. For example, a cultural pattern of the United States is individualism. Americans highly value their individualism and their freedom to act differently within the limits set by the social structure. In contrast, many Asian cultures value collectivism, where group membership and group harmony prevails. Cultural patterns influence a person's life script, master contract, episodes, speech acts, and content.

V. Life Script: Clusters or patterns of episodes and actions that make up an individual's self-concept. The life script comprises the individual's expectations for the kinds of communicative events that can and probably will occur. In a sense, the life script is the culmination of all the previous episodes in which one has acted.

IV. Relationship/Master Contract: Master contracts are defined as the implicit agreements between people that establish the relational boundaries and how they define their relationship. The meaning of an episode depends on the master contract between the interactants.

III. Episode: Episodes are communicative routines that people view as whole and are comprised of reciprocal speech acts characterized by their constitutive and regulative rules. Episodes are characterized by their special rules of verbal and nonverbal behavior and are often distinguished by clearly recognizable opening and closing sequences. The episode is the most important key to understanding meaning.

II. Speech Act: Pearce defines the speech act as comprising the verbal and nonverbal "things," that people do to each other (e.g., compliment, insult, etc.). For example, saying to someone "You are beautiful" is a compliment. The speech act is a compliment. The meaning is in the act itself, not in the referent.

I. Content: The content level describes the referential function of verbal and nonverbal communication. This is the message separated from context.

Based on CMM's hierarchy of meaning the meaning of a particular person, event, object, word, or happening is based on an individual's culture, life script, master contract, episodes, speech acts, and content. The higher levels of the hierarchy provide a context for the lower levels. For example, Jim tells Jan "I love you." In determining what the phrase "I love you" means, Jim and Jan can use the hierarchy.

At the content level "I love you" is simply three words in the English language. Without context this phrase is simply recognized for its referential value. Said to no one, "I love you" is relatively meaningless. Both Jim and Jan understand the language but do not have a proper context in which to place it. As a speech act, the phrase "I love you" could be interpreted as term of endearment or an expression of affection. As indicated in the previous list, an episode is a communication routine with a definite beginning and ending point. Hypothetically, the episode might look something like this:

Jim: "I'm leaving now."

Jan: "O.K., I'll see you tonight."

Jim: "I love you."

Jan: "I love you, too."

Jim: "Bye."

Jan: "Bye."

In the case of Jim and Jan, the episode is Jim leaving to go to work. In this scenario the master contract/relationship is husband and wife. This kind of interaction might seem strange if exchanged between nonintimates (e.g., roommates, etc.). The life script includes all the episodes Jim and Jan have encountered separately and together. Finally, the cultural patterns for Jim and Jan are American. Americans frequently verbally express their love for one another. Culturally, Americans are much more verbally oriented than are other cultures, particularly Asian ones. In such cultures, the phrase "I love you" might be misunderstood or even thought of as unnecessary. Japanese couples, for example, rarely verbally express their love for each other in this way. They see their behaviors as symbols of their love. The phrase "I love you" takes on its own meaning for Jim and Jan because of the unique hierarchy. The same phrase may mean something quite different to another couple with different hierarchies.

Usually the higher levels of the hierarchy determine how to interpret meaning at lower levels. For example, in most cases, one's life script will dictate how to interpret a specific episode. Occasionally, however, lower levels reflect back and affect the meaning of higher levels.[18] For example, at times some episode may occur that alters the person's life script, particularly if it is quite dramatic or recurs with some regularity. The process of lower levels reflecting up to higher levels is called a loop. Loops are not particularly troublesome for people unless the meanings at lower levels are inconsistent or contradictory with higher levels. When this occurs, Pearce calls it a "strange loop." Graphically, a strange loop looks like this:[19]

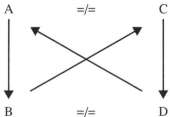

A common type of strange loop forms when one's life script becomes influenced by reflecting episodes. In the strange loop presented above, the letters A and C represent the life script while B and D represent specific episodes. Pearce offers the case of an alcoholic whose periods of sobriety are followed by periods of heavy drinking. Pearce's strange loop is presented below:[20]

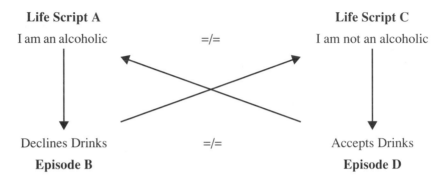

| Life Script A | | Life Script C |
| I am an alcoholic | =/= | I am not an alcoholic |

| Declines Drinks | =/= | Accepts Drinks |
| **Episode B** | | **Episode D** |

Beginning with the upper left quadrant, the person's life script contains the notion that the person is an alcoholic. The life script manages the meaning during specific episodes, which are depicted in the lower left quadrant. At some point the episodic behavior becomes incorporated into the life script which begins to take on new meaning. Armed with new meaning "I am not an alcoholic" the person begins to drink. Eventually, the drinking will reflect back to the life script and the strange loop repeats.

Management

By management, Pearce and his associates contend that individuals have the ability to manage their own meanings; that is, people themselves can determine what a term means. Pearce argues that although people may not be able to change their environment or themselves, they can "transcend" their culture.[21] This simply means that particular words can take on very private idiosyncratic meanings that may be quite different than the normative (i.e., cultural) usage. For example, the word *college* has a standardized meaning in American culture. Most people understand it to refer to the four or so years of education a person may pursue after high school. Although the word means basically the same thing to you as it does to others in this culture, it also has some very unique meanings to you. For example, the word probably meant something very different when you were a freshman in high school than what it means to you today. In this sense, you have managed the meaning of the term. To be sure, your hierarchy of meaning certainly has changed since high school. The number of speech acts, episodes, and relationships in which the term *college* is associated has grown over the years. When you say the word *college,* your meaning of the term is based on all of the speech acts, episodes, and master contracts you have experienced while there. Thus, when you say "college" you may think of professors, final exams, poor food, boy/girlfriends, or late-night study sessions. Consider what the term means to your high school friends who decided not to attend college after high school graduation. They have not had the same experiences and, hence, have different hierarchies. When your friends think of "college," they may think of a four-year paid vacation from work. You and your friends manage the meaning of "college" quite differently. For you and your friends to communicate about "college" requires all of you to coordinate your management of meaning.

Coordination

CMM describes communicants as actors attempting to achieve social coordination,[22] although coordination does not necessarily mean mutual understanding. Sometimes coordination is achieved because people have different meanings for different terms. An attempt at coordination occurs whenever two or more persons come together, engage in interaction, create an episode, and attempt to interpret the sequence of actions.[23] Cronen, Pearce, and Harris cite an example of two motorists who coordinate their cars at an intersection:

> *two motorists coordinate their encounter at an intersection by avoiding each other even though they inhabit different "realities." One driver is dutifully obeying the system of traffic laws that specifies which car should proceed first, while the other is spontaneously responding to the behavior of others.*[24]

Coordination is viewed as people communicating wherein individuals interpret and respond to the behaviors of others based on their own management of meaning. Coordination, which takes on an inherent ethical dimension, is a process whereby people collaborate to create social reality. Collaboration requires that each person brings his or her own notion of what is moral, ethical, and necessary to create the episode. This is not unlike the playing of a game of chess or poker. Sometimes interaction is well-coordinated, as in the following exchange:

Jim: Are you enjoying the evening?

Jan: Yes, are you?

Jim: Yes, it is beautiful out here with the moon and all.

Jan: Yeah, it is so quiet, I just love it.

Here, the two interactants have coordinated their meanings of a nice evening. The contributions of each mesh together to create a complete episode. Sometimes interaction is not well-coordinated. For example:

Jim: Are you enjoying the evening?

Jan: What makes you think I'm not?

Jim: I didn't say you weren't, aren't you?

Jan: Why would you ask if you thought I was?

Jim: Never mind...

In this scene there is a sense of incompleteness. Both interactants are now probably uncomfortable not having coordinated their meanings.

CMM and Rules

How interactants go about managing meaning and coordinating it with others depends on the following of rules. CMM's conception of rules is fairly unique. Rules are descriptions of how people process information. Rules are seen as organizations of cognitions; that is, they exist in the heads of individual communicants. People are viewed as organized clusters of rules which enable them to interpret others' acts.[25]

Rules within CMM are graphically and structurally represented by a series of logical, symbolic operators outlined in Figure 9.1.

The CMM conception of rules is based on a structural-functional approach whereby two types of rules are defined, including constitutive and regulative rules.[26] Constitutive rules are rules of meaning and indicate meaning at the various levels of the hierarchy. They do not prescribe appropriate behavior; they describe the assignment of meaning. For example, the phrase "I love you" takes on different meanings in different episodes and master contracts. Between husband and wife versus between granddaughter and grandmother the phrase takes on different meaning. The most basic or primitive form of a constitutive rule is outlined in Figure 9.2.

In this example, the episode is play, the antecedent conditions are that your spouse has just insulted your mother. An insult at the i level of the hierarchy may be defined as an at-

---

$\supset$ =   disjunctive operator; similar to the conditional in logic to be read as "if... then." In CMM it is to be read "if an entity perceives X as having occurred, that entity perceives that it should do Y."

$\rightarrow$ =   "counts as" operator; denotes the meaning of one event as equivalent to the meaning of another.

$\neg$ =   hierarchical operator; to be read as "in the context of..."

Examples:

1. Marriage

"I love you" $\rightarrow$ Term of endearment

In the context of a marriage, the phrase "I love you" counts as a term of endearment.

2. Marriage

Spouse is leaving for work $\supset$ Hug spouse

In the context of a marriage, if a spouse is leaving for work, then one should hug him or her.

FIGURE 9.1 Logical Operators for Representing Rules

From *Communication, Action, and Meaning: The Creation of Social Realities,* by W. B. Pearce & V. E. Cronen. Copyright © 1980 by Praeger, (p. 140). Reprinted by permission from W. Barnett Pearce.

$$CR = \frac{MC_k}{A \supset \{MC_i \rightarrow MC_j\}}$$

Where:

CR = Constitutive Rule

A = Antecedent conditions

MC_k = Meaning in this episode at this time

MC_i = Meaning at i level of the hierarchy (e.g., speech act, master contract but different than i level)

MC_j = Meaning at the j level of the hierarchy (e.g., speech act, master contract but different than i level)

Read: If antecedent conditions A occur, then MC_i counts as MC_j.

Example:

$$CR = \frac{\text{Episode Play}}{\text{Spouse insults Mother-in-law}} \supset \text{Insult} \rightarrow \text{Joke}$$

FIGURE 9.2   Basic Form of Constitutive Rule

From *Communication, Action, and Meaning: The Creation of Social Realities,* by W. B. Pearce & V. E. Cronen. Copyright © 1980 by Praeger, (p. 142). Reprinted by permission from W. Barnett Pearce.

tack or derogatory remark. Taken within the context of play, however, the constitutive rule prescribes that the insult should be interpreted at the j level of the hierarchy, which in this case means that it is a joke. Try not to be confused by the terms i and j level of the hierarchy. These are simply ways of denoting different levels. In the above example the i level of the hierarchy may be the speech act level which stipulates that an insult is a derogatory remark. The j level, however, might be the episode or the master contract level which prescribes that the insult should be interpreted differently; that is, as a joke.

Regulative rules are different than constitutive rules. Regulative rules guide sequential action by prescribing what behavior is appropriate in what contexts. These rules are based on the constitutive rules operative in any given interaction. The basic or primitive form of a regulative is outlined in Figure 9.3 on page 242.

In this example, the antecedent conditions are that you have burped while in the context of an expensive restaurant. Wanting to be perceived as polite and having proper etiquette, you say "excuse me." The regulative rule is that people should say "excuse me" after they burp.

Regulative rules evolve out of constitutive rules. Figure 9.4 on page 243 demonstrates how the regulative rule from Figure 9.3, that one should say "excuse me" after burping, evolved out of constitutive rules.

$$RR = \frac{}{[\, A \supset \{Do(ACTN_i)\}\,] \supset c}$$

Where:

RR	=	Regulative Rule
A	=	Antecedent condition
DO	=	Deontic Operator (prescribes what action is obligatory, prohibited, or preferred)
ACTN$_i$	=	Action; a specific act at the i level of the hierarchy (e.g., speech act, episode etc.)
C	=	Intended Consequences (the expected results of the prescribed action)

Read: If antecedent conditions occur, then engage in action to achieve the desired consequences.

Example:

$$\frac{\text{Expensive Restaurant}}{\text{Burp} \supset \{\, \text{Say ("excuse me")}\,\} \supset \text{Polite}}$$

Read: If in the context of an expensive restaurant you burp, then say "excuse me" if you want to be perceived as polite.

FIGURE 9.3   Basic Form of a Regulative Rule

From *Communication, Action, and Meaning: The Creation of Social Realities,* by W. B. Pearce & V. E. Cronen. Copyright © 1980 by Praeger, (p. 142). Reprinted by permission from W. Barnett Pearce. See also Cronen, V. E., Pearce, W. B., & Harris, L. M. (1982), "The Coordinated Management of Meaning: A Theory of Communication," in F. E. X. Dance, (Ed.), *Human Communication Theory: Comparative Essays,* (pp. 61–89), Cambridge: Harper and Row, (pp. 75–76).

The Logical Force of Rules

Constitutive and regulative rules guide preferred and obligatory action. Regulative rules guide the selection of the next action while constitutive rules describe the "way" to enact the next action.[27] The motivation or "force" to enact rule-governed behavior is called logical force and CMM theorists outline four types.[28] The first type, prefigurative force, is similar to a laws-like explanation where a person is motivated to enact rule-governed behavior because of some set of antecedent conditions. The sense of obligation is located in the past. This is called the "because" motive. When asked, "Why did you do that?" the person responds, "I did that because it is cold outside." The second type, called practical force, is the "in order to" motive. Here, rule-governed behavior is enacted to achieve some future goal. "I did that in order to get a good grade." The third type of logical force is called contextual force. Here one feels obliged to act in order to be consistent with one's definitions of the self, episode, relationship, and life script. "Why did you do that?" "Because I am the type of person who does this sort of thing." Finally, implicative force is operating when one acts

$$CR_1 + CR_2 = RR_1$$

$$CR_1 = \frac{\text{Expensive Restaurant}}{\text{Burping} \rightarrow \text{Prohibited}}$$

$$CR_2 = \frac{\text{Expensive Restaurant}}{\text{Burping} \rightarrow \text{Rude, low class, \& unintelligent}}$$

$$RR_1 = \frac{\text{Expensive Restaurant}}{\text{Burping} \supset \{\text{Say (``excuse me'')}\} \supset \text{Do not want to be perceived as}}$$
rude, low class, or unintelligent

FIGURE 9.4   Evolution of Regulative Rules from Constitutive Rules

From *Communication, Action, and Meaning: The Creation of Social Realities,* by W. B. Pearce & V. E. Cronen. Copyright © 1980 by Praeger, (p. 142). Reprinted by permission from W. Barnett Pearce.

to change the definitions of the self, episode, or relationship. "Why did you do that?" "Because I want to be seen as different than people see me now."[29]

Complex Rule Systems and Communication Competency

Whenever two or more persons combine to create social reality they create what is called an interpersonal system of rules. Each individual brings to the interaction his or her own set of regulative and constitutive rules. The individual systems are called intrapersonal rules. When systems of intrapersonal rules combine, the interpersonal system is created. Intrapersonal rule systems vary from person to person and from simple to complex. The competent communicator is the one who can move in and out of various interpersonal systems by maintaining a flexible intrapersonal rule system. Pearce and Cronen provide a fascinating example of how this might look.[30] Their example requires some abstract thinking. Assume that there are only four symbols in a hypothetical language:

*0   []   *   ^*

Assume also that the following three people speak the language but have different rules for using the language:

Intrapersonal Rules for Person A:

*if 0 then [] or * or ^*

*if * then 0 or ^ or **

if ^ then 0 or [] or * or ^

if [] then 0

Intrapersonal Rules for Person B:

if 0 then []

if [] then * or [] or ^

if * then 0 or ^ or []

if ^ then 0 or [] or * or ^

Intrapersonal Rules for Person C:

if 0 then 0

if [] then 0

if * then ^

if ^ then []

In the hypothetical language and rule systems, all conversations must start by using the 0 symbol. The goal of every conversation is to use all four of the language shapes as soon as possible. Persons A, B, and C must follow their own rules in coordinating conversations.

At first glance it seems obvious that Persons A and B have complex rule systems and that Person C has a relatively simple system. Based on their complex rule systems it would appear that Person A and Person B would be able to achieve the goal of using all four of the shapes if they were to converse with each other. This is not the case, however. Notice that based on A and B's rule system, should they converse, their conversation would look like this (A speaks first): 0, [], 0, [], 0, [], 0.... Should Persons A and C converse, however, their conversation could take many forms, including (A speaks first): 0, 0, *, ^, []. The goal of using all four language symbols is easily met in only a few turns. The point here is that communication with another is a function of the rules one brings to the interaction. The competent communicator is not necessarily the one with the most complex rule system, but the one who has flexible rules that allow for a variety of ways to coordinate with others.

CMM and the Critics

CMM is perhaps the most complete rules theory of human communication. Since the early 1970s, Pearce, Cronen, and their associates have modified and refined the theory based on criticisms. Because CMM is so different from other theories, even other rules theories, it can be misunderstood. Many find it confusing. Relative to other theories, CMM is still young and will continue to develop. Many new applications are being developed now, including work with intercultural communication.[31] As the field matures, we can look forward to more from CMM.

CASE STUDY 12   Intercultural Communication and the Coordinated Management of Meaning

Key Terms

Hierarchy of Meaning

Constitutive Rules

Regulative Rules

Coordination

The coordinated management of meaning (CMM) rules approach can be a very useful tool for explaining intercultural communication. Most communication scholars agree that communication is culture bound, or that the symbol system used in one culture is unique to that culture and that a message sent from one culture to another may have a very different meaning in each culture. Intercultural communication occurs whenever two persons, from different cultural groups, come together, usually in face-to-face settings, and exchange verbal and nonverbal messages.

Because communication is governed by rules, and is culture bound, many of the rules for communicating are also culture bound. Thus, during intercultural communication, coordination may be difficult, but certainly not impossible. In this case study we will see interaction between David Jones, a sales representative for a U.S. auto parts manufacturer, interacting with Hamad Abdi, the head of the sales department for a Saudi Arabian auto parts distributor. Mr. Jones is in Saudi Arabia hoping to secure a huge sale from the Saudi Arabian company. Unfortunately, in this case, the interaction between Jones and Abdi is not coordinated, mainly because Jones is not sensitive to the Saudi Arabian rules for interacting. In the end, it is very unlikely that Abdi will agree to the terms of the sale. To begin the case study, let's look at Jones's and Abdi's hierarchy of meaning. Recall that in CMM the meaning of a particular communicative act is managed by the individual based on his or her hierarchy of meaning. Outlined below is a brief sketch of the top three levels of their hierarchies.

The Top Three Levels of Jones's and Abdi's Hierarchies of Meaning

Cultural Patterns

David Jones. The United States, as a culture, values democracy, individuality, and equality between sexes and races. Americans place importance on planning for the future and, in a sense, believe they can control their destiny to a certain degree. Like other Western cultures, Americans believe they control their own time. A dominant cultural value is to "be all that you can be." As a cultural group Americans are goal and achievement oriented, highly organized, freedom-loving, and self-reliant. Responsibility lies with the individual. Although Americans reject traditional privileges of royalty and class, they will defer to those with wealth and power.

Hamad Abdi. Almost 100 percent of Saudi Arabians practice Islam, thus are called Muslims. To Muslims, religion and law are one. Saudi Arabians of all professions and social

Continued

CASE STUDY 12 *Continued*

levels firmly believe that "there is no God but Allah and Mohammed is his messenger." In just fifty years, Saudi Arabia has gone from rags-to-riches because of its huge oil reserves. But even so, most Saudis will not depart from traditional ways. Another expression of many Arabs is "Bukra insha Allah" which means "tomorrow if God wills," which they believe literally. Arab society demands a high degree of conformity. The Saudi interpretation of Islam imposes several restrictions on women. They are not allowed to drive cars, to travel, or to live abroad without a male member of the family. When they leave their homes they must cover their heads, arms, and legs with black veils.

Life Scripts

David Jones. David Jones was born and raised in the United States in a moderately sized city in Indiana. He grew up in a middle-class family with two sisters. David's father managed a grocery store and his mother worked part-time at the local library. All three of the Jones children went to college. David majored in business, while his sisters have their law degrees and are attorneys in Chicago. David is married with two children. His wife works full time as an accountant. Both of his children are in high school with plans to go to college. David has worked for the auto parts manufacturer for only four years but has managed to move up in the company rather rapidly. If successful as its international sales representative, David could be promoted to the national office.

Hamad Abdi. Hamad Abdi was born and raised in Saudi Arabia. Hamad was born into a Bedouin family, thus he moved from place to place as a child depending on the weather, etc. He is the only member of his family to go to school. Neither his mother, father, nor two brothers can read. Hamad is married with one child, a daughter. His wife does not work. Hamad is very proud of his culture and religion. Like other Arabs, he prefers aural and oral communication and will not make decisions unless in person. Like other Arabs, Hamad honors honor. To Hamad, shame is a very powerful force that dictates many of his behaviors. An individual committing an act that brings upon him shame loses face, power, and influence. Hamad can speak English.

Relationship/Master Contract

The master contract between Jones and Abdi is that each represents his company and culture on an international level. The two men have interacted indirectly through the mail but have never actually met face-to-face. The purpose of their meeting is to close a major deal. Jones wants to establish a permanent arrangement whereby his company will sell auto parts to Abdi's company who subsequently distributes them to its affiliates throughout Saudi Arabia.

With the top levels of the hierarchy defined, the interaction between Jones and Abdi can be examined. Remember that the actual interaction is called the episode, or the communicative routine that people view as whole. Episodes are comprised of reciprocal speech acts characterized by their constitutive and regulative rules. During episodes individual communicants try to coordinate their management of meaning. Clearly, in the episode below Jones and Abdi are not coordinated. The problem here is that Jones does not have an understanding of the rules guiding Abdi's meaning. The episode is presented below.

The Episode between Jones and Abdi

The meeting between Jones and Abdi takes place in Saudi Arabia and is scheduled for a Tuesday morning. Jones arrives on Monday. On Tuesday morning he receives a message that Abdi cannot meet with him. Jones is simply told to wait. On Wednesday and Thursday Jones hears nothing from Abdi. Finally on Friday, Jones receives a call from Abdi's company indicating that he is ready to meet with him.

When Jones arrives at Abdi's company, he is told to wait in a lobby. He sits on a pillow on the floor. Someone hands him a small coffee cup and fills it with coffee. He immediately finishes it whereby the same person fills it. Jones indicates that he does not want any more coffee. The staff person fills his cup nevertheless. Abdi enters the lobby and greets Jones:

ABDI: Ah . . . Mr. Jones, it is nice to meet you.	1
JONES: Hamad! What is going on? I've been here since Monday!	2
ABDI: Please Mr. Jones, come into my office. Here, please have a seat. Please have some coffee.	3
JONES: No . . . no . . . I've had enough. (Staff person fills his cup)	4
ABDI: You seem very anxious, Mr. Jones. Please sit down.	5
JONES: (Sits with legs crossed on the pillow facing Abdi) What's going on?	6
ABDI: I'm sorry to have kept you waiting but some important business came about.	7
JONES: Well, OK, it's good to finally meet you. How's your wife and family?	8
ABDI: Mr. Jones, how was your trip across the ocean?	9
JONES: Well, it was fine, now . . . about the contract . . . I've had some papers drawn up by our attorney, here. (Hands them to Abdi with his left hand)	10
ABDI: (Does not take the paper) Mr. Jones, please have some more coffee. Tell me about your trip.	11
JONES: No . . . no thanks, I've had enough coffee. My trip was fine. Now . . . about the sales contract, I'm wondering if we could close the deal by the beginning of next week, say on Monday.	12
ABDI: Excuse me, Mr. Jones, I must take a phone call.	13

By looking at the individual speech acts within the episode, several constitutive and regulative rules can be deduced. For example, Mr. Jones does not understand why he waited for two days to see Mr. Abdi. In Saudi Arabia, one of the fundamental qualities for doing business is patience. Thus, for Mr. Jones the constitutive rule is:

Saudi Arabia

Doing business $\supset$ Impatience $\rightarrow$ Rude

When Jones violates this rule, Mr. Abdi is suspicious of him; remember "Bukra insha Allah."

Continued

CASE STUDY 12 *Continued*

Upon the initiation of a meeting, which may be held in a group setting with many inter-ruptions, the guest will always be offered refreshments. They should always be accepted. Coffee, for example, is the ultimate expression of hospitality. Thus, the regulative rule here is:

Saudi Arabia

Offered Coffee ⊃ Say "yes" ⊃ Gracious

In Saudi Arabia, exposing the soles of one's foot is considered very rude. Yet, Jones sits with his legs crossed facing Abdi. The constitutive rule is:

Saudi Arabia

Exposing sole of foot → Rude

Questions about one's wife or family is also considered impolite. The constitutive rule is:

Saudi Arabia

Questions about wife/female children → Rude

The right hand is for public matters and business transactions. The left hand is for private matters such as cleaning oneself. When Mr. Jones hands Abdi the contract with his left hand, Abdi will not take it. The regulative rule is:

Saudi Arabia

Doing business ⊃ Use right hand ⊃ Polite

Finally, initial business meetings are designed for the interactants to become acquainted with one another. Foreigners should avoid pressing the issue. Because things occur with the will of God, there is no hurry. To look to the future is considered sacrilegious. Thus, when Jones presses the issue about closing the deal on the following Monday, Abdi simply refuses to acknowledge the request and takes a phone call.

The content in the above episode is the individual speech acts separated from the context and the rules, and have little meaning. Thus, line 8 is simply "How is your wife and family?"

Reardon's Regulative Rule Model

Kathleen Kelley Reardon is a rules theorist who uses the rules approach to explain the pro-cess of persuasion.[32] Her theory begins with the notion that people construe reality differ-ently. No two people see the same event exactly the same way. In order to interpret reality Reardon argues that people develop mental maps of the world around them, sometimes called *constructs* or *schemata*. They are basically the ways people mentally represent the world around them and they serve as a basis for making decisions and inferring meaning. People use their mental maps in the development of personal goals, the interpretation of events and others around them, and to guide social behavior. For example, you have a mental map of your life at college that you use to help you determine your career path, to understand happenings on campus, to develop relationships with others, and to guide your own social behavior.

Consistent with the rules approach, Reardon asserts that social action is based on an individual's mental map of the situation and the subsequent following of rules. Rules that guide social action are called regulative rules. Reardon's regulative rule model is presented in Figure 9.5.

Reardon's model depicts how one might choose a particular action over another. The antecedent conditions refer to how the person perceives the situation at hand. This would be his or her "mental map" of the particular situation. The desired consequences refer to the person's goal; what he or she wants to achieve. Given these two sources of input, certain behavioral options emerge; that is, certain actions will be perceived as more appropriate than others. Rules will prescribe which behavioral options are more appropriate.

The decision to engage in one action over another is based on its perceived appropriateness, consistency, and effectiveness.[33] Appropriateness refers to the social acceptability of the behavior. Consistency refers to whether the behavior is personally acceptable. Effectiveness is the degree to which the behavior will achieve the intended result.

Reardon applies this model to the process of persuasion. Persuasion is viewed as a special type of social behavior. She defines persuasion as "the activity of attempting to change the behavior of at least one person through symbolic interaction."[34] Persuasion is a conscious activity that is necessitated by the fact that our goals differ and frequently conflict. When two or more people come together with conflicting goals, one person will use persuasion to try and change the other's goals and hence, the other's behavior. The successful persuader helps the persuadee change his or her mental map; that is, his or her view of the antecedent conditions, desired consequences, and what is perceived to be the most appropriate, consistent, and effective behavior. Reardon argues that the most successful persuader recognizes what rules the persuadee is following and the specific conditions the persuadee uses to apply the rule.

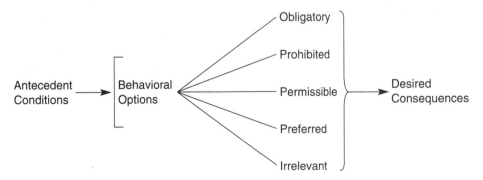

FIGURE 9.5   Reardon's Regulative Rule Model

Regulative Rule Model, from Kathleen Kelley Reardon, *Persuasion in Practice,* (p. 22), copyright © 1991, Sage Publications. Reprinted by permission from Sage Publications, Inc.

The following example may help to demonstrate Reardon's model. Imagine that two friends, Bruce and Jim, are going to lunch. Remember that people construe reality differently. To Jim, smoking cigarettes is unacceptable. Bruce, on the other hand, enjoys smoking. After lunch Bruce decides to smoke. His perception of the situation (i.e., the antecedent conditions) and his desired consequences (to ward off the tiring effects of eating a big lunch) lead him to apply the rule: "If one is tired after eating a big lunch, then smoke a cigarette." Jim, however, has a conflicting goal. Jim dislikes smoking and wants to breathe clean air after his meal. Jim is also familiar with Bruce's application of smoking rules. Jim knows that Bruce's decision to smoke (i.e., his behavioral option) is based on his perception of the situation and intended consequences. Jim has also perceived the situation differently than Bruce. Thus, Jim mentions to Bruce that there is a "No Smoking" sign in the lobby of the restaurant, that there are no ashtrays on any of the tables, and that no one else is smoking. Jim is trying to help Bruce revise his perception of the situation (i.e., the antecedent conditions). Jim also mentions that to smoke in such circumstances would be perceived as socially unacceptable. Hearing this, Bruce alters his perception of the situation and thus revises the number of behavioral options available to him. Given this revision, he decides not to smoke.

Smith's Contingency Rules Theory

Mary John Smith, a leading rules theorist, has also applied rules theory to persuasive communication in a theory she calls the contingency rules theory.[35] Smith theorizes that persuasive behaviors are goal-based actions that are governed antecedently by their intended consequences,[36] which serve as the antecedent conditions to overt persuasive behavior. Rules link the intended consequence and the overt persuasive behavior. Smith calls these rules behavioral contingency rules, which take the form: "If expected consequence X, in context Z, then persuasive message Y."[37] Smith uses the word contingency to mean that one's persuasive message choice is contingent on the applicable rules for the given context. According to the theory, two general categories of rules guide persuasive behavior, including self-evaluative contingency rules and adaptive contingency rules.[38] Self-evaluative rules link persuasive messages to self-generated criteria for appropriate behavior. There are two types of self-evaluative contingency rules, including self-identity rules and image-maintenance rules. Adaptive rules link persuasive behavior with those goals that are external to the maintenance of the self-concept. There are three types of adaptive contingency rules, including environmental contingency rules, interpersonal relationship rules, and social normative rules. The following list presents the various self-evaluative and adaptive contingency rules.

Self-Evaluative Contingency Rules

1. *Self-Identity Rules:* These rules link persuasive behavior to personal values ethics and mores that make up the individual's self-concept. These rules are typically very personal and private and represent an individual's self-definition (e.g., "This behavior is consistent with how I see myself").

2. *Image-Maintenance Rules:* These rules connect persuasive behavior to those qualities associated with one's self-image, including the public presentation of the self and impression-management. These rules guide behavior that reflects important aspects of the physical, social, and personal self (e.g., "This is how I want others to see me").

Adaptive Contingency Rules

1. *Environment Rules:* These rules guide persuasive behavior to concerns about the physical well-being and safety of the self and significant others, including health, safety, and general well-being (e.g., "This behavior helps me to achieve physical and environmental benefits for myself and others I care about").

2. *Interpersonal Relationship Rules:* These rules link persuasive behavior to the maintenance of personally satisfying relationships with significant others (e.g., "This behavior helps me to maintain the relationships I have with good friends, family, and romantic partners").

3. *Social Normative Rules:* These rules are associated with persuasive behaviors that are consistent with the general societal and cultural norms operating in the given context. These rules guide behavior that leads to acceptable status and success in one's community (e.g., "This action represents something I 'must' do to be a member of the community").[39]

Although any of the rules may be operative, the application of specific contingency rules depends on the context in which persuasive messages are exchanged between people. For example, interpersonal relationship rules are more likely to be applied in those situations where intimates rather than strangers are engaged in persuasive interaction. Based on prior research, the theory outlines three situational dimensions that influence the application of specific contingency rules.[40] The first dimension is the actual relationship between the interactants, including such relational aspects as intimacy (high/low), resistance (agreeable/disagreeable), power (equal/unequal), and relational consequences of compliance (short/long term). The second dimension is the intentions of the interactants, including such aspects as who personally benefits from compliance (selfish/altruism), rights to make persuasive requests (high/low), and temporal objectives (short/long term). The third dimension is how the interactants actually view the situation, including their individual ego-involvement (high/low), situational complexity (many/few situational beliefs), emotional orientation (favorable/unfavorable), and their level of situational apprehension (high/low). These eleven situational factors combine in complex ways to determine which contingency rule operates during persuasive interaction.

For example, consider how the following two situations differ along these dimensions. The first situation entails an undeserving employee trying to persuade her boss for a raise. This situation could be characterized as low intimacy, unagreeable resistance, unequal power, short-term consequence, selfish benefits, low rights, short-term objective, high ego-involvement, few situational beliefs, unfavorable emotional orientation, and high situational apprehension. The second situation involves a spouse trying to persuade a spouse to have sex. This situation could be characterized as high intimacy, equal power, agreeable resistance, short-term consequence, altruistic benefits, high rights, short-term objective, low ego-involvement, many situational beliefs, favorable emotional orientation, and low situational apprehension. Note that on nine of the eleven situational factors the two situations differ. Based on these differences, different contingency rules will operate in each situation.

Available data suggest that the theory is valid. In her research, for example, Smith found that the situational dimensions did in fact influence what rules people apply to their persuasive behavior. In one study, Smith examined the influence of intimacy, rights, and personal benefits on the application of the two self-evaluative and three adaptive contingency rules. The other eight situational factors were held constant. Smith asked participants to imagine themselves in a hypothetical situation in which they were being persuaded to do something. The participants were then asked to respond exactly as they thought they would if the situation were actually occurring. Smith's results are presented in the following list.[41]

The Impact of Three Situational Factors on Contingency Rule Application

Situation 1: (Intimate, High Rights to Resist, Self-Benefits)

You are a homeowner and you are planning to cut down a large shade tree at the edge of your property, near your neighbor's property, in order to build a new two-car garage. Your neighbor, who is a good friend of yours, wants to persuade you to not cut down the tree. Your neighbor says you should leave the tree standing because it enhances the beauty and marketability of his home. *Operative Rules:* Interpersonal Relationship, Image-Maintenance.

Situation 2: (Intimate, High Rights to Resist, Mutual Benefits)

You are a homeowner and you are planning to cut down a large shade tree at the edge of your property, near your neighbor's property, in order to build a new two-car garage. Your neighbor, who is a good friend of yours, wants to persuade you to not cut down the tree. Your neighbor says you should leave the tree standing because it enhances the beauty and marketability of both of your homes. *Operative Rules:* Interpersonal Relationship.

Situation 3: (Intimate, Low Rights to Resist, Self-Benefit)

You are a smoker and you enjoy smoking. The person with whom you work, and who sits next to you, is a good friend of yours and has asked you to cut down on your smoking. The coworker says that your smoking endangers his or her health, so please cut down. *Operative Rules:* Environmental Contingency.

Situation 4: (Intimate, Low Rights to Resist, Mutual Benefit)

You are a smoker and you enjoy smoking. The person with whom you work, and who sits next to you, is a good friend of yours and has asked you to cut down on your smoking. The coworker says that your smoking endangers your health as well as his or her health, so please cut down. *Operative Rules:* Environmental Contingency.

Situation 5: (Nonintimate, High Rights to Resist, Self-Benefits)

You are a homeowner and you are planning to cut down a large shade tree at the edge of your property, near your neighbor's property, in order to build a new two-car garage. Your neighbor, who you do not know very well, wants to persuade you to not cut down the tree. Your neighbor says you should leave the tree standing because it enhances the beauty and marketability of his home. *Operative Rules:* Image-Maintenance, Self-Identity, Environmental Contingency.

Situation 6: (Nonintimate, High Rights to Resist, Mutual Benefits)

You are a homeowner and you are planning to cut down a large shade tree at the edge of your property, near your neighbor's property, in order to build a new two-car garage. Your neighbor, who you do not know very well, wants to persuade you to not cut down the tree. Your neighbor says you should leave the tree standing because it enhances the beauty and marketability of both of your homes. *Operative Rules:* Social Normative.

Situation 7: (Nonintimate, Low Rights to Resist, Mutual Benefit)

You are a smoker and you enjoy smoking. The person with whom you work, and who sits next to you, who you do not know very well, has asked you to cut down on your smoking. The coworker says that your smoking endangers his or her health, so please cut down. *Operative Rules:* Social Normaltive.

Situation 8: (Nonintimate, Low Rights to Resist, Mutual Benefit)

You are a smoker and you enjoy smoking. The person with whom you work, and who sits next to you, who you do not know very well, has asked you to cut down on your smoking. The coworker says that your smoking endangers your health as well as his or her health, so please cut down. *Operative Rules:* Environmental Contingency.

Smith's theory is an important part of the literature on both rules and persuasion. Unlike some research, Smith's studies provide an explanation as to why people choose certain persuasive messages over others. Her theory identifies rules as a primary motivating force for social action. In addition, the theory points out the importance of context in the application of rules.

Conversation Analysis

Bobby: Hey Suzy.

Suzy: Hi.

Bobby: What's up?

Suzy: Oh . . . not much, how 'bout you?

Bobby: Nuthin' . . . man, you look great today!

Suzy: Thanks.

Bobby: Uh . . . wanna come over to the room tonight?

Suzy: Well yeah . . . sure, what'll we do?

Bobby: Ah . . . we'll think of somethin'

Suzy: O.K., (laughs) see you tonight, then?

Bobby: Yeah, ah . . . 'bout seven?

Suzy: Sounds good, see ya.

To the casual observer, the above conversation between Bobby and Suzy seems quite ordinary. Upon closer inspection, however, you can discover that their behavior is complex and requires that both Bobby and Suzy have an immense amount of knowledge about each other, the world around them, verbal and nonverbal language, social rules, and simple manners. What appears to be a commonplace activity is actually a highly structured and managed sequence of rule-governed behavior called conversation.

The establishment, maintenance, and termination of our relationships requires the ability to converse. For the most part, our everyday conversations flow smoothly even though they are almost always impromptu. Our ability to create smooth flowing conversations has fascinated scholars for decades and has created a fruitful area of research known as conversational coherence.[42] A coherent conversation is one in which the discourse is said to "hang together," where the interactants cooperate with one another by making relevant contributions to the conversation.[43] Conversations are coherent because the interactants obey certain rules. Occasionally, however, we experience trouble in our conversations and feel that with some people we just "can't communicate." This is usually the result of some rule violation.

Robert E. Nofsinger, an expert in conversation analysis, outlines three characteristics of conversations that distinguish them from other forms of communication (e.g., debate, public speaking, interviewing, etc.).[44] First, the primary characteristic of a conversation is that it is interactive; that is, it requires at least two people. During conversations people contribute and respond to each other in a turn-taking sequence. Typically, one's turn in a conversation reflects on something just said while simultaneously projecting ahead. For example, in Bobby and Suzy's conversation, Bobby invites Suzy over to his room. When she accepts the invitation, Suzy's response reflects on Bobby's invitation and projects ahead by asking for more information about the evening.

The second characteristic of conversations is that they are "locally managed." The conversants themselves determine the rules of the conversation including such things as the topic and speaking turns. Within their relationship, for example, it is acceptable for Bobby to comment on Suzy's physical appearance. In addition, both Bobby and Suzy exchange an equal number of speaking turns. In face-to-face conversations there are also nonverbal rules that are followed by the conversants. These might include eye contact and distance. If Bobby were conversing with the president of his university, for example, different conversational rules might apply. Bobby probably would not comment on the president's physical appearance, for example.

The third aspect of conversations is that they are characteristically mundane. Most of our conversations with others are not about critical affairs of state or the world; they more likely involve "small talk" about such topics as the weather and other local interests. Note that the conversation between Bobby and Suzy is a simple exchange of greetings, followed by a compliment, continuing with an invitation and acceptance, and ending with a brief farewell. Their conversation is interactive, locally guided, brief, and mundane. You have probably found that most of your conversations are quite similar.[45]

Although conversations appear commonplace and simple, they require a great deal of communication competence. Specifically, this competence includes the knowledge and practice of rules. Since most conversations are not rehearsed, the participants actively and spontaneously apply myriad rules to generate coherent talk. Communication scholars have spent a considerable amount of time studying how people converse with each other. Much of this research can be categorized into five areas, including (a) the relationship between conversation and language, (b) conversation as gameplaying, (c) conversational actions, sequences, and coherence, (d) turn taking in conversations, and (e) conversational alignment.

Language and Conversation

Perhaps the most important prerequisite for engaging in conversation is language. A language is defined as a system of sounds along with a set of rules for combining them for the sole purpose of communicating.[46] Languages consist of three major components, including sounds, syntax, and semantics.[47] Sounds, the most basic units of language, are used to create speech. The most basic unit of sound is called a phoneme.[48] Most sounds are symbolized by individual letters in the alphabet (e.g., *k, s,* and *b*). Some sounds are combinations of letters, however (e.g., *ly, ph*). The English language has forty speech sounds.

In combination, sounds form words. When words are combined, they form sentences. In order to combine sounds and words a language must have a set of rules, called syntax or grammar. Syntax prescribes exactly how to combine sounds and words in order to produce grammatically correct sentences. Syntax tells the speaker how to assemble sentences, how to express the proper tense, gender agreement, etc. Syntax does not prescribe meaning. A perfectly meaningless sentence may be grammatically correct.

The third component of language, semantics, refers to the meaning of words and sentences. For example, the individual sounds *a, t,* and *c* are meaningless until combined in the order of *c-a-t*. In English the combination of the three sounds *c, a,* and *t* refers to a fuzzy little animal.

The study of language, called linguistics, is an incredibly vast subject that can be approached in a variety of ways. One of the most influential voices from a rules perspective is that of Noam Chomsky.[49] Chomsky believes that language separates humans from other life forms. Language, according to Chomsky, is innately human. He argues that humans are born with a "blueprint" for language and that the structure of language is deeply embedded in the human mind. Chomsky calls this the "deep structure" of language. Deep structures form the basic structure of a sentence that, when ready for utterance, is called the "surface structure." To move from deep structure to surface structure, the native speaker performs a series of transformations.[50]

Chomsky is particularly interested in the creativity or "open-ended-ness" of language.[51] According to Chomsky, the majority of sentences produced by speakers of language are ones that have never before been spoken. In addition, Chomsky argues, speakers have little difficulty understanding never before spoken utterances. For example, the conversation between Bobby and Suzy may be the very first time those exact sentences have ever before been uttered and yet few native speakers of English have difficulty comprehending them. The words and sentences in this very paragraph are combined in such a way as never before and yet are fully understandable to native speakers of English. To explain this phenomena, Chomsky asserts that native speakers of a language must possess a finite set of linguistic rules that allow them to generate an infinite number of sentences.[52] Think for a moment about the game of chess. The rules for the game of chess are finite but can produce an almost infinite number of games. A single game of chess has probably never been played the exact same way twice. Chomsky also contends that the general principles which determine the rules for any particular language (e.g., Japanese, English, Arabic) are to some extent common to all languages.[53] He refers to this as a "universal grammar" which is based on the deep structure of language inherent in humans.[54] The specific rules for any individual language are, of course, different from other languages. These rules, however, are deeply embedded but are learned through enculturation and socialization.

The set of rules that allows a speaker to create new sentences is called generative grammar. Chomsky's goal is to describe this grammar. Chomsky is careful to distinguish between descriptive generative grammar and traditional prescriptive grammar, like that you learned in grade and high school. Chomsky's generative grammar describes how people speak, not how they ought to speak.[55] In defense of his descriptive grammar, Chomsky argues that there are many examples of prescriptive rules established by grammarians that are not reflected in the normal usage of the language. For example, when asked "Who's there?" we typically answer "It's me." From the standpoint of traditional prescriptive grammar this is grammatically incorrect. The grammatically correct response would be "It is I." Chomsky is not interested in the grammarian's prescription on how people "ought" to speak. Instead he was interested in what native speakers of a language actually say and what rules they follow to generate their sentences. In this sense, Chomsky's grammar is neutral with respect to the correct and incorrect production of sentences. The deep structure linguistic rules generate only correct sentences.[56]

Chomsky is convinced that native speakers of a particular language have intuitions that tell them when a sentence is acceptable or unacceptable. Take the following two sentences:

A: *The cat played with the ball.*

B: *Cat the played ball with the.*

If asked which of the two sentences is acceptable, even illiterate speakers of the language with no knowledge of traditional prescriptive language will choose Sentence A as the more acceptable or correct sentence.

Native speakers of a language may produce ungrammatical sentences, however (although not as ungrammatical as Sentence B). To explain why, Chomsky distinguishes between language competence and language performance. Language competence refers to one's knowledge of the rules whereas performance refers to one's actual application of the rules. Hence when one produces an ungrammatical sentence it is due to an error in the application of the rules.[57]

Chomsky's Rules

Chomsky's generative grammar consists of two parts, including phrase structure grammar and transformational grammar. Although phrase structure grammar, which was developed by structural linguists in an attempt to describe the structure of language, cannot account for an infinite number of sentences, Chomsky used it as the basis for his transformational grammar.

Imagine that you have something in mind that you want to say. Exactly how that thought is mentally represented is unknown to us but think of it as kind of a "lump of meaning" in your head.[58] In order to express this "lump" in your head, it needs some structure.

The goal of phrase structure grammar is to provide a set of rules for giving the "lump" of meaning in your head some structure. A representative list of six basic rules for simple phrase structure grammar follows:[59]

S	=	Sentence	N	=	Noun
NP	=	Noun Phrase	P	=	Phrase
VP	=	Verb Phrase	→	=	Counts as
Rule 1:		S	→		NP + VP
Rule 2:		NP	→		T + N
Rule 3:		VP	→		V + NP Phrase
Rule 4:		T	→		the
Rule 5:		N	→		{cat, ball,...}
Rule 6:		V	→		{likes, wants,...}

This set of rules will generate only a finite set of sentences in English but demonstrates simple phrase structure grammar. The rules are to be applied as follows: Rule 1 tells us that a sentence is written as a noun phrase plus a verb phrase. Note that Rule 1 is accomplished by following other rules (i.e., either Rule 2 or 3). Rule 2 requires us to apply Rule 4 and Rule 5. Rule 3 requires us to apply Rule 6 and Rule 2. These rules will permit the generation of some sentences but not others. For example, by following these rules, the following sentences can be generated:

A: The cat likes the ball.

B: The cat wants the ball.

Both of these sentences would seem acceptable to native speakers of English. The rules will not permit the generation of the following sentences:

A: Wants the ball the cat.

B: Likes the cat the ball.

Both of these sentences would be perceived as unacceptable or incorrect to native speakers. Sentences in phrase structure grammar are usually represented in a tree diagram.

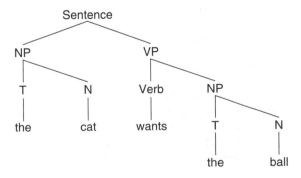

Transformational Grammar

The second part of Chomsky's theory is transformational rules, which take the result of the phrase structure rules and change, or transform, it. Take the following two sentences:

> A: *The cat wants the ball.*

> B: *The ball the cat wants.*

Sentence A is the result of the phrase structure rules presented in the above list. Sentence B is the result of applying a transformational rule to Sentence A. Sentence B could not be generated from only the phrase structure rules. Transformational rules can (a) move, (b) delete, (c) insert, or (d) substitute parts of the sentence.[60] In the case of the example above, the transformational rule moved the two noun phrases. For example:

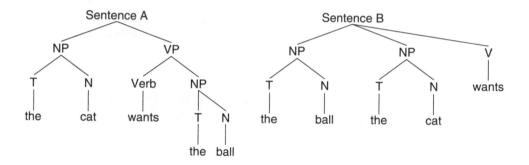

An example of a deletion rule would be to transform the sentence "I like chicken and rice" to "I like rice." An example of a substitution rule could be "Jim behaved himself" to "Jim behaved Jim." An example of an insertion rule could be to put the word "To" at the beginning of the sentence "To err is human." Though transformational rules certainly change sentences, a major point about transformational rules is that they may not change the meaning of a sentence.[61]

Recall that transformation rules allow the speaker to move from deep structures to surface structure by transforming the deep structure into acceptable sentences. Perhaps the most important aspect of transformational grammar is that it demonstrates how two similar sentences have different meanings based on their transformations. To demonstrate this Chomsky used the following two examples:[62]

> A: *John is eager to please.*

> B: *John is easy to please.*

Using phrase structure grammar, these two sentences would be diagrammed identically except for the spellings of "eager" and "easy." Clearly, however, these two sentences have different "deep" structures. The meaning of Sentence B is that: "For somebody to please John is easy." By applying the deletion rule to "For somebody" and the movement rule to "to please" we can create the sentence "John is easy to please." A major contribution of transformational grammar is that it tries to explain surface structure language through the transformation of deep structure. Not all linguists accept Chomsky's ideas but few of them can ignore their impact on linguist theory. In order to be on the cutting edge of their field, linguists from the various schools of thought become well versed in Chomsky's ideas.

Conversation as Game Playing

Many communication scholars are interested in the actual use of language in communication. This area of study is generally known as pragmatics and one of the dominant theories in this area is known as speech act theory. In 1916 the linguist Ferdinand de Saussure compared language to the game of chess. He argued that like the game of chess, language consists of a set of rules which can generate an infinite number of moves between the players.[63] Conversation, too, is analogous to a game. According to Jacobs and Jackson:

> *Games are social activities defined by rules; their players are held accountable to the rules. Players have knowledge of the rules and varying degrees of skill in using the rules to make moves that realize their goal. Games are characterized by varying degrees of mutual constraint: Each player's action will constrain, in some degree, the actions of the other.*[64]

Conversation, like most games, exists only if certain rules are followed. In addition, many of the terms used to describe a game can be used to describe conversation.[65] These terms include (a) moves, (b) turns, (c) goal, and (d) strategy. Moves refer to the set of behaviors required to play the game. In football, for example, this includes passing, blocking, kicking, and running. In conversation, moves are the verbal and nonverbal statements people make to each other. In most games and in conversation behaviors are performed in some specified order or sequence called turns. Turns, of course, must be made according to the rules. Generally, turns are performed to achieve some goal. In football, the goal is to outscore the opponent. In conversation, it may be to persuade someone to go out on a date or to compliment someone. Finally, when players perform their turns, they do it strategically in order to more effectively accomplish the goal. For example, a football team may decide to pass on only certain plays and run on others depending on the strengths and weaknesses of the opponent. Likewise, a person may decide to use a number of different persuasive strategies in order to persuade someone to go out on a date (e.g., begging).[66]

Rules and Conversational Action, Sequence, and Coherence

As mentioned above, conversations, like games, consist of rule-governed moves performed in a turn-taking sequence to accomplish some goal. Again, moves are verbal and nonverbal statements people contribute to the conversation. Moves in conversation are called utterances.[67] An utterance may or may not be a complete grammatically correct sentence. For example, the following two statements are considered utterances but are not grammatically acceptable.

A: Want this?

B: Nah . . .

For the most part, conversation analysts focus their attention on verbal utterances. J. L. Austin distinguishes between two types of utterances. The first type, called a locution, refers to the actual message itself, the words and sounds (i.e., phonemes) used to produce it, and what it means. The second type of utterance is called an illocutionary act. Here, emphasis is placed not so much on the actual message content but on what the message actually does; that is, its function. In the above example Utterance A acts as an offer; its function is to present something for acceptance or rejection. Utterance B acts as a rejection of the offer made in Utterance A.[68]

Several scholars have proposed taxonomies (i.e., lists) of illocutionary acts. Three of these taxonomies are presented below:

Taxonomies of Illocutionary Acts

Bach & Harnish (1979)[69]

1. Constatives: Acts that express the speaker's belief as well as his or her intent that others will adopt the same belief (e.g., suggesting, asserting).

2. Directives: Acts that express the speaker's intent that the receiver perform some act (e.g., requests, advice, prohibitions).

3. Commissives: Acts that express a speaker's intention to perform some future action (e.g., promising, offering).

4. Acknowledgments: Acts that recognize a receiver's act (e.g, thanking, apologizing, congratulating).

Searle (1979)[70]

1. Commissives: Acts that commit the speaker to some future action (e.g., promises, offers).

2. Directives: Acts designed to influence the receiver to perform action (e.g., orders, requests).

3. Assertives: Acts that describe the speaker's belief in something (e.g., descriptive statements, speculations).

4. Expressives: Acts that express the speaker's attitude or feeling about something else (e.g., compliments, thanks).

5. Declarations: Acts that in themselves simultaneously perform a corresponding act via their utterance (e.g., "I quit," "you're fired").

Fraser (1975)[71]

1. Asserting: Acts that express the speaker's level of knowledge about something else (e.g., remark, comment, state).

2. Evaluating: Acts that express the speaker's critical assessment of something (e.g., appraise, characterize).

3. Reflecting: Acts that express the speaker's attitude about some prior action (e.g., oppose, denounce).

4. Stipulating: Acts designed to express the speaker's agreement with some other act (e.g., define, specify).

5. Requesting: Acts designed to express the speaker's desire that someone else perform some action (e.g., direct, beg).

6. Suggesting: Acts that express the speaker's preferences (e.g., advise, warn).

7. Exercise of Authority: Acts that express the speaker's role of authority (e.g., approve, nullify).

8. Committing: Acts that pledge the speaker to a course of action (e.g., promise, swear to).

The individual categories in the above taxonomies are based on the function performed by the act. What an act means, what it counts as, or how it functions is based on a set of constitutive rules that must be followed by the speaker. Constitutive rules are rules of meaning that prescribe what behaviors actually mean by accomplishing certain functions. For example, the phrase "Hello" counts as, or functions as, a greeting. John Searle, one of the primary theorists of speech act theory, argues that constitutive rules guide and define all illocutionary acts. Sometimes called preconditions, constitutive rules prescribe the appropriate performance of the act.[72] These conditions are sometimes called felicity conditions (i.e., that which promotes aptness or grace especially in art or language) and include (a) sincerity conditions, (b) preparatory conditions, and (c) essential conditions.[73] Speakers must follow each of these conditions in order to successfully perform an illocutionary act. Sincerity rules refer to the internal states of speakers regarding their commitment to perform the act. For example, a speaker must actually intend to keep a promise. Preparatory rules refer to any prerequisite conditions that are needed to perform the act. For example, a violation of some social rule is a prerequisite for an apology. Essential conditions refer to the strategic point of the act; that is, the intent of the speaker in performing the act. For example, when performing a compliment, the essential condition is that the speaker gives the receiver a positive "face" by communicating approval for the receiver's appearance or behavior.

A second type of rule, regulative rules, also pertain to the performance of illocutionary acts. Unlike constitutive rules that prescribe how to perform a specific act, regulative rules prescribe when to use illocutionary acts. For example, if one violates a social norm—for example, burping out loud at a restaurant—then the regulative rule indicates that one should perform the act of excusing oneself.

Conversational Action Sequences

By definition, conversations consist of more than one illocutionary act. Combinations of at least three or more conversational acts are called conversation action sequences.[74] Conversational sequences, like illocutionary acts, are rule governed. The most common type of action sequence is called the adjacency pair. McLaughlin defines an adjacency pair as: "Expandable pairs of adjacently placed speech acts in which the first establishes a slot for the performance of the second, and the second satisfies the demand expressed in the first."[75]

McLaughlin describes adjacency pairs as having the following features, including (a) two-act length, (b) adjacent positioning of the two acts, (c) different speakers performing each act, (d) first act precedes second act, and (e) the first and second acts must be relevant to each other. Some of the most common types of adjacency pairs include question-answer, greeting-greeting, request-grant/refusal, invitation-acceptance/refusal, accuse-deny/confess, apology-accept/refuse, goodbye-goodbye, etc.[76]

One theory that explains how adjacency pairs operate in conversations is the sequencing rules model developed by Emmanuel Schegloff and his associates Harvey Sacks and Gail Jefferson.[77] They argue that adjacency pairs consist of two parts, including the first pair part and the second pair part, and that these two parts are defined by two rule-governed sequential properties. The first rule is called the conditional relevance rule.[78] This means that when a first pair part is uttered it creates a demand, or force, for a relevant second pair part. Any given second pair part, then, is conditional upon the preceding first pair part. Take the following two examples. Note that in Example One conditional relevance has been satisfied whereas in Example Two conditional relevance is violated.

Example One	*Example Two*
A: What time is it?	A: What time is it?
B: About three o'clock.	B: Did you wash your hair today?

In addition to conditional relevance, adjacency pairs are also governed by a "preference for agreement" between the first pair and second pair parts.[79] This means that although there may be a variety of relevant second pair parts available to a speaker, some are preferred over others; specifically those that are in agreement with the intentions of the speaker who utters the first pair part. For example, Speaker A utters the first pair part "Wanna go to lunch?" to Speaker B. There are many equally relevant second pair parts available to Speaker B (e.g., "Yes," "Maybe," "No," "I don't know," etc.), but the preferred second pair part (based on A's intentions) would be the answer "Yes." Jacobs and Jackson contend that this rule creates a force whereby interactants work to avoid those relevant second pair parts that are in disagreement with, or negate, first pair parts.[80]

In addition to identifying the rules of conditional relevance and preference for agreement, the sequencing rule model has also articulated the notion that adjacency pairs themselves occur in rule-governed sequences; that is, conversations are made up of multiple sequential adjacency pairs. Two of these sequences include presequences and embedded expansions.[81]

Presequences are those illocutionary acts that "set up" or precede adjacency pairs; that is, they serve as a preface to the adjacency pair. For example, continuing with the examples above, Speaker A might precede his or her request in a presequence:

Speaker A: Are you hungry?

Speaker B: Yeah sort of . . .

Speaker A: Wanna go to lunch?

Speaker B: Sure.

Embedded expansions, also called insertions, are adjacency pairs which occur within other adjacency pairs. In a sense, embedded expansions interrupt first pair and second pair parts of primary adjacency pairs. Embedded expansions are subordinate to the primary adjacency pair. For example:

Presequence

> *Speaker A:* Are you hungry?
>
> *Speaker B:* Yeah, sort of . . .
>
> *Speaker A:* Wanna go to lunch?
>
> *Speaker B:* What time is it?

Embedded Sequence

> *Speaker A:* Ah . . . seven 'til twelve.
>
> *Speaker B:* OK. . . . Sure.

In the above example the primary adjacency pair is the request-acceptance preceded by a presequence and interrupted by an embedded sequence.[82]

Rules and Conversational Turn Taking

One of the most distinguishing characteristics of conversation is turn taking. Many aspects of our lives are conducted via turn taking, including such activities as games; waiting in line at the post office, doctor's office, or supermarket; traffic stop signs; etc. Conversations, too, are conducted via turn taking. Like most other aspects of conversation, turn taking is highly rule governed.

Perhaps the most widely cited model of conversational turn taking is called the simplest systematics model developed by Harvey Sacks, Emmanuel Schegloff, and Gail Jefferson.[83] Sacks and his associates begin their treatment of turn taking by articulating what they call "grossly" apparent facts about conversation, which are listed below:[84]

1. Speaker change recurs, or at least occurs.
2. Overwhelmingly, one party talks at a time.
3. Occurrences of more than one speaker at a time are common, but brief.
4. Transitions (from one turn to the next) with no gap and no overlap are common. Together with transitions characterized by slight gap or slight overlap, they make up the vast majority of transitions.
5. Turn order is not fixed, but varies.
6. Turn size is not fixed, but varies.
7. Length of conversation is not specified in advance.
8. What parties say is not specified in advance.
9. Relative distribution of turns is not specified in advance.
10. Number of parties can vary.
11. Talk can be continuous or discontinous.

12. Turn-allocation techniques are obviously used. A current speaker may select a next speaker (as when he addresses a question to another party); or parties may self-select in starting to talk.
13. Various 'turn-constructional units' are employed; e.g., turns can be projectedly 'one word long', or they can be sentential in length.
14. Repair mechanisms exist for dealing with turn-taking errors and violations; e.g., if two parties find themselves talking at the same time, one of them will stop prematurely, thus repairing the trouble.

Sacks et al. note that the above-listed facts about conversation, especially turn taking, distinguish it from many other forms of communication. For example, the length and allocation of turns is prespecified in many other forms of interaction (e.g., debates, meetings, symposia). They argue that conversation "occupies a central position among the speech-exchange system; perhaps its turn-taking system is more or less explanatory of that centrality."[85] The simplest system model of turn-taking (SSM) outlines three aspects of conversational turn taking, including (a) the construction of turns, (b) the allocation of turns, and (c) a set of rules.

SSM indicates that there are various "unit-types" of turns. This is called the turn-construction component of the model. Unit-type refers to the syntactical structure of the turn. Turns may be sentences, phrases, clauses, or single words. In general, turns are quite short in length. James Deese found, for example, that of the twenty thousand utterances he recorded, 20 percent of them lasted fewer than one second and 90 percent of them lasted fewer than ten seconds.[86] Examples of single word-turns include:

Bruce: You want a single or double?

Jim: Double.

Jan: Did you walk the dog last night?

Marlene: Yeah.

Examples of single-phrase turns include:

Wayne: I paid for the whole thing in cash.

Larry: You what?

Mary Alyce: I was out really late last night.

Kathi: On Wednesday?

Examples of single-clause turns include:

Kevin: The loon is out on the water.

Donna: Near the dock.

Karen: Where is it—that snake!?

Dave: Jist teasin' ya.

Examples of single-sentence turns include:

Bobby: You look great today!

Suzy: Thanks.

Jan: The cat is on the counter again.

Jim: I let her on there at night.

SSM also describes a turn-allocation component. SSM specifies that turn allocation is determined by the current speaker who may select the next speaker or by the other potential speakers who may select themselves in what is called self-selection allocation. In the following example, the speaker who "holds the floor" (i.e., is taking a turn) selects the next speaker:

Ken: Hey Marijean, what's the deal here . . .

Marijean: The deal is—you lose.

In the next example, the speakers self-select their turns:

Jim: It's a good idea.

Bob: I never know 'bout these things.

Mary: I think so, I mean, I guess.

Larry: Yeah, it'll probably work.

SSM offers a set of four rules regarding conversational turn taking. The rules apply in the order in which they are stated; that is, Rule 1 applies before Rule 2, etc. Rule 1 indicates that during the performance of a turn if the speaker holding the floor selects the next speaker then that speaker has the right and obligation to take the next turn. No others have the right to take a turn. Rule 2 indicates that if the speaker holding the floor does not select the next speaker, then self-selection may proceed. The speaker who self-selects first has the floor. Rule 3 states that if the speaker holding the floor does not select the next speaker then he or she may continue, but need not continue, unless another speaker self-selects. Finally, Rule 4 states that if during a turn neither Rule 1 nor Rule 2 has applied and the current speaker continues with another turn, then during that second turn, Rule 1 and Rule 2 reapply at the next turn-taking transition.[87]

Although SSM is highly regarded as one of the best models of conversational turn taking, it is not without its limitations. Some have argued the SSM's turn-construction component is poorly defined. Others have argued that the model does not clearly distinguish between turns and nonturns. Another criticism is that the model does not take into account cultural differences that might affect the rules of turn taking. Still others have criticized the model for its lack of attention to the receiver's role in turn taking.[88] These limitations notwithstanding, SSM provides a very practical model with which researchers can study and analyze conversations.

Rule Violations and Conversational Alignment

Recall from Chapter 8 that a rule was defined as a "followable prescription that indicates what behavior is preferred, obligated, or prohibited."[89] Recall also that followability implies that rules are breakable. Without a doubt, the rules of conversation are frequently broken. Whether it be mispronounced words, ungrammatical sentences, or speaking out of turn, conversants make mistakes during interaction. Research indicates that in most cases people correct their errors. In fact, Deese found that less than 2 percent of the utterances he recorded that included errors were left uncorrected.[90] The study of how interactants go about correcting their rule violations is called conversation alignment. Ragan defines alignment talk as "verbal strategies that communicators can use to repair misunderstanding or disruptions in conversations."[91] In her research Ragan studied the use of alignment talk during job interviews. Her analysis uncovered seven aligning strategies, including accounts, formulations, metatalk, side sequences, metacommunicative digressions, qualifiers, and "you knows." These strategies are below:

Accounts
Statements offered to explain unanticipated or questionable behavior (e.g., justifications, excuses).

Sandra: So that's why he did it.

Jim: That's bullshit!

Sandra: Wha . . . ?

Jim: Oh . . . sorry about that . . . it's just that this guy pisses me off.

Formulations
Statements that summarized previous statements or offered interpretations of the conversation in progress.

Jill: Is it OK if I miss class today?

Dr. Wong: When someone misses my class—in a sense they cheat themselves out of their tuition. Besides, they may miss important material. Participation is important also. Ah . . . one cannot participate if one is not in class.

Jill: So you don't want me to miss class.

Dr. Wong: Well . . . right.

Metatalk
Metatalk is talk about talk. These statements refer explicitly to the verbal properties of a message in the conversation. Metatalk can come in a variety of ways, including:

Clarifying: "I assume you mean that . . ."

Remediating: "This is gonna sound funny . . ."

Directing: "Let me interrupt . . ."

Requesting: "What else do you want me to say?"

Agendizing: "Let me introduce myself."

Side Particles: "Quite frankly..."

Side Sequences

These are statements that constitute a metacommunicative break in the conversation after which the conversation resumes.

Jan: Got it?

Jim: Got it.

Jan: You sure?

Jim: Sure.

Metacommunicative Digressions

These are statements that constitute a metacommunicative break in the conversation after which the conversation resumes but are more elaborate than side sequences and less ritualized.

Sven: So we've covered what's botherin' you?

Lisa: I think we have.

Sven: I've asked you everything?

Lisa: You've just about covered it.

Sven: Anything else we should talk about?

Lisa: That should just about do it.

Sven: Should we go on?

Lisa: No...that's OK.

Qualifiers

Words or phrases that explicitly manifested tentativeness, uncertainty, and nonassertiveness. Qualifiers typically evade or dilute the issue or statement of opinion.

Jenny: I don't know...I sorta just feel like kinda quittin' or somethin.

You Knows

These are metacommunicative expressions said to the receiver for the purpose of conversation tracking or emphasis.

Jenny: Ya know...that's just great, I mean ya know what I mean?

Although defined as repair strategies, alignment strategies can be used as preventative strategies within conversations.[93] Preventative strategies are used in anticipation of potential problems during conversations. For example, when speakers believe that what they are about to say may break a rule or cause confusion, they may engage in preventative alignment talk to prevent the problem. Accounts, for example, are frequently employed as preventative strategies. Repairs are those alignment strategies that occur after a violation has occurred. Most alignment strategies are used as repair strategies.

Conversation is a highly ruled-governed mode of communication that requires a great deal of knowledge about language, syntax, and rules. During conversation, interactants engage in a gamelike activity whereby they exchange turns by following the rules in hopes of achieving some goal. As Nofsinger states, conversations are "some of the most important moves of the broader game of everyday life.'"[94]

CASE STUDY 13   Interpersonal Rule-Based Conversation

Key Terms

Illocutionary Acts

Action Sequences

Turn Taking

Conversational Alignment

A considerable portion of this chapter is devoted to the study of rules as they pertain to everyday conversation. This case study focuses on a "normal" conversation between Kevin and Donna. Much, if not all, of the dimensions of conversation analysis can be applied to their conversation, including (a) illocutionary acts, (b) turn taking, (c) alignment strategies, and (d) action sequences.

In order to apply the concepts from conversational analysis, Kevin and Donna's conversation will be presented four times so that individual applications can be made. In the first application each utterance will be labeled according to Searle's typology of illocutionary acts. The second application will point out the various styles and types of turn taking. In the third application several alignment strategies will be demonstrated. Finally, the fourth application will show the various action sequences in the conversation. You may want to refer back to the chapter for specific definitions.

Application 1: Illocutionary Acts in Kevin and Donna's Conversation

DONNA: Are we going over to Jim and Jan's tomorrow? **(Directive)**	1
KEVIN: Donna, can I pour you some more wine? **(Commissive)**	2
DONNA: Ah...yeah. **(Expressive)**	3
KEVIN: Here ya go. **(Declaration)** Oops! Sorry. **(Expressive)**	4
DONNA: What? **(Directive)**	5
KEVIN: I spilled some wine on the table. **(Assertive)**	6
DONNA: Good one. **(Expressive)**	7
KEVIN: Sorry, yeah, ya know, I'm really talented. **(Assertive)**	8
DONNA: That's OK, I'll get a rag. **(Commissive)**	9

KEVIN: Thanks. **(Expressive)**   10
DONNA: Here. **(Declarative)**   11
KEVIN: Got it, thanks. **(Expressive)**   12
DONNA: Got it? **(Directive)**   13
KEVIN: Got it. **(Directive)**   14
DONNA: Are we going to Jim and Jan's tomorrow? **(Directive)**   15
KEVIN: I don't care. **(Expressive)** Do you want to? **(Directive)**   16
DONNA: Huh? **(Directive)**   17
KEVIN: Quite frankly, I don't care. **(Expressive)**   18
DONNA: I'd like to, they're fun. **(Expressive)**   19
KEVIN: So, we're going? **(Directive)**   20
DONNA: Yeah, let's. **(Expressive)**   21
KEVIN: Sure, anything else? **(Directive)**   22
DONNA: OK, so, I assume we're going? **(Directive)**   23
KEVIN: I guess so. **(Assertive)**   24
DONNA: We'll go out to eat, then to their house? **(Directive)**   25
KEVIN: You got it. **(Expressive)**   26
DONNA: So, we're set? **(Directive)**   27
KEVIN: Yeah. **(Expressive)**   28

Application 2: Turn Taking in Kevin and Donna's Conversation

DONNA: Are we going over to Jim and Jan's tomorrow? **(Self-Selected Turn)**   1
    (Rule 1)
KEVIN: Donna, can I pour you some more wine?   2
DONNA: Ah . . . yeah. **(Single-Word Turn)**   3
KEVIN: Here ya go. Oops! Sorry.   4
DONNA: What?   5
KEVIN: I spilled some wine on the table.   6
DONNA: Good one. **(Single-Phrase Turn)**   7
KEVIN: Sorry, yeah, ya know, I'm really talented.   8
DONNA: That's OK, I'll get a rag.   9
KEVIN: Thanks.   10
DONNA: Here.   11
KEVIN: Got it, thanks.   12
DONNA: Got it?   13
KEVIN: Got it.   14
DONNA: Are we going to Jim and Jan's tomorrow?   15
KEVIN: I don't care. Do you want to? **(Self-Selected 2nd Statement) (Rule 3)**   16
DONNA: Huh?   17
KEVIN: Quite frankly, I don't care.   18
DONNA: I'd like to, they're fun. **(Single-Sentence Turn)**   19
KEVIN: So, we're going?   20
DONNA: Yeah, let's.   21

Continued

CASE STUDY 13   *Continued*

KEVIN: Sure, anything else?	22
DONNA: OK, so, I assume we're going? **(Single-Clause Turn)**	23
KEVIN: I guess so.	24
DONNA: We'll go out to eat, then to their house?	25
KEVIN: You got it.	26
DONNA: So, we're set?	27
KEVIN: Yeah.	28

Application 3: Alignment Talk in Kevin and Donna's Conversation

DONNA: Are we going over to Jim and Jan's tomorrow?	1
KEVIN: Donna, can I pour you some more wine?	2
DONNA: Ah . . . yeah.	3
KEVIN: Here ya go. Oops! Sorry.	4
DONNA: What? **Account**	5
KEVIN: I spilled some wine on the table.	6
DONNA: Good one.	7
KEVIN: Sorry, yeah, ya know, I'm really talented. **(Metatalk = ya knows)**	8
DONNA: That's OK, I'll get a rag.	9
KEVIN: Thanks.	10
DONNA: Here.	11
KEVIN: Got it, thanks.	12
DONNA: Got it? **(Side Sequence)**	13
KEVIN: Got it.	14
DONNA: Are we going to Jim and Jan's tomorrow?	15
KEVIN: I don't care. Do you want to?	16
DONNA: Huh?	17
KEVIN: Quite frankly, I don't care.	18
(Metatalk = Side Particle)	
DONNA: I'd like to, they're fun.	19
KEVIN: So, we're going?	20
DONNA: Yeah, let's.	21
KEVIN: Sure, anything else? **Metacommunicative**	22
DONNA: OK, so, I assume we're going? **Digression**	23
(Metatalk = Clarifying)	
KEVIN: I guess so.	24
DONNA: We'll go out to eat, then to their house?	25
KEVIN: You got it.	26
DONNA: So, we're set?	27
KEVIN: Yeah.	28

Application 4: Action Sequences in Kevin and Donna's Conversation

DONNA: Are we going over to Jim and Jan's tomorrow?   1

KEVIN: Donna, can I pour you some more wine?	2
DONNA: Ah...yeah. **(Invitation/Acceptance)**	3
KEVIN: Here ya go. Oops! Sorry.	4
DONNA: What?	5
KEVIN: I spilled some wine on the table.	6
DONNA: Good one.	7
KEVIN: Sorry, yeah, ya know, I'm really talented. **(Apology/Accept)**	8
DONNA: That's OK, I'll get a rag.	9
KEVIN: Thanks.	10
DONNA: Here.	11
KEVIN: Got it, thanks.	12
DONNA: Got it?	13
KEVIN: Got it.	14
DONNA: Are we going to Jim and Jan's tomorrow?	15
KEVIN: I don't care. Do you want to?	16
DONNA: Huh?	17
KEVIN: Quite frankly, I don't care.	18
DONNA: I'd like to, they're fun.	19
KEVIN: So, we're going?	20
DONNA: Yeah, let's.	21
KEVIN: Sure, anything else?	22
DONNA: OK, so, I assume we're going?	23
KEVIN: I guess so. **(Question/Answer)**	24
DONNA: We'll go out to eat, then to their house? **(Presequence)**	25
KEVIN: You got it.	26
DONNA: So, we're set?	27
KEVIN: Yeah.	28

Summary

Since its inception into the communication field during the early 1970s, the rules approach has blossomed into a substantial body of research that, although not accepted by all, is too important to be ignored by any communication student or theorist. This chapter offers a look into only some of the rules theory applications, including the basic assumptions of the rules approach as they apply to communication, the coordinated management of meaning, Reardon's regulative rule model, Smith's contingency rules theory, and conversational analysis. The rules approach is thought to be a superior metatheoretical approach for communication because it focuses on symbolic interaction itself.[95] Critics, however, maintain that the definition of rule is vague and thus difficult to identify. The efforts described in this chapter attest that rules can be precisely defined, however. The job of the communication researcher is to go out and observe behavior from which rules can be identified and continue developing, clarifying, and using this important heuristic metatheoretical base so that human communicative behavior can be adequately explained.

Glossary

Adjacency Pair: A type of conversational action sequence such as hello/good-bye, question/answer.

Conversational Action Sequences: Combinations of three or more conversational acts.

Conversational Alignment: The study of how interactants correct errors during conversation.

Constitutive Rules: Rules prescribing meaning based on the different episodes and master contacts between interactants.

Contingency Rules Theory: Developed by Mary John Smith, this theory maintains that a person's choice of persuasive messages are goal-based actions that are governed antecedently by their intended consequences. Contingency rules provide the link between the intended consequences and the overt persuasive behavior.

Coordinated Management of Meaning: A theory of communication developed by Barnett Pearce and Vernon Cronen. The theory maintains that communication actually creates social reality. Social interaction is a process of coordinating meaning between people. Individuals manage their own meanings based on their individual hierarchy.

Coordination: From the coordinated management of meaning, coordination is the process of using rules to manage meaning during social interaction.

Generative Grammar: Based on the work of Noam Chomsky, generative grammar is the finite set of rules that allows a speaker of any particular language to generate an infinite number of sentences; consists of phrase structure and transformational grammar.

Hierarchy of Meaning: From the coordinated management of meaning, a six-level organizational scheme by which meaning is categorized hierarchically. The hierarchy includes cultural patterns, life script, master contract, episode, speech acts, and content.

Illocutionary Act The function of an utterance in a conversation. "Hello" functions as a greeting.

Locution An utterance within a conversation, the actual message itself.

Management: From the coordinated management of meaning, management refers to the evolution of meaning through an individual's hierarchy of meaning. Any particular word has different meanings for each person.

Regulative Rule: Rules that guide sequential action by prescribing what behavior is appropriate in what contexts.

Regulative Rule Model: Developed by Kathleen Reardon, this model describes how people choose persuasive messages based on antecedent conditions, behavioral options, and the desired consequences.

References

1. Cushman, D. P., & Whiting, C. (1972). "An Approach to Communication Theory: Toward Consensus on Rules," *Journal of Communication, 22,* 217–238.

2. Pearce, W. B., & Wiseman, R. (1983). "Rules Theories: Varieties, Limitations, and Potentials," in W. Gudykunst, (Ed.), *Intercultural Communication Theory,* (pp. 79–88), Beverly Hills: Sage.

3. Cushman, & Whiting, "An Approach to Communication Theory," 217–238.

4. Cushman, D. P. (1977). "The Rules Perspective as a Theoretical Basis for the Study of Human Communication," *Communication Quarterly, 25,* 30–45.

5. Ibid.

6. Cushman, D. P., Valentinsen, B., Dietrich, D. (1982). "A Rules Theory of Interpersonal Communication," In F. E. X. Dance, (Ed.), *Human Communication Theory: Comparative Essays,* (pp. 90–119), Cambridge: Harper and Row, (p. 93).

7. Cushman, & Whiting, "An Approach to Communication Theory," 217–238.

8. Ibid.

9. Cushman, "The Rules Perspective," 30–45; Cushman, & Whiting, "An Approach to Communication Theory," 217–238.

10. Pearce, W. B. (1976). "The Coordinated Management of Meaning: A Rules Based Theory of Interpersonal Communication," in G. R. Miller, (Ed.), *Explorations in Interpersonal Communication,* (pp. 17–36), Beverly Hills: Sage.

11. Pearce, W. B., & Cronen, V. E. (1980). *Communication, Action, and Meaning: The Creation of Social Realities,* New York: Praeger.

12. Pearce, W. B. (1989). *Communication and the Human Condition,* Carbondale, IL: Southern Illinois University Press, (p. 11).

13. Ibid., (p. 14).

14. Pearce, & Cronen, *Communication, Action, and Meaning,* (p. 120).

15. Ibid., (pp. 120–121).

16. Cronen, V. E., Pearce, W. B., & Harris, L. M. (1982). "The Coordinated Management of Meaning: A Theory of Communication," in F. E. X. Dance, (Ed.), *Human Communication Theory,* (pp. 67–68).

17. Ibid., (pp. 61–89); Griffin, E. (1994). *A First Look at Communication Theory,* (2nd Ed.), New York: McGraw-Hill.

18. Griffin, *A First Look at Communication Theory.*

19. Pearce, *Communication and the Human Condition,* (pp. 47–48).

20. Ibid., (pp. 47–48).

21. Ibid.

22. Cronen, Pearce, & Harris, "The Coordinated Management of Meaning," (pp. 61–89).

23. Ibid.; Pearce, *Communication and the Human Condition.*

24. Cronen, Pearce, & Harris, "The Coordinated Management of Meaning," (p. 68).

25. Ibid., (pp. 61–89); Pearce, & Cronen, *Communication, Action, and Meaning.*

26. Cronen, Pearce, & Harris, "The Coordinated Management of Meaning," (pp. 61–89).

27. Ibid.

28. Pearce, *Communication and the Human Condition.*

29. Ibid.

30. The following discussion of the hypothetical language is based on Pearce, & Cronen, *Communication, Action, and Meaning,* (pp. 154–158).

31. Cronen, V. E., Chen, V., & Pearce, W. B. (1988). "Coordinated Management of Meaning: A Critical Theory," in Y. Y. Kim & W. B. Gudykunst, (Eds.), *Theories in Intercultural Communication,* (pp. 66–98), Newbury Park, CA: Sage.

32. Reardon, K. K. (1991). *Persuasion in Practice,* Newbury Park, CA: Sage.

33. Ibid.

34. Ibid., (p. 3).

35. Smith, M. J. (1982). *Persuasion and Human Action: A Review and Critique of Social Influence Theories,* Belmont, CA: Wadsworth; Smith, M. J. (1982). "Cognitive Schemata and Persuasive Communication:

Toward a Contingency Rules Theory," in M. Burgoon, (Ed.), *Communication Yearbook 6,* (pp. 330–362), Beverly Hills: Sage.

36. Smith, M. J. (1984). "Contingency Rules Theory, Context, and Compliance Behaviors," *Human Communication Research, 10,* 489–512.

37. Ibid., (p. 491).

38. Ibid., (pp. 489–512).

39. Ibid.

40. Ibid.

41. Ibid., (p. 498).

42. Three excellent sources for information regarding conversation analysis include Craig, R. T., & Tracy, K. (Eds.) (1983). *Conversational Coherence: Form, Structure, and Strategy,* Beverly Hills: Sage; Nofsinger, R. E. (1991). *Everyday Conversation,* Beverly Hills: Sage; McLaughlin, M. L. (1984). *Conversation: How Talk Is Organized,* Beverly Hills: Sage.

43. McLaughlin, *Conversation;* Nofsinger, *Everyday Conversation.*

44. Nofsinger, *Everyday Conversation.*

45. Ibid.

46. Goss, B., & O'Hair, D. (1988). *Communicating in Interpersonal Relationships,* New York: Macmillan.

47. Ibid.

48. Ellis, A., & Beattie, G. (1986). *The Psychology of Language and Communication,* New York: Guilford Press.

49. Ibid.

50. Lyons, J. (1970). *Noam Chomsky,* New York: Viking Press.

51. Ibid.

52. Ellis, & Beattie, *The Psychology of Language and Communication.*

53. Lyons, *Noam Chomsky.*

54. Trenholm, S. (1991). *Human Communication Theory,* Englewood Cliffs, NJ: Prentice Hall.

55. Ellis, & Beattie, *The Psychology of Language and Communication.*

56. Lyons, *Noam Chomsky.*

57. Ibid.

58. This specific example is from Elgin, S. H. (1975). *A Primer of Transformational Grammar for Rank Beginners,* Urbana, IL: National Council of Teachers of English.

59. This example is from Lyons, *Noam Chomsky,* who adapted it from Chomsky's original work.

60. Elgin, *A Primer of Transformational Grammar for Rank Beginners.*

61. This example is from Elgin. *A Primer of Transformational Grammar for Rank Beginners.*

62. These are from Lyons, *Noam Chomsky,* and Elgin, *A Primer of Transformational Grammar for Rank Beginners.*

63. Collett, P. (Ed.) (1977). *Social Rules and Social Behaviour,* Totowa, NJ: Rowman and Littlefield; de Saussure, F. (1960). *Course in General Linguistics,* London: Peter Owen.

64. Jacobs, S., & Jackson, S. (1983). "Speech Act Structure in Conversation: Rational Aspects of Pragmatic Coherence," in Craig & Tracy, *Conversational Coherence: Form, Structure, and Strategy,* (pp. 47–66).

65. Nofsinger, *Everyday Conversation.*

66. Ibid.

67. Ibid.

68. Austin, J. (1975). *How to Do Things with Words,* Cambridge, MA: Harvard University Press.

69. Bach, K., & Harnish, R. M. (1979). *Linguistic Communication and Speech Acts,* Cambridge, MA: The MIT Press.

70. Searle, J. (1969). *Speech Acts,* Cambridge: Cambridge University Press.

71. Fraser, B. (1975). "Hedged Performatives," in P. Cole and J. L. Morgan, (Eds.), *Syntax and Semantics, Vol. 3: Speech Acts,* (pp. 186–194), New York: Academic Press.

72. Jacobs, Jackson, "Speech Act Structure in Conversation," (pp. 47–66).

73. Ibid.

74. McLaughlin, *Conversation: How Talk Is Organized.*

75. Ibid., (p. 269).

76. From McLaughlin, *Conversation: How Talk Is Organized,* Jacobs, & Jackson, "Speech Act Structure in Conversation," (pp. 47–66).

77. Schegloff, E. A. (1972). "Sequencing in Conversational Openings," in J. A. Fishman, (Ed.), *Advances in the Sociology of Language,* (pp. 75–109), The Hague: Mouton.

78. Ibid.

79. Schegloff, E. A. (1988). "On an Actual Virtual Servo-mechanism for Guessing Bad News: A Single Case Conjecture," *Social Problems, 35,* 442–457; see also Jacobs, & Jackson, "Speech Act Structure in Conversation, (pp. 47–66).

80. Jacobs, & Jackson, "Speech Act Structure in Conversation," (pp. 47–66).

81. Ibid.

82. Ibid.

83. Sacks, H., Schegloff, E. A., & Jefferson, G. (1974). "A Simplest Systematics for the Organization of Turn-Taking for Conversation," *Language, 50,* 696–735.

84. Ibid. Simplest Systematics Turn-Taking Model, from H. Sacks, E. Schegloff, & G. Jefferson, (1974). "A Simplest Systematics for the Organization of Turn-Taking for Conversation," *Language, 50,* 696–735. Reprinted by permission from the Linguistic Society of America.

85. Ibid., (p. 700).

86. Deese, J. (1978). "Thought into Speech," *American Scientist, 66,* 314–321.

87. Sacks, Schegloff, & Jefferson, "A Simplest Systematics for the Organization of Turn-Taking for Conversation," 696–735.

88. For a summary of these criticisms, see McLaughlin, *Conversation: How Talk Is Organized.*

89. Shimanoff, S. B. (1980). *Communication Rules: Theory and Research,* Beverly Hills. Sage, (p. 57).

90. Deese, "Thought into Speech," 314–321.

91. Ragan, S. L. (1983). "Alignment and Conversational Coherence," in Craig and Tracy, *Conversational Coherence: Form, Structure, and Strategy,* (pp. 157–173).

92. These definitions are from Ragan, "Alignment and Conversational Coherence," (pp. 157–173), but the examples presented here are from the author.

93. McLaughlin, *Conversation: How Talk Is Organized.*

94. Nofsinger, *Everyday Conversation,* (p. 10).

95. Shimanoff, *Communication Rules.*

The Systems-Interactional Approach

[M]an lives by those propositions whose validity is a function of his belief in them.[1]—GREGORY BATESON

The systems-interactional approach is a general theoretical orientation that encompasses a very wide variety of academic disciplines ranging from mathematics to communication. Commonly referred to as "general systems theory," and more recently called "modern systems theory," and "living systems theory," this perspective is a metatheory. Kenneth Boulding describes the systems approach as a "skeleton of science."[2] Walter Buckley refers to the systems approach as a "world view."[3] The systems approach does not belong to any one academic discipline. In keeping with this thinking, throughout this chapter, the term "approach" rather than "theory" will be used to describe this particular perspective. This chapter will profile the historical foundations of the systems approach so that when it is presented as a communication theory in the next chapter you will have a better grasp of its background and philosophical underpinnings and it will help you apply this theory in your everyday life. In doing so, this chapter is organized into four major sections. Section one traces the historical roots of systems thinking with an emphasis on a major systems thinker, Ludwig von Bertalanffy. Section two presents some definitions of systems. Section three outlines the basic assumptions that any systems thinker must accept and understand is to utilize a systems approach in the theory building process. Finally, section four demonstrates how a scientist can use the systems perspective to facilitate explanation, prediction, and control of phenomena.

The Historical Roots of Systems Thinking

In comparison with causal process or human action approaches, the systems approach is a relatively new perspective. The notion of a system is not new and systems have been studied for centuries, but the study of systems in the twentieth century focuses on the system as a whole rather than on its individual parts. For example, centuries ago theorists might have studied the individual parts in an economical system without focusing on the entire system, as Karl Marx studied the labor force.

A fundamental assumption of contemporary systems thinking is that all phenomena are essentially interrelated and interdependent of all other phenomena whether they be physiological or social.[4] Put simply, the general orientation of this approach is on the organization of and the relationships between parts of the system. The systems approach is based on the premise that phenomena/entities should be viewed as complete wholes (i.e., as a system). An important and often neglected point about systems is that systems theorists search for system laws.

Ludwig von Bertalanffy and the Beginnings of Systems Thinking

Ludwig von Bertalanffy, a professor of theoretical biology and considered one of the foremost biologists of our time, is generally regarded as a founder of general systems theory. He formally outlined systems thinking in his seminal book *General System Theory.*[5] von Bertalanffy, whose thinking was influenced by many noted theorists and philosophers including Leibniz, Nicolas of Cusa, Marx, and the German philosopher Hegel, describes modern science as disciplines of specialization. Scientists, both in the natural and social sciences, who are actively engaged in scientific activity are encapsulated in their own private worlds virtually unaware of what is going on around them in other disciplines. In addition, most of these scientists are entrenched in the search for lawlike statements that reflect their reductionistic mechanistic paradigm. von Bertalanffy observed that scientists became specialists in their field happily following the established paradigm who focus on only a few areas of study. He noticed, for example, that during this time the physicists were busy dealing with the derivation of the second law of thermodynamics (i.e., closed physical systems progress toward states of disorder) and trying to isolate particles. In biology, the biologists, practicing their reductionistic bent, were engaged in reducing organisms into the smallest entity possible, the atom. Even in the social sciences psychologists were reducing human behaviors into stimulus and response patterns and trying to isolate certain behavioral patterns.

In the midst of all this, an unusual event began to take shape. von Bertalanffy discovered that these scientists, in each of their respective fields, began to focus on similar kinds of problems, those of wholeness and organization. The physicists began to focus on the relationships between particles in thermodynamics rather than individual particles, and the biologists investigated not only individual atoms in isolation but their interaction with other atoms as well. The psychologists began taking interest in something called Gestalt psychology (i.e., the psychology that sees that a whole is something more than the sum of its parts). It became evident to von Bertalanffy and others that there may be models, principles, and possibly even laws that apply to all areas of science and that a general theory is needed to express these similarities and possibly unify science. Thus, von Bertalanffy began his notion of a general system theory, one that would go beyond the discipline of physics and extend into many other fields.[6] von Bertalanffy writes:

Nothing prescribes that we have to end with the systems traditionally treated in physics. Rather, we can ask for principles applying to systems in general, irrespective of whether they are of physical, biological or sociological nature.... A consequence of general system properties is the appearance of structural similarities or isomorphisms in different fields.[7]

von Bertalanffy thought of systems theory as a general science of wholeness and that such a theory could bring about an integration of natural and social science. In fact, von Bertalanffy argued that the systems approach could be a way for the nonphysical sciences (i.e., social sciences) to become more exact.

von Bertalanffy envisioned three major goals for his systems approach. First, because of the increasing development in the biological, behavioral, and social sciences, he believed that similar models, laws, conceptualizations, and a vocabulary that could be used by all the scientists, regardless of their particular field of study, was needed. Second, at the time of his writing, the behavioral and social sciences were developing at a fast pace but were unable to adopt the mechanistic models of their natural science counterparts. The search for natural laws provided no useful model for the social sciences. Thus, von Bertalanffy called for an expansion of categories. He did not dismiss the utility of laws; instead he proposed new categories that would include lawlike statements *about systems* but not about any particular area of study. Third, to combat the progressive specialization he observed, the new theory would need to be interdisciplinary. In other words, the same abstract models should apply to all the sciences in such a way to point out isomorphisms (i.e., having identical or very similar form or shape but from different ancestry) in their formal structure. Given these motivations, the road map for a systems approach had been drawn.[8]

Definitions of System

The term *system* is used frequently by people in many academic disciplines From a systems perspective, it is important to exclude the colloquial use of the term and clearly articulate what is meant by systems thinkers when using it. Several definitions of system from various sources are listed below:

1. von Bertalanffy: "A system is defined as a complex of components in interaction ... the components need not be material, as, for example, in the system analysis of a commercial enterprise where components such as buildings, machines, personnel, money and good will of customers enter."[9]

2. von Bertalanffy: "sets of elements standing in interaction."[10]

3. Buckley: "[A] complex of elements or components directly or indirectly related in some causal network, such that each component is related to at least some others in a more or less stable way within any particular period of time."[11]

4. Hall & Fagen: "A system is a set of objects together with relationships between the objects and between their attributes."[12]

5. Fisher: "[a] whole, the 'all of a thing'."[13]

6. Rapoport: "[a] whole which functions as a whole by virtue of the interdependence of its parts."[14]

7. Capra: "Systems are integrated wholes whose properties cannot be reduced to smaller units."[15]

Certain dimensions of these definitions best characterize a system, such as the notion of wholeness, relationship, and interdependency, as well as the fact that systems contain parts, components, items, entities, elements, or units.

Wholeness, Relationship, and Interdependency

Perhaps the most important concept to understand about the systems approach is that of wholeness. Remember that the underlying premise of systems thinking is that phenomena are interrelated and interdependent of other phenomena whether it is an atom's relationship with other atoms, an animal's relationship with other animals, the part of a machine's relationship with some other part, or a human's relationship with another human. These relationships make up the wholeness of the system. Almost anything imaginable—animate or inanimate—can be a system as long as its parts (i.e., its components) interact with one another interdependently. In fact, the components of the system are actually less important than the relationship between them. As Fisher argues, the components of the system do not actually characterize the systemic nature of the whole, but is the relationships between the parts of the system that make the system uniquely whole.[16] Interdependency means that each component of the system is mutually dependent on the other parts to function properly. Any change in one part produces a change in another part. For example, an automobile can be thought of as a system. The auto's component parts include the engine, tires, body, and gas tank. Without the engine, the tires could not function. Without tires, the engine would not function properly either. The human body is often thought of as a system. A few of the body's interdependent parts include the skeleton, muscles, arms, and legs. A family is a social system. The parts here include the father, mother, and children. Even the human mind can be thought of as a psychological system made up of attitudes, emotions, beliefs, and thoughts.

Notice that each of these systems is made up of component parts and that each component part is mutually dependent (interdependent) on each of the other component parts in order to function properly. For example, a boy cannot be a brother unless he has a sibling. In a single-child family, the child cannot be a brother or sister. The unique mutually dependent relationship that each part has with the other parts produces this quality of wholeness discussed above. Eliminate any of the component parts from the system and the system changes drastically. In fact, in some cases, to remove a single component part destroys the system. For example, the human body cannot survive without the skeleton. The automobile cannot function without the engine. The human mind cannot function properly without personality traits, and a family without siblings may not be a family at all. Keep in mind that the relationships, not the parts individually, define the nature of the system. For example, consider any two families and note their differences. Each family may have a mother, a father, a daughter, and a son. Each family is quantitatively equal. Upon further investigation of these families you will soon notice very different relationships between mother and father, brother and sister, sister and mother, brother and father, etc. In Family A, for example, the mother and father get along very well and rarely argue or yell at each other. In Family B, however, the mother and father argue frequently and sometimes the father physically hits the mother. These are two very different mother/father relationships. The differences in these relationships differentiate the families from one another. And it is these relationships that define the qualitative nature of the family. Physically separate the four members of the families from each other and you no longer have a complete whole.

Another important dimension in this discussion of wholeness is that the sum of the components in any system is qualitatively different than the actual unique whole system itself. If you were to take the parts of a system and separate them (i.e., not allow them to interact or relate) you would eliminate and/or destroy the system itself. The sum total of the parts in isolation (e.g., four people) is qualitatively less than the sum total of the parts of the system when interacting interdependently (e.g., a family). Imagine two other systems, the human body and an automobile—one animate, one inanimate. Two components of the human body include the lungs and muscles. Two components of the car include the engine and the tires. Notice that these components are related to one another. The lungs are related to the muscles in such a way that without the chest and diaphragm muscles, the lungs could not expand with air. Likewise, the muscles are related to the lungs in such a way that without the oxygen supplied to the blood by the lungs, the muscles could not extend. Both are related to one another and both are dependent on one another (interdependent). In isolation the lungs and the muscles cannot work. Likewise, with a car, the parts are related and interdependent. The engine cannot propel the car without tires. The tires of a car cannot function without the engine. Together, the engine and the tires (and many other components) make up the unique system of a car. Taken apart and separated, each component cannot function. Again, the tires are related and dependent on the engine (and many other parts) and vice versa. If you were to completely dismantle a car and place all the components in front of you on the ground, the sum total of these parts is quantitatively equal but qualitatively less than when each part is allowed to interact with the other parts interdependently. The car cannot function as a system when laid out in front of you in pieces and is actually no longer a system as defined by systems thinkers. In summary then, a system is a unique whole of interrelated components that operate interdependently.

Components of the System

Each definition from the previous list mentions that systems are made up of interdependent relationships between components, parts, items, units, elements, or objects. Whatever term you prefer, the objects of a system are simply its parts. A system can have an unlimited variety of components. The human body, for example, has arms, legs, blood vessels, hairs, teeth, toenails, and a veritable plethora of other parts. The parts of a system can be either physical, like the ones just mentioned making up the human body, or abstract, such as mathematical variables, human communication, behaviors, and even feelings and attitudes.[17]

Regardless of whether a particular system has many or few components, each component is defined by its properties or qualities. Teeth, for example, are physically rigid and hard whereas hair is soft and flexible. Teeth and hair, though component parts of the same system, have very different properties and qualities.[18]

Basic Assumptions of the Systems Approach

In order to be a practicing systems thinker and theorist, you must accept many assumptions, including the dimensions of (a) closed and open systems, (b) equifinality, (c) feedback, self-regulation, and homeostasis, (d) environment, self-organization, and change, and (e) hierarchy. Each of these dimensions is outlined below.

Closed and Open Systems

Perhaps the main departure of the systems approach from conventional theories in natural science concerns the principle of open systems. In conventional physics, closed systems are studied. A closed system is one that does not interact with or exchange anything with its environment—it is a system in isolation. The boundaries of a closed system are impermeable (i.e., do not permit passage, are not penetrable). The laws of thermodynamics, for example, apply only to closed systems. Chemists, for example, observe chemical reactions that occur within a test tube (i.e., a closed system) and derive their theories from their observations of this closed system. The glass boundaries of the test tube are impermeable and do not allow the chemicals within its boundaries to interact with the environment.[19]

The study of closed physical systems has dominated the natural sciences since the time of Descartes and Newton. During this time one of the greatest achievements was the discovery of the laws of thermodynamics. These laws are considered to be the most fundamental laws of physics but they only apply to closed systems. The first law of thermodynamics, the law of conservation, states that the total amount of energy involved in a process never lessens but is always conserved. The form of energy might change during a process, but the amount of energy remains constant. For example, the energy involved in the combustion of a car's engine is transformed into heat and exhaust. Certainly the quality and utility of the energy changes, but the amount of energy in the process stays constant. In the case of an automobile's engine, the amount of useful energy decreases because it has dissipated into heat and exhaust.

The first law of thermodynamics led scientists to formulate the second law of thermodynamics, which states that in nature there is an irreversible yet natural tendency for closed physical systems to progress toward disorder. For example, if you mix equal amounts of cold and hot water, the result is lukewarm water and the two liquids become one and cannot be separated.[20] Likewise, if you were to take a bag of white sand and mix it with a bag of black sand, the result would be gray sand. Rather than remaining close together and organized, the black grains become disorganized with the white grains. Note that when you first began mixing the two sands, there were dominant areas of white and black sand. If you poured the black sand on top of the white sand, there would be an unequal distribution of black sand on the top and white sand on the bottom. Upon continued mixing, however, the two sands would become more uniformly gray. When the bag is completely mixed and you have a consistently gray sand, equilibrium is said to have occurred. Equilibrium is a state of balance between two opposing forces (e.g., the two different kinds of sand). This process, according to the second law of thermodynamics, is irreversible. In fact, no matter how much we continue to mix the sands, they will never separate spontaneously into half white and half black sand. Then these two processes both proceed from a process of order to dis-

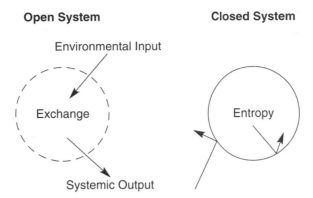

FIGURE 10.1   Open versus Closed Systems

order. In this example, the gray sand is considered a total disordering or disorganization of equal parts of white and black sand. The second law of thermodynamics states that any closed physical system progresses to total disorganization. The actual amount of disorder in a closed system is called entropy, a term that stems from a combination of the words *energy* and *tropos*. *Tropos* is the Greek word for evolution or transformation. Thus, the natural evolution of energy (i.e., entropy) is such that disorder continues to increase in a closed system until it reaches a state of maximum entropy and the system dies. All closed systems eventually die as a result of maximum entropy because a system can take only a certain amount of disorder. According to this second law of thermodynamics, the earth and the universe are headed in this direction.[21]

Now, you are asking yourself what all this has to do with systems thinking and your communication course. The major point here is that the systems approach focuses on open systems. Systems are by nature open. All living organisms are open systems and many inanimate systems are as well. As Figure 10.1 indicates, an open system exchanges and interacts with its environment through its permeable boundaries. In other words the system has input from and produces output to the environment, hence an open system is not subject to the laws of thermodynamics. This fact is a major ingredient in systems thinking. In fact, because of some other qualities of open systems, they can combat and even reverse the effects of entropy. Closed systems can delay disintegration via a process known as negentropy (i.e., negative entropy) but they cannot reverse entropy. Open systems, on the other hand, can avoid the increase of entropy and even move toward states of increased order and organization.[22]

Equifinality

The final state of a closed system is determined by the initial conditions of the system. For example, our bag of consistently gray sand was determined by adding the equal amounts of white and black sand. If we had put unequal amounts of black and white sand into the bag, the end result would have been different. If, for example, we mixed two parts of white sand with one part of black sand, the result would have been a lighter gray than our mixing of equal amounts. The point here is that prior conditions (i.e., amounts of white and black sand) determine the final outcome of the system (i.e., the color of the sand after mixing). Thus, in many instances it is possible to calculate the precise final state of a closed system given the initial conditions. This is not true of open systems because they can reach a final state in a variety of ways. von Bertalanffy referred to the process as equifinality (equal-ends), which he defined as "the tendency towards a characteristic final state from different initial states and in different ways, based upon dynamic interaction in an open system attaining a steady state."[23]

For example, say that it is about noon and you are getting hungry. Your body tells you that it is time to eat. You can eat any number of things to satisfy your hunger. You can go to the university cafeteria and eat there or to a fancy restaurant. In either case, the final state (satisfaction of hunger) would be met. This is characteristic of open systems and not closed systems because open systems are said to be teleological, or directed toward an end by a purpose. They are goal directed and exist for a reason. For living systems, the basic purpose and/or goal is to survive. This kind of thinking is in opposition to the mechanistic view of nature with its universally invariant laws. Recall that, from a mechanistic point of view, events and behaviors (closed systems) are governed by laws, not purposes or goals. From a pure laws perspective, nature has no choice but to act in accordance with natural laws and organisms are passive receivers of input from the environment. In fact, the notion of teleology was discounted in the natural sciences as another form of metaphysics. Because systems exist with a goal and/or purpose, they can reach their final state in any number of ways and are not subject to universally invariant (i.e., one way and only one way) end states. Equifinality does not occur in inanimate systems and is thus reserved for living systems. But in a sense, nonliving systems, when at the mercy of humans, can be said to reach final end states in different ways.

Feedback, Self-Regulation, and Homeostasis

In the discussion of equifinality, the example of how a person satisfies hunger was presented to demonstrate the process. The fact that a person senses hunger and responds to it by eating demonstrates several other important dimensions of open systems, including feedback, self-regulation, and homeostasis. One of the ways a living open system fights entropy is by exchanging matter with its environment (i.e., its openness). The decision to input or output matter to or from the environment is based on the ability of parts of the system to communicate with each other. Unlike closed systems, open systems are able to generate and produce their own information. Central to the notion of a system's parts communicating with each other is feedback. The study of information and feedback in systems is called cybernetics. Although a complete review of the development of cybernetics exceeds the scope and purpose of this book, it is important to know that systems theory is often identified with cybernetics and information theory.[24] But, as von Bertalanffy indicates, this is an incorrect assumption to make. Cybernetics is a theory of control mechanisms in technology and nature and was founded on the concepts of information and feedback and is really only a part of the general systems approach. Cybernetic systems are a special case of systems that show self-regulation. The notion of feedback is critical to the systems approach, but one need not be an expert in cybernetics to understand and employ a systems approach in build-

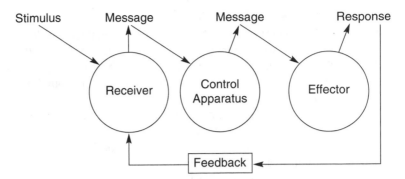

FIGURE 10.2   Simple Feedback Scheme

Adapted from von Bertalanffy, L. (1968). *General System Theory: Foundations, Development, Applications,* New York, George Braziller.

ing theory. To get back the point of feedback in systems, Figure 10.2 presents a simple feedback scheme.

This model applies specifically to human systems. Here, the system is made up of a receiver, a control apparatus, and an effector. The receiver receives a stimulus from another part of the system. The receiver translates the stimulus into message form for the control apparatus. Here the control apparatus could be the human brain. The control apparatus relays the message to the effector. An effector is a bodily organ, like a gland or muscle, that becomes active when stimulated. The effector's actions return to the receptor as feedback. This feedback is actually another stimulus on which the receiver will act.

Another example of how the principle of feedback operates is the heating system that operates in most homes.[25] Figure 10.3 presents a closed loop heating control system. During the winter months the desired temperature of most homes is approximately 78 degrees Fahrenheit. According to Figure 10.3, the actual temperature of the home is monitored by the thermostat which can sense the air temperature. When set to 78 degrees Fahrenheit, the thermostat compares the air of the room to the setting of 78 degrees. If the thermostat senses that the air temperature is less than 78 degrees Fahrenheit, it will (a) send an electrical sig-

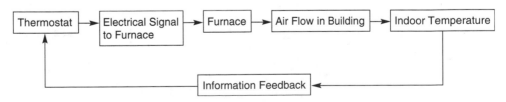

FIGURE 10.3   Closed Loop Heating Control System

Adapted from Porter, A., (1969). *Cybernetics Simplified,* New York: Barnes & Noble.

nal to the furnace, which turns on the furnace, (b) the furnace pumps warm air into the building, which will (c) change the air temperature in the home. The thermostat continuing to compare the air temperature to the 78 degree setting will sense the change in air temperature and will (a) shut off the electrical signal to the furnace which (b) subsequently shuts off the furnace, and (c) no longer sends warm air into the building which eventually will cool down and the process begins all over again.

The feedback function can easily be applied to living systems as well as a home heating system. There are probably millions of feedback systems in the human body. Take, for example, the throwing of a baseball.[26] Figure 10.4 presents how this physiological process can be diagrammed as a feedback loop.

The decision to throw a baseball is made in the brain which (a) sends a message via the spinal cord to a particular set of nerve cells, which (b) activates nerves in the muscles of the arm and hand, which (c) extends the arm and hand and the throw is made. A feedback signal stimulated by other nerve cells in the arm sends a signal back to the spine to communicate that the act has been carried out.

The two types of feedback in living open systems are negative and positive feedback. Negative feedback occurs when there is a deviation in the system. Air temperature below 78 degrees would be considered negative feedback in the temperature control feedback loop. Positive feedback occurs when the system is signaled to maintain its current state. In the home heating example, when the comparator unit senses that the air temperature is at 78 degrees, it signals the system that everything is running smoothly and that there is no need to change. When the heat turns on in your home it remains on for awhile. The signal to keep the heat on could be considered positive feedback, sometimes known as amplification. When the house becomes too warm, negative feedback will signal the comparator unit to shut off. Negative feedback is perhaps the most important kind of feedback because it allows the system to self-regulate, which ensures that the system stabilizes and reaches what is called homeostasis. Say, for example, that your home's thermostat malfunctioned and your system was unable to regulate when to turn the heat on or off. Your home would either freeze, because the system cannot monitor the temperature and regulate when the heat comes on, or it would become unbearably warm, because the system is unable to shut the heat off. In either situation, the system certainly is not stabilized. When your home heating feedback system functions properly, your home is comfortable. This is the level of homeostasis. Homeostasis is the maintenance of balance in living systems. Through the processes of feedback, self-regulation, and homeo-

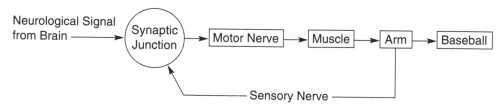

FIGURE 10.4   Diagram of a Physiological Feedback System

Adapted from Porter, A., (1969) *Cybernetics Simplified,* New York: Barnes & Noble.

stasis, the system is actually generating its own information (e.g., it is too hot or too cold) and is able to combat entropy and maintain and increase order. As soon as the system experiences entropy, parts of the system feedback to other parts to make adjustments and maintain order. This process cannot happen in closed systems. The ability of open systems to generate their own information enables them to survive.

Systemic Environments, Self-Organization, and Change

Open living systems do not exist within a vacuum or in isolation. Part of the system's survival is dependent on the environment in which it lives. Likewise, any particular environment is dependent on its systems for its survival. Hall and Fagen define the environment of a system as: "For a given system, the environment is the set of all objects a change in whose attributes affect the system and also those objects whose attributes are changed by the behavior of the system."[27]

The system and its environment can be said to make up a universe. Like systems themselves, an environment can be physical, social, or psychological. An example of a physical environment could be a human body organ. The environment of a human heart, for example, would be the chest cavity of the human body. An example of a social system environment could be a state in which individual cities are the systems. The human mind could be an example of a psychological environment with attitudes, personality traits, and beliefs as individual systems. The environment is the home of the system—the surroundings, atmosphere, neighborhood, vicinity, setting, or medium in which the system functions. To thoroughly profile a system's environment you would have to know all of the variables that affect or are affected by the particular system itself.[28]

Although it is difficult to completely specify a system's environment, it is clear that the environment and system are interdependent and that the environment changes. It is precisely because of a dynamic environment that a system must be self-regulating and adaptive if it is to survive. The flexibility of a system to change and adapt to its environment does not mean that the system's internal organization and makeup is totally dependent on the environment, however. A living open system is a self-organizing system in that its internal order and structure is established, not only by the environment, but by the system itself. Thus, the system has a degree of autonomy from its environment. The two main principles of systemic self-organization include, (a) self-renewal, the ability of open systems to continuously renew their components while maintaining their overall structure, and (b) self-transcendence, the ability of systems to reach out creatively beyond their environment to learn, develop, and evolve.[29]

The self-renewal process can easily be seen within the human body. The human body is in a constant state of self-renewal as cells, tissues, and organs continuously break down and build back up. Your physical body is in a constant state of change. Literally from one day to another you are not the same person either physiologically or psychologically. The pancreas, for example, replaces almost all of its cells in less than twenty-four hours. The lining in your stomach has completely replaced itself in the last three days. Our white blood cells are replaced every ten days or so and almost all of the protein in our brain is renewed approximately once a month. What is truly amazing about this renewal process is that it never ceases, yet the overall appearance of the system remains constant. A friend who you have not seen in a year would easily recognize you and yet you have replaced your brain almost twelve times, your pancreas approximately three hundred and sixty-five times, your blood about thirty times, and your stomach lining almost one hundred times. The hair on your head is not the same hair you had a year ago (unless you rarely get a haircut) and you have shed your skin a number of times. In systems terminology, the technical word for those self-renewal processes that tend to preserve and maintain a system's form and organization is is morphostasis.[30] Another amazing part of this self-organization process is evolutionary changes that take place in systems. Both similar and different to morphostasis, this type of change occurs as the system continues to adapt in changing environmental conditions. These types of environmentally influenced changes tend to alter or elaborate a system's form, organization, or structure. For example, the coat of many animals becomes much thicker and fuller during the winter months. This type of change is called morphogenesis.[31]

The other type of self-organized change mentioned above is self-transcendent change, which is not influenced by the environment and entails creative change by the system itself. For example, a self-transcendent change could be striving for a college degree or to physically developing your body via weight lifting and bodybuilding. Neither of these changes are necessitated by the environment but both reflect creative attempts by the living system to change its basic organization.

Hierarchy

The universe of a system is a multileveled stratified ordering of systems whose levels differ in degrees of complexity. At each level are open living self-organizing whole systems that are simultaneously the smaller part of a larger system (i.e., a subsystem) and the larger part of a smaller system (i.e., suprasystem).[32] This ordering is called a hierarchy. Typically, hierarchies are represented symbolically as pyramids. Simply put, systems tend to be embedded within each other and the hierarchy provides an organization of complexity.[33] As we move along from level to level we observe differing degrees of complexity. A unit belonging to one system may belong to the universe of another system. A hierarchy is simply an ordering of suprasystems, systems, and subsystems and any particular system is simultaneously all three. A subsystem is a system that is embedded in a larger system. A suprasystem is a system that has smaller systems embedded within it. Whether a particular system is considered a suprasystem, system, or subsystem depends on the observer. If, for example, you are observing the engine of a car, the engine would be considered the system. If you are observing the entire car, the engine is considered a subsystem. If you are observing the distributor cap, the engine is the suprasystem. Like systems themselves, there are physical, social, and psychological hierarchies.

The human body can easily be seen as a hierarchy of suprasystems, systems, and subsystems. Figure 10.5 presents a very simplified hierarchy of the human body's systems.

Different types of social systems are also hierarchically arranged. Your state's government, for instance, is a good example of a social hierarchy. Figure 10.6 presents a hierarchy of how many state governments are systematically ordered.

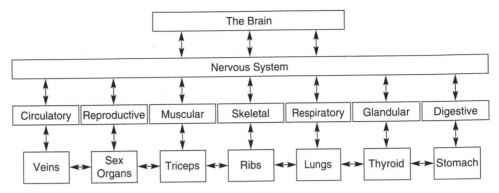

FIGURE 10.5   The Systems of the Human Body

Keep in mind that whether it is the levels of the universe, systems of the human body, or your state's government, the observer is always observing at the system level. Thus, if investigating the lungs, the lungs are the system. If investigating the human body, the lungs are a subsystem. If observing the individual air passages, the lungs are the suprasystem.

Up to this point, we have seen the historical development of systems thinking, discussed several definitions of systems, and outlined the basic assumptions of the systems ap-

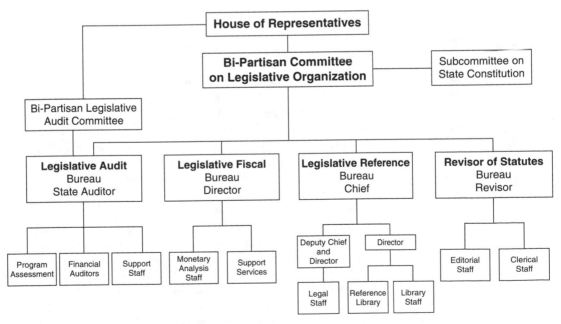

FIGURE 10.6   Hierarchy of Hypothetical State Government

proach. Remember that the overall goal of the systems approach is to develop a unified theory of science based on the notion of system. Recall that a system is a unique whole consisting of interrelated and interdependent parts. The systems we investigate are open systems that are goal directed and produce their own information (i.e., feedback) in order to self-regulate, control, and maintain balance (homeostasis). Keep in mind that each system exists in some environment and is capable of self-organization, self-renewal, and change. Finally, remember that systems exist simultaneously as subsystems, systems, and suprasystems in a hierarchy.

Armed with all of this information about the systems approach, what is it that scientists from different branches of science do? Recall from Chapter 2 that the three major functions of a theory are to explain, predict, and control phenomena. The final section of this chapter outlines how scientists can and are using the systems approach in this way.

CASE STUDY 14   The Systems Approach in Health Care

Fritjof Capra, a high-energy physicist, presents a compelling argument for the adoption of a systems approach in the field of health care. This application would affect an enormous amount of people working within the health care field, including all types of physicians, nurses, surgeons, psychiatrists, therapists, and psychologists, and would also probably affect those persons working indirectly with the field, such as clergy, social workers, and perhaps even the insurance industry.[a]

Because of the wide diversity of persons employed in the health care field, there are many ways of approaching health that are based on differing views and philosophies of health care. By adopting a systems approach, the field would become unified, an original goal of von Bertalanffy.

For about the last three centuries the pervasive approach toward health care in this country has been based on the mechanistic philosophies of Descartes and Newton. Remember from Chapter 1 that it was Descartes who argued that the body and mind are separate and that the body should be viewed as a machine with machinelike operations. In fact, it was Descartes who compared a well-made clock to a well-built human. Physicians and other health care professionals treat illness and disease consistent with this mechanistic philosophy, by focusing on individual parts of the body and treating them individually. If you have a stomach ailment, for example, it is the stomach, in isolation, that is treated. If you break your arm, the individual bone is set and cast. Simply stated, persons in the medical profession treat that part of the body that is sick without much attention on the whole organism. Once the particular body part is healed or is well, the patient is no longer considered sick. In other words people are either sick or well. This approach is certainly not in keeping with the systems view of life. If a systems point of view were adopted by the health care profession, the emphasis would shift from focusing on the individual parts of the body to focusing on the entire body as a whole organism. This approach reflects what is called a "holistic" method of health care and is entirely consistent with systems thinking. Systems thinkers in the health care field do not separate the mind from the body but treat the person as a complete whole. Thus, sickness would be explained by examining the whole organism not simply an individual body part.

In addition to the notion of holistic medicine, the concept of health would shift from dichotomizing a person's condition as being either (a) in good health or (b) sick and instead view the health of a person as an ongoing process. Health care, from a systems point of view, would be seen as a multidimensional phenomena that looks at the relationships between the person and his or her natural and social environment. The system is the person. The person exchanges matter with the environment (naturally and socially) and adapts accordingly. In some cases, the system becomes unbalanced and illness sets in. A person's illness is the result of interrelating with natural and social aspects of the environment. The person is then treated with the environmental conditions in mind. For example, a person can become ill due to natural environmental conditions, as in the case of pollution, a high pollen count, or very cold weather. Likewise, the social conditions of one's environment can lead to illness, as in the loss of a loved one, a divorce, or being terminated from a job. All of these examples would be considered entropy (disorder/disorganization) in the system which knock it out of balance. Health care professionals, from a systems view, then treat the whole individual with a conscious effort to consider the system's environment. Thus, therapy (e.g., with drugs or otherwise) would be prescribed that attempts to balance the system with its environment. Illness is viewed as a result of the whole system's interaction, relationship, and interdependency with its environment.

Keep in mind that the mental aspects of illness are considered as important as are the physical manifestations of ill health. The process of healing is as much a mental as it is a physical phenomena. This is not a new idea. Hippocratic medicine, which dates back to pre-Hellenic times and was subsequently developed in ancient Greece, was a system that viewed the process of healing as a spiritual phenomena. In Chinese culture health is a combination of harmony with oneself and society. The Chinese conception of the human body focuses on the interrelationships between parts rather than on anatomy. To them, the body in an indivisible system of interdependent parts. Getting sick and becoming well are integral parts of a system's self-organization, and the mind is a central component of the dynamics of self-organization. Thus, from a systems view, the person (i.e., the system) is seen as a dynamic system that has physical, social, and psychological components interrelating interdependently. All three of these components must be in balance for the system to maintain good health.

An excellent example of the systems approach in the health field is a program of cancer therapy initiated by O. Carl Simonton and Stephanie Matthews-Simonton. Dr. Carl Simonton (M. D.) is a radiation oncologist (i.e., cancer treatment) and Stephanie Matthews-Simonton is a psychotherapist. Both are regarded as worldwide leaders in the holistic health field. To be sure, the Simontons do not dismiss or even discount the vital importance of traditional medicine, including the use of drugs, surgery, and physical therapy. Holistic medicine should not confused with "faith healing" or "witch doctoring." The Simontons view both illness and health holistically.

Continued

CASE STUDY 14   *Continued*

> *It is our central premise that an illness is not purely a physical problem but rather a problem of the whole person, that it includes not only body but mind and emotions. We believe that emotional and mental states play a significant role both in susceptibility to disease, including cancer, and recovery from all disease . . . if the total integrated system of mind, body and emotions, which constitute the whole person, is not working in the direction of health, then purely physical interventions may not succeed.*[b]

The Simontons do not view the human body as an object with replaceable parts (i.e., like a machine). Instead, they view the mind and the body as an integrated system. They believe that the mind can and does exert some influence on the physiological processes of the human body and that people are able to influence their own internal body processes via biofeedback. Feedback, a central concept in systems thinking, refers to the system's ability to generate its own information in order to maintain homeostasis. Biofeedback refers to the mind's ability to generate information to the body in order to influence physiological states. From the Simonton's systemic perspective, cancer is the result of a state of imbalance in the system. This state is the result of either natural environmental conditions (e.g., exposure to harmful chemicals) or social environmental aspects (e.g., stress) that are exchanged with the system and disrupt homeostasis. To combat the disease via biofeedback, the mind sends information to the body. One type of biofeedback is visual imagery, which involves a period of relaxation whereby the patient tries to visualize the cancer, the treatment destroying it, and most importantly, the body's natural defenses assisting in recovery.[c] Clearly the Simontons do not view cancer as a purely physical problem but as a problem of the whole person. Indeed, their treatment of the problem also stresses the importance of the whole human being.

a. Capra, F. (1988). *The Turning Point; Science, Society, and the Rising Culture,* Toronto: Bantam.
b. Simonton, O. C., Matthews-Simonton, S., & Creighton, J. L. (1978). *Getting Well Again,* Toronto: Bantam.
c. Ibid.

Summary

Hopefully by this point you have an understanding of the fundamental concepts of the systems approach. This chapter has presented a historical picture of the development of systems theory and several definitions of system, pointed out the basic assumptions of a systems thinker, and presented an application of the approach from the health care field. The systems approach offers a flexible and broad perspective from which to study natural and social phenomena, but critics of the approach argue that the whole notion of system is vague. Some argue, for example, that the approach presents little more than ill-defined analogies and that it does not yield much explanatory power and has not produced a significant body of empirical evidence.[34] The purpose of this chapter is not to persuade you to adopt the systems approach but to present an unbiased sketch of one possible theoretical orientation. The next chapter discusses how the systems approach is utilized in the communication field. After reading that chapter, you will be able to make an informed choice when deciding which theory will guide you in your study of human communication.

Glossary

Closed System: A theoretically isolated system that does not exchange matter with its environment. A closed system is subject to the second law of thermodynamics.

Cybernetics: The study of control mechanisms in technology and nature. The study of information and feedback.

Entropy: The amount of chaos and/or disorder in a system.

Environment: The "home" of a system. All of those external factors that influence the system are a part of its environment.

Equifinality: A characteristic of open systems; a tendency towards a characteristic final state from different initial states and in different ways.

Feedback: In systems terminology, feedback is short for "information feedback." Feedback refers to the ability of open systems to generate their own information as a way of maintaining balance and control.

First Law of Thermodynamics: A natural law of physics that states that the total energy involved in a process is conserved. The energy may change its form and subsequently its utility, but it is not lost.

Hierarchy: A multileveled structure of systems whose levels of complexity differ from simple to complex in stratified order.

Homeostasis: The state of balance in a living system.

Interdependency: A characteristic of the objects in a system to be mutually dependent on each other.

Isomorphism: Having similar or identical shape or form but of different ancestry. A one-to-one correspondence.

Morphogenesis: The processes in systems which tend to change a system's given form or structure usually in an effort to adapt to environmental changes.

Morphostasis: Those processes in systems that tend to preserve the system's form, organization, and state.

Open System: A living system having permeable boundaries which allow for the exchange of matter with the environment. Open systems are not subject to the second law of thermodynamics and are capable of combating entropy and can actually increase order and organization.

Second Law of Thermodynamics: A natural law of physics that states that there is a natural tendency in closed systems to progress toward a state of entropy (i.e., disorder or disorganization).

Self-Organization: The ability of living systems to combat the natural tendency of entropy. Living systems generate information and can actually increase order. The order in a system is determined by the system rather than by its environment.

Self-Regulation: The ability of a system to control the actions of its component parts. A system restricts and limits the actions of parts in order to maintain homeostasis.

Self-Renewal: A critical aspect of self-organization whereby the system maintains and repairs its deteriorating parts.

System: A whole that consists of entities, parts, components, objects, or elements that are interdependently interrelated in such a way that allows for the generation of information, self-organization, self-renewal, change, and homeostasis. Systems exist in hierarchies and exchange matter with their environment.

Systems Approach: A general theoretical orientation of wholeness that stresses isomorphisms between the various branches of science by way of systems.

Teleology: The doctrine that explains that systems are guided toward final states by a purpose or goal.

Wholeness: A characteristic of all systems such that the whole is more than the sum of its parts. There is a qualitative difference between the parts of the system operating interdependently and the parts of the systems in isolation.

References

1. Bateson, G. (1951). "Conventions of communications: Where Validity Depends upon Belief," in J. Ruesch, & G. Bateson, *Communication: The Social Matrix of Psychology,* (pp. 212–227). New York: W.W. Norton, (p. 212).

2. Boulding, K. E. (1968). "General Systems Theory—The Skeleton of Science," in W. Buckley, (Ed.), *Modern Systems Research for the Behavioral Scientist,* (pp. 3–10). Chicago, IL: Aldine, (p. 3).

3. Buckley, W. (1967). *Sociology and Modern Systems Theory,* Englewood Cliffs, NJ: Prentice Hall, (p. 36).

4. Capra, F. (1988). *The Turning Point; Science, Society, and the Rising Culture,* Toronto: Bantam.

5. von Bertalanffy, L. (1968). *General System Theory: Foundations, Development, Applications,* New York: George Braziller.

6. Ibid.

7. Ibid., (p. 33).

8. von Bertalanffy, L. (1967). *Robots, Men, and Minds,* New York: George Braziller; von Bertalanffy, *General System Theory.*

9. von Bertalanffy, *Robots, Men, and Minds,* (p. 69).

10. von Bertalanffy, *General System Theory,* (p. 38).

11. Buckley, *Sociology and Modern Systems Theory.*

12. Hall, A. D., & Fagen, R. E. (1968). "Definition of System," in Buckley, *Modern Systems Research for the Behavioral Scientist,* Chicago, IL: Aldine (pp. 81–92).

13. Fisher, B. A. (1978). *Perspectives on Human Communication,* New York: Macmillan, (p. 197).

14. Rapoport, A. (1968). "Forward," in W. Buckley, (Ed.), *Modern Systems Research for the Behavioral Scientist,* (pp. viii-xxii). Chicago, IL: Aldine, (p. xvii).

15. Capra, *The Turning Point,* (p. 226).

16. Fisher, *Perspectives on Human Communication.*

17. Hall, & Fagen, "Definition of System," (pp. 81–92).

18. Ibid.

19. von Bertalanffy, *General System Theory.*

20. Capra, *The Turning Point.*

21. Ibid.

22. von Bertalanffy, *General System Theory.*

23. Ibid., (p. 46).

24. Littlejohn, S. W. (1992). *Theories of Human Communication,* (4th Ed.), Belmont, CA: Wadsworth.

25. Porter, A. (1969). *Cybernetics Simplified,* New York: Barnes & Noble.

26. Ibid.

27. Hall, & Fagen, "Definition of System," (pp. 81–92).

28. Ibid.

29. Capra, *The Turning Point.*

30. Ibid., Buckley, *Sociology and Modern Systems Theory.*

31. Buckley, *Sociology and Modern Systems Theory.*

32. Capra, *The Turning Point.*

33. Boulding, "General Systems Theory" (pp. 3–10).

34. Infante, D. A., Rancer, A. S., & Womack, D. F. (1993). *Building Communication Theory,* (2nd Ed.), Prospect Heights, IL: Waveland.

Systems Approaches to Communication

[M]an's awareness of himself is essentially an awareness of functions, of relationships in which he is involved, no matter how much he may subsequently reify this awareness.[1]
——*PAUL WATZLAWICK, JANET BEAVIN, & DON JACKSON*

Thirty years ago a group of psychotherapists working at the Mental Health Institute in Palo Alto, California, began investigating the behavioral effects of human communication specifically as they related to psychopathological disorders. Under the leadership of Paul Watzlawick, this group became known as the Palo Alto Group and were the first to articulate a systems approach to human communication. Many of their ideas stemmed from anthropologist Gregory Bateson. The result of their work culminated in what now is considered a seminal work in systems thinking and human communication titled *Pragmatics of Human Communication: A Study of Interactional Patterns, Pathologies, and Paradoxes.*

The Palo Alto Group argued that human communication can be viewed as an open system and that all of the fundamental assumptions underlying systems thinking, particularly those articulated by von Bertalanffy, applied to the study of human interaction. In addition, the Palo Alto Group laid the foundation for what is known in the communication literature as the "pragmatic" perspective on human communication theory.[2]

Following the work of Charles Morris, the Palo Alto Group argued that the study of language and human communication can be divided into three areas, including: (a) syntactics, (b) semantics, and (c) pragmatics. Syntactics is the study of the rules of language (e.g., grammar). Semantics is the study of the meaning of words and the relationship between words and their referents. Pragmatics, then, is the study of how communication affects behavior.[3] Although Watzlawick and his associates were specifically interested in the pragmatic study of human communication (i.e., communication's affect on psychopathology), their work has been extended into the field of human communication by such scholars as B. Aubrey Fisher, Frank Millar, Edna Rogers, Peter Monge, and Bill Wilmot. Communication systems theorists apply the basic assumptions of wholeness, relationship, interdependency, openness, equifinality, feedback, self-regulation, control, and hierarchy to many human communication contexts, including interpersonal communication, small group communication, and organizational communication. By employing a systems approach, these theorists are able to explain, predict, and control the social phenomena of human interaction.

This chapter is organized into three sections. Section one presents some of the basic assumptions of the pragmatic approach as originally presented by Watzlawick and his associates. Section two defines communication as a system, outlines the components of the system, and applies the notions of wholeness, relationship, interdependency, equifinality, feedback, self-regulation, control, hierarchy, and environment to human interaction. Section three presents several alternative themes of the pragmatic approach currently operating in various contexts in the communication field, including interpersonal, small group, and organizational communication.

Basic Assumptions of the Palo Alto Group

In their classic text, Watzlawick, Beavin, and Jackson outline some of the fundamental assumptions underlying systems theory and communication.[4] They refer to these fundamental assumptions as axioms (i.e., a statement or proposition widely accepted on its intrinsic merit and/or self-evident truth).

Axiom One: The Impossibility of Not Communicating

The initial axiom is that one cannot not communicate and that all behavior should be regarded as communicative. Any behavior can fall under one of two categories, verbal or nonverbal. According to Watzlawick et al.:

> behavior has no opposite. In other words, there is no such thing as nonbehavior or, to put it even more simply, one cannot not behave. Now, if it is accepted that all behavior in an interactional situation has message value, i.e., is communication, it follows that no matter how one may try, one cannot not communicate.[5]

Thus, according to the axiom, all behaviors are communicative. This means that even a person's silence is meaningful. Indeed, all behaviors have message value even if the person behaving does not intend to send a message. Note that in their explanation, Watzlawick et al. argue that all behavior in an "interactional situation" has message value. Thus, for behavior to be communicative, another person must witness that behavior. Behavior is not communicative until someone other than the person emitting the behavior perceives it.

Axiom Two: The Content and Relationship Levels of Communication

The second axiom is that all communication defines the relationship between the interactants and occurs at two levels, the report and the command level.[6] The report level is the actual content of the message and the command level is how the message is to be interpreted. The interpretation of any message is dependent on the relationship between the two interactants and also serves to further define that relationship. Thus, the command level of a message varies from relationship to relationship.

For example, Jim and Jan are a married couple who own a cat. Jan typically gets out of bed before Jim every morning and it has become her task to feed the cat. That Jan feeds the cat every morning has become a defining characteristic of Jim and Jan's relationship. On this particular morning, Jim gets up at his usual time (i.e., after Jan) and finds the cat sitting next to her empty food bowl crying rather irritatingly for someone to feed her. After feeding the cat Jim confronts Jan and asks, "Did you feed the cat this morning?" The report level of the message "Did you feed the cat?" is an interrogative expression of whether or not Jan has fed the cat; it is a question. Obviously, since the cat's bowl was empty, Jim knew, in fact, that Jan had not fed the cat. Thus, the command level of the message defines the relationship. Jim's interrogative expression, at the command level, is interpreted as "You usually feed the cat, why didn't you do it this morning?" The command level of the message communicates how the interactants define the relationship and include such aspects as "This is how I see myself . . . this is how I see you . . . this is how I see you seeing me." Interactants rarely deliberately define the relationship, however. Thus, the command levels of messages are often very subtle, unspoken, and unconscious. In essence, the command level of any message is actually a message about a message and thus is considered metacommunication.

For example, think how your communication professor might respond to your request to miss class because you want to study for an examination in some other class. The professor might respond with a simple, soft-spoken "No. . . . " Perhaps the professor might respond by loudly yelling "No!" while simultaneously pounding his or her fist on the desk. In the first instance, you might interpret the professor's soft-spoken "No . . ." as meaning you should not miss class but also that your professor does not consider it all that important. In the second instance, where the professor yells at you, you may interpret the message as meaning that you had better attend class or else. In each case, the report level of the message is synonymous. In the second instance, the command level is much different, however. The yelling and pounding of the fist are additional messages about the message; they are metamessages. In this case these metamessages are telling you that the professor really means what he or she is saying and that you had better listen. Thus, a metamessage is one that complements, supplements, or accents another message. The report level of a message is sometimes called the "content" level or the "data." The command level of the message is sometimes called the "relational" level or the "instructions." Some scholars have even referred to the report level as the verbal and/or digital message and the command level as the nonverbal and/or analogic message. In other words the report level is *what* is said and the command level is *how* it is said. Wilmot argues that it is impossible to relate to another with only the content of a message. The content and relationship level of messages are inseparable. Whenever people communicate with each other they communicate not only their content, but their definition of the relationship.[7]

Axiom Three: The Punctuation of the Sequence of Events

The third axiom outlined by Watzlawick et al. regards the relationship among the messages exchanged between interactants. A healthy relationship is one in which the participants punctuate their message exchanges similarly. Watzlawick et al. argue that it is impossible to determine the starting and ending point of any particular message exchange. Any one message sent between persons is simultaneously: (a) a stimulus for another message, (b) a response to a previous message, and (c) a reinforcement of the overall interaction. Take, for example, a simple greeting between a student and his or her professor. When the student and professor meet one another the student says "Good Morning, Professor" and the professor says "Good Morning, Scholar." Each message is a stimulus, response, and reinforcement. The student's message "Good Morning, Professor" is a stimulus for the professor's message, it is also a response to seeing the professor in the hallway, and it reinforces the relationship between the student and professor who have defined their relationship such that they greet each other when they pass in the hallway because they have developed a civil student/professor relationship. Thus, the simple greeting expressed by each interactant is much more than a simple two-message exchange. The student and professor agree on the punctuation of their sequence of messages and their relationship flows smoothly.

When the interactants disagree on the punctuation, communication problems arise. For example, when one interactant defines a particular message as only a stimulus and the other defines it as only a response, relational distress can result. Take, for instance, a couple arguing about the other's behavior at a cocktail party. The wife says, "You avoided me all night," to which the husband responds, "I only avoided you because you were too busy talking with Tom," which is met with, "I only spoke with Tom because you avoided me." Here, it is clear that each participant defines the stimulus differently. The husband argues that his avoidance behaviors were a response to his wife's attention to Tom (the stimulus). On the other hand, to the wife, her behavior is a response to her husband's avoidance behavior (the stimulus). Thus, the couple experiences a disagreement about how to punctuate their interaction. The error they make is that they presuppose that interaction has a distinct beginning point. According to the third axiom, however, this is not how interaction evolves since any message within an exchange is simultaneously a stimulus, response, and reinforcement.

Axiom Four: Digital and Analogic Communication

Like computers, humans interact on a digital and analogic level. Simply put, digital communication is verbal communication. Following the computer analogy, words are similar to digits; they have specific beginning and ending points and arbitrarily represent something else. The word *cat,* for example, clearly begins with the symbol "c" and ends with the symbol "t." Its meaning is derived out of socially negotiated norms. There is no natural connection between the letters "c a t" and the cute fuzzy little animal that complains when her food bowl is empty. The only reason "c a t" represents the little animal is because a group of people (English speaking) have agreed to allow such symbols to represent that particular referent. The symbols "c a t" do not represent a cute little fuzzy animal in Russia. That humans communicate digitally is probably the single most significant aspect that separates us from other living organisms. We allow symbols to arbitrarily represent something else.

Digital communication, however, is only one of two ways humans communicate. The other way is analogically. Unlike digital communication which *symbolically* represents some- thing else, analogic communication *signals* something else. There is a difference between a symbol and a signal. A symbol is an *arbitrarily* learned stimulus representing something else. A signal is a *natural* sign of something else. Shivering is a sign of being cold, thunder is a sign of an oncoming storm, and sweating is a sign of being too hot. Each sign is naturally connected to its referent. Most, if not all, analogic messages are nonverbally communicated and are more representative of the relationship than is digital communication. To tell someone how much you love them (digital communication) is meaningless unless your actions (analogic communication) complement your words. Thus, analogic communication is nonverbal and relational communication. It has no clear beginning and ending point. Our nonverbal behaviors seem to flow from one sentence to the next. We are always behaving nonverbally.

Axiom Five: Symmetrical and Complementary Communication

The final axiom contends that all relationships revolve around a pattern of symmetry or complementarity. A symmetrical relationship is one in which the behaviors of one person elicit similar or like behaviors of another. Thus, if one person becomes assertive, the other responds with assertiveness. A complementary relationship is one where assertive behavior from one might be met with submissive behavior from the other. Symmetrical relationships are characterized by equality and the minimization of difference and complementary relationships are characterized by inequality and maximization of difference. Systems thinkers argue that relationships tend to gravitate toward symmetry or complementarity.

Most systems theorists within the communication field abide by the above outlined axioms of communication. Communication "pragmatists" agree that (a) one cannot not communicate, (b) all messages are sent on two levels, a report and a command level, (c) all messages are simultaneously a stimulus, response, and reinforcement, (d) humans communicate in a digital and analogic mode, and (e) relationships revolve around a pattern of symmetrical or complementary message exchanges.[8]

Communication as a System

Recall from Chapter 10 that almost anything imaginable can be a system as long as the components interact with one another interdependently. Thus, a person, place, or thing can be a system. A system can be physical, social, or psychological. In the case of communication, the system is *social* interaction. Figure 11.1 on page 298 presents a diagram of communication as a social system.

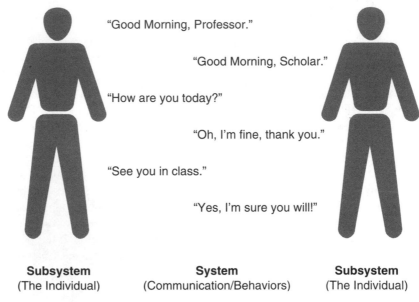

Subsystem (The Individual)   **System** (Communication/Behaviors)   **Subsystem** (The Individual)

FIGURE 11.1   **Communication as a Social System**

Whenever two or more persons come together and exchange messages (verbal and/or nonverbal) a social system has been created. The messages and/or behaviors exchanged between the two communicants are called *acts*. The individual persons are the subsystems. The unit of analysis (i.e., the actual system itself) is not the person, but the person's behaviors—in this case, the nonverbal and verbal message acts generated by the individual. Remember that to the systems theorist, behavior and communication are synonymous. Although the individual persons in the interaction are the subsystems, the systems theorist focuses his or her analysis on the interaction at the system level. Individuals are not studied in isolation. The pragmatic theorist is not interested in unobservable phenomena (e.g., attitudes, beliefs, motivations, dispositions) of the individual within whom the communication begins. While the pragmatic theorist understands that such aspects may be important in influencing the kind of messages expressed, such aspects are beyond sensory perception. For example, an individual's personality cannot be observed, while an individual's behaviors, which may be influenced by the personality, can be. The individual's attitudes, personality, beliefs, and all other internalized phenomena enter the system via behavior. The behaviors themselves, the acts, which are empirically assessable to the theorist, are the crucial elements that make up the system.

Communication systems theorists focus on information processing at the systemic level and not the level of the subsystem. Because the social system allows for interaction with the environment, it is an open system. In the exchange presented in Figure 11.1, for example, at any point the participants can add new information to the system. Indeed, the system is open enough to allow another subsystem to enter in the exchange. Another student, for example, might pass by just as the professor and the first student exchange greetings. The third student could insert information (e.g., another greeting) and the system would continue to function.[9]

Wholeness, Relationship, and Interdependency

What makes a communication system whole is the interdependent relationships between the components. This wholeness, however, is qualitatively more than two individuals. When the individuals come together they create something (i.e., a social system) that did not exist before. They create, what Miller and Steinberg call, a unique, functioning behavioral unit—a system.[10] The social system and the individual people that create it are different entities, because there are characteristics attributable to the system that cannot be attributed to either individual separately which come about as the result of interaction. If one member is considered politically liberal and the other conservative, their relationship (i.e., the system) might be characterized by conflict. Not until the liberal and conservative come together and interact does conflict emerge. Thus, the social system is composed of individual acts that are related to and interdependent of each other. The subsystems, too, are considered components of the system and are also related interdependently. Notice in Figure 11.2 the message exchange between the two subsystems, Jim and Jan.

The system in Figure 11.2 includes Acts 1 through 6 that occur in a patterned sequence. To remove any particular act changes the nature of the system. Act 1, for example, is Jim's response to noticing Jan at the bus stop. Jan's nonverbal behavior was communicative. Indeed, Act 2 is dependent on Act 1. Likewise, Act 3 is dependent on Act 2. In a sense, Act 2

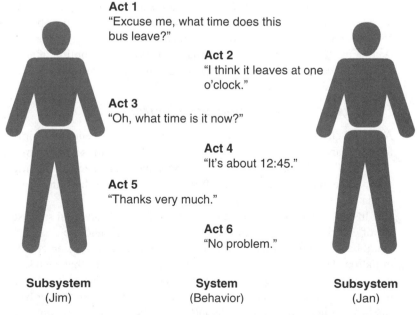

Act 1
"Excuse me, what time does this bus leave?"

Act 2
"I think it leaves at one o'clock."

Act 3
"Oh, what time is it now?"

Act 4
"It's about 12:45."

Act 5
"Thanks very much."

Act 6
"No problem."

Subsystem
(Jim)

System
(Behavior)

Subsystem
(Jan)

FIGURE 11.2   Message Exchange between Jim and Jan

requires a response like Act 3 and thus depends on some response to take on any meaning. Hence, any two acts are interdependent. Taken together, two sequential acts produce what is called an *interact*. Systems researchers generally study the patterns of interacts rather than individual acts in isolation. Recall that any message is simultaneously a stimulus, response, and reinforcement. Thus, Act 2 is a response to Act 1 and a stimulus for Act 3. Act 2 also reinforces the relationship between the components, which in this case are two commuters at a bus stop. By studying their interacts a systems theorist can deduce the exact relationship between the persons. Eventually, we could conclude that the two are strangers, acquaintances, or perhaps even intimates. Their talk will eventually lead us to that conclusion because messages are sent on a content and relational level and define the relationship. In addition, by studying the sequence of interacts we could also conclude whether their relationship was symmetrical or complementary.

Because the wholeness of the system depends on the relationship between acts, to select a particular act and examine it in isolation destroys the system. In fact, in isolation, these messages have very little, if any, meaning. For example, we glean very little information from examining only Act 1. When taken together as interacts and examined systematically, one can easily determine the context and the meaning. Over time it is possible to determine at what level of probability one type of act will follow another. For example, upon examining numerous interacts such as those in Figure 11.2, we might conclude that at a certain degree of probability (e.g., 90 percent of the time) Act 5 is followed by Act 6.

Equifinality

The message exchange displayed in Figure 11.2 could have reached its conclusion in any number of ways. Jim's goal was to determine at what time the bus leaves. He could have asked someone other than Jan and still accomplished his goal or he could have asked Jan for the same information but in a different way. For example, we can replace Act 1 with the statement, "Do you know when this bus will leave?" The notion of equifinality means that the system could have reached its final state in a variety of ways.

Feedback, Self-Regulation, and Control

A crucial characteristic of open systems is that they can generate their own information via feedback and thus regulate and control their balance. Jim's subsystem was imbalanced because he didn't know when the bus left. Sensing that he needed this information (a form of internal feedback), he asked Jan. After the exchange with Jan, Jim's subsystem was back to a balanced state.

In the interaction presented in Figure 11.2, each individual subsystem is clearly capable of contributing more information to the system should the system need it. Jim and Jan could have continued their discussion for several minutes or Jan could have ignored Jim's initiation. That the discussion ended when it did indicates that each subsystem felt that the goal had been reached appropriately; the system was balanced via self-regulation. Jim tells himself that his goal has been accomplished and thanks Jan for her help. Jan registers that she has met her obligation and the interaction stops (a form of control).

Environment and Hierarchy

The interaction depicted in Figure 11.2 presents a system living in a particular environment, a bus stop. In this case, the interaction was dependent, to some extent, on the environmental conditions. If Jim had asked for the same information of Jan during an airplane flight, she would have thought his behavior inappropriate. The interaction shown in Figure 11.2 is not totally dependent on the bus stop environment, however. Jim could have struck up a conversation about the weather or any other local guidelines typical of small talk.

The environment presented in Figure 11.2 also helps demonstrate the notion of systems hierarchy. In this case the subsystems are the individuals and the individual acts. The system is the entire exchange between the two. The suprasystem is all the other interaction going on around Jim and Jan. One might think of the society to which Jim and Jan belong as a suprasystem. Watzlawick et al. contend that the suprasystem might be the family, the hometown, or the society in which the subsystems survive.

A Working, Living, Open Communication System

In the following conversation between a student and a professor a working, living, social communication system is presented. The student is questioning his or her grade on an exam.

Environment: The professor's office

Subsystems: The Social System

Student A: Hmmm . . . can I talk to you about my exam?

Stimulus, Response, Reinforcement: This message is a stimulus for the professor, a response to the professor's evaluation of the exam, and a reinforcement of the student/teacher relationship.

Professor: Sure c'mon in, just let me save this on the disk . . . (Pause while professor saves file)

Wholeness: Without each person, the interaction would not occur, thus, no system would exist.

Student A: Ya know on that exam you handed back yesterday?

Professor: Ah . . . yeah . . .

Student A: Well . . . I was wondering why I got so few points on this one question.

Imbalance: The system is in a state of imbalance, thus the student asks for more information.

Professor: Here, let me read your answer. (Pause) Yeah, OK. . . .I remember this one.

Student A: I mean is it because I didn't, I didn't give enough examples because I know . . . I mean you really like it when there's examples.

(Interuption)

Student B: Here are those copies you wanted ... oops, sorry to interrupt. (Laugh)

Openness: The system allows for another person to contribute information to the system.

Professor: No problem ... thanks.

Student A: (Makes a giggling sound)

Professor: The reason for the number of points awarded on this question is because you only discuss four of the dimensions we discussed in class. Remember when we discussed those five communication dimensions?"

Information: The system generates its own information.

Student A: Oh ... you wanted us to talk about all of them?

Feedback: The system responds.

Professor: Yeah ... see ... that's what the question says 'Discuss each of the five dimensions mentioned in class'.

Student A: Hmm ... yeah ... oh ... OK ... yeah, OK, I guess I see what you mean. (Slight giggling sound)

Professor: Yeah ... see if you had discussed all five dimensions, then you would have, ah ... you would have received more points.

Student A: So I should have discussed all five parts?

Professor: Dimensions, yes ... all five dimensions, just as the question asks.

Student A: Hmmm ... well ... OK, I just thought I'd ask ... hmmm ... OK ... thanks.

Self-Regulation: The system is now back to a balanced state.

Professor: Sure ... anytime.

Student A: OK ... thanks, I guess I'll see you tomorrow.

Relationship: The interaction indicates that the subsystems are related.

Professor: That's right, in class.

Student A: OK then, see ya.

Interdependence: The professor's acts are interdependent with the student's acts.

Professor: Bye.

Control: The system, now balanced, needs no more information at this time, so the interaction ceases, temporarily.

Hierarchy: The population of the school.

CASE STUDY 15   Interethnic Conflict

Key Terms

Interethnic Conflict

Subsystem (Microlevel) Conditions

System (Intermediary-level) Conditions

Suprasystem (Macrolevel) Conditions

This case study centers on one of the most dramatic instances of interethnic conflict in American history. On March 3, 1991, Los Angeles, California, motorist Rodney King, a six-foot-three-inch, 250-pound African American, legally drunk, led police on a high-speed car chase, reaching speeds of 155 miles per hour while committing numerous traffic offenses. When King was finally caught and subdued, four white Los Angeles County police officers proceeded to beat him, hitting him over fifty times with their police batons. Unknown to the police officers, a passerby noticed the beating and recorded it on his video camera. The videotaped beating was aired on newscasts all over the country. The nation was stunned at what appeared to be blatant police brutality. Many felt it was racially motivated. That the police were white and the motorist was African American served to further outrage the public. The four police officers were subsequently charged with police brutality and the videotape was used as evidence both by the prosecuting and defense attorneys.

Because of the amount of pretrial exposure, the trial of the four police officers was held outside the city of Los Angeles in the suburban, dominantly white Simi Valley community. The jury consisted of ten whites, one Hispanic, and one Asian. On April 29, 1992, the jury acquitted the four officers of all charges. News of the acquittal quickly spread across the country and induced a seventy-two-hour convulsion of violence in Los Angeles that left forty-four persons dead, over two thousand injured, and an estimated $1 billion in damages, primarily to stores that had been looted and set afire. By 10:00 P.M. that evening, over twenty-five square blocks of south central Los Angeles were on fire. Though the rioters were primarily African Americans, many Hispanics and some whites joined in the rioting. Throughout the city African American store owners spray painted the fronts of their businesses "Black—don't burn" to distinguish them from white- and Asian-owned businesses. Though many argued that the riot was not a race but a class riot, clear racial tensions emerged especially between whites, African Americans, and Asian Americans, primarily of Korean descent. Over one hundred Korean-owned businesses were destroyed in the violence. As Asian American stores became the target of violence, vigilante-style groups of Korean shop owners armed with semiautomatic high-powered guns took to the streets to defend their properties. Other riots broke out in San Francisco, Seattle, and Atlanta. Even in Madison, Wisconsin, several police cars had their windshields smashed. Though some discount the influence of race on the riots, others contend that at the core of the problem is racial injustice that has been a part of U.S. history over the past two centuries.[a]

Continued

CASE STUDY 15 *Continued*

This incident can be described as an extreme case of interethnic conflict. Like other forms of social conflict, interethnic conflict is the result of strained relationships between the involved parties. In this case, the parties are members of different ethnic groups. A prominent systems theorist, Young Yun Kim, has developed a systems model of interethnic conflict that attempts to explain how, why, and with what effects different ethnic groups and individuals come into conflict with one another, and how such conflicts can be managed.[b]

Kim sees ethnicity as more of a social phenomena than simply a biological one. She contends that ethnicity refers to a set of physical and social attributes shared by some social group that differentiate it from other social groups. Kim views interethnic conflict as simultaneously a group and an individual phenomena. Interethnic conflicts are always a group phenomenon experienced by individuals. As Kim argues: "An assault to an ethnic individual 'becomes' an assault to that ethnic group as soon as it is experienced as an 'interethnic' (as opposed to interpersonal) conflict."[c]

Kim's model of interethnic conflict is presented below:

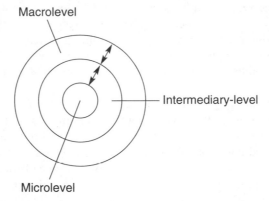

According to the model, interethnic conflict can be viewed on three levels, including the subsystem or microlevel, system or intermediary-level, and suprasystem or macrolevel. All three levels are interdependent and interact to facilitate interethnic conflict. Remember that the analysis of the systems theorist is done at the system level. In communication the system is a social system. In the case of the Los Angeles riots, the actual riot is the system, the behaviors of the rioters. The system is affected by the subsystem and suprasystem.[d]

Recall that the subsystem of any social system is the individual. According to the model four key attributes of subsystems are most likely to contribute to interethnic conflict, including cognitive simplicity/rigidity, ingroup bias, insecurity/frustration, and divergent behavior. Cognitive simplicity/rigidity refers to the degree of rigidity and simplicity in which individuals process information about members of different ethnic groups—that is, outgroups. Simplistic information processing refers to gross stereotyping of outgroup members based on ignorance. Because many feel that the riots were class and race related, some rioters may stereotype all whites as rich and racist, for example. Cognitive rigidity refers to inflexible cognitive categories in which outgroup members are placed. For example, "all whites are bad" would represent a rigid category in which to place all members of the outgroup.

Ingroup bias refers to the degree to which individuals have an unreasonable or unjustifiable form of ingroup favoritism—that is, ethnocentrism. Ethnocentrism is defined as viewing one's own group as at the center of everything and using the standards of one's own group to measure or gauge the worth of all other groups. Insecurity and frustration refer to the degree to which individuals have high levels of uncertainty about and fear of outgroup members. During the riots, for example, thousands of people clogged the highways to get out of town. Like gross stereotypes, fear is many times based on ignorance.

Divergent behavior refers to the behavioral patterns of group members that clearly differentiate and distance them from outgroup members. For example, obviously different speech patterns or accents may ostensively separate groups from one another. Inner-city African Americans may have developed slang words and phrases that others do not understand.

At the system or intermediary level is the actual interaction. In this example, the riot is the system. Three components of the system foster interethnic conflict, including segregation and contact, intergroup salience, and status discrepancy. These conditions mediate the subsystem and suprasystem levels. Perhaps the most basic condition for interethnic conflict is contact between diverse ethnic identities on a day-to-day basis. The schools and neighborhoods of many of major cities, such as Los Angeles, are racially segregated. Many journalists and politicians have noted the striking differences between south central Los Angeles, where the riots began, and Simi Valley, where the trial was held. Segregated communities do not allow for much interaction and hence components at the subsystem level (e.g., cognitive rigidity, ingroup bias, etc.) tend to develop and escalate to intolerable levels thus facilitating interethnic conflict.Intergroup salience refers to the observable physical and social differences between conflicting ethnic groups. Such ethnic markers include distinct physical and behavioral differences such as race, language, and speech patterns. As Kim notes, to the extent that the groups are ethnically distinct (i.e., the more intergroup salience), the communicative skills of the minority ethnic group that are used within the home or local communities clash with those of the majority that are used in public contexts, where the majority group's symbol system is dominant. In the Los Angeles situation, there was a high degree of intergroup salience between the minority (i.e., African American) and majority (i.e., white) groups on several dimensions, including distinct physical and socioeconomic differences.

The third system level condition that facilitates interethnic conflict is status discrepancy; that is, the degree to which conflicting parties differ in status along ethnic lines. In the case of Los Angeles, and in many other communities, African Americans perceive an asymmetrical power structure. In a sense the riots were based on this sense of powerlessness. In addition, the four police officers had higher legal status/power. That they were white and Rodney King was African American exacerbated the conflict. If the police officers had been African American or if King had been white, chances are good that the riots may not

Continued

CASE STUDY 15   *Continued*

have occurred. In the case of Los Angeles, two segregated groups with much intergroup salience and status discrepancy clashed.

The suprasystem in which the system survives and exchanges inputs and outputs represents the environmental constraints that foster interethnic conflict at the system and subsystem level. According to the model, the macrolevel conditions that foster interethnic conflict include the history of subjugation, ideological/structural inequality, and minority group strength.

The history of subjugation of one group by another is a key environmental condition in interethnic conflict. African Americans have long been subjugated by whites in America. Historically, African Americans were slaves. Even upon emancipation, they were not allowed to vote. As late as the 1960s restaurants in the southern United States had separate bathrooms, seating areas, and drinking fountains. As Elaine King, professor of Asian American studies at the University of California-Berkeley argues

> *The tensions of people of color are rooted in racial violence woven into U.S. history for the past 500 years and evidenced today in a judicial system that can allow the men who beat Rodney King to escape conviction.*[e]

Ideological and structural inequality refers to societal differences regarding power, prestige, and economic reward. Historically, whites have held most of the power positions and gained most of the economic reward. Hence, there is a vast ideological and structural difference between whites and African Americans, particularly between those African Americans in south central Los Angeles and the whites in Simi Valley. In fact, several journalists characterize the riot in Los Angeles as a class riot.

The third component of the suprasystem that facilitates interethnic conflict is minority group strength. Minority groups vary in their ability to rally their members against structural inequalities. Minority group strength varies as a function of the status of the group's language within the society, the sheer numbers of members in the group, and forms of societal support (e.g., governmental services designed specifically for the group). The African American community, relative to other ethnic groups, is economically and politically quite powerful. Political scientists argue, for example, that the 1992 presidential election may have been swung by the African American voting block. According to Young Kim, the stronger the ethnic group, the more likely the individual will take actions in interethnic conflict situations. This seemed to be the case in Los Angeles as African Americans made up the majority of rioters.

From a systems perspective, conflict arises out of discrepancies between the needs and capacities of the system and suprasystem; that is, it is a form of negative feedback. As Kim notes:

> *The system experiencing conflict then acts on the discrepancy, striving to adapt to the new reality by closing the gap. Conflict, therefore, can be viewed as a crucial force for the system's change, growth, and evolution, as well as a defense against its stagnation, detachment, and entropy.*[f]

Systems theory offers a useful tool for communication researchers to explain communication phenomena. Whether in dyadic, small group, organizational, or cultural contexts, the systems approach is applicable.

[a]Mathews, T., Meyer, M., Foote, D., Murr, A., Wright, L., Hammer, J., Mabry, M., Manly, H., Springen, K., & Crandall, R. (1992). "The Siege of L.A.," *Newsweek, 69,* (pp. 30–38).
[b]Kim, Y. Y. (1990). *Explaining Interethnic Conflict: An Interdisciplinary Overview.* Paper presented at the annual convention of the Speech Communication Association, Chicago.
[c]Ibid.
[d]Ibid.
[e]Kim, E. H. (1992). "They Armed in Self-Defense," *Newsweek, 69,* (p. 10).
[f]Kim, *Explaining Interethnic Conflict,* (p. 13).

Although the concept of equifinality is not demonstrated in this conversation, it can be assumed that the conversation could have taken any number of directions and reached the same goal. For example, the student could have telephoned the professor and received essentially the same information. In any case, the system eventually reaches balance.

Systems Approaches in Communication Contexts

In their seminal work, Watzlawick, Beavin, and Jackson argue that their conceptualization of the pragmatic approach to interaction is only introductory. The principles of systems theory are so new and so abstract that they can be and probably are applied in numerous ways by different theorists. In this section of the chapter, numerous systems approaches will be examined within three communication contexts, including (a) interpersonal, (b) small group, and (c) organizational communication.

Context I: Interpersonal Communication and Systems Theory

Communication theorists applying the general systems theory to interpersonal communication tend to refer to their area of study not as interpersonal communication but rather as relational communication. Fisher argues that the terms *interpersonal communication* and *human relationship* are synonymous.[11]

One of the major assumptions of the relational communication systems theorist is that relationships are defined by the interaction between the participants. In other words, if one were to describe his or her relationship with another person as intimate, it is only because the interaction between the participants is intimate. In order to describe a relationship one must look not at isolated individuals, but at the interaction between the individuals. As Miller and Steinberg argue:

> *If we can assign some characteristics (even intangible) to a relationship at all, we must first admit that we cannot account for these characteristics solely by accounting for the characteristics of either member of the relationship. A relationship is not person A nor person B; rather it emerges from transactions of person A and person B.[12]*

Although relational theorists study all types of relationships, most of their work focuses on interpersonal relationship development.

Relational Development

A major assumption of relational theorists is that relationships develop over time. Relationships progress from noninterpersonal to interpersonal in a gradual stage-by-stage process. In some cases this process can take months or even years, in others, a few days.

Because relationships are open systems that exchange information with their environment, they are in a constant process of development; they are dynamic. Several theorists, not all of them avowed systems theorists, have proposed models of relational development. In addition, systems theorists have developed their own models of relational growth, each of which is a descriptive account of the developmental phases of relationships. Although not all of these models originated with pure systems theorists, systems theory provides a useful explanation of the process. Table 11.1 provides a brief summary of each model.

Notice that each model of relational development in Table 11.1 describes the stages a little differently. The Altman and Taylor model, for example, describes relational development in four stages. Phillips and Wood describe six stages while Wilmot proposes only two. Regardless of which model you follow, systems theorists contend that the relational development process is gradual. A relationship, for example, does not move from stage 1 to stage 2 overnight. In fact, it may not even be apparent to the participants when they have moved from one stage to another until long after it has happened. The point is that as an open system the relationship is in a constant state of change, process, and development. Because interaction constantly changes, the nature of the relationship is always changing.

Because of its precision and applicability to systems theory, Knapp and Vangelisti's model provides a particularly useful explanation of the systemic nature of relationships. According to them, relationships progress through five stages when developing toward in-

TABLE 11.1   Models of Relational Development

Altman & Taylor	Knapp & Vangelisti	Phillips & Wood	Wilmot
Orientation	Initiation	Individuals Alone and Receptive	Initiation
Exploratory Affect	Experimenting	Invitational Communication	Stabilization
Affective Exchange	Intensifying	Exploratory Communication	
Stable Exchange	Integrating	Intensifying (Euphoria)	
	Bonding	Revising Communication	
		Bonding Communication	

Altman, I., & Taylor, D. A. (1973). *Social Penetration,* Monterey, CA: Brooks Cole; Knapp, M. L., & Vangelisti, A. L. (1992). *Interpersonal Communication and Human Relationships,* Boston: Allyn & Bacon; Phillips, G., & Wood, J. (1983). *Communication and Human Relationships: The Study of Interpersonal Relationships,* New York: Macmillan; Wilmot, W. (1987). *Dyadic Communication,* New York: Random House.

timacy—initiation, experimenting, intensifying, integrating, and bonding. Keep in mind that each particular stage is defined by the interaction. If one describes their relationship as in the experimenting stage, it is because of the interaction.[13]

Initiation

The first stage of relational development is initiation. Knapp and Vangelisti argue that this phase incorporates the processes enacted when we first come together with other people. The system begins to function when interaction starts. Imagine someone with whom you consider yourself intimate. Keep in mind that intimacy does not necessarily mean sexual intimacy. Try to remember the very first time you interacted. At the moment you first spoke with each other, the relationship/system began to function. The process of initiating interaction for the first time is very complex. In fact, Wilmot argues that a number of requirements must be met for the creation of a functioning relationship/system. First, you and the other person must be behaving. This requirement is not particularly hard to meet since a fundamental assumption of systems theory is that one cannot not behave. Second, in order for the system to begin functioning, however, you must be aware of the other's behavior and simultaneously the other person must be aware of your behavior. As a result, you are aware that he or she is aware of you and he or she is aware that you are aware of him or her. Wilmot refers to this process as the perception of being perceived. Such reciprocal awareness is a critical requirement for a system to form and is what makes the system whole. Hence, an individual simply observing another person without that person's knowledge is not a system. The relationship between two people is uniquely different from the act of one person observing another.[14]

During the initiation stage, people generally engage in cultural or sociological data exchange, thus the relationship is noninterpersonal. It is important to note, however, that *any time* interaction is initiated, a system is created. Thus, when you enter a store to buy a six-pack of beer, a relationship between you and the clerk begins. The relationship is noninterpersonal, but it is nevertheless a fully legitimate operating system. If you frequent the same store, you will begin to notice how the interaction between you and the clerk develops. At first, the interaction will be very restricted. After a while, however, the topics of interaction may begin to change and develop.

Initiation is a very short stage whose interaction is restricted to greetings. One might initiate conversation with a simple verbal salute such as "Hello!" or one might greet another by asking a question such as "Haven't I seen you before?" The specific greeting changes with the nature of the relationship and situation. Knapp and Vangelisti argue that such aspects as the kind of relationship (formal or informal), the time allowed for interaction (passing in the hallway or sitting next to one another on a transatlantic flight), the situational context (in an elevator or at a rock concert), or any special codes that might be needed to engage in interaction (fraternity handshake) will influence the type of greeting. Once interaction has begun and the system is operating, the relationship quickly moves to the second stage—experimenting.

Experimenting

Experimenting, which immediately follows initiation, is where the participants attempt to reduce uncertainty about each other and typically engage in the exchange of cultural and sociological data. The system generates its own information and adapts accordingly. Knapp and Vangelisti refer to this as the "name, rank, and serial number" stage. In fact, they liken it to the sniffing ritual performed by animals. Interaction at this stage is limited to small talk. For example, whenever you meet someone new at a party, you quickly initiate the relationship with a greeting and move into the small talk stage. You begin by exchanging names ("Oh hi, I'm Jim"), rank ("I'm a junior"), and serial number (". . . and a communication major").

Although small talk can sometimes be tedious and mundane, it serves several important functions, including that (a) it keeps the system open, (b) it serves as an audition for later "big" talk, (c) it is relative safe talk, and (d) it allows the system to grow and remain alive. Remember that for a system to survive it must generate its own information and adapt accordingly. Commitments at the experimenting stage are very limited and most of our relationships do not progress past this point. Hence, most of our relationships are noninterpersonal.

Intensifying

Should the participants decide to develop the system further, they may move into the intensifying, or "close friends" stage, and is very much contingent on the interaction. Verbally, the participants begin to exchange psychological data in the form of self-disclosure. Forms of address (nicknames), private symbols (slang or jargon), and expressions of commitment ("I enjoy going out with you") become the focus of the interaction. In addition, nonverbal interaction becomes sophisticated. We may begin to dress alike, stand close together, hug when we meet, kiss when we depart, and hold hands with some regularity.

Integrating

The integrating stage is characterized by very intimate psychological data exchange. Self-disclosure reaches its zenith, intimate trophies are exchanged (rings or pins), common property is designated ("our song" or "our park"), and even more importantly, other people treat us as one (one invitation, one present, one letter).

Bonding

The final stage in the relational development model is bonding. Here the participants legalize their relationship (i.e., marriage). Typically, this stage is reserved for systems consisting of one male and one female, although the legal definitions of marriage are changing in some states. The interaction at the integrating and bonding stages is very similar. The institutionalization of the relationship acts as a powerful force in the development of the system. Legally, for example, it is now much more difficult to get out of the relationship. In addition, each participant takes on a new role, that of spouse. Because of this new role, interaction regarding the acting out of such roles may dominate communication.

Because of the dynamic self-regulating nature of open systems, relationships move in and out of stages with some degree of regularity. In other words a relationship may move from intensifying to integrating and then back to intensifying. Whether the movement is forward (from initiating to experimenting to intensifying) or backward (integrating to intensifying to experimenting), movement is typically gradual and systematic. Usually, relationships do not skip stages, although such movement is possible (from experimenting to bonding). In addition, movement can occur within stages as well. Wherever movement occurs, however, it is always to a new place. Because the system constantly adapts with the interaction, any interaction changes the system forever. A relationship could move backward from integrating to intensifying to experimenting and then forward again to integrating. But the nature of the relationship during its second integrating stage is altered by its first journey there. A couple who has bonded (marriage), for example, may divorce from each other and then decide to remarry each other and return to the bonding stage. Although they return to the bonding stage, their earlier divorce changes the nature of their relationship forever. The system constantly adapts.[15]

Relational Maintenance: Social Exchange Theory

Regardless of the stage a relationship reaches, the dyadic system must maintain its balance and fight against entropy or it will cease to exist. Like any other open system a dyad fights entropy by exchanging inputs and outputs from the environment. Within communication systems, the primary resource exchanged with the environment is interaction. Social psychologists Thibaut and Kelley have developed a theory which explains the process by which dyadic systems maintain their balance via environmental exchange. It is called "social exchange theory" and has been adopted by many systems theorists.

According to the theory, relationships function much in the same way as an economic system, via a ratio of assets and liabilities. An economic system survives as long as its liabilities (e.g., costs) do not exceed its assets (i.e., profits or rewards). Likewise, relationships evolve around the exchange of costs and rewards. Thibaut and Kelley refer to relational costs and rewards as resources. A resource can be anything exchanged between the system and its environment (e.g., subsystems). As a result of the exchange, the system gains something (i.e., a reward), but it must also give something back (i.e., a cost). As long as there is a balanced ratio between costs and rewards, the system functions properly and can reduce entropy. A reward is any resource input into the system that provides pleasures, satisfaction, gratifications, or anything that fulfills a need. A cost, on the other hand, is defined as anything that inhibits the performance of the system. In any relationship, the participants are giving to and taking from the system any number of different types of resources. For example, communication, love, time, money, and sex are critical resources exchanged in a dyadic system. As long as the system perceives an equal ratio of costs versus rewards, it maintains its homeostasis (e.g., positive feedback). However, when there is an unequal distribution of costs and rewards, the system becomes imbalanced (e.g., negative feedback) and must adapt to maintain homeostasis. Within any dyadic system communication is a vital resource to exchange. Figure 11.3 on page 312 presents two dyadic systems—one balanced, the other imbalanced.[16]

The resources exchanged in each dyadic system include small talk, psychological data, self-disclosure, and intimate touch and represent only a sample of the potential resources that could be exchanged. Small talk is characterized by breadth not depth and is generally limited to superficial topics such as the weather, what happened at work, and other local guidelines. Psychological data involves the exchange of information regarding attitudes, motivations, dispositions, feelings, etc. Self-disclosure occurs whenever a person tells someone else psy-

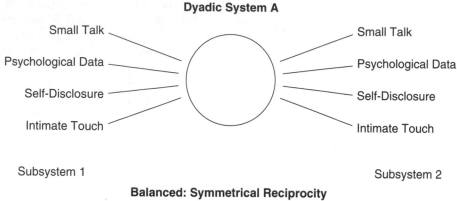

Dyadic System A

Small Talk

Psychological Data

Self-Disclosure

Intimate Touch

Subsystem 1

Small Talk

Psychological Data

Self-Disclosure

Intimate Touch

Subsystem 2

Balanced: Symmetrical Reciprocity

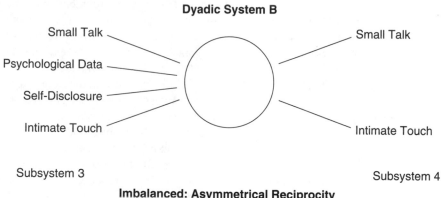

Dyadic System B

Small Talk

Psychological Data

Self-Disclosure

Intimate Touch

Subsystem 3

Small Talk

Intimate Touch

Subsystem 4

Imbalanced: Asymmetrical Reciprocity

FIGURE 11.3   Balanced and Imbalanced Dyadic Systems

chological data about themselves that would otherwise be unavailable to the other person. Finally, intimate touch could involve hand-holding, hugging, kissing, lovemaking, and so on.

Notice that Dyadic System A is balanced. Each of the subsystems contributes equally to the system—there is symmetrical (balanced proportions) reciprocity (mutual exchange) of the resources. It should be noted here that symmetrical reciprocity does not necessarily mean that each subsystem must exchange exactly the same resources immediately upon receipt. In fact, as relationships develop and grow intimate, the exchange of resources becomes delayed and may not be equal. For example, one subsystem may contribute five parts self-disclosure and five parts intimate touch whereas the other subsystem may contribute three parts self-disclosure and seven parts intimate touch. In the end, each subsystem has contributed ten parts of its resources to the system. In addition, the exchange may be delayed. Subsystem 1 may self-disclose on Tuesday and Subsystem 2 may self-disclose on Friday. The point here is that eventually the exchange is perceived as symmetrical.

On the other hand, Dyadic System B is not balanced. Subsystem 3 seems to be contributing much more to the system than is Subsystem 4. In this scenario, it is likely that Subsystem 3 will begin to perceive that he or she is giving (costs) more than receiving (rewards); there is asymmetrical (unequal proportions) reciprocity. In this case, the system is imbalanced and must adapt accordingly if it is to survive. At some point, Subsystem 3 might try to persuade Subsystem 4 to contribute more to the system. If unsuccessful, Subsystem 3 might decide to leave the system, in which case it would no longer be whole and would disintegrate.

Perhaps all dyadic systems tolerate a certain degree of asymmetrical reciprocity in their resources exchange. The stronger the bond between the participants, the more tolerant they may be of each other's unequal exchange. For example, if one member of a dyadic system is experiencing severe mental depression and is unable to contribute much, the healthy subsystem will contribute much more knowing that it will keep the system alive. This is a form of adaptation characteristic of most open living systems. When someone breaks their right leg, for example, the left leg takes on much more weight than is normally expected but is required if the human body system is to survive.

Relational Maintenance: Control, Trust, and Intimacy

Perhaps those scholars in the communication field who are doing the purist form of systems research include Frank Millar and Edna Rogers. Frank Millar is a professor of communication at the University of Wyoming and Edna Rogers is a professor of communication at the University of Utah. Both have been influenced by the writings of Ludwig von Bertalanffy, Paul Watzlawick, Gregory Bateson, and sociologist Georg Simmel. Keeping in line with the fundamental assumptions of systems theory, Millar and Rogers argue for a shift away from the individual as a unit of analysis in communication (what they term a monadic approach) to a focus on the dyad as the unit of analysis. According to Millar and Rogers:

> *The unit of analysis in a transactional perspective is a minimum of two, a dyad; and the focus of analysis is on the systemic properties that the participants have collectively, not individually. The system is viewed as a joint product of behavior, a product admittedly made up of individual actions, but one that has a "life" of its own which goes beyond the sum of its constituent parts.[17]*

Millar and Rogers contend that an individual's identity is created and sustained through ongoing interaction with others and that an individual's self-concept is not formed through personal introspection (i.e., monadically) but is constructed and maintained via social contact with others. For example, if individuals perceive of themselves as good students, it is because others (e.g., teachers, parents, friends) have provided repetitive and consistent input or feedback about their scholastic ability. A student knows he or she has done well in school when the teacher gives an A on a report card, for example. The student and teacher have interacted about the student's identity. In addition, because individuals are goal-oriented and purposeful and because, at least at a subconscious level, they understand the socialness of their identity, they seek out others who will be dependable sources of information about themselves. Thus, to Millar and Rogers it is the social relationship, not the individual, that is the fundamental unit of analysis.

In describing the nature of relationships, Millar and Rogers implement a spatial metaphor. They contend that in any relationship individuals maintain a certain space or "distance" from each other. In long-term intimate interpersonal relationships, for example, the individuals are physically, socially, and psychologically quite close, whereas in short-term noninterpersonal relationships the interactants are usually physically, socially, and psychologically distant. Through ongoing interaction, the participants are constantly defining their distance from each other.

Given the above description regarding the nature of relationships, Millar and Rogers have outlined three distancing dimensions of relationships, including control, trust, and intimacy. They state:

> *These dimensions, control, trust, and intimacy, are not intended to be an exhaustive list of relational variables. They are intended to be viewed as three basic joint products of behavior that emerge, have "life," and fluctuate through the exchange of messages—basic products in the sense that, given the advent of precise operations, all social relationships can be usefully described and differentiated over time and situations.*[18]

Control

The control dimension refers to the "process of establishing the right to define, direct, and delimit the actions of the dyad at the current moment."[19] When an individual attempts to assert relational definitions, he or she is exerting control over the relationship. Statements such as "I will make the decision," "I know what's best here," "You don't have the right to speak to me like that," "I'll say whatever I please," and "I have the right to say what I think" are all declarations of control called "one up" statements. Statements that relinquish control to the other, such as "Sure, we'll do it your way," "Whatever you want is fine with me," or "You should make the decision," are considered "one down" utterances. Control, the most dynamic of the three dimensions, varies with the topic and situation and from dyad to dyad. Thus, when making financial decisions the husband might assert control whereas during discussions regarding childrearing practices, the wife might assert control. In conceptualizing control as a distance variable, Millar and Rogers metaphorically refer to it as vertical distance between interactants. Thus, the more control one has in a relationship, the more height he or she is said to have.

Relational control can be assessed in any relationship by studying the interaction of a dyad over an extended time period and by measuring patterns of redundancy, dominance, and power in the communication. Redundancy refers to the variability and frequency of definitional rights asserted by the members of the system. If one member consistently utters "one up" statements with more frequency than the other, the system is said to have a rigid control pattern; the control attempts are redundant. On the other hand, if "one up" statements vary in consistency and frequency between members, the system is said to have a flexible control pattern; the control pattern is chaotic.

The second index of control, dominance, refers to how a member's assertion of control (i.e., a "one up" utterance) is reciprocated. In some relationships, "one up" statements are answered with similar replies. For example, "I'll make the decision"/"Oh no you won't" would be considered a "one up/one up" exchange, but "I'll make the decision"/"That's all right by me" would be considered a "one up/one down" exchange. Relationships characterized by "one up/one up" exchanges are said to be symmetrical. Relationships wherein "one up" utterances are frequently and consistently met with "one down" statements are said to be complementary. Recall back to section one of this chapter where one of the major axioms of Watzlawick et al. was that relationships gravitate toward complementarity or symmetry. Millar and Rogers are perhaps the first to clearly articulate and measure this fundamental axiom of systems theory.

A third index of the control dimension in relationships is power, which refers to the potential of one member's behaviors to influence the other's. A dyadic member is influenced by the other to the extent that he or she perceives the other to have adequate resources (e.g., money, education, etc.) and personal attributes (e.g., intelligence, willpower) to exert power. Based on the member's assessment of the other's power, he or she will decide to resist or submit.

Trust

The second distance dimension described by Millar and Rogers is trust. Remember that because relationships are conceptualized as dyadic systems, they are in a constant state of change. Systems are open and always adapting to and interacting with their environment. Because of this, all dyadic systems have a certain degree of what Millar and Rogers call inherent fragility. That is to say that it is impossible to predict with 100 percent accuracy each other's behavior. Naturally, however, human beings are uncomfortable with uncertainty and desire a certain degree of predictability in their lives and especially in their relationships with others. Trust represents this notion of predictability. Because a dyadic system's components (e.g., two people in a relationship) are interdependent and mutually influence each other, each subsystem has a vested interest in the other's behaviors since such behaviors will, to some extent, determine one's own behavioral choices. In terms of the metaphorical spatial distance, where control is conceptualized as height, trust represents the horizontal width between people. Where there is a great deal of horizontal width between interactants, there is much trust and little uncertainty. In contrast, where there is little horizontal width between persons, there is little trust and much uncertainty. Utterances such as "He's a really reliable guy," "I can always rely on her," and "I'd trust him with my wife" are examples of interaction expressing trust in another. Like the control dimension, trust can be assessed in a number ways but requires a longitudinal study of ongoing interaction in the dyad.

The amount of trust in a dyadic system can be assessed in terms of vulnerability, reward dependability, and confidence. Vulnerability refers to the accepted ratio of costs and rewards by either member of the dyadic system. For example, whenever a dyadic member incurs a cost (e.g., self-disclosing a very personal and perhaps negative aspect about the self) he or she becomes very vulnerable. Thus, by so disclosing, the one member places a great deal of trust in the other. So far as this vulnerability is not taken advantage of by the other, trust builds between the interactants. Reward dependability refers to the frequency with which one is rewarded for placing him- or herself in vulnerable positions. For example, if one member assumes a vulnerable position by disclosing very personal negative aspects of the self and the other responds by accepting the information and providing reciprocal therapeutic interaction, the discloser feels rewarded. The more common such rewards become, the more dependability within the relationship and thus trust.

The final indice of trust is confidence. Confidence refers to one member's "subjective probability estimate of nonbetrayal" by the other. The more confidence in the other, the more trust one has in that person.[20]

Intimacy

The final dimension articulated by Millar and Rogers is that of intimacy, which refers to the sentiments associated with the relationship. Intimacy is not based on the content of interaction but on the degree to which each member uses the other as a source of self-confirmation and his or her subsequent self-evaluation based on the other's definition. Intimacy also refers to the strength of attachment each member has toward the other. The sentiments and degree of attachment are built on a backlog of interaction and past history. In terms of the metaphorical space analogy, intimacy represents the depth of the relationship and can be assessed by characterizing the transferability, attachment, and knowledge of the participant's relationship.

Transferability refers to the number of people that a person can rely on for self-confirmatory interaction. Persons know themselves via social interaction and depend on such interaction to confirm and create self-definitions. The more people with which one can interact, the more transferable the relation and the less dependent the person is on any particular relationship. In contrast, the fewer people from which to obtain self-confirmatory interaction, the less transferable the relation and thus a more intimate and intense relationship develops with those few people providing the self-confirmatory interaction.

Attachment refers to a person's evaluation of the other's self-confirmation. Remember that if each of us uses interaction with someone else to help us confirm our own self-definitions, then the other person is also using that same interaction as a way to evaluate their own self-definition. To the extent that we positively evaluate the other's identity, we become attached to that person.

The knowledge index refers to the extent that each member of the dyadic system understands and realizes that he or she has been understood by the other. When this type of event occurs, the relationship is said to possess knowledge. The greater the knowledge in a relationship, the more intimate it becomes.

Relational Level Research: Measuring Relational Control

Millar and Rogers and their associates (e.g., John Courtright, Roger Farace, and Malcolm Parks) have developed a method for coding relational control patterns in ongoing dyadic interaction. This coding scheme was designed to: (a) focus on relational control rather than on message content, (b) define message sequences (i.e., interacts) rather than individual messages in isolation, and (c) chart interactional patterns as they progress over time so as to be sensitive to the dynamic nature of the control dimension in a relationship.[21]

The coding scheme is restricted to verbal messages. A message is defined as each verbal contribution of an interactant in a conversation. The message may be a single phrase or

TABLE 11.2   Message Code Categories

Digit One	Digit Two (Format)	Digit Three (Response Mode)
1. = Speaker 1	1. = Assertion	1. = Support
2. = Speaker 2	2. = Question	2. = Nonsupport
	3. = Successful Talk-Over	3. = Extension
	4. = Unsuccessful Talk-Over	4. = Answer
	5. = Noncomplete	5. = Instruction-Other
	6. = Other	6. = Order
		7. = Disconfirmation
		8. = Topic Change
		9. = Self-Instruction
		0. = Other

From *Relational Communication Control Coding Manual: RC²*, by L. Edna Rogers. Copyright © 1982 L. Edna Rogers. Unpublished manuscript, University of Utah. Reprinted by permission from L. Edna Rogers.

a string of continuing utterances. According to the scheme, each message is categorized according to a three-digit code (see Table 11.2). The first digit designates the speaker (1 or 2). The second digit categorizes the message format (1 to 6), and the third digit categorizes the response mode (1 to 10).

As indicated in Table 11.2, since most coding is done on dyadic systems, the first digit is almost always a 1 or a 2. The second digit can vary from 1 to 6 depending on the message format. The following list provides definitions of each of the six message formats.[22]

Definitions of Message Format/Digit Two

1. **Assertion:** Any message stated in declarative or imperative form that clearly indicates a control function.
2. **Question:** Any message that takes an interrogative form.
3. **Successful Talk-Over:** Any interruption or verbal intervention made while the other is speaking and results in the first speaker relinquishing the floor to the interrupter.
4. **Unsuccessful Talk-Over:** Any interruption or verbal intervention made while another person is talking and the other speaker continues to speak despite the interruption.
5. **Noncomplete:** Any utterance other than those coded as talk-overs that are initiated but not completed.
6. **Other:** Any utterance that is indistinguishable or grammatically unclassifiable.

The third digit varies from 1 to 10 depending on the response mode. Messages are considered as both a stimulus for furthering interaction and a response to an earlier message. The following list provides definitions of each of the ten response modes.[23]

Definitions of Message Response Mode/Digit Three

1. Support: Any message seeking or giving agreement, assistance, or approval.
2. Nonsupport: Any message that is a disagreement, rejection, demand, or challenge.
3. Extension: Any message that continues the flow or theme of the preceding message.
4. Answer: Any message that is a definitive response to a question.
5. Instruction-Other: Any message that is a regulative response but is in the form of a suggestion instructing the other how to feel and/or act.
6. Order: Any message that is a regulative response but is in the form of an unqualified command.
7. Disconfirmation: Any message that ignores or bypasses the request of the previous message.
8. Topic Change: Any message that has little continuity with the preceding message.
9. Self-Instruction: Any message that is regulative in function and instructs the self how to feel and act.
10. Other: Any message that is unclear and unclassifiable.

Once each message has been categorized according to its three-digit code, the next step is to code each message according to its control mode. As mentioned earlier, a message that attempts to assert definitional rights is coded as a one up ($\uparrow$) message. A message that is a request or an acceptance of the other's definition of the relationship is designated as a one down ($\downarrow$) message. Finally, a message that is nondemanding or nonaccepting is designated as one across ($\rightarrow$). Control directions are given in Table 11.3.

The six possible message formats (digit two) and the ten possible message response modes (digit three) represent sixty different combinations, each with its own control designation. Thus, if a particular message was coded as an assertion in nonsupport, its control direction would be designated as one up. Conversely, if a message were coded as a question of support its control direction would be designated as one down. Finally, if a message were coded as an unsuccessful talk-over, that is an extension, its control direction would be one across.

The coding scheme is designed to locate patterns of control directions. Patterns, rather than individual messages, tell much more about the control dimension in a relationship. Control patterns can be determined by combining the control direction of one message with the control direction of the following message. Recall that two contiguous message acts make up an interact. Interacts, not acts, are the primary concern in defining control patterns in relationships. Table 11.4 presents the control configurations of the nine types of possible interact pairings.

Thus, if Message 1 and Message 2 are coded as one up control messages, then the interact represents competitive symmetry. By coding ongoing interaction between dyadic partners over time, patterns of complementarity or symmetry can be determined.

Table 11.5 on page 320 presents a hypothetical conversation between Jim and Jan. Each message is assigned a three-digit code and control mode designate.

TABLE 11.3   Control Direction of Message Types

		Support	Nonsupport	Extension	Answer	Instruction	Order	Disconfirmation	Topic Change	Self-Instruction	Other
		1	2	3	4	5	6	7	8	9	0
Assertion	1	↓	↑	→	↑	↑	↑	↑	↑	→	→
Question	2	↓	↑	↓	↑	↑	↑	↑	↑	↓	↓
Successful Talk-Over	3	↓	↑	↑	↑	↑	↑	↑	↑	↑	↑
Unsuccessful Talk-Over	4	↓	↑	→	↑	↑	↑	↑	↑	→	→
Noncomplete	5	↓	↑	→	↑	↑	↑	↑	↑	→	→
Other	6	↓	↑	→	↑	↑	↑	↑	↑	→	→

From *Relational Control Coding Manual: RC²*, by L. Edna Rogers. Copyright © 1982 L. Edna Rogers. Unpublished manuscript, University of Utah. Reprinted by permission of L. Edna Rogers.

In this exchange between Jim and Jan are examples of competitive symmetry (↑↑), neutralized symmetry (→→), complementarity (↓↑), and transition (↓→). Because this is only a very brief message exchange, conclusions about the nature of the control dimension in this relationship should be avoided. However, if we were to code ongoing interaction between Jim and Jan over an extended period of time and find a similar pattern of control, we

TABLE 11.4   Transactional Control Codes

	Speaker A		
	One Up ↑	**One Down** ↓	**One Across** →
Speaker B ↑ One Up	↑↑ Competitive Symmetry	↑↓ Complementarity	↑→ Transition
↓ One Down	↓↑ Complementarity	↓↓ Submissive Symmetry	↓→ Transition
→ One Across	→↑ Transition	→↓ Transition	→→ Neutralized Symmetry

From *Relational Control Coding Manual: RC²*, by L. Edna Rogers. Copyright © 1982 L. Edna Rogers. Unpublished manuscript, University of Utah. Reprinted by permission of L. Edna Rogers.

TABLE 11.5   Conversation with Message Codes and Control Modes

Speaker	Message	Message Code/Control Direction
Jim	Do you have time to help with the dishes?	121 ↓
Jan	Sure, I don't mind helping, ya know.	214 ↑
Jim	I'm not saying you don't help.	113 →
Jan	Well . . . it's when you ask, it makes it sound like I don't help much.	213 →
Jim	What's wrong with my asking?	123 ↓
Jan	It's the implication, it's like you think I just sit around and watch you do all the work all the time.	214 ↑
Jim	I'm sorry, I don't mean to sound that way.	113 →
Jan	That's OK, you don't have to apologize.	211 ↓
Jim	In that case, would you vacuum the house, wash my car, press my shirts, and paint the house so that I can relax? (Laughter)	125 ↑
Jan	Sure, I'll be back in five minutes when I'm done!	214 ↑

might conclude that Jim and Jan both make control attempts and that both accept the control definitions of the other. Thus, their relationship, in terms of the control dimension, could be characterized as flexible since both assert definitional rights and because both symmetrical and complementary patterns of control emerge.

The work of Rogers and Millar and their associates is one of only a few theory-driven programs of research and it has done much to advance the field of communication in terms of the systems perspective. Unlike most other research efforts, their program focuses specifically on interaction as a unit of analysis rather than on individual (monadic) dimensions; thus, it can be legitimately labeled a communication perspective. Their work, however, is far from complete. As Millar and Rogers state:

> *Our empirical findings are meager compared with our discoveries about the paradoxical nature of human interactions. As we have investigated communicative patterns, we have become painfully aware of the limitations of our efforts and humbled by the enormity of the task.*[24]

Relational Disengagement

Systems theory also provides a useful theoretical explanation of relational termination, or the ending of relationships, an unfortunate, but inevitable, reality of all dyadic systems. Although all eventually die, the process of death may be different for each system (equifinality). Like the process of relational development, systems theorists argue that relationships progress through a series of stages as they break up. In the case of a breakup, relationships regress from interpersonal to noninterpersonal in a gradual stage-by-stage process. This process can occur almost simultaneously or can take months or even years (e.g., a long, drawn-out separation and divorce).[25]

Passing away Termination

Many systems theorists refer to the gradual ending of a relationship as its "passing away." Passing away is the long, drawn-out process of relational dissolution whereby the relationship very slowly decreases in intimacy (i.e., one of the three relational dimensions discussed by Millar and Rogers). Davis argues that the passing away phase of relational dissolution is usually, though not always, precipitated by one of the following three events: (a) the introduction of a new intimate other to one of the relational partners which leads to jealousy by the other and conflict, (b) an increase in interaction distance as a result of physical and/or psychological separation and the relationship fades away, and (c) a natural process whereby each relational partner simply grows and changes such that each develops different needs and interests that are no longer compatible.[26]

Sudden Death Termination

In some cases, this process of relational dissolution can occur spontaneously. This "sudden death" phenomena can be the result of both people, one person, or, as in the case of the literal death of one of the partners, neither person. When two people decide to suddenly end their relationship, it usually comes as a surprise to their friends and family. The typical scenario involves a couple that, over time, has lost the feelings of intimacy but continues to act out their roles as relational partners because their past history and social and perhaps legal commitments (home mortgage payment) make it very difficult to break up. Eventually, the couple realizes that the relationship is going nowhere and decides to terminate it. In other cases, sudden death syndrome may come about from the efforts of only one member of the dyad and may come as a complete surprise to the other. Usually one member has been experiencing levels of dissatisfaction for some time but never communicated those feelings to the other. Suddenly one day this partner decides that he or she can no longer continue in the relationship and simply walks away.

Models of Relational Termination

Systems theory literature on relational termination uses a number of terms used to describe the ending of a relationship, including (a) relational termination, (b) relational disengagement, (c) relational de-escalation, and (d) relational dissolution. Although everyone has probably experienced the pain of a relationship breakup, Wilmot contends that relationships never actually end. Wilmot argues that:

> *Actually, when a relationship is "terminated" it is usually redefined. The uncoupling process will drastically alter the patterns of interaction and put the dyadic participants at different places geographically, but in a very real sense, the old re-*

lationship cannot be stopped dead in its tracks. The influence of the other lives on, even in minute amounts, throughout the person's lifetime.[27]

Thus, perhaps it is appropriate to think of a breakup not as a death, but as a redefined relationship, one defined by a lack of interaction.

Because relationships are open systems that exchange information with their environment, they are in a constant process of development; they are dynamic even through the breakup process. Several theorists, not all of them avowed systems theorists, have proposed models of relational termination. In addition, systems theorists have focused on actual interaction during the disengagement process. Table 11.6 presents three models of the relational disengagement process. Each of which is a descriptive account of the disengagement phases of relationships. Although not all of these models originated with pure systems theorists, systems theory provides a useful explanation of the process. In addition, each model is different from the others in mostly subtle ways.

Because of its comprehensiveness, precision, and applicability to systems theory, Duck's model provides a particularly useful explanation of the systemic nature of relational termination. Box 11.1 provides a more detailed account of Duck's model of termination. Keep in mind that movement from stage to stage is gradual and developmental. Like relational development, the interactants may not be aware that they have entered a particular stage until after they have been in it for awhile. Also keep in mind the interaction defines the stage. The only way a relationship reaches any particular stage is because interaction takes it there.

The first stage is the breakdown stage, during which the participants become dissatisfied with the relationship, perhaps because of asymmetrical reciprocity of resources. Interaction here is only slightly different from normal interaction during intimate stages. In fact, since the system may not experience any interactional changes, this stage may occur only at the subsystem level.

TABLE 11.6   Models of Relational Disengagement

Duck	Knapp & Vangelisti	Lee
Breakdown	Differentiation	Dissatisfaction
Intrapsychic Stage	Circumscribing	Exposure
Dyadic Phase	Stagnating	Negotiation
Social Phase	Avoiding	Resolution
Grave Dressing Phase	Terminating	Transformation

Duck, S. (1982). "Typography of Relationship Disengagement and Dissolution," in S. Duck, (Ed.), *Personal Relationships 4: Dissolving Personal Relationships,* New York: Academic Press, (pp. 1–30); Knapp, M. L., & Vangelisti, A. L. (1992). *Interpersonal Communication and Human Relationships,* Boston: Allyn & Bacon; Lee, L. (1984). "Sequences in Separation: A Framework for Investigating Endings of the Personal (Romantic) Relationship," *Journal of Social and Personal Relationships,* 1, 49–73.

BOX 11.1   Duck's Model of Relational Termination

BREAKDOWN: *Dissatisfaction with relationship*

THRESHOLD: *"I can't stand it anymore."*

> *Intrapsychic Stage*
> Personal focus on Partner's behavior
> Assess adequacy of Partner's role performance
> Depict and evaluate negative aspects of being in the relationship
> Assess positive aspects of alternative relationships
> Face "express/repress dilemma"

THRESHOLD: *"I'd be justified in withdrawing."*

> *Dyadic Phase*
> Face "confrontation/avoidance dilemma"
> Confront Partner
> Negotiate in "Our Relationship Talks"
> Attempt repair or reconciliation
> Assess joint costs of withdrawal or reduced intimacy

THRESHOLD: *"I mean it."*

> *Social Phase*
> Negotiate postdissolution state with partner
> Initiate gossip/discussion in social network
> Create publically negotiable face-saving/blame-placing stories and accounts
> Consider and face up to implied social network effects
> Call in intervention team?

THRESHOLD: *"It's now inevitable."*

> *Grave Dressing Phase*
> "Getting Over" activity
> Retrospection; reformulative postmortem attribution
> Public Distortion of own version of break up story

From *Personal Relationships 4: Dissolving Personal Relationships,* by Steve Duck. Copyright © 1982 Academic Press, (p. 16). Reprinted by permission from Academic Press and the author.

During the intrapsychic phase, one or both participants begin to focus on the other's behavior. As they observe the other, they may assess the other's role performance and actively assess the relative costs and rewards that the relationship provides. The cost of withdrawal from the relationship and the potential rewards of entering into another relationship may be assessed. During this phase the partners also face the dilemma of expressing or repressing their dissatisfaction. This phase is basically an intrapersonal, and thus subsystem, phase. Baxter and Wilmot contend that interaction about the relationship at this stage may be characterized by "secret tests" of the other. In other words, one partner may actually test the other's devotion or contribution to the relationship. For example, a husband might say to himself, "If she ignores my sexual advances one more time, I'm asking for a divorce." Like the breakdown phase, there is no overt discussion of the relationship.[28]

If one or both relational partners fail the "secret tests" administered by the other, the relationship moves into the dyadic phase. Here overt interaction regarding the dissatisfaction occurs. A shift from a focus on oneself to a focus on the relationship occurs and the couple redefines their relationship and may attempt to repair and/or reconcile the problem. A possible outcome of this interaction may be an alteration of the cost/reward ratio. The couple may also assess the joint costs of termination.

If a reconciliation was not reached during the dyadic phase, the couple moves into the social phase, during which, according to Duck, relational termination is accepted by each partner. Because termination seems inevitable, each will begin to establish new social networks and will attempt to justify the termination to others via face-saving mechanisms such as blaming the other for the dissolution and initiating gossip. Also during this stage, the couple negotiates their postdissolution state. For example, will the couple still interact? Will the couple remain friends?

The grave dressing phase is not an actual "relational" stage, but is essentially a subsystem phase. After the social phase is complete, the system no longer exists. But as Wilmot says, the relationship is not actually over but rather redefined. The influence of the relationship remains forever. Because of the relationship's lasting effects, each person progresses through the grave dressing phase concentrating on getting over the hurt. New systems are generated and one tries to make sense of the relationship and may even publicly distribute his or her own version of the termination. According to Duck, one's version of the termination may change upon reaching the grave dressing phase.

Interaction during Termination

A number of systems theorists in the communication field have investigated interaction during termination. Most relational termination talk probably occurs during the dyadic phase of Duck's relational dissolution model. At this stage the dyadic partners must negotiate the relationship and decide whether to proceed with or terminate the relationship. While researchers have devised numerous labels for the kind of messages people use to terminate relationships, people employ basically three general types of disengagement strategies, including direct, indirect, and positive, tone strategies. As a group of messages, direct strategies typically involve some sort of open confrontation with the other telling them directly that the relationship is over. In some cases direct strategies are used by only one of the partners (i.e., unilaterally). In other cases, direct strategies are used by both members of the dyadic system (i.e., bilaterally).

Indirect strategies are those which provide only subtle hints that the relationship is in trouble. In some cases a relational partner may actually engage in behaviors to stimulate the other to dissolve the relationship.

With positive tone strategies, the relational partner attempts to let the other down as softly as possible and in a positive way by emphasizing concern for the other. Positive tone strategies may involve recounting the positive dimensions of the relationship and how much one regrets leaving it.[29]

Reconciliation versus Termination

Continuing with their focus on dyadic systems and control dynamics, Courtright et al. recently studied interaction that occurs during relational termination. The purpose of their work was to describe control patterns which characterize and differentiate couples during Duck's dyadic phase of relational dissolution. Specifically, they examined and compared the conversations of those couples in the dyadic phase of relational dissolution who eventually terminated their relationship with those who eventually reconciled. Table 11.7 summarizes their findings.

As can be seen in Table 11.7 the control dimension articulated by Millar and Rogers seems to operate differently for those couples who eventually terminate their relationship versus those who reconcile. From the results of their study, couples who eventually reconcile do not give up control but move instead toward transition types of statements (i.e., one across), whereas couples who terminate tend to give up control (i.e., one down).

Systems Theory and Relational Communication

Those scholars adopting a systems view of interpersonal communication have taken a clear departure from traditional interpersonal communication theories. Systems theorists prescribe to the notion that the relationship is the fundamental unit of analysis and that, in and of itself, interaction and relationship are synonymous. Systems theory provides a useful explanation for how relationships initiate, develop, maintain intimacy, and dissolve. Although systems theory is perhaps the youngest of the theoretical approaches described in this book, it has nevertheless provided a rich and heuristic framework for explaining and predicting dyadic human interaction.

TABLE 11.7   Interaction Patterns of Terminated versus Reconciled Couples

Terminated Couples	Reconciled Couples
Avoidance and indirect behaviors	Directness of interaction
Decreased involvement	Increased involvement
Use of questions to serve purposes other than extensions	Use of questions primarily as extensions
Substitution of one down for one up movements	Substitution of one across for one up movements
Frequent complementary transacts	Frequent statements of support
	Less frequent complementary transacts
	More structured and more predictable interacts

*Copyright, © J. A., Millar, F. E., Rogers, L. E., & Bagarozzi, D. (1990). "Interaction Dynamics of Relational Negotiation: Reconciliation versus Termination of Distressed Relationships," *Western Journal of Speech Communication,* 54, 429–453.

CASE STUDY 16   Relational Maintenance and Control

Key Terms

Dominance

Control

Competitive Symmetry

Complementarity

This case study centers on Rick and Carol who have been involved in a romantic relationship for almost two years. Rick is twenty-one years old and Carol is twenty. Both are feeling some dissatisfaction with their relationship, although they have not expressed it directly. They are in the final phases of the intrapsychic stage of relational termination. During this stage relational partners focus on each other's behavior, assess each other's role performance, and actively appraise the balance of costs and rewards associated with the relationship, but they typically do not openly express their dissatisfaction with the relationship. Although Rick and Carol have strong feelings for each other and want the relationship to continue, they know that something must change if the relationship is to survive. Neither understands why they do not seem to get along.

In the following interaction Rick and Carol begin to initially express their dissatisfaction with the relationship. Hence, they are moving from the intrapsychic into the dyadic phase of relational termination. Here, overt interaction about dissatisfaction is expressed and the couple may try to redefine the relationship.

The relational control coding scheme developed by Millar and Rogers provides a very useful diagnostic tool for assessing the communication between Rick and Carol. By looking at their interaction and coding it, clues can be uncovered as to the status of their relationship.

Scene: Rick and Carol's apartment on a Tuesday evening immediately following dinner. Both are sitting at the dinner table discussing the next day's plan.

RICK: So, what time will you be home tomorrow? (**121↓**)	1
CAROL: I work late. (**214↑**)	2
RICK: Yeah, I know that, you work late every night. (**112↑**)	3
CAROL: Then why did you ask? (**223↓**)	4
RICK: I just thought maybe, for once, you could come home and be with me. (**115↑**)	5
CAROL: C'mon, it's not my fault. We're short staffed and someone has to do it. (**212/214↑↑**)	6
RICK: And it's always you. (**113→**)	7
CAROL: As soon as we hire someone it'll help. (**213→**)	8
RICK: Yeah, I've heard that one before. (**112↑**)	9
CAROL: It's true. (**213→**)	10
RICK: Obviously it's you that counts. (**113→**)	11

CAROL: What's that mean? **(222↑)**   12

RICK: Do you ever think about me? I think about you all the time. **(121/111↓↓)**   13

CAROL: Of course I think about you. **(214↑)**   14

RICK: When? **(122↑)**   15

CAROL: All the time. **(214↑)**   16

RICK: Sure doesn't seem like it. Work always comes first. **(112/112↑↑)**   17

CAROL: I can't help it if my job needs me right now. **(213→)**   18

RICK: Maybe I need you sometimes too. **(112↑)**   19

CAROL: I'm trying. You can't admit I'm trying. You refuse to give me credit for   20
anything.**(212↑)**

RICK: I haven't seen much change. **(112↑)**   21

CAROL: Damnit! I've changed a lot! **(212↑)**   22

   (Phone rings)

RICK: Must be work. You answer it. **(115↑)**   23

Obviously Rick and Carol are experiencing some problems in their relationship. By looking closely at the message format, message response modes, message control direction, and transactional control codes, it is easily seen that this interaction is characterized as competitive symmetry. Assertions of nonsupport—that is, one up statements—dominate much of their conversation. Rick and Carol each assert relational control; that is, each asserts his or her definition of the relationship via verbal messages. Their messages indicate that each has a different definition of the relationship and this is at the center of their problems.

On the surface, it appears that Rick and Carol simply disagree about her work schedule, but by employing the relational coding scheme, a different picture emerges. Actually, each person is declaring control without compromise—that is, competitive symmetry—and relational problems result. Try not to be misled by Rick and Carol's talk, it is more than a disagreement about her work schedule.

Context II: Small Group Communication and Systems Theory

As with the study of interpersonal communication, systems theory provides a unique and heuristic framework for the study of small group interaction. Although not shared by everyone in the field, several small group communication scholars have adopted the systems approach in guiding their research. These researchers recognize that adopting the systems approach necessitates omitting other approaches. Hence, while reading this chapter, recognize that certain aspects of small group interaction found in many small group communication textbooks are not addressed by systems theorists. Fisher and Ellis argue, however, that an understanding of communication and the group process depends on the perspective with which one chooses to view it.[30] Thus, while these researchers understand that not everyone adheres to the tenets of systems theory, they believe it offers the best approach to the study of small group interaction. In fact, Beebe and Masterson contend that:

Perhaps the most prevalent approach to small group communication is that of systems theory. In many respects, systems theory represents the most promising perspective on small group communication because it is flexible enough to encompass the vast array of variables that influence small group interaction.[31]

Conceptualizing the Small Group as a System

The principal assumptions regarding systems theory presented in Chapter 10 and those presented earlier in this chapter are exercised by small group researchers adopting a systems approach. But because small groups differ from dyads in important ways, small group system theorists sometimes apply the theory's assumptions differently. Two important ingredients distinguishing the dyad from the small group include the number of available communication channels and coalition formation (see Table 11.8).

As shown in Table 11.8, dyads and groups, as systems, differ regarding the number of potential communication channels and the ability to form coalitions. In a dyadic system, only two possible communication channels exist (it could be argued that only one channel exists), whereas in a small group with a minimum of three people, the number of possible communication channels is tripled by adding only one more person. This results in the possibility of the formation of a communication network, something a dyad cannot form and will be discussed in detail later.

The second important difference is that, with a minimum of three people, the group can engage in an important process known as coalition formation. Often groups are called upon to make decisions, whose importance can range from extremely important (a group of doc-

TABLE 11.8 Dyadic versus Small Group Systems

Channels		Coalition Formation	
Dyad	**Group**	**Dyad**	**Group**
A → B	A → B	A	AB C
A ← B	A ← B	B	AC B
	A ← C		BC A
	B → C		
	B ← C		
	A		

B   C

tors deciding patient therapy) to relatively unimportant (a group of friends deciding where to eat lunch). Many times, group members have different opinions on what the final decision should be. Ideally, the goal of the group is to achieve the best possible solution. In some cases, however, the group is divided and must conduct a kind of vote to decide what to do. In these cases, the majority (i.e., the coalition) wins the right to make the decision. Thus, coalitions occur when three or more persons are involved in the decision-making process and two or more act as a unit against at least one other. Regardless of the outcome, a system still exists. Unlike a dyad where if one person leaves the system dies, group members can leave the system and the system, though changed, remains alive.[32]

Mortensen argues that another important difference between a dyadic and group system is that dyadic systems are vulnerable to highly complementary (one up versus one down) interaction and are much more likely than groups to gravitate toward dominant-submissive interactive patterns. In essence, Mortensen believes this renders the dyad more unstable than a group.[33]

Fisher and Ellis believe that perhaps the most important difference between a dyadic and group system is the feeling of identification one experiences as a member of a group that is absent as a member of a dyad. This identification stems from the interdependency of group members, sometimes referred to as a part of the "groupness" phenomena.[34]

The Small Group as a System

Though small groups and dyads are different kinds of systems, perhaps all of the concepts of general systems theory apply to the small group. From a systems perspective a small group is defined as an open system of behaviors emitted from at least three to as many as ten interdependent components interacting among themselves and with their environment in a self-regulating fashion so as to maintain homeostasis.

Like a dyadic system, the group system is made up of verbal and nonverbal behaviors, not individuals. Although behaviors are intangible (i.e., they cannot be touched or felt), they are observable and are the only way a group can be formed. A very important note to make here is because it is the interdependency of behaviors, and not the individuals themselves, that define a group, it is possible to distinguish between just any collection of people standing around a street corner and a small group system as conceived here. Fisher and Ellis use a basketball team as a good analogy to exemplify this definition. A basketball team does not become a team until their behaviors (running, shooting, and rebounding) are enacted and coordinated interdependently. Five athletes standing around a gymnasium do not constitute a group until they emit their athletic skills interdependently on the court.

The above example leads to an important point about groups not explicitly mentioned in the definition. Another aspect of a small group that separates it from just any collection of people is the notion of a common goal or purpose. While it is the behaviors that make up the system, there must be a reason for these behaviors and this reason must be perceived by each group member. Like a dyad, a group does not become a system until each member recognizes each other and recognizes that each of the other group members recognizes him or her as part of the group. In this way behaviors become interdependent and the group comes into being. For example, five athletes running around shooting baskets in a gymnasium do not become a group system until they come together and coordinate their behaviors interdependently. This notion demonstrates the idea of wholeness. The team is a separate entity, whole by itself, and qualitatively more than the sum of its parts (i.e., five athletes).[35]

Like any other system, groups maintain their homeostasis via self-regulation and control. An important aspect of self-regulation and control involves how a system adapts to its environment based on feedback. Using the basketball team analogy, imagine a team that is losing a game. Losing represents negative feedback, which stimulates some sort of adaptation in the system. As a response to this feedback, the team members perform some self-regulating functions by running faster, increasing their shooting percentage, and grabbing more rebounds. This effort leads to more points and the team begins to win the game. As long as the team continues winning, no change is necessary since they regard winning as their balanced or homeostatic state. Winning can be thought of as a positive feedback.

Keep in mind that an open system can combat entropy via its exchange with the environment. Like any other system, the basketball team is subject to entropy (i.e., disorganization and the tendency toward chaos). Most basketball teams fight off entropy by practicing frequently, which keeps the system in a steady state. Without regular practice, team members might forget plays, defense formats, and the general strategies of play (i.e., become disorganized).

Groups, like any other open system, can reach their goal in any number of ways. Again, a basketball team, whose goal is to win the game, might change its game plan depending on who they are playing. Whenever two teams play each other, and no matter how many times they might play each other, the game will always be different. Keep in mind the old saying that any team can beat any other team on any particular day. To be sure, the end result will always be the same (i.e., one team wins and one loses) but the process by which they achieve the final state (i.e., the end of the game) will be different each time. This represents the idea of equifinality.

Groups exist within a hierarchy of subsystems and suprasystems. The basketball team has at least five subsystems (i.e., the players) and exists within a suprasystem (i.e., a conference). Likewise, the basketball conference consists of subsystems (i.e., the individual teams) and exists within a suprasystem (e.g., a league or division).

Input, Process, and Output Variables

As an open living system, each group is different because it is made up of different inputs, it processes these inputs differently, and it creates different outputs. Input variables are those components from the environment from which a small group is formed, and can include such things as the actual members, resources, the reason for the group's formation, as well as environmental conditions. Process variables are those produced as a function of the group's interaction, including roles, rules, norms, procedures, and relationships between persons. Output variables are those tangible and intangible outcomes that the group produces as a result of its processes. Tangible output variables might include reports or other physical objects (e.g., a car). Intangible output variables might include personal satisfaction, group decisions, recommendations, and group development. Table 11.9 presents a model of the group as an open system of inputs, processes, and outputs.

TABLE 11.9   A Small Group Open System of Inputs, Processes and Outputs

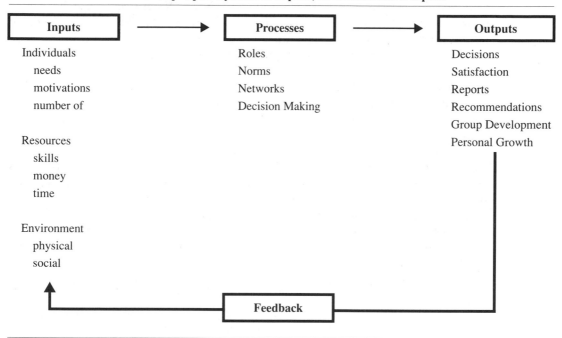

This model is adapted from Brilhart, J. K., & Galanes, G. J. (1989). *Effective Group Discussion,* Dubuque, IA: Brown.

Input Variables

The formation of a group depends on a number of environmental conditions. These conditions, called input variables, are what constitute the group. Perhaps the most important input variable for the formation of a small group system is the individual members. The actual number of members is an important input variable since this will directly impact on the interaction. Earlier a group was defined as having at least three but not more than ten members. The upper limit of ten is rather arbitrary. Some researchers argue that the upper limit of a group is nine, or eleven, or even twelve. Although the exact number is difficult to pin down, most small group researchers agree that the upper limit is somewhere around the number ten, because at about that number, the small group tends to become two small groups. In other words, at or around the number ten, subgroups begin to form.

Many small group researchers agree that the members' needs and motivations, beliefs and attitudes, and values make up another important input variable. Pure systems theorists agree that these may be important areas of research but disregard these variables from their analysis. Recall back to the earlier part of this chapter where Fisher and Ellis argued that since psychological dispositions such as attitudes and beliefs are not perceptibly observable they are not a part of the system itself. Remember that an individual's attitudes or beliefs cannot affect the system, only his or her behaviors can. Internalized phenomena enter the system as behaviors or they do not enter the system at all.[36]

Other input variables investigated by systems theorists include observable physical environmental conditions such as the physical space allowed for interaction and the number of available resources (e.g., facts, media, funds). Also regarded as important is whether or not the group members understand the purpose of the group and its goal. Members whose personal attitudes are at odds with the overall group goal may inhibit the group's progress.[37]

Process Variables

To systems theorists, process variables are perhaps the most important aspects of small group communication. The four process variables to be discussed here include roles, norms, the decision-making process, and networks.

By definition, a role is an expected set of behaviors. The role that one assumes in a group is a function of that person's behavioral contributions to group interaction. If a group member is described as the leader, it is because of that person's interaction. As Cragan and Wright argue, roles can be described as large chunks of one kind of communication coming from a person. Remember, the only thing a person can give to the system is behavior. Because each group member interacts differently, each member assumes a different role, although some roles are shared from time to time. A member's role can be determined by looking at the frequency (i.e., how much), distribution (i.e., to whom), and content (i.e., about what) of his or her communication. Indeed, most systems researchers would rather view group systems as being made up of roles than individuals.[38]

Generally, there are two types of roles, formal and informal. Formal roles are those that have a formally prescribed set of behavioral expectations, such as the president of a bank or a police officer. When one assumes a formal role, behavioral expectations have been drawn up and may even exist in writing. The president of your university or college, for example, is assuming a formal role and is expected to behave in a certain prescribed way. Any severe deviation from the prescribed set of expectations could lead to dismissal.

Informal roles are much less structured and are learned through experience. For example, most of you are assuming the role of son or daughter, brother or sister right now. Your definition of son, daughter, brother, or sister is probably somewhat different from that of the person sitting next to you. Although you both assume the same role, your behavioral expectations are different. You may have experienced a parent saying something like "No child of mine is going to behave like that!" In such cases, the parent is claiming his or her idiosyncratic definition of what is means to be his or her child.

For the most part, group systems create and develop their own group roles, thus they are informal. The college or university group to which you belong may have handed you a "list" of duties to perform when you were elected to a position, but the realization of the role can come about only through your communicative behaviors in the group, thus will be somewhat unique to you. As Fisher and Ellis argue, group members recognize the roles of individuals and develop a set of expectations about each other retrospectively. In other words, after the behaviors have been performed and the expectations have been developed, each member's role becomes easily identified. It is important to note that from a systems perspective any one individual's role is dependent on the interaction of the others in the group. A group member can assume a dominant role only if someone assumes a submissive one. Likewise, a leader cannot lead without followers. Thus, because roles are the product of interaction, they, like interaction, are mutually interdependent. This interdependency renders the group a network of roles, but each group member enacts a role that distinguishes him or her from others in the group.

Benne and Sheats distinguish between task, maintenance, and individual roles as shown in Table 11.10. Benne and Sheats classify twenty-five different roles positions. Task roles are those defined by behaviors that contribute directly to the accomplishment of the group's goal. For example, an information-seeker is one whose interaction is probably characterized by frequent questions. Maintenance roles, sometimes called interpersonal or socioemotional roles, are defined by behaviors that assist in maintaining harmonious and cohesive relationships between group members. For example, a harmonizer engages in interaction that reduces tensions and promotes compromise. Individual roles are those defined by behaviors which are not group oriented but self-centered. The self-centered person performs behaviors that meet his or her personal needs rather than the group's needs. A blocker, for example, interacts in such a way as to prevent progress toward the goal by instigating conflict or topic shifting.

A central notion of systems theory is that interaction, over time, becomes patterned and predictable (e.g., complementary/symmetrical). Likewise, in groups, once the roles have become established, norms begin to emerge. Galanes and Brilhart state that norms establish limitations and restrictions on behavior by specifying what behaviors are not permitted. Fisher and Ellis assert that norms represent conformity by group members to certain behavioral conventions, specified or unspecified.[39] Norms also represent the group's standards. Thus, like roles, norms vary from group to group and can be formally stated, as in the bylaws of an organization, or informally defined, as in the case of a group of friends who agree not to use profanity in front of each other.

Norms develop out of a pattern of repetitious behaviors enacted by group members and through the process of self-regulation, control, and feedback. As group members interact, the system is created. During interaction, certain behaviors will receive positive sanctions (i.e.,

TABLE 11.10   Task, Maintenance, and Individual Roles

Task	Maintenance	Individual
Initiator	Encourager	Aggressor
Information-Seeker	Harmonizer	Blocker
Opinion-Seeker	Compromiser	Recognition-Seeker
Information-Giver	Gatekeeper	Self-Confessor
Elaborator	Group Observer	Playboy
Coordinator	Follower	Dominator
Orienter		Help-Seeker
Evaluator-Critic		Special-Interest pleader
Energizer		
Recorder		
Procedural technician		

Benne, K. D., & Sheats, P. (1948). "Functional Roles of Group Members," *Journal of Social Issues, 4,* 41–49.

positive feedback) while others receive negative sanctions (i.e., negative feedback). The system will adjust to this feedback by continuing to enact those behaviors receiving positive feedback and eliminating or controlling those behaviors receiving negative feedback. Hence, over time, positively sanctioned behaviors are enacted again and again (i.e., they become repetitious and patterned) and eventually become norms for the group. Figure 11.4 presents a simple feedback model of the norming processes in small group systems.

Perhaps the most important process in which a group engages is the decision-making process, a subset of problem solving. Problem solving is a comprehensive multistage procedure which usually requires that a group make several decisions. Decision making, on the other hand, involves the group selecting between two or more alternatives. Typically, in decision-making situations, at least two alternatives exist from which the group is to select one. In problem-solving situations, the group may have to not only select a solution, but also create one. Fisher and Ellis define a decision as the outcome of group interaction and is inevitably a choice made by group members. They also contend that groups do not make decisions but rather that decisions emerge from group interaction. After observing the acts and interacts of decision-making groups, they discovered that most decisions emerge from groups gradually and cumulatively through a series of four phases. Table 11.11 profiles the four-phase decision-making model they developed. In phase one of the model the group is said to experience primary tension, which is defined by Beebe and Mastersen as tension or anxiety that occurs when a group first meets. Once the group moves into the second phase, Fisher and Ellis observed that the group experiences secondary tension, which occurs when the group experiences conflict over norms, roles, and differences among members' opinions. In the third phase of the model, both primary and secondary tension recur. Finally, in phase four, most of the tension is gone and the group achieves consensus.

The final group process to be discussed here is the formation and development of system networks. From a systems perspective, a network is what the system looks like struc-

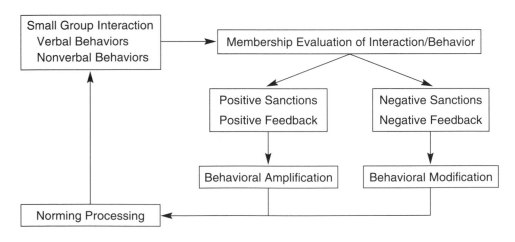

**FIGURE 11.4   A Feedback Loop Model of Small Group Interaction
Norming Processes**

Based on Fisher, B.A., & Ellis, D. G. (1990). *Small Group Decision Making: Communication and the Group Process,* New York: McGraw-Hill.

TABLE 11.11   Four-Phase Model of Group System Decision Making

Phase 1: Orientation	Phase 2: Conflict Phase
Initial Period of Awkwardness	Ideational Conflict
Nervous Apprehensive Interaction	Group Direction Is Clear
Primary Tensions	Polarization of Attitudes
Few Assertions	Coalition Formation
Tentative Opinion Giving	Assertive Interaction
Ambiguous Opinions Expressed	Opinions Clearly Expressed

Phase 4: Reinforcement	Phase 3: Emergence
Achieve Consensus	Conflict & Dissent Dissipate
Positive Reinforcement of Others	Coalitions Weaken
Expressions of Agreement	Recurrence of Ambiguity
Dissent Is Gone	One Decision Emerges
Spirit of Unity	Support of Decision Ignites
Little Tension	Leadership Emerges
Group Commitment of Decision	
Happy Interaction	

Fisher, B. A., & Ellis, D. G. (1990). *Small Group Discussion Making: Communication and the Group Process,* New York: McGraw-Hill.

turally; how the system is put together. Fisher and Ellis describe a network as a pattern of channel linkages among individual members of the group.[40] Without regard to the content of a message, a network outlines a system in terms of who is sending messages to whom. As the process of group interaction develops, some members interact with certain members quite frequently and with others much less frequently. As the pattern of interaction stabilizes, the communication network begins to emerge and reflects the social structure of the group. Figure 11.5 presents five of the most common networks in small groups.

Systemic networks differ from one another in terms of each member's centrality and distance from each of the other members in the system. Distance refers to the sum of the communicative links required for a message sent from one person to reach the intended receiver. The minimum distance between two group members would be one. In a five-member group, the maximum distance would be four. Centrality refers to the sum of the distances between a member's position in a group and all of the other positions in the network. The lower the sum, the more central the position. The numbers in parentheses represent each member's centrality. Of the groups represented in Figure 11.5, the wheel and chain networks are regarded as the most centralized networks and the circle is the least centralized, or decentralized. Centralized networks function with more speed and efficiency and are faster and more accurate at solving simple problems, although decentralized networks seem to be better at solving complex problems. Members of decentralized networks are more satisfied with their group than are members of centralized networks. In essence,

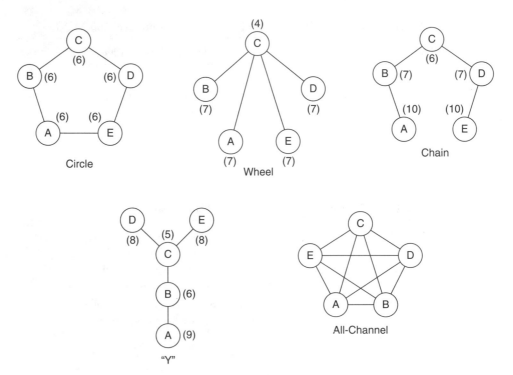

FIGURE 11.5   Five Common Small Group System Networks

Small Group Decision Making; Communication and the Group Process, by B. A. Fisher and D. G. Ellis. Copyright © 1990, McGraw-Hill. Reprinted with permisson from McGraw-Hill.

centralized networks appear to be superior at task-related functions, whereas decentralized networks may be more cohesive in the long run.

Output Variables

Output variables are the outcome of the combination of group inputs and processes. Outputs are oftentimes called the group's product. Group products can be tangible outputs—such as a report, paper, car, or building—or intangible outputs—such as membership satisfaction, individual growth, and the development of interpersonal relationships. In addition, the product of a group can be a restructuring of the group itself. For example, a group may decide to change its roles, norms, decision-making process, or network. Obviously, depending on the inputs and group processes, the product of each particular group varies.

Measuring Group System Behavior: Interaction Analysis

B. Aubrey Fisher developed a method for observing small group interaction, some of which resembles that of Millar and Rogers's method of analyzing the control dimension in dyadic systems. Fisher's method is called "interaction analysis" and is based on the "system interact model," or the idea of taking the whole system and breaking it down into its component parts. By definition, the component parts of a communication system are behaviors. Recall that any particular behavior is called an act and that two contiguous acts are called an inter-act. Thus, like Millar and Rogers, Fisher breaks down the small group system into a series of interacts, thus the name "interact system model."

Recall that in the Millar and Rogers relational control coding scheme, acts were as-signed a three-digit code based on the speaker, the act's grammatical form (e.g., assertion, question, etc.), and the act's response mode (e.g., support, nonsupport, etc.). Following this, and based on the three-digit code, each act was assigned a control designation code (one up, one down, etc.). Fisher's scheme, though different, follows a similar logic in coding small group interaction. Whenever a group member contributes an act to the small group discussion, his or her contribution is coded into one of six categories defined in Table 11.12.

Given the coding scheme in Table 11.12, the following segment of group interaction provides an example of how acts can be coded. The symbols to the left of each act indicate that act's classification based on the coding scheme.

TABLE 11.12   Message Categories in Fisher's Interaction Analysis

Code	Category	Definition
1	Interpretation f—favorable toward the decision u—unfavorable toward decision ab—ambiguous toward decision with bivalued (both favorable and unfavorable) evaluation an—ambiguous toward the decision with neutral evaluation	A simple value judgement without evidence, reasons, or explanations.
2	Substantiation	A value judgment that includes supporting evidence or reasons
3	Clarification	An act that restates some previous act in more concrete language
4	Modification	An act that functions to amend a decision under consideration
5	Agreement	An act that expresses support to the immediately preceding act
6	Disagreement	An act that expresses nonsupport to the immediately preceding act
0	Initiation	Used in conjunction with the above symbols to indicate that act as the one which originates a new decision proposal. The symbol will appear with a subscript indicating which new decision proposal it is.
D	Reintroduction	Indicates when a decision proposal has been reintroduced that has previously been discussed by the group. The symbol will have a subscripted number showing how many times it has been reintroduced.

Fisher, B. A., & Ellis, D. G. (1990). *Small Group Discussion Making: Communication and the Group Process,* New York: McGraw-Hill.

1an0	A: Do we want to spend another $100 to upgrade our computer software?
3	B: The upgrade of what?
3	A: For our computer software, how much should we budget?
1u	C: I'd rather not discuss it now.
1u	B: Let's drop it, not talk about it.
2f	A: But if we're setting the budget, we need to know how much we're planning on allocating to software. I think we need to know it, anyway.
6	C: No.
2u	D: But knowing the amount won't influence our decision to buy another computer or not.
5	C: Yep, that's right.
2ab	A: Well, the good thing about discussing it is that we'll know, the bad thing is that it probably won't matter anyway.
5 C:	Yes, exactly.

Once the acts are coded into categories, they are divided into interacts. The interacts are then tabulated into the following 12 by 12 grid (see Figure 11.6). Thus, a possible 144 interacts could occur during group interaction. Along the first row (the side) of the matrix

Subsequent acts

Antecedent acts	1f	1u	1ab	1an	2f	2u	2ab	2an	3	4	5	6
1f												
1u		1			1							
1ab												
1an									1			
2f						1						1
2u						1	3		1	2		
2ab												
2an												
3		1			1				2			
4												
5						1						
6						1						

FIGURE 11.6   Matrix of Interacts

From *Small Group Decision Making: Communication and the Group Process* by B. A. Fisher and D. G. Ellis. Copyright © 1990, McGraw-Hill. Reprinted with permission from McGraw-Hill.

are the categories of the interaction analysis pertaining to the first act of the interact, which are called the antecedent acts. Along the first column (the top) of the matrix are the same categories as in the first row, but these are used to code the second act of the interact, called the subsequent act. Interacts are charted on this matrix so that patterns and quantities of interacts can be seen.[41] Finally, the acts are coded according to the following relational interaction analysis (REL/COM) which is very similar to the Millar and Rogers control dimension coding scheme.

Like the Millar and Rogers control coding scheme, each act is assigned a REL/COM code in terms of how it relates to the immediately preceding act. Any two acts are then combined into interacts whereby it is possible to find patterns of dominance, submissiveness, deference, and equivalence in small group decision-making processes.

CASE STUDY 17   Small Group Input-Process-Output Decision Making

Key Terms

Inputs

Process

Outputs

Roles

Negative Feedback

Norming

In this case study a small group of students has gathered to discuss where they are going to study for an upcoming examination in a class in which they are all enrolled. The systems concepts of inputs, processes, outputs, role, and norm development and negative feedback can be applied to this interaction.

Scene: A group of students sitting together in a classroom immediately following class where an examination is scheduled for the next day.

BRIAN: Man... Neuliep's class really sucks. (Sighs)	1
TONY: No kiddin' it's *the* worst... woooo... really lame.	2
HEIDI: Oh, I don't know... I'm learning something.	3
BRIAN: (Fade)... women.	4
HEIDI: (To BRIAN) Go away... (Sighs)	5

(Angie enters)

ANGIE: Hello scholars! (Very chipper and alert)	6
BRIAN: Hey baby. (Thinks he's being cool)	7
ANGIE: BRIAN, you're weird.	8
HEIDI: I agree. Hello, ANGIE.	9

Continued

CASE STUDY 17   *Continued*

TONY: (To ANGIE) What's hapnin'?	10
ANGIE: So...where are we going to study? (Smiles)	11
BRIAN: Why study? We'll all flunk.	12
HEIDI: I don't think I will flunk, BRIAN.	13
BRIAN: Take a hike.	14
TONY: Wanna go to the library?	15
HEIDI: The library can be awfully busy and cumbersome at times, not at all condu- cive to studying.	16
BRIAN: Yeah...but all my friends meet there. We could throw books an' stuff...	17
TONY: Hey man, lighten up, do you wanna be in this group or not?	18
BRIAN: Sure I do...alright, I know what ya mean. I'm sorry.	19
ANGIE: Well...does anyone have a house or dorm we could go to?	20
HEIDI: I have a nice place to study. We could meet there.	21
ANGIE: I vote we go to HEIDI's house.	22
TONY: Sounds good.	23
BRIAN: Yeah...good idea.	24
ANGIE: This will be great! We'll do better on the test!	25
HEIDI: I'm glad we got together to figure out what we're going to do.	26

Many of the small group systems concepts can be applied to this interaction. The system is the group itself and the behaviors contributed by each member. The subsystems include the individuals and the suprasystem could be the entire class. Openness is demonstrated by Angie's entrance between lines 5 and 6; the system allows others to enter. The goal is to find a place to study. The goal can be reached in a number of ways, including going to the library, Heidi's house, or someplace else, hence equifinality is demonstrated. Each act is interdependent on the others. For example, Angie tells Brian he is weird because he calls her "baby." She probably would not call Brian weird if he had responded in a more appropriate manner.

The group can be seen as a system of inputs-processes-outputs. The inputs include the individual members of the group. The members bring with them certain similar needs and goals. Each needs to study for exam and each has a goal of performing well on the exam. They each bring to the group individual resources to accomplish the goal. For example, each can offer his or her own dorm or apartment as a location for the group to study. The physical environment serves as an input to the group as well. Here the "academic" environment influences the group's behavior; that is, to find a place to study. The social environment also contributes to the group's behavior. These members have a student-to-student relationship. This affects their decision to study in a quiet place rather than the library for the upcoming examination.

Two group processes that can be seen in the interaction include role performance and norming behaviors. Recall that there are three main types of roles, including task, maintenance, and individual roles. Brian takes on the task role of evaluator-critic (line 1), and the individual roles of blocker (line 11), aggressor (line 13), and playboy (lines 4 and 7). Heidi assumes the task role of information-giver (lines 12, 15, and 20) and the maintenance role of compromiser (line 20). Tony takes on the task role of opinion-seeker (line 14) and the maintenance role of harmonizer (line 17). Finally, Angie assumes the task role of initiator (line 10) and information-seeker (line 19) and the maintenance role of encourager (line 6).

Throughout the interaction a group norm is established as a result of Brian's inappropriate behavior. Brian's behavior in lines 4, 7, 11, and 16 is met with negative feedback in lines 5, 8, 12, and 17. As Fisher and Ellis's feedback loop model of small group interaction norming processes indicates, such negative feedback should result in Brian modifying his behavior, thus establishing the norm or acceptable pattern of behavior for the group. No one except Brian acts as he does. Finally, in line 18 Brian modifies his behavior with an apology and indicates that the decision to study at Heidi's house is a good idea (line 23). Neither of those two behaviors are met with negative feedback indicating to Brian that such behaviors are acceptable.

Two group outputs seen in this interaction include the final decision to study at Heidi's house (lines 20 through 25) and the satisfaction that the members express about their group meeting and the decision (lines 22 through 25). For Brian an additional output is personal growth. If the group comes together and has a productive study session and the members eventually perform well on the exam, this will feedback to each member and serve as an input the next time the group comes together.

Context III: Organizational Communication

Many communication scholars adopting a systems perspective focus their attention on communication as it exists within the organization. Viewing the organization as a system did not originate with communication scholars, however. Perhaps the first to articulate systems terminology with organizations were Daniel Katz and Robert Kahn. They argued that an organization was an open system that ingested energy from its environment, transformed the energy, and expended it back into the environment. This notion has been called the input-throughput-output cycle and conceptually is very similar to the small group input-process-output model discussed above. But, as will be shown in this chapter, dyads, small groups, and organizations are different kinds of systems. Organizational communication scholars focus on the input, throughput, and output of information in organizations.[42]

In addition to the input-throughput-output model, some systems theorists studying organizational communication adopt what is called a structural-functional perspective.[43] The structure of a communication system (or of any system) is the set of connections or relationships among the component parts. For example, the connection or relationship between the engine and the wheels (two component parts of an automobile) is that the engine rotates the transmission which is connected to the axle which turns the wheels which propels the system. In the dyadic communication system, the two most basic component parts are the individuals and the talk between them. The structure of a small group might be its particular network. A structural analysis of a system answers the question, "How is the system put together?"

In addition to its structural qualities, systems theorists following a structural-functional perspective examine the function of a system, or of a part of the system. Simply defined, the function of a system is simply whatever it does. More specifically, it is something that the system must do such that if the function were not performed, the system would break down.[44] A functional analysis of a system answers the question, "What does the system do?" Dyads develop relationships, small groups make decisions, organizations control and coordinate people and resources via the communication process. Thus, many systems theorists studying organizational communication focus on how the system's communication is structured and how it functions.

Organizations as Systems

When defined as systems, organizations are open systems composed of component parts that interrelate to form a whole. Like dyads and small groups, however, the nature of the component parts and their interrelationships in the organization are different than in other types of communication systems. Lawrence and Lorsch define an organization as:

> At the most general level we find it useful to view an organization as an open system in which the behaviors of members are themselves interrelated. The behaviors of members of an organization are also interdependent with the formal organization, the tasks to be accomplished, the personalities of other individuals, and the unwritten rules about appropriate behavior from a member.[45]

Given their definition, the behavior of any individual in the organization is determined by the personalities of other individuals, the nature of the task performed, and the rewards associated with task completion. In other words, they are all interrelated and interdependent.

Like other systems discussed in this chapter, an organization is an open system, which means that its boundaries permit interaction with the environment. Organizations must be open systems if they are to survive. They receive energy from the environment (i.e., inputs) in the form of workers, raw materials, and information, and they send energy back into the environment (i.e., outputs) in the form of products, services, pollution, and information. In the middle of this process, the organization transforms the inputs. Constant interaction with its environment keeps the organization dynamic and alive.[46]

Two other factors that ensure the survivability of an organizational system are feedback and balance. Remember that systems combat entropy by maintaining a balanced or homeostatic state. Such balance is achieved by constant feedback accompanied by self-regulation. In organizational systems, some of the system's outputs are fed back into the organization as new inputs. Keep in mind that the organizational system affects and is influenced by its environment. Thus, whenever the system exports energy into its environment it alters the environment; the same environment from which it imports its energy. Goldhaber points to the example of a college or university where students who receive an education regenerate the college or university by getting jobs and paying taxes, some of which are appropriated to support higher education. The organizational system (i.e., college) must maintain a balanced flow of inputs (i.e., new students), transform them (i.e., educate them), and export them back into the environment. As long as the college imports more energy than it exports, it can survive. Any college that graduates one thousand students one year but enrolls only two hundred the next is not maintaining a balanced state and cannot survive very long.[47]

Organizational systems are whole because of the relationship between and interdependency of their component parts. A college or university can be thought of as an open system that enrolls, educates, and graduates students. The system has many component parts working interdependently to see that this process continues in a homeostatic state. The college's admissions office works closely with the external environment to gather inputs, the faculty transforms the inputs, and the administration graduates them and sends them back into the environment. None of this process would be possible without the support of the physical maintenance of the campus, the food services, student life offices, alumni offices, and the library staff to name only a few. Remove any one of these ingredients and every other aspect of the process is affected. Without the faculty there would be no students. Without students there would be no need for faculty. Without the physical college, there would be no need for students or faculty. Without students or faculty, we would not need a physical campus, and the list of interdependent relationships within an organizational system goes on and on.

Farace, Monge, and Russell indicate that there are four major organizational communication system levels. Figure 11.7 on page 344 outlines each of these levels.

While all four systems levels are important areas of study for the systems theorist, the individual level is perhaps the least important. At this level, the focus is on individual differences rather than on the individual as an interdependent part of the system.

Perhaps more than either a dyadic or small group system, the organizational system depends on the environment for its ultimate survival. An organizational system's environment includes all of the physical and social factors that affect the decision-making behaviors of individuals in the system. Organizations have both an internal and external environment. The internal environment includes the physical layout, workers, managers, and administration components. The external environment includes the geographical location, weather, customers, suppliers, competitors, and technology. Organizations are more sensitive to their environment because they exist by exchanging environmental inputs with outputs. When the external environment changes, the inputs available to the organization (and critical for its survival) also change. The organization is in a constant state of uncertainty. Organizational systems must constantly monitor the external environmental changes because they place new demands on the organization. Organizations must respond by creating and exchanging information with their internal and external environment.[48]

Organizational Communication

Systems theorists in the communication field studying organizations focus their attention on communication within the organizational system. Organizational communication is both similar to and different from other kinds of communication and it involves the encoding and decoding of messages within a specified context. Wilson, Goodall, and Waagen define organizational communication as "an evolutionary, culturally dependent process of sharing information and creating relationships in environments designed for manageable, cooperative, goal-oriented behavior."[49] Reflecting a systems perspective, Goldhaber defines orga-

Level One: The Individual

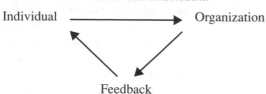

How does the individual communicate to and receive communication from the organization?

How much communication is there between the individual and the organization (e.g., duration and frequency of interpersonal contacts and exposure to organizational printed material)?

What channels does the individual use to interact with the organization?

What are the effects of organizational information on the individual's opinions, knowledge, or behaviors?

Level Two: The Dyad

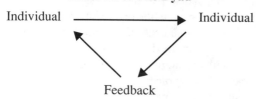

Focus on relational control: How much influence or direction does one member have on another?

Are relationships complementary or symmetrical?

What are the rules that guide and shape interaction between dyads?

How do managers and subordinates interact?

Level Three: Groups

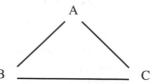

What kinds of groups exist in the organization (e.g., work, friends, kinships?)

What are the networks in organizational groups?

Level Four: The Organization

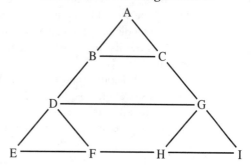

How does the organization interact with its environment?

What is the network of interaction within the organization?

What are the relationships between the individual group networks and other organizational activities?

FIGURE 11.7   Four Organizational System Levels

Based on Farace, R. V., Monge, P. R., & Russell, H. (1977). *Communicating and Organizing.* Reading, MA: Addison-Wesley.

nizational communication as "the process of creating and exchanging messages within a network of interdependent relationships to cope with environmental uncertainty."[50] In addition, Goldhaber stresses that organizational communication occurs (a) in an open system that is influenced by its environment, (b) involves the flow, purpose, direction, and medium of messages, and (b) includes people and their attitudes, feelings, relationships with others, and skills.

Central to the study of organizational communication is the input, throughput, and output of information. Shockley-Zalabak argues that understanding the relationship between external environment information and internal information processing is key to understanding organizational communication. Information from the external environment is called communication inputs. This kind of information affects the organization by influencing the decision-making process of the entire organizational system. For example, a new law restricting the amount of pollution an organization can produce would be considered a communication input. Communication throughputs are the transformations that the organization makes on the communication inputs. An organization may decide, for example, to drastically change its manufacturing process based on the new law restricting pollution amounts. Communication outputs are messages sent to the external environment from within the organization. Outputs are the result of the input and throughput process. The organization may hold a press conference to announce its new manufacturing process and to show its publics how little pollution it will produce.[51]

The Structure of Organizational Systems and Organizational Communication

As mentioned earlier, the structure of an organization or of organizational communication refers to what the system looks like. Figure 11.8 on page 346 presents a hypothetical organizational structure. In this hypothetical organization, we can see that its structure is made up of six components, including (a) social system, (b) technology, (c) external environment, (d) dominant coalition, (e) formal organizational arrangements, and (f) employees and other tangible assets. Relating to organizational communication, structure refers to the patterns and regularities of interaction between the organization's components. How information travels through these components defines the structure of the communication, or the movement, rather than the content, of messages. In studying an organization's communication structure, the systems theorist examines the movement of messages through various channels (e.g., networks), message direction in networks, and the persons influential in the network (i.e., network roles).[52]

Like a dyadic and small group system, organizational systems are defined by the interactions of the individual members. According to systems theory, and other organizational approaches, the channels people use to interact in an organization are called networks. Simply stated, networking is concerned with who communicates with whom; who is sending the messages and who is receiving them. Farace et al. define a network as a pattern of repetitious interaction. Shockley-Zalabak defines a network as a formal or informal pattern of communication that links organizational members. Formal networks are the official channels through which messages are exchanged (e.g., a letter from the accounts payable department inquiring about certain charges). Informal networks are the unofficial channels through which communication flows (e.g., employees exchanging rumors about layoffs). Unofficial networks, sometimes called "the grapevine," emerge from formal networks and are formed by organizational members who develop interpersonal relationships.

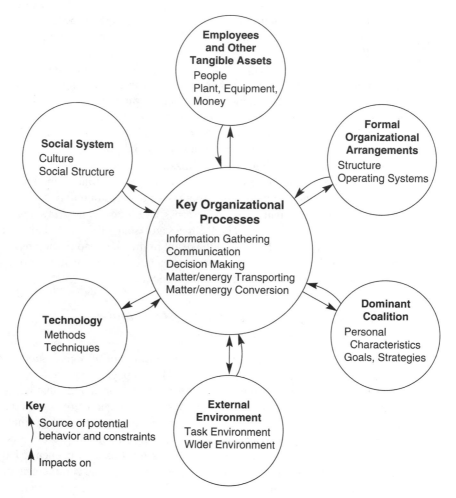

FIGURE 11.8 **Hypothetical Organizational Structure**

John P. Kotter, *Organizational Dynamics: Diagnosis and Intervention* (pg. 24), © 1978 by Addison-Wesley Publishing Company, Inc. Reprinted by permission of the publisher.

Most organizational networks are made up of several channels, but as Goldhaber indicates, a network can be defined by as few as two people. Communication channels between two or more individuals are called network links. In examining networks, Farace et al. point to three important characteristics of communication links, including symmetry, strength, and reciprocity. Symmetrical links are those in which the individuals equally exchange information with each other. The most common form of symmetrical link occurs in an informal network where friends exchange information on an equal basis. An asymmetrical link is established when there is an unequal exchange of information between organizational members—for example, a boss giving instructions to his or her subordinates. Asymmetrical links are typically one-way communication channels.

The second link property is strength. Link strength refers to the frequency and length of interaction between individuals. Strong links are those characterized by high frequency and duration. Weak links are those characterized by low frequency and short duration of interaction. The final property is reciprocity, which describes the agreement among organizational members about their networks links. For example, organizational members may totally disagree about their interaction with each other or they may be in complete agreement. Figure 11.9 presents several different organizational networks.

As can seen in Figure 11.9, messages generally flow in three directions—up, down, and across. The direction of the information exchange can usually help determine the relationship between interactants. For example, downward communication generally refers to messages which flow from superiors to subordinates, such as in relationships of authority, tradition, and prestige. Katz and Kahn provide five examples of downward communication including job instructions, job rationale, procedures and practices, feedback, and the indoctrination of goals.

Upward communication is that which originates in lower levels of the organization and travels toward the top. As with downward channels, upward channels define levels of authority. Upward communication, which serves as a source of feedback for management and as a morale builder for subordinates, comes in the form of questions, feedback, and suggestions. Upward and downward communication are said to exist in vertical or hierarchical organizational networks.

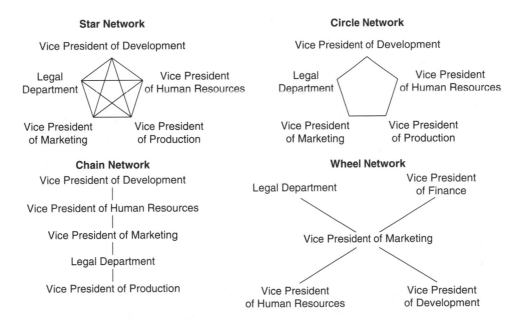

FIGURE 11.9   Organizational Communication Networks

Cummings, H. W., Long, L. W., & Lewis, M. L. (1987). *Managing Communication in Organizations: An Introduction,* Dubuque, IA: Gorush Scarisbrick Publisher; Goldhaber, G. M. (1993). *Organizational Communication,* (6th Ed.), Madison, WI: Brown & Benchmark.

Horizontal communication flows laterally across the organization through members of equal status. Goldhaber indicates that horizontal communication usually relates to task or human purposes, coordination, problem solving, conflict resolution, and information sharing. Goldhaber, Shockley-Zalabak, and others indicate that horizontal communication is usually quicker than vertical communication.[53]

In all organizational networks, members assume certain roles, and these roles determine how the information flows through the system. Shockley-Zalabak and others have distinguished between six network roles, including liaisons, bridges, isolates, gatekeepers, participants, and nonparticipants. Remember that roles are defined as expected sets of behaviors. Shockley-Zalabak defines a liaison as someone who links or connects groups with common information without being a member of either group. A bridge is a member of one group and sends information from that group to another group. An isolate is an individual with very little or no communication links in the organization. Individuals become isolated because of fear or apprehension about communicating in the network. In Figure 11.10, the role of liaison, bridge, and isolate can be seen.

The gatekeeper in a communication network controls the flow of information through the channels. They serve an important filtering function since they receive information from several sources and then decide who else should receive it. Managers are gatekeepers

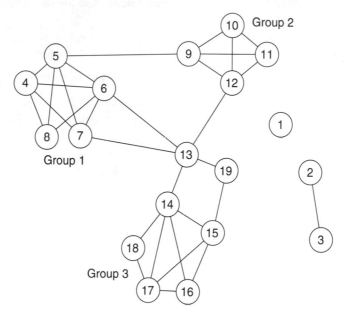

Groups	Group Linkers	Isolates
Group 1 – 4, 5, 6, 7, 8	Bridges – 5, 9	True Isolate – 1
Group 2 – 9, 10, 11, 12	Liaison – 13	Isolated Dyad – 2, 3
Group 3 – 14, 15, 16, 17, 18	Other – 19	

FIGURE 11.10   Communication Network Link Roles

From *Communicating and Organizing,* by R. Farace, P. Monge, & H. Russell. Copyright © 1977 Addison-Wesley. Reprinted by permission from McGraw-Hill who owns the copyright.

in relation to their subordinates, just as secretaries are gatekeepers controlling who can interact with the boss. The other individuals in the organizational network who are neither bridges, liaisons, isolates, nor gatekeepers are called participants. They interact within the network but with less influence than the above-described roles. Nonparticipants are those individuals who belong to the network but do not interact as much as participants. Isolates and nonparticipants differ in the extent that nonparticipants have communication abilities but do not use them by choice, not out of fear or apprehension.

The Function of Organizational Communication

The third area of focus in a structural-functional systems perspective is the function. Whereas structure refers to the system's interaction patterns and regularities, the function of the system refers to the use of interaction to achieve different goals and purposes. In other words, what does communication do in an organizational system and how does it contribute to the overall functioning of the system?

Many researchers in the organizational communication field have devised their own classification schemes of organizational communication functions (see Table 11.13).

Although all of the authors classify organizational communication functions under different headings, there is a clear pattern. While they may quibble over titles, it appears clear that there are at least three basic functions of organizational communication, including production, maintenance, and innovation.

Production messages are those that facilitate the achievement of the organization's overall goal or product. Farace et al. state that messages serving a production function are those that direct, coordinate, regulate, and facilitate the output or product. Such messages may include official policies, organizational rules and regulations, employee handbooks, and those messages that specify the type or amount of output required of all organizational members. Shockley-Zalabak argues that the effectiveness of an organization's production messages can be evaluated by how well members understand and perform their tasks. Most production messages flow through formal communication networks.

TABLE 11.13   Functions of Organizational Communication

Authors	Communicative Functions			
Redding	Task	Maintenance	Human	
Katz & Kahn	Production	Maintenance	Adaption	Management
Shockley-Zalabak	Organizing	Relationship	Change	
Berlo	Production	Maintenance	Innovation	
Farace, Monge, & Russell	Production	Maintenance	Innovation	

Redding, W. C. (1972). *Communication within the Organization,* New York: Industrial Communication Council; Farace, R. V., Monge, P. R., & Russell, H. (1977). *Communicating and Organizing,* Reading, MA: Addison-Wesley; Shockley-Zalabak, P. (1991). *Fundamentals of Organizational Communication,* New York: Longman; Berlo, D. K. (1969). *Human Communication: The Basic Proposition,* Unpublished paper. Department of Communication, Michigan State University; Katz, D., & Kahn, R. (1977). *The Social Psychology of Organizations,* New York: Wiley & Sons.

Maintenance messages serve an interpersonal function. They help establish and maintain (a) members' self-concept, (b) interpersonal relationships among members, and (c) the production of the organization. In addition, these messages are designed to help the individual member feel a part of the system and that he or she belongs in the organization and is an important ingredient. Maintenance messages can range from informal conversations between horizontal role positions, to vertical communication between superior and subordinate. Whereas production messages are sometimes thought of as "organizational messages," maintenance messages are sometimes called "human messages."

The final category is innovation messages, sometimes called change messages. These help the system adapt to both internal and external environmental changes. Farace et al. suggest that there are two aspects of innovation messages. The first function is to elicit new ideas for changing the organization from within the system in order to increase efficiency, morale, or other goals. The second function is to influence organizational members to adopt new policies, procedures, or practices.

The Structural-Functional Approach

The structural-functional approach to organizational communication helps the organizational communication researcher describe and understand how organizational messages are put together and how they function to produce, maintain, and change organizations. Researchers exercising this approach should allow the theory to guide their work and help them make decisions about the nature of organizational communication.

CASE STUDY 18   Information Flow at St. Academia College

Key Terms

System, Subsystem, Suprasystem

Feedback, Equifinality, Inputs/Outputs

Star Network

Network Roles

Organizational Communication Functions

This case study centers around St. Academia College (hereafter called St. A.), a small parochial liberal arts college with about two thousand students in the midwestern United States. Tuition at St. A. is competitive with other parochial liberal arts colleges but relatively high compared with state institutions. Almost 70 percent of the total operating budget is based on student tuition. The student population at St. A. is homogeneous. Approximately 90 percent of the students have similar racial, religious, and socioeconomic backgrounds. Unfortunately for St. A. and the other similar colleges, recent demographic trends have led to lower enrollments. Because St. A.'s budget is tuition driven, lower enrollments have led to budget cuts and possible layoffs.

St. A. is the system, its subsystems include the administration, faculty, students, support staff, and facilities. The suprasystem is the environment within which St. A. exchanges matter. In this case the suprasystem is the local community. St. A. is an open system. Perhaps the most important input is new students (i.e., freshmen) who enter the system from the environment. The most important output is also students (i.e., seniors) who leave the system as they graduate. St. A. receives a variety of other kinds of environmental input as well, including new faculty members, information from the local community in the form of positive or negative feedback, and money in the form of tuition, grants, and donations. In addition to graduating seniors, St. A. has various other forms of output, including community service projects and money in the form of wages and salaries. The foremost goal of St. A. is to educate students. How the students become educated varies. Students can major is a variety of areas, including biology, business, communication, education, math, physics, and zoology. Hence, the goal of educating students is accomplished in a variety of ways; that is, equifinality.

Various forms of feedback occur at St. A. Students receive feedback from their professors in the form of grades. Professors receive feedback from students in the form of teacher evaluations. Recently a national magazine cited St. A. as one of the best small colleges in its region; a form of positive feedback from the environment. Also recently, local citizens complained to the president of St. A. that student parties were out of control; a form of negative feedback.

The different subsystems within St. A. are interdependent. For example, without students, the faculty could not teach. Without faculty, the students could not learn. The various subsystems at St. A. formally interact with one another in a star network.

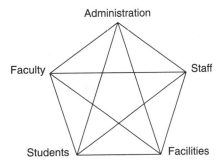

Like most organizations, informal interaction channels include the St. A. grapevine. For example, a recent memo was sent to all administration, faculty, and staff, but not students. The memo was sent from Robert Parker, an associate vice president, and was quite brief and simply read:

> *John Smith has resigned his position as director of admissions effective immediately. Susan Jones has been named acting director of admissions and will be happy to work with you on matters related to admissions.*

Continued

CASE STUDY 18   *Continued*

Because the memo came from an associate vice president it represented downward communication. As an associate vice president, Parker's network role is that of bridge. Recall that a network bridge is a member of one group who communicates information from his or her group to another group or groups. Because the memo was so brief, Parker also serves as a gatekeeper; the reason for Smith's resignation is not disclosed. The actual message functions primarily as a production message since it relays information about official college business. The information functions in a maintenance capacity as well since it deals with the relationships. For example, if a member of the college community deals directly with the director of admissions, his or her relationship with that person has changed.

Once the memo was received by the various subsystems, the grapevine went into operation. Because the memo lacked any explanation for John Smith's resignation, many felt that he had actually been fired. Members of the admissions staff, for example, thought there may be more layoffs. Some members of the faculty felt that perhaps Smith had committed some impropriety.

Summary

The systems approach to communication offers one of the most promising and heuristic theoretical frameworks for the field of human communication. Unlike other approaches, systems theory specifically focuses on interaction, thus is truly a communication theory. Although this theory has much to offer, critics argue that it is far too broad and general. Some have argued that the term *system* itself is vague and lacks definitional boundaries. Indeed, others contend that if systems terminology can be applied to all scientific disciplines, then it really applies to none of them.

The purpose of this book and of this chapter is not to influence your choice of theoretical perspectives but only to inform you of the choices you have in communication to guide your thinking about the subject. In this chapter, you have seen how one theoretical approach applies to communication in general and as well as to specific communication contexts. The choice to adopt or abandon the approach is up to you.

Glossary

Analogic Communication: Nonverbal communication that defines the relationship between the interactants. Analogic communication signals something.

Asymmetrical Reciprocity: The unequal exchange of relational costs and rewards.

Complementary Communication: Communication wherein the interactants' behavior tends to complement each other and is based on the maximization of differences. A pattern of complementary communication is sometimes characterized as "one up" and "one down."

Digital Communication: Verbal communication, sometimes called the content/report aspect of a message. The literal information of a message.

Input Variables: Components in the system's environment that make up a small group, including people and other tangible and intangible resources.

Network: Channels of repetitive communication between group or organizational members.

Norm: A regular pattern of behavior that evolves from positive and negative feedback in a small group.

Output Variables: The end result of small group interaction, including such things as decisions, membership satisfaction, reports, and productivity.

Process Variables: Processes that emerge out of small group interaction, including roles, norms, decision making, and networks.

Relational Control: The process of establishing the right to define and direct the actions of the dyad. The vertical distance between relational partners.

Relational Disengagement: The process whereby a relationship terminates or ends.

Relational Intimacy: The depth distance in a relationship. The degree to which members of a dyad use each other as a basis of self-confirmation.

Relational Trust: The horizontal distance between relational partners that represents the amount of predictability in the other's behavior.

Role: An expected set of behaviors; defined either formally or informally. A prescription for how one ought to act.

Social Exchange Theory: A systems-based theory that asserts that relationships function much in the same way as economic systems, via a ratio of assets and liabilities or relational costs and rewards.

Social System: A system whereby the relationship between the interactants and their communicative behaviors define the system. The focus is not on the subsystem—that is, the individual—but on their social roles and defining behaviors. In communication a social system is defined by the verbal and nonverbal acts committed by the interactants.

Structural-Functional Approach: A systems approach to organizational communication that describes how organizations are put together and how they function to produce outcomes, maintain their structure, and change to meet the demands of the environment.

Symmetrical Communication: Communication wherein the interactants tend to mirror each other's behavior. Communication is characterized by equality and the minimization of differences.

Symmetrical Reciprocity: A term used to describe the a relationship whereby there is an equal exchange of costs and rewards.

References

1. Watzlawick, P., Beavin, J. H., & Jackson, D. D. (1967). *Pragmatics of Human Communication: A Study of Interactional Patterns. Pathologies, and Paradoxes,* New York: Norton, (p. 28).

2. Ibid.

3. Morris, C. (1938). "Foundations of the Theory of Signs," in O. Neurath, R. Carnap, & C. Morris, (Eds)., *International Encyclopedia of Unified Sciences,* Chicago: University of Chicago Press.

4. Watzlawick, Beavin, & Jackson, *Pragmatics of Human Communication.*

5. Ibid. (pp. 48–49).

6. Ibid.

7. Wilmot, W. W. (1987). *Dyadic Communication,* New York: Random House.

8. Watzlawick, Beavin, & Jackson, *Pragmatics of Human Communication.*

9. Fisher, B. A. (1978). *Perspectives on Human Communication,* New York: Macmillan.

10. Miller, G. R., & Steinberg, M. (1975). *Between People: A New Analysis of Interpersonal Communication,* Chicago: Science Research Associates.

11. Fisher, B. A. (1987). *Interpersonal Communication: Pragmatics of Human Relationships,* New York: Random House.

12. Miller, & Steinberg, *Between People,* (p. 51).

13. Knapp, M. L., & Vangelisti, A. L. (1992). *Interpersonal Communication and Human Relationships,* Boston: Allyn & Bacon.

14. Wilmot, *Dyadic Communication.*

15. Knapp, & Vangelisti, *Interpersonal Communication and Human Relationships.*

16. Thibaut, J. W., & Kelley, H. H. (1959). *The Social Psychology of Groups,* New York: Wiley.

17. Millar, F. E., & Rogers, L. E. (1976). "A Relational Approach to Interpersonal Communication," in G. R. Miller, (Ed.), *Explorations in Interpersonal Communication,* (pp. 87–104), Beverly Hills: Sage, (pp. 89–90).

18. Ibid., (p. 90).

19. Millar, F. E., & Rogers, L. E. (1987). "Relational Dimensions in Interpersonal Dynamics," in M. E. Roloff & G. R. Miller, (Eds.), *Interpersonal Processes: New Directions in Communication Research,* (pp. 117–139), Newbury Park: Sage, (p. 120).

20. Ibid., (p. 123).

21. Millar, & Rogers, "A Relational Approach to Interpersonal Communication," (pp. 87–104).

22. From Rogers, L. E. (1982). *Relational Communication Control Coding Manual: RC²* Unpublished manuscript: University of Utah; Reprinted with permission.

23. Ibid.

24. Millar, & Rogers, "Relational Dimensions in Interpersonal Dynamics," (p. 118).

25. Courtright, J. A., Millar, F. E., Rogers, L. E., & Bagarozzi, D. (1990). "Interaction Dynamics of Relational Negotiation: Reconciliation Versus Termination of Distressed Relationships," *Western Journal of Speech Communication, 54,* 429–453.

26. Davis, M. S. (1973). *Intimate Relations,* New York: Free Press.

27. Wilmot, *Dyadic Communication,* (p. 211).

28. Baxter, L. A., & Wilmot, W. W. (1984). "Secret Tests: Social Strategies for Acquiring Information about the State of the Relationship," *Human Communication Research, 11,* 171–201.

29. Baxter, L. A. (1979). "Self-disclosure as a Relationship Disengagement Strategy: An Exploratory Investigation," *Human Communication Research, 5,* 215–222; Baxter, L. A. (1982). "Strategies for Ending Relationships: Two Studies," *Western Journal of Speech Communication, 46,* 223–241; Baxter, L. A. (1985). "Accomplishing Relationship Disengagement," in S. Duck & D. Perlman, (Eds.), *Understanding Personal Relationships: An Interdisciplinary Approach,* Beverly Hills: Sage, (pp. 243–266); Baxter, L. A., & Philpott, J. (1982). "Attribution Based Strategies for Initiating and Terminating Relationships," *Communication Quarterly, 30,* 217–224; Courtright, Millar, Rogers, & Bagarozzi, "Interaction Dynamics of Relational Negotiation," 429–453; Cody, M. J. (1982). "A Typology of Strategies and an Examination of the Role Intimacy Reactions to Inequity and Relational Problems Play in Strategy Selection," *Communication Monographs, 49,* 148–170; Fisher, *Interpersonal Communication: Pragmatics of Human Relationships.*

30. Fisher, B. A., & Ellis, D. G. (1990). *Small Group Decision Making: Communication and the Group Process,* New York: McGraw-Hill.

31. Beebe, S. A., & Masterson, J. T. (1994). *Communicating in Small Groups,* (4th Ed.), New York: HarperCollins, (p. 35).

32. Shaw, M. E., (1981). *Group Dynamics; The Psychology of Small Group Behavior,* New York: McGraw-Hill.

33. Mortensen, D. C. (1972). *Communication: The Study of Human Interaction,* New York: McGraw Hill.

34. Fisher, & Ellis, *Small Group Decision Making;* Brilhart, J. K. (1978). *Effective Group Discussion,* Dubuque, IA: Brown.

35. Fisher, & Ellis, *Small Group Decision Making;* Galanes, G. J., & Brilhart, J. K. (1991). *Communicating in Groups: Applications and Skills,* Dubuque, IA: Brown.

36. Fisher, B. A. (1982). "The Pragmatic Perspective of Human Communication: A View of System Theory," in F. E. X. Dance, (Ed.), *Human Communication Theory: Comparative Essays,* (pp. 192–219), New York: Harper & Row.

37. Brilhart, J. K., & Galanes, G. J. (1989). *Effective Group Discussion,* Dubuque, IA: Brown.

38. Cragan, J. F., & Wright, D. W. (1991). *Communication in Small Group Discussions,* St. Paul, MN: West.

39. Fisher, & Ellis, *Small Group Decision Making.*

40. Fisher, & Ellis, *Small Group Decision Making.*

41. Ibid.

42. Katz, D., & Kahn, R. (1977). *The Social Psychology of Organizations,* New York: Wiley & Sons.

43. Cummings, H. W., Long, L. W., & Lewis, M. L. (1987). *Managing Communication in Organizations: An Introduction,* Dubuque, IA: Gorush Scarisbrick Publisher; Farace, R. V., Monge, P. R., & Russell, H. (1977). *Communicating and Organizing,* Reading, MA: Addison-Wesley; Shockley-Zalabak, P. (1991). *Fundamentals of Organizational Communication,* New York: Longman.

44. Cushman, D. P., & Craig, R. T. (1976). "Communication Systems: Interpersonal Implications," in G. R. Miller, (Ed.), *Explorations in Interpersonal Communication,* (pp. 37–58), Beverly Hills: Sage.

45. Lawrence, P. R., & Lorsch, J. W. (1977). *Organization and Environment,* Homewood, IL: Irwin, (p. 6).

46. Goldhaber, G. M. (1993). *Organizational Communication,* (6th Ed.), Madison, WI: Brown & Benchmark.

47. Ibid.

48. Duncan, R. (1972). "Characteristics of Organizational Environments and Perceived Environmental Uncertainty," *Administrative Science Quarterly, 17,* 313–327; Goldhaber, *Organizational Communication.*

49. Wilson, G. L., Goodall, H. L., Jr., & Waagen, C. L. (1986). *Organizational Communication,* New York: Harper & Row.

50. Goldhaber, *Organizational Communication.*

51. Shockley-Zalabak, P. (1991). *Fundamentals of Organizational Communication,* New York: Longman.

52. Ibid.

53. Ibid.; Goldhaber, *Organizational Communication.*

Name Index

Subject Index